COMPULSORY PURCHASE
AND COMPENSATION

COMPULSORY PURCHASE AND COMPENSATION

(Seventh Edition)

by

BARRY DENYER-GREEN, LLM, PhD, FRICS

of Middle Temple, Barrister
Chartered Surveyor

2003

ESTATES GAZETTE
151 WARDOUR STREET, LONDON W1F 8BN

First edition 1980
Second edition 1985
Third edition 1989
Fourth edition 1994
Fifth edition 1998
Sixth edition 2000
Seventh edition 2003

By the same author: *Development and Planning Law* (1999)

ISBN 0 7282 0397 9

British Library Cataloguing-in-Publication Data
A catalogue record for this book is available
from the British Library

Typesetting by Amy Boyle, Rochester, Kent
Printed and bound in Finland by WS Bookwell, Juva

Contents

	Page
Preface	xiii
Table of Cases	xv
Table of Statutes	xliii
Table of Statutory Instruments	lvii
Table of Circulars	lviii

PART I
THE POWER TO COMPULSORILY PURCHASE LAND

Chapter 1	**Introduction**	3
	The use of compulsory acquisition powers	3
	Compensation and compulsory acquisition	4
	Compulsory acquisition and the law	5
	Human rights	6
	Law reform	6
Chapter 2	**The Need for Statutory Powers**	9
	How can land be expropriated?	9
	Public benefit and compensation	11
	Compulsory purchase outlined	14
	Acquisition of rights other than full ownership	15
	The need for statutory powers	15
	Purchase by agreement	17
Chapter 3	**The Sources of Compulsory Purchase Powers**	19
	Introduction	19
	Royal prerogative	19
	Private Act of Parliament	20
	Public General Act of Parliament	21
	Public General Act of Parliament and provisional order	22

Public General Act of Parliament and
   compulsory purchase order   22
Transport and Works Act 1992 and works
   order   23
Common acquisition and compensation
   procedures   24
Summary   25

Chapter 4   **Compulsory Purchase and Works Orders**   27
Introduction   27
Preparation and making of an order   28
Objections and confirmation of an order   32
Special kinds of land   38
Special Parliamentary procedure   38
Works orders   38
The role of the confirming minister   41
Challenging an order in the High Court   49

Chapter 5   **Purchase and Blight Notices**   57
Introduction   57
Purchase notices under the planning Acts   57
Purchases notices under the housing Acts   61
Blight notices   62

Chapter 6   **Purchase and Disposal by Agreement**   73
Introduction   73
Contractual rights and the exercise of
   statutory powers   74
Purchase by agreement: no compulsory
   purchase order   75
Purchase by agreement: compulsory purchase
   order in the background   77
Disposal of land   80

PART II
EXERCISING THE POWERS OF COMPULSORY PURCHASE

Chapter 7   **Commencing a Compulsory Purchase**   85
Introduction   85
Notice to treat   86
Deemed notice to treat   97
General vesting declaration   98

Chapter 8	**The Land: What is Acquired**	103
	Introduction	103
	The definition of land	104
	Interests in land that can be acquired	106
	Severed land	109
	Power to override third party rights	117
	Omitted land	120
Chapter 9	**Taking Possession and Conveyance**	121
	Introduction	121
	Survey and preliminary works	121
	Entry under the Compulsory Purchase Act 1965	122
	Entry under a general vesting declaration	125
	Consequences of entry	125
	Advance payment of compensation	125
	Unlawful entry	126
	Enforcing entry	128
	Absent or untraced owners	128
	Compelling an authority to take possession	128
	Conveyance	129
Chapter 10	**The Lands Tribunal**	
	Introduction	131
	Reference to the Lands Tribunal	135
	Valuation methods and evidence	142
	Small claims	148
	Appealing an award	150

PART III
COMPENSATION FOR THE COMPULSORY PURCHASE OF LAND

Chapter 11	**Introduction to the Assessment of Compensation for Land Acquired**	155
	Introduction	155
	The purpose of compensation	155
	Legal presumptions in favour of compensation	156
	Meaning of compensation	158
	The development of the market value rule	159
	The present statutory entitlement to compensation and the basic rules of valuation	170
	Persons entitled to compensation	171

Date of valuation or assessment of
compensation 174

Chapter 12 **Compensation for Land Acquired:
Market Value** 181
Introduction 181
The market value rules 182
Development and hope value 192
Marriage and ransom value 192
The *Stokes* principle 196
Lotting 197
Special types of properties 198

Chapter 13 **Statutory Planning Assumptions** 199
Introduction 199
Planning assumptions: general 199
Assumptions not directly derived from
development plans 201
Special assumptions derived from
development plans 204
Certificate of appropriate alternative
development 206
Compensation for additional development
permitted after acquisition 212

Chapter 14 **The Effect of the Scheme** 217
Introduction 217
Statutory rules for disregarding the 'scheme' 218
Section 9 of the Land Compensation Act 1961 221
The *Pointe Gourde* principle 223
Summary 230

Chapter 15 **Depreciation or Enhancement of Retained
Land: Compensation or Set-off** 233
Introduction 233
Severance and injurious affection 233
Set-off 247
Subsequent acquisition of retained land: section
8 of the Land Compensation Act 1961 252

Chapter 16 **Compensation for Land Acquired:
Special Cases** 255

Introduction 255
Equivalent reinstatement 255
Houses unfit for human habitation 260
Listed buildings 261

Chapter 17 **Compensation for Disturbance** 263
Introduction 263
Principle of equivalence 263
Persons entitled to disturbance compensation 268
The general principles of the disturbance claim 272
Disturbance: particular compensatable losses 280
Other matters under rule(6) 293

Chapter 18 **Additional Payments** 295
Introduction 295
Legal costs and other fees and losses 295
Home-loss payments 297
Statutory disturbance payments 301
Statutory discretionary payments, re-housing
    duty and loans 305
Interest 306
Loss payments 308

Chapter 19 **Compensation for Leasehold Interests
and Tenancies** 309
Introduction 309
Compensation for leasehold interests 310
Compensation for short tenancies: section 20
    basis 312
Compensation for reversionary interests 315
Business tenancies 319
Additional payments 321

Chapter 20 **Compensation for the Acquisition of
Agricultural Land** 323
Introduction 323
Land acquired from an owner-occupier 323
Land acquired from a landlord 328
Land acquired from a tenant 329
Farm loss payment 342
Severance of an agricultural unit 344

Chapter 21 **Special Compensation Procedures**   347
Introduction   347
Minerals   347
Common land   348
Land of statutory undertakers   350
Land subject to mortgage   351
Interests omitted from purchase   353
Accommodation works   353

Chapter 22 **Compensation and Tax**   355
Introduction   355
Compensation sums subject to tax   355
Allowance for tax in assessing compensation   357
Value added tax   359

PART IV
WORSENMENT: COMPENSATION AND MITIGATION

Chapter 23 **Compensation for Activities**   365
Introduction   365
Nuisance   367
Compensation for injurious affection caused
    by execution of works: Compulsory
    Purchase Act 1965, section 10: the
    McCarthy Rules   370
Compensation for depreciation caused by the
    use of public works: Land Compensation
    Act 1973, Part I   380
Compensation for street lights   392

Chapter 24 **Mitigation of Injurious Effect of Public
    Works**   393
Introduction   393
Sound-proofing of buildings affected by public
    works: section 20   394
Sound-proofing of buildings affected by the
    use of aerodromes   395
Acquisition of land: 396
    (A) In connection with highways   396
    (B) In connection with public works
       other than highways   398
Execution of works   398

Expenses of persons moving temporarily
during construction works 399

Chapter 25 **Compensation for Decisions** 401
Introduction 401
Interference to property rights: is there a
right to compensation? 402
Compensation for refusal of planning
permission 404
Compensation for revocation, modification
and discontinuance under the Planning Acts 406
Compensation in connection with listed
buildings and ancient monuments 409
Compensation in respect of tree preservation
orders, control of advertisements and stop
notices 412
Compensation for highway decisions 415

Chapter 26 **Statutory Utilities: Compensation for
Wayleaves and Damages** 421
Introduction 421
Oil exploration and exploitation 422
Coal mining subsidence 423
Land drainage work 424
Sewers and water pipes 425
Gas pipelines 427
Telecommunications 429
Electricity 431
Pipe-lines Act 1962 434

Chapter 27 **Human Rights** 437
Introduction 437
Human Rights Act 1998 437
European Convention on Human Rights 438
Article 1 of First Protocol: protection of
property 439
Article 6(1) of the Convention: right to
a fair trial 443
Article 8: right of respect to home 443

Index 445

Preface

This is the now the seventh edition of a book that I first wrote for students some 24 years ago. This edition includes a substantial amount of new material, particularly decisions of the courts and of the Lands Tribunal. Since the last edition there has been much debate about the reform of compulsory purchase and compensation procedures. The Law Commission has published two substantial and well researched reports containing a number of proposals for reform. Readers should look out for legislative changes in due course.

At the date of writing this Preface, a Planning and Compulsory Purchase bill is before Parliament. This contains proposals for amending section 226 of the Town and Country Planning Act 1990, and for the introduction of a new and additional scheme of loss payments. These payments, up to a maximum of £25,000, are intended to 'sugar the pill' of compulsory purchase.

Once again, I am grateful to Navjit Ubhi, barrister, for her considerable help in the preparation of the various tables and the index.

Barry Denyer-Green
March 2003

Table of Cases

Abbreviations

AC:	Appeal Cases (Law Reports)
Ch or ChD:	Chancery (Law Reports)
QB (or KB):	Queens (or Kings) Bench (Law Reports)
All ER:	All England Law Reports
WLR:	Weekly Law Reports
LT:	Law Times
LGR:	Local Government Reports
P&CR:	Property and Compensation Reports
JPL:	Journal of Planning and Environment Law
EG:	Estates Gazette
EGD:	Estates Gazette Digest
EGLR:	Estates Gazette Law Reports
Lloyd's Rep:	Lloyd's Law Reports
RVR:	Rating and Valuation Reports
CSW:	Chartered Surveyor Weekly
PLR:	Planning Law Reports

A

A&B Taxis Ltd *v* Secretary of State for Air [1922] 2 KB 328 278

Abbey Homesteads (Developments) Ltd *v* Northamptonshire County
Council [1992] 2 EGLR 18 on appeal from [1991] 1 EGLR 224
following [1986] 1 EGLR 24; (1986) 53 P&CR 1, CA 150, 186, 223,
. . . . 225, 228

Abbey Homesteads Group Ltd *v* Secretary of State for Transport
(1982) 263 EG 983; [1982] 2 EGLR 198 . . . . . . 185, 210, 237, 239, 241, 242

Aberdeen City District Council *v* Sim (1982) 264 EG 621; [1982]
2 EGLR 22 275

Ackerman *v* Secretary of State for the Environment (1980) 257 EG 1037;
[1981] 1 EGLR 13. 53

Acquilina *v* Havering London Borough Council (1993) 66 P&CR 39;
[1992] RVR 21; [1993] 05 EG 139; [1993] 1 EGLR 33 on appeal from
[1991] 2 EGLR 209. 150

ADP & E Farmers *v* Department of Transport (1988) 28 RVR 58; [1988]
1 EGLR 209. . . . . 146, 211, 239, 242

Advance Grounds Rents Ltd *v* Middlesbrough Borough Council
    [1986] 2 EGLR 221 . . . . 87, 127, 353
Afzal *v* Rochdale Metropolitan Borough Council [1980] RVR 165;
    [1980] 1 EGLR 157 . . . . 168, 282
Aka *v* Turkey [2001] (19639/92) (2001) 33 EHRR 27; [1998] HRCD 866
    441
Alfred Golightly & Sons Ltd *v* Durham County Council (1981) 260
    EG 1045 . . . . 77, 358
All Souls College, Oxford *v* Middlesex County Council 54 TLR 667;
    [1938] 2 All ER 586 77
Allen *v* Department of Transport, unreported, 14 June 1994 382
Allen *v* Gulf Oil Refining Ltd [1981] AC 1001; [1981] 1 All ER 353
    . . . . 17, 368, 369, 371, 376
Amalgamated Investment and Property Co Ltd *v* John Walker &
    Sons Ltd (1976) 235 EG 565; [1976] 2 EGLR 153 411
Anderson *v* Glasgow Corpn (1976) SLT 225 Ct of Sess 303, 329
Anderson *v* Moray District Council (1980) RVR 19 . . . . 332, 335
Andreae *v* Selfridge & Co Ltd [1938] Ch 1 . . . . 369, 373
Argyle Motors *v* Birkenhead Corpn [1974] 1 All ER 201; 229 EG 1589
    . . . . 373, 375, 379
Arkell *v* Department of Transport (1983) 267 EG 855; [1983] EGLR 181
    388
Arrondelle *v* UK Government [1982] JPL 770 . . . . 366, 403, 443
Ashbridge Investments Ltd *v* Minister of Housing and Local
    Government [1965] 3 All ER 371; [1965] 1 WLR 1320 . . . . 43, 46, 48
Aslam *v* South Bedfordshire District Council [2000] 40 RVR 121 285
Associated Provincial Picture Houses *v* Wednesbury Corpn [1948]
    1 KB 223; [1948] 2 All ER 680 . . . . 46, 48, 50, 51
Aston Charities Trust Ltd *v* Stepney Corpn (1952) 3 P&CR 82 . . . 256, 257
Atkinson *v* National Coal Board [1974] RVR 350 424
A-G *v* De Keysers Royal Hotel Ltd [1920] AC 508; [1920] All ER
    Rep 80 20
A-G *v* Horner (1884) 14 QBD 245 366
Ayr Harbour Trustees *v* Oswald (1883) 8 AC 623 . . . . 74, 76, 117

B
Bailey *v* Derby Corpn [1965] 1 All ER 443; (1964) 16 P&CR 192;
    192 EG 817 . . . . 276, 281
Baird's Exors *v* Commissioners of Inland Revenue [1991] 1 EGLR
    201 333
Balco Transport Services Ltd *v* Secretary of State for the Environment
    [1985] 3 All ER 689; (1985) 50 P&CR 423; [1985] 2 EGLR 187 59
Baker Britt & Co Ltd *v* Hampsher (VO) (1976) 19 RRC 62 150
Bamlings (Washington) Ltd *v* Washington Dev Corpn; *sub nom*
    Washington Dev Corpn *v* Bamlings (Washington) Ltd [1985]

1 EGLR 16 on appeal from (1982) 43 P&CR 427 79

Banham *v* Hackney London Borough Council (1970) 22 P&CR 922 92

Bannocks *v* Secretary of State for Transport [1995] 2 EGLR 157. 381

Barb *v* Secretary of State for Transport (1978) 247 EG 473; [1978]
2 EGLR 171 . . . . 386, 388

Barclays Bank *v* Kent County Council [1998] 2 EGLR 14 142

Barlow *v* Hackney Corporation (1954) 5 P&CR 129 279

Barstow *v* Rothwell Urban District Council (1970) 22 P&CR 942;
[1970] EGD 648 189

Batchelor *v* Kent County Council [1992] 1 EGLR 217 (LT) on remission
from [1990] 1 EGLR 32 (CA) on appeal from (1988) 56 P&CR 320
. . . . 187, 196, 224, 438

Bateman *v* Lancashire County Council [1999] 2 EGLR 203. . . . . . . 134, 392

Beckett *v* Midland Rly Co (1867) LR 3 CP 82 . . . . 374, 379

Bede Distributors Ltd *v* Newcastle-upon-Tyne Corpn (1973) 26
P&CR 298. . . . . 276, 280, 287

Belfast Corpn *v* OD Cars Ltd [1960] AC 49; [1960] 1 All ER 65 . . . 166, 402

Bell *v* Canterbury City Council [1988] 1 EGLR 205; on appeal from
(1986) 16 CSW 420 413

Bennett *v* Wakefield Metropolitan District Council [1997] 37 RVR 32. . . 71

Bestley *v* North West Water Ltd [1998] 1 EGLR 187 . . . . 308, 427

Bibby & Sons Ltd *v* Merseyside County Council (1979) 251 EG 757;
[1977] 2 EGLR 154. . . . . 273, 277, 289

Bigg *v* London Corpn (1873) LR 15 Eq 376. 418

Binns *v* Secretary of State for Transport [1986] 2 EGLR 207 67

Bird *v* Eggleton (1885) 29 ChD 1012 117

Bird *v* Great Eastern Rly Co (1865) 34 LJCP 366, 13 LT 365 375

Bird *v* Wakefield Metroplitan District Council (1978) 248 EG 499;
[1978] 2 EGLR 16 (CA) on appeal from [1977] 2 EGLR 158 226

Birmingham City Corpn *v* West Midland Baptist (Trust) Association
Inc [1970] AC 874; [1969] 3 All ER 172; 20 P&CR 1052; [1969]
EGD 704 . . . . 90, 91, 175, 178, 259, 275, 313

Birmingham City District Council *v* Morris & Jacobs Ltd (1976) 33
P&CR 27; [1975] 2 EGLR 173 (CA); [1976] 2 EGLR 143. 228

Birrell Ltd *v* City of Edinburgh District Council (1982) Scots Law
Times 111 . . . . 178, 228, 306

Biscoe *v* Great Eastern Rly Co (1873) LR 16 Eq 636. 372

Bisset *v* Secretary of State for Scotland [1992] RVR 98 272

Blackadder *v* Grampian Regional Council [1992] 2 EGLR 207 . . . . 179, 230

Blake *v* Newcastle-upon-Tyne Corpn (1966) 198 EG 155 288

Blamires *v* Bradford Corpn [1964] Ch 585; [1964] 2 All ER 603; (1964)
16 P&CR 162. 88

Blandrent Investment Developments Ltd *v* British Gas Corporation
[1978] 2 EGLR 10; (HL), [1979] 2 EGLR 18; (1979) 252 EG 267. 188,
. . . . 189, 190

Blower *v* Suffolk County Council (1994) 67 P&CR 228; [1994] RVR
    78; [1994] 47 EG 168; [1994] 2 EGLR 204 . . . . 381, 388
Blundell *v* R [1905] 1 KB 516 . . . . 158, 432
Bollans *v* Surrey County Council (1968) 20 P&CR 745 413
Bolton *v* North Dorset District Council [1997] 2 EGLR 180 191
Bolton *v* Southern Electric plc [1999] 1 EGLR 177 432
Bolton Corpn *v* Owen [1962] 1 QB 470 62
Bolton Metropolitan Borough Council *v* Secretary of State for the
    Environment (1990) 71 P&CR 309; [1995] JPL 1043; [1995] 3
    PLR 37 53
Bolton Metropolitan Borough Council *v* Secretary of State for the
    Environment and Greater Manchester Waste Disposal Authority
    (1990) 61 P&CR 343;[1991] JPL 241 48
Bolton Metropolitan Borough Council *v* Tudor Properties Ltd
    (2000) 80 P&CR 537 227
Bolton Metropolitan Borough Council *v* Waterworth (1981) 259 EG
    625; [1981] 2 EGLR 7; on appeal from (1978) 37 P&CR 104; (1978)
    251 EG 963 (*sub nom* Waterworth *v* Bolton Metropoliltan Borough
    Council) 195, 237, 243
Bostock Chater & Sons Ltd *v* Chelmsford Corpn (1973) 26 P&CR 321
    . . . . 86, 275
BP Petroleum Developments Ltd *v* Ryder [1987] 2 EGLR 233; (1987)
    28 RVR 211 . . . . 186, 196, 239, 423
Bradford *v* Mayor of Eastbourne [1896] 2 QB 205 422
Bradford Property Trust Ltd *v* Hertfordshire County Council (1973)
    27 P&CR 228 . . . . 91, 92
Bremer *v* Haringey London Borough Council (1983) Chartered
    Surveyor Weekly 19 May, 401 . . . . 61, 86, 96
Brickell *v* Shaftesbury Rural District Council (1955) 5 P&CR 174 272
British Coal Corpn *v* Gwent County Council [1995] NPC 103; [1995]
    EGCS 104 308
British Electricity Authority *v* Cardiff Corpn (1951) 158 EG 233 191
British Transport Commission *v* Gourley [1956] AC 185; [1955] 3 All
    ER 796 357
Brookdene Investments Ltd *v* Minister of Housing and Local
    Government (1969) 21 P&CR 545 59
Brown *v* Heathlands Mental Health National Service Trust [1996] 1
    All ER 133 376
Brown *v* Secretary of State for the Environment (1978) 40 P&CR 285 . . . 44
Bryan *v* United Kingdom (1995) 21 EHRR 342, [1996] 1 PLR 47 443
Buccleuch (Duke) *v* Inland Revenue [1967] 1 AC 506; [1967] 1 All
    ER 129 HL 183, 197, 237
Buccleuch (Duke) *v* Metropolitan Board of Works (1872) LR 5 HL 237
Buckingham Street Investments Ltd *v* Greater London Council (1975)
    31 P&CR 453; [1976] EGD 397; [1976] 1 EGLR 178 177

Buckle *v* Holderness Borough Council [1996] 2 EGLR 133; [1996] 1
 PLR 66 413
Budgen *v* Secretary of State for Wales [1985] 2 EGLR 203 . . . . 66, 272, 292,
 . . . . 326, 373
Burmah Oil Co *v* Lord Advocate [1965] AC 75; [1964] 2 All ER 348 20
Burn *v* North Yorkshire County Council [1992] 2 EGLR 193; 60
 P&CR 81 68
Burroughs Day *v* Bristol City Council [1996] 1 EGLR 167; [1996] 1
 PLR 78 410
Burson *v* Wantage Rural District Council (1974) 27 P&CR 556 124
Burton *v* National Coal Board [1983] RVR 140. 423
Burton *v* Secretary of State for Transport [1988] 2 EGLR 35; (1988)
 31 EG 50 CA 45
Bushell *v* Secretary of State for the Environment [1981] AC 75; [1980]
 2 All ER 608; [1980] JPL 458. . . . . 33, 41, 42, 43,53
Butcher Robinson & Staples Ltd *v* London Regional Transport [1999]
 3 EGLR 63; (1999) 79 P&CR 523 369
Buttle *v* Saunders [1950] 2 All ER 193. 81
Bwllfa and Merthyr Dare Steam Collieries (1891) Ltd *v* Pontypridd
 Water Works Company [1903] AC 426. . . . . 145, 146, 147, 244

C
Caledonian Railway *v* Turcan [1898] AC 256 111
Cameron *v* Nature Conservancy Council [1992] 1 EGLR 227. 334
Campbell Douglas & Co Ltd *v* Hamilton District Council (1983) 267
 EG 953; [1983] 2 EGLR 183. 271
Camrose (Viscount) *v* Basingstoke Corpn [1966] 3 All ER 161; [1966]
 1 WLR 1100; [1966] RVR 459; [1966] EGD 469 . . . . 220, 229
Canterbury City Council *v* Colley [1993] 1 All ER 591; [1993] 1 EGLR
 182 407
Capital Investments Ltd *v* Wednesfield Urban District Council [1965]
 Ch 774; [1964] 1 All ER 655; 15 P&CR 435 . . . . 93, 96
Caplan *v* Secretary of State for the Environment (1980) 5 HLR 104. . . . 299
Cardiff Corpn *v* Cook [1923] 2 Ch 115; [1922] All ER Rep 651 89
Cardigan Timber Co *v* Cardiganshire County Council (1957) 9 P&CR
 . . . . 158, 413
Carrell *v* London Underground (1995) 70 P&CR 135 71
Cary-Elwes Contract, Re [1906] 2 Ch 143; 4 LGR 838; 70 JP 345 94
Carnochan *v* Norwich & Spalding Railway Co (1858) 26 Beav 169 89
Cawoods *v* Southwark London Borough Council (1982) 264 EG 1087;
 [1982] 2 EGLR 222. 408
Cedar Rapids Manufacturing and Power Co *v* Lacoste [1914] AC 569;
 [1914–15] All ER Rep 571 . . . . 162, 188
Central Control Board *v* Cannon Brewery [1919] AC 744; 17 LGR 569
 158

Chamberlain *v* West End of London and Crystal Palace Rly Co (1863)
    B&S 617; 2 New Rep 182; 32 LJQB 173; 8 LT 149; 9 Jur (NS) 1051;
    11 WR 472 affirming (1862) 2 B&S 605 377
Chapman, Lowry & Puttick Ltd *v* Chichester District Council (1984)
    269 EG 955; [1984] 1 EGLR 188. 133, 190, 194, 227
Charman *v* Dorset County Council (1986) 52 P&CR 85 70
Chiltmead Ltd *v* Reading Borough Council (1981) 258 EG 1191;
    [1981] 1 EGLR 183. 288
Chilton *v* Telford Development Corpn (1985) 47 P&CR 674; [1985]
    1 EGLR 195; on appeal [1987] 1 EGLR 12 . . . . 123, 124, 177, 306
Ching Garage *v* Chingford Corpn [1961] 1 WLR 470, [1961] 1 All ER
    671 418
Chocolat Express *v* London Passenger Transport Board (1935) 152 LT
    63; 50 TLR 490. 95
Christos *v* Sectary of State for the Environment, Transport and the
    Regions [2002] (unreported, 1 July 2002) 112
City of Glasgow District Council *v* Mackie [1992] 20 EG 114. 305
Citypark Properties Ltd vBolton Metropolitan Borough Council
    [2000] RVR 343 418
Clark *v* School Board for London (1874) 9 Ch App 120. . . . . . . 87, 107, 117
Clarke *v* Highways Agency (LCA/92/1999 – unreported 10/1/2000)
    388
Clarke *v* Wareham and Purbeck Rural District Council (1972) 25
    P&CR 423 244
Cleaners (JV) *v* Luton County Borough Council (1968) 20 P&CR 465. . . 92
Clibbert (W) Ltd *v* Avon County Council (1976) 16 RVR 131; [1976]
    1 EGLR 171 135
Clift *v* Welsh Office [1999] 1 WLR 796 373
Clouds Estates Trustees *v* Southern Electricity Board [1983] 2 EGLR
    186 433
Cohen *v* Haringey London Borough Council (1981) 42 P&CR 6; (1981)
    258 EG 165; [1981] 1 EGLR 17; [1982] JPL 35 . . . . 92, 127
Colac (President, etc of) *v* Summerfield [1893] AC 187; [1891–1894]
    All ER Rep Ext 1655; 68 LT 762; 62 LJPC 54, PC. 372, 377
Cole *v* Southwark London Borough Council (1979) 251 EG 477; [1979]
    2 EGLR 162 . . . . 292, 293
Coleen Properties Ltd *v* Minister of Housing and Local Government
    [1971] 1 All ER 1049; [1971] 1 WLR 433; 69 LGR 175; 22 P&CR 417
    . . . . 43, 47
Colley *v* Secretary of State for the Environment, Transport and the
    Regions (1998) 77 P&CR 190 . . . . 58, 59
Collins *v* Thames Water Utilities Ltd [1994] 2 EGLR 209 427
Collector of Land Revenue *v* Kam Gin Paik [1986] 1 WLR 412 95
Commissioner of Highways *v* Shipp Bros Pty Ltd (1978) 19 SASR 215
    279

Cook *v* Southend Borough Council [1990] 2 QB 1; [1990] 1 All ER 243 262
Cook *v* South West Water [1995] (Unreported) 427
Cook *v* Winchester City Council (1995) 69 P&CR 99; [1995] 1 EGLR 179 .... 58, 141
Cooke *v* Secretary of State for the Environment (1973) 27 P&CR 234 .... 242, 250, 251, 324
Co-operative Insurance Society Ltd *v* Hastings Borough Council [1993] 2 EGLR 19 .... 85, 99
Co-operative Retail Services Ltd *v* Wycombe District Council [1989] 30 RVR 110 143
Co-operative Wholesale Society *v* Chester-le-Street District Council [1996] 2 EGLR 143; on appeal [1998] 3 EGLR 11 .... 101, 133,134
Corrin (Trustees of Northampton Church Charities) *v* Northampton Borough Council (1980) 253 EG 489; [1980] 1 EGLR 148........... 192
Conservative and Unionist Club *v* Manchester City Council (1975) 235 EG765 256
Cowper Essex *v* Acton Local Board (1889) 14 App Cas 153, [1886–90] All ER Rep 901 .... 234, 236
Crabb *v* Surrey County Council (1982) 44 P&CR 119 .... 79, 206
Craske *v* Norfolk County Council [1991] 1 EGLR 221............... 151
Crista *v* Highways Agency (Acq/132/1998–unreported 6/4/2000) ... 285
Cunningham *v* Sunderland City Borough Council (1963) 14 P&CR 208 260
Cuthbert *v* Secretary of State for the Environment (1979) 252 EG 921 325
Currie's Exors *v* Secretary of State for Scotland [1993] 2 EGLR 221.... 412

D
de Rothschild *v* Secretary of State for Transport [1989] 1 All ER 933; (1989) 6 EG 123; [1988] 1 EGLR 11; (CA), [1989] 1 EGLR 19 .... 45, 47, 48, 52
DHN Food Distributors Ltd *v* Tower Hamlets London Borough Council [1976] 3 All ER 462; [1976] 1 WLR 852; (1976) 32 P&CR 240; 239 EG 719; 1 EGLR 168; (CA), [1976] 2 EGLR 7... 87, 107, 174, 270, 271
Davies *v* Mid-Glamorgan County Council (1979) 251 EG 65; [1979] 2 EGLR 158 .... 384, 391
Davies *v* Powell [1977] 1 WLR 258 357
Davy *v* Leeds Corpn [1965] 1 All ER 753; [1965] 1 WLR 1218; 17 P&CR 83; [1965] EGD 57 220
Dawson *v* Great Northern City Rly [1905] 1 KB 260 CA; reversing on other grounds [1904] 1 KB 277, 73 LJKB 174, 90 LT 20, 20 TLR 87; 68 JP 214.. 89, 93
Dawson *v* Norwich City Council (1979) 250 EG 1297; [1979] 1 EGLR 204 340

Day & Sons *v* Thames Water Authority (1984) 270 EG 1294; [1984] 1
  EGLR 197. 424
Delaforce *v* Evans (1970) 22 P&CR 770. 143
Department of Transport *v* North West Water Authority [1983] 3 All
  ER 273 370
Derby & Co Ltd *v* Weldon (No 9) The Times, 9 Nov 1990 148
Devotwill *v* Margate Corpn; see Margate Corpn *v* Devotwill
  Investments 204, 205
Dhenin *v* Department of Transport (1990) 60 P&CR 349. . . . . 144, 146
Dicconson Holdings Ltd *v* St Helens Metropolitan Borough Council
  (1979) 249 EG 1075; [1979] 1 EGLR 180. . . . . 190, 194
Dingleside Development Co Ltd *v* Powys County Council [1995]
  1 EGLR 183 . . . . 145, 196
Director of Buildings and Lands *v* Shun Fung Ironworks [1995] 2 AC
  111; [1995] 1 All ER 846; [1995] 19 EG 147; [1995] RVR 124; [1995]
  ECGS 35; [1995] 1 EGLR 19. . . . . 157, 168, 249, 264, 265, 273, 275,
  . . . . 277, 278, 288, 279, 318, 264
Dixon *v* Allgood (1981) 257 EG 1268. 312
Dodd Properties (Kent) Ltd *v* Canterbury City Council [1980] 1 All
  ER 928; [1980] 1 EGLR 15. 377
Donaldson *v* Hereford and Worcester County Council [1997] RVR 242
  385
Donovan *v* Welsh Water (1993) 67 P&CR 233; [1993] RVR 126, LT;
  [1994] 05 EG 163; [1994] 1 EGLR 203 . . . . 132, 427
Douglas *v* London NW Rly Co (1857) 3 K&J 173; 69 ER 1069 128
Dowty Boulton Paul Ltd *v* Wolverhampton Corpn [1971] 1 WLR 204;
  [1971] 2 All ER 277; (1970) 69 LGR 192; affirmed [1972] 2 All ER
  1073. . . . . 74, 75, 76, 117
Drake *v* Manchester City Council (1980) 256 EG 615; [1980] 2
  EGLR 162. 318
Durnford *v* Avon County Council (unreported, 18 November 1994) . . 388
Durnsford *v* South Gloucestershire County Council [1999] 39 RVR 70
  142
Duttons Breweries Ltd *v* Leeds City Council (1982) 261 EG 885 and
  989; [1980] 2 EGLR 21; (CA), [1982] 1 EGLR 27 . . . . 78, 94, 177

E

Eagle *v* Charing Cross Rly Co (1867) LR 2 CP 638. . . . . 379, 387
Eden *v* N E Railway Co [1907] AC 400. 347
Edge Hill Light Rly Co *v* Secretary of State for War (1956) 6 P&CR 211
  258 . . . .
Edmonstone *v* Central Regional Council (1984) 271 EG 901; [1984]
  2 EGLR 189 188
Edmunds *v* Stockport Metropolitan Borough Council [1990] 1 PLR 1. . 119
Edwards *v* Bairstow [1956] AC 14 150

Edwards *v* Minister of Transport [1964] 2 QB 134, 15 P&CR 144; [1963]
EGD 123; *sub nom* Minister of Transport *v* Edwards [1964] 1 All ER
483, 14 P&CR 364, [1963] EGD 244. 245
Elcock *v* Newham Borough Council [1996] 2 EGLR 13 62
Ellesmere (Earl) *v* Commissioners of Inland Revenue [1918]
2 KB 735. 197
Ellis *v* Rogers (1885) 29 ChD 661 . . . . .107, 197
Elm Avenue, New Milton, *ex parte* New Forest District Council, Re
[1984] 3 All ER 632 . . . . .76, 371
Elmer-Smith *v* Stevenage Development Corpn (1972) 23 P&CR 371;
[1972] EGD 500. 271
Emslie & Simpson Ltd *v* Aberdeen City District Council [1994]
1 EGLR 33. . . . . 275, 318, 438
Emslie & Simpson Ltd *v* Aberdeen City District Council (No 2) [1995]
35 RVR 159. 140
English Exporters (London) Ltd *v* Eldonwall Ltd [1973] ChD 415. 137
Enterprise Inns plc *v* Secretary of State for the Environment, Transport
and the Regions (2001) 81 P&CR 236 49
Entwistle Pearson (Manchester) Ltd *v* Chorley Borough Council
(1993) 66 P&CR 277; [1993] RVR 220. 68
EON Motors Ltd *v* Secretary of State for the Environment (1981) 258
EG 1293; [1981] 1 EGLR 19. 31
Eronpark Ltd *v* Secretary of State for Transport [2000] 2 EGLR 165 . . . 260
Essex County Council *v* Essex Congregational Church [1963] AC 808;
[1963] 1 All ER 326 . . . . .69, 260
Essex Incorporated Congregational Union *v* Colchester Borough
Council [1983] RVR 267; (1982) 263 EG 167 LT; [1982]
2 EGLR 178 142
Evans *v* City of Glasgow District Council (1977) LTS 1977/2. 304
Evans (FR) (Leeds) Ltd *v* English Electric Co Ltd (1977) 36 P&CR 184;
245 EG 657. . . . . .184, 185
Evis *v* Commission for New Towns [2002] 2 EGLR 167 302

F

Factorset Ltd *v* Selby District Council [1995] 2 EGLR 190; [1995]
2 PLR 11. 413
Fagan *v* Knowsley Metropolitan Borough Council (1985) 50 P&CR
363; (1985) 83 LGR 782; [1985] 2 EGLR 39 86
Fairmount Investments Ltd *v* Secretary of State for the Environment
[1976] 2 All ER 865; [1976] 1 WLR 1255; [1976] EGD 82, 98; CA,
[1976] 1 EGLR 7; (HL) [1976] 2 EGLR 18 53
Fallows *v* Gateshead Metropolitan Borough Council (1993) 66 P&CR
460; [1993] JPL 1157. 387
Farmers (ADE&P) *v* Department of Transport see ADE&P Farmers *v*
Department of Transport [1988] 1 EGLR 209 . . . . .239, 242

Farr *v* Millersons Investments Ltd (1971) 22 P&CR 1061 144
Fawcett *v* Newcastle-upon-Tyne Metropolitan Borough Council (1980)
    256 EG 615; [1977] 1 EGLR 24 141
Fennessy *v* City Airport Ltd [1995] 31 EG 76, LT; [1995] 2 EGLR 167
    387
Festiniog Rly Society Ltd *v* Central Electricity Generating Board (1962)
    13 P&CR 248; [1962] RVR 202; [1962] EGD 125 . . . . 258, 278
Finsbury Business Centre *v* Mercury Communications Ltd [1994] 34
    RVR 108. . . . . 132, 430
First Garden City Ltd *v* Letchworth Garden City Corpn [1966] RVR 633
    197
First Leisure Trading Ltd *v* Dorita Properties [1991] 1 EGLR 133 184
Fisher *v* Great Western Railway [1911] 1 KB 551. . . . . 141, 236
Fitzwilliams (Earl) Wentworth Estates Co *v* British Rail Board (1967) 19
    P&CR 588 325
Flanagan *v* Stoke-on-Trent City Council (1982) 262 EG 1201; [1982]
    1 EGLR 205. . . . . 374, 377, 379, 417, 419
Fleming *v* Newport Rly Co (1883) 8 AC 265 320
Fletcher *v* Chelmsford Borough Council [1991] 2 EGLR 213 413
Fletcher Estates (Harlescott) Ltd *v* Secretary of State for the
    Environment [2000] 1 All ER 929; [2000] 2 WLR 438; [2000] 1 EGLR
    13; [2000] 1 PLR 93 on appeal from [1999] QB 1144; [1998] 4 All
    ER 838; [1998] 3 EGLR 13; [1998] 3 PLR 99. 210
Follows *v* Peabody Trust (1983) 10 HLR 65 299
Ford *v* Metropolitan and Metropolitan District Rly Cos (1886) 17 QBD
    12; 55 LJQB 296; 54 LT 718; 2 TLR 281; 50 JP 661; 34 WR 426 373
Fox *v* Secretary of State for the Environment [1991] 2 EGLR 13 209
Fox (Lady) Exors *v* Commissioners of Inland Revenue [1994] 2 EGLR
    185 . . . . 183, 185
Francis *v* Harris [1989] 07 EG 70; [1989] 1 EGLR 45 296
Frank Warr & Co Ltd *v* LCC [1904] 1 KB 713 375
Frederick Powell & Son Ltd *v* Devon County Council [1979]
    RVR 127. 243
Freedman *v* British Railways Board [1992] EGCS 55. 82
Freeman *v* Middlesex County Council (1965) 16 P&CR 253. 350
Frisby *v* Chingford Corpn (1957) P&CR 423, HL. 313

G

Gaganus *v* Turkey [2002] (unreported: 5 May 2001) 441
Garland J and Re J [1990] FCR 193. 148
Garrett *v* Department of the Environment for Northern Ireland [1985]
    RVR 73. . . . . 245, 417
Gately *v* Central Lancashire New Town Development Corpn (1984)
    270 EG 1197; [1984] 1 EGLR 195. . . . . 179, 230

Gaze *v* Holden [1983] I EGLR 147. 147

Genders *v* London County Council [1915] 1 Ch 1 111

General Estates Co Ltd *v* Minister of Housing and Local Government
   [1965] EGD 98 58

George *v* Secretary of State for the Environment (1979) 38 P&CR 609;
   [1979] JPL 382 [1979] 1 EGLR 30 reversing 37 P&CR 188; 250 EG
   399; (QB), [1978] 2 EGLR 8; (CA). 31, 54

George *v* Southwest Electricity Board [1982] 2 EGLR 214 433

George Whitehouse Ltd *v* Anglian Water Authority (1978) 247 EG
   223; 35 P&CR 230 425

Glasgow City *v* Secretary of State for Scotland [1990] 2 EGLR 18 55

Glasshouse Properties Ltd *v* Department of Transport (1994) 66 P&CR
   285; [1994] 1 EGLR 207 . . . . 110, 111, 113

Glossop Sectional Buildings Ltd *v* Sheffield Development Corpn,
   sub nom Sheffield Development Corpn *v* Glossop Sectional
   Buildings Ltd [1994] 2 EGLR 29 282

Gooderam *v* Department of Transport [1994] 35 RVR 12 336

Goss *v* Paddington Churches Housing Association (1982) 261
   EG 373 304

Gozra *v* Hackney London Borough Council [1988] 2 EGLR 20 305

Grafton (Duke of) *v* Secretary of State for Air (1956) 6 P&CR 374, CA;
   reversing (1955) 5 P&CR 290; [1955] CLY 387, LT 296

Grampian RC *v* Secretary of State for Scotland [1983] 3 All ER 673;
   (HL), [1984] 2 EGLR 175 . . . . 209, 210

Grape Bay Ltd *v* Attorney-General of Bermuda [2000] 1 WLR 575 440

Graysmark *v* South Hams District Council [1989] 03 EG 75; [1989]
   1 EGLR 191 415

Greater London Council *v* Holmes [1986] QB 989; [1986] 1 All ER
   739; [1986] 1EGLR 22; (1985) 277 EG 641; reversing [1984] 2 All
   ER 743. 298

Green *v* Secretary of State for Environment (1984) 271 EG 550; [1984]
   2 EGLR 27; [1985] JPL 119 (QB) 45

Greenbank *v* Pickles [2001] 1 EGLR 1. 334

Greenwich London Borough Council *v* Secretary of State for the
   Environment (1993) The Times March 2. 39

Greenwoods Tyre Service Ltd *v* Manchester Corpn (1971) 23 P&CR
   246 [1972] EGD 205 313

Grice *v* Dudley Corpn [1958] 1 Ch 329; [1957] 2 All ER 673; [1957]
   3 WLR 314. 93

Griffith *v* Richard Clay & Sons Ltd [1912] 2 Ch 291 378

Grimley *v* Minister of Housing and Local Government [1971] 2 QB 96;
   [1971] 2 All ER 431; 22 P&CR 339; [1971] EGD 282 31

Grosvenor Motor Co *v* Chester Corpn (1963) 14 P&CR 478; [1963]
   EGD 215 252

H

Halil *v* Lambeth London Borough Council [2001] RVR 18 285
Halliday *v* Secretary of State for Transport [1991] RVR 40 111
Hallows *v* Welsh Office [1995] 1 EGLR 191 144
Halstead *v* Manchester City Council [1998] 1 EGLR 1. .... 260, 307, 308
Hammersmith and City Rly Co *v* Brand (1869) LR 4 HL 171; [1861–73]
    All ER Rep 60. .... 17, 368, 375, 376
Hanks *v* Minister of Housing and Local Government [1963] 1 QB 999;
    [1963] 1 All ER 47; 15 P&CR 246 52
Harding *v* Metropolitan Rly Co (1872) 7 Ch App 154 .... 93, 176
Harford *v* Birmingham City Council (1993) 66 P&CR 468; [1993]
    RVR 119 132
Harris *v* Commissioners for Inland Revenue (1961) 177 EG 365
    .... 186, 316
Harris *v* Welsh Development Agency [1999] 3 EGLR 207 .... 280, 289,
    .... 291, 292, 358
Harrison & Hetherington Ltd *v* Cumbria County Council [1985]
    2 EGLR 37; (1985) 275 EG 457, HL. 137, 257
Harvey *v* Crawley Development Corpn [1957] 1 QB 485; [1957] 1 All
    ER 504. .... 273, 275, 290, 304
Hayes Will Trusts, in Re [1971] 1 WLR 758 145
Hearts of Oak Benefit Society *v* Lewisham Borough Council (1979)
    249 EG 967; [1979] 1 EGLR 178 .... 193, 315
Heffron *v* City of Liverpool (unreported: 7 September 1989). 90
Herring *v* Metropolitan Board of Works (1865) 144 ER 886 373
Hibernian Property Ltd *v* Liverpool Corpn [1973] 2 All ER 1117. 316
Hillingdon Estates Co *v* Stonefield Estates Ltd [1952] Ch 627; [1952]
    1 All ER 853; 2 P&CR 415. .... 89, 316
Hillingdon London Borough Council *v* ARC Ltd [1997] 29 EG 125; on
    appeal [1998] 3 EGLR 18 134
Hillingdon London Borough Council *v* ARC Ltd (No 2) [2000] 3
    EGLR 97. 134
Hitchins Builders Ltd *v* Secretary of State for the Environment (1979)
    251 EG 467; 37 P&CR 40. 209
Hoare *v* National Trust [1999] 1 EGLR 155. 185
Hobbs (Quarries) Ltd *v* Somerset County Council (1975) 30 P&CR
    286; [1975] EGD 466; [1975] 1 EGLR 189 .... 169, 407
Hoddom & Kinmount Estates *v* Secretary of State for Scotland [1992]
    1 EGLR 252 .... 273, 324
Holloway *v* Dover Corpn [1960] 2 All ER 193; [1960] 1 WLR 604;
    [1960] EGD 23 .... 92, 172, 311
Holditch *v* Canadian Northern Ontario Railway [1916] 1 AC 536
    .... 234, 235
Holt *v* Gas Light and Coke Co (1872) 8 LR 728. .... 235, 236
Holy Monasteries *v* Greece (1994) 20 EHRR 1 443

Horn *v* Sunderland Corpn [1941] 2 KB 26; [1941] 1 All ER 480 . . . 157, 168,
. . . . 169, 186, 239, 217, 238, 239, 249, 266, 267, 268, 324, 334, 266,
. . . . 267, 357, 433
Horton *v* Colwyn Bay Urban District Council [1908] 1 KB 327 . . . 378, 432
Hoveringham Gravels Ltd *v* Chiltern District Council (1979) 252 EG
815; [1979] 2 EGLR 182; remitted by CA (1977) 243 EG 911; [1977]
2 EGLR 17; on appeal from LT (1976) 237 EG 811; [1976] 1 EGLR
185. . . . . 178, 195, 211, 237, 239, 241
Hoveringham Gravels Ltd *v* Secretary of State for the Environment
[1975] QB 764; [1975] 2 All ER 931; 73 LGR 238; 30 P&CR 151, CA;
(1975) 235 EG 217, 295; [1975] 2 EGLR 123. 404
Hull and Humber Investment Co *v* Hull Corpn [1965] 2 QB 145; [1965]
1 All ER 429; 16 P&CR 201; [1964] EGD 206 . . . . 86, 209, 274
Hughes *v* Doncaster Metropolitan Borough Council [1991] 1 AC 382;
[1991] 1All ER 295; [1991] 1 EGLR 31 . . . . . . 160, 168, 191, 239, 265, 266,
. . . . 265, 266, 361
Hussain *v* Oldham Metropolitan Borough Council (1981) 259 EG 56;
[1981] 2 EGLR 17. . . . . 101, 178
Hutchinson (doe d) *v* Manchester (1845) 15 M&W 314. 128
Hutton *v* Esher Urban District Council [1972] Ch 515; [1972] 3 All ER
504; 24 P&CR 20; [1972] EGD 659 109

I

Ikarian Reefer [1993] 2 EGLR 183 148
Imperial Gaslight & Cooke Co *v* Broadbent (1859) 7 HLC 600. 372
Inland Revenue Commissioners *v* Clay & Buchanan [1914] 3 KB 466;
[1914–15] All ER Rep 882 on appeal from [1914] 1 KB 339 . . . . . 182, 189
Ingle *v* Scarborough Council [2002] 2 EGLR 161 299
Islington London Borough Council *v* Secretary of State for the
Environment [1980] JPL 739. 55
Ivens & Sons Ltd *v* Daventry District Council (1975) 31 P&CR 480;
[1976] 1 EGLR 195 203

J

James *v* UK Government [1986] 14 CSW 782 . . . . . . 5, 12, 13, 403, 441, 442
JA Pye (Oxford) Ltd *v* Kingswood Borough Council [1998] 2 EGLR 159
. . . . 225
Jelson Ltd *v* Blaby District Council [1978] 1 All ER 548; (1977) 243
EG 47; [1977] 2 EGLR 14. . . . . 222, 227, 241
Johns *v* Edmonton Corpn (1958) 171 EG 515 296
Johnson (B) & Co (Builders) Ltd *v* Minister of Health [1947] 2 All ER
395, CA 42
Johnson *v* North Yorkshire County Council (1992) 65 P&CR 65; [1992]
RVR 184. 115

Johnson (E) & Co (Barbados) Ltd *v* NSR Ltd [1996] 3 WLR 583, PC
.... 89, 93
Johnson *v* Sheffield City Council (1981) 260 EG 931; [1981] 2 EGLR 188
.... 311
Jolliffe *v* Exeter Corpn [1967] 2 All ER 1099; 18 P&CR 343; [1967]
     EGD 312 .... 376, 417
Jubb *v* Hull Dock Co (1846) 9 QB 443 .... 265, 268

K

K&B Metals Ltd *v* Birmingham City Council (1977) 33 P&CR 135;
     [1976] 2 EGLR 180 409
Kayworth *v* Highways Agency (1996) 72 P&CR 433 70
Keary Developments Ltd *v* Tarmac [1995] 3 All ER 534; [1995] 2 BCLC
     395; 73 BLR 115, CA 142
Ken Newbridge Ltd *v* Ipswich Borough Council (1983) 267 EG 605 . . . 143
Kettering Borough Council *v* Anglian Water Services plc [2001]
     2 EGLR 157 426
King, Re [1963] Ch 459, on appeal from [1962] 1 WLR 632 .... 316, 317
King *v* Dorset County Council [1997] 1 EGLR 245 .... 386, 388, 390
Kirby *v* School Board for Harrogate [1896] 1 Ch 437 .... 107, 371
Klein *v* London Underground [1996] 1 EGLR 249 284
Knibb *v* National Coal Board [1986] 2 EGLR 11 408
Koch *v* Greater London Council (1968) 20 P&CR 472; [1969] JPL 277
.... 281
Kolbe House Society *v* Department of Transport (1994) 98 P&CR 569
.... 259
Korogluyan *v* Matheou [1976] 2 EGLR 157 .... 93, 259

L

Laing Homes Ltd *v* Eastleigh Borough Council (1979) 250 EG 350;
     [1979] 1 EGLR 187 .... 195, 250
Lake *v* Cheshire County Council (1976) 32 P&CR 143, LT 67
Lamba Trading Co Ltd *v* Salford City Council [1999] 3 EGLR 186 279
Lambe *v* Secretary of State for War [1955] 2 QB 612; [1955] 2 All ER
     386; 5 P&CR 227 .... 187, 193
Landlink Two Ltd *v* Sevenoaks District Council [1985] 1 EGLR 19
.... 89, 171
Landau *v* Secretary of State for the Environment [1991] EGCS
     119 .... 44, 46
Lay *v* Norfolk County Council [1997] RVR 9 349
Layzell *v* Smith Morton & Long [1992] 1 EGLR 169 333
Leake *v* Wirrall MB [1977] 2 EGLR 117 375
Leicester City Council *v* Leicestershire County Council (1995) 70
     P&CR 435; [1995] 2 EGLR 169 251
Lee *v* Minister of Transport [1966] 1 QB 111; [1965] EGD 176; *sub nom*

Minister of Transport *v* Lee [1965] 2 All ER 986; 17 P&CR 181, [1965]
EGD 8. 296

Leek *v* Birmingham City Council (1982) 261 EG 1101; [1982]
1 EGLR 185 . . . . 222, 316

Leggat *v* Secretary of State for the Environment [1991] 1 PLR 103 52

Leonidis *v* Thames Water Authority [1979] 2 EGLR 8. 425

Lesquende *v* Planning and Environmental Committee of the State of
Jersey [1998] 1 EGLR 137. . . . . 139, 297

Lewars *v* Greater London Council (1981) 259 EG 500; [1981]
2 EGLR 178 . . . . 143, 178

Lewis *v* Hackney London Borough Council [1990] 2 EGLR 15 86

Lewis *v* Mid-Glamorgan County Council [1995] 1 All ER 760 350

'Liesbosch', the [1933] AC 449. 415

Line (John) & Son *v* Newcastle upon Tyne Corpn (1956) 6 P&CR 466;
168 EG 63. 279

Lindon Print Ltd *v* West Midlands County Council (1987) 283 EG
70; [1987] 2 EGLR 200 LT 276, 277, 279, 282

Lingké *v* Christchurch Corpn [1912] 3 KB 595. 373

Lion Nathan Ltd *v* CC Bottlers [1996] 1 WLR 1438. 283

Lithgow *v* United Kingdom (1986) 8 EHRR 329 . . . . 440, 442

Livesey *v* CEGB [1965] EGD 205. 188

Livingston *v* Rawyards Coal Co (1880) 5 App Cas 25. 157

Llanelec Precision Engineering Co Ltd *v* Neath Talbot County
Borough Council (unreported: 3 August 2000) 78, 94

London CC *v* Tobin [1959] 1 All ER 649; [1959] 1 WLR 354; 10 P&CR
79; [1959] EGD 22. . . . . 146, 283, 293, 296

London & Clydeside Estates Ltd *v* Aberdeen District Council [1979]
3 All ER 876; (1979) 253 EG 1011; [1980] 1 EGLR 11. 208

London & Winchester Properties Ltd's Application (1983) 45 P&CR
429; [1983] EGD 717; [1983] 2 EGLR 201; [1983] JPL 318 132

London Regional Transport *v* Imperial Group Pension Trust Ltd (1987)
284 EG 1593; [1987] 2 EGLR 20 88

London Tilbury and Southend Rly Co and Gower's Walk Schools
Trustees, Re (1889) 24 QBD 326. 378

London Transport Executive *v* Congregation Union of England and
Wales (1979) 249 EG 1173 111

London Welsh Association *v* Secretary of State for the Environment
(1979) 252 EG 378; [1979] 2 EGLR 22 QB; [1980] 2 EGLR 17 CA 51

Long Eaton Recreation Grounds Co *v* Midland Rly Co [1902]
2 KB 574 . . . . 107, 374, 376

Lonsdale (Earl of) *v* Attorney General [1982] 1 WLR 887; [1982] 3 All
ER 579; (1983) 45 P&CR 1. 348

Loosemore *v* Tiverton & North Devon Rly Co (1884) 9 App Cas 480 . . 128

Lorbright Ltd *v* Staffordshire County Council [1980] 1 EGLR 156;
[1980] RVR 139. 252

Loromah Ltd *v* Haringey London Borough Council (1978) 248 EG 877;
  [1978] 2 EGLR 202. 408
Louisville Investments Ltd *v* Basingstoke District Council (1976) 31
  P&CR 419; [1976] 2 EGLR 172 69
Lucas and Chesterfield Gas and Water Board Re [1909] 1 KB 16,
  99 LT 767. . . . . 161, 188, 228, 228

M

M&B Precision Engineers *v* Ealing London Borough Council (1972)
  225 EG 1186. 291
Macleod *v* National Grid Co plc [1998] 2 EGLR 217 . . . . 433, 435
Mahood *v* Department of the Environment for Northern Ireland
  (1986) 277 EG 652; [1986] 1 EGLR 207. 296
Maidstone Borough Council *v* Secretary of State for the Environment
  [1996] 3 PLR 66; [1996] 1 EGLR 29. 211
Maile *v* West Sussex County Council [1985] RVR 52; [1984]
  1 EGLR 194 . . . . 387, 388
Mallick *v* Liverpool City Council [1999] 2 EGLR 7 292
Malmesbury (Countess) *v* Secretary of State for Transport [1982] 2
  EGLR 188. 246
Malvern Hills District Council *v* Secretary of State for the Environment
  [1982] 1 EGLR 175; [1982] JPL 439. 415
Manchester Homeopathic Clinic (Trustees) *v* Manchester Corpn (1970)
  22 P&CR 241; see Trustees of the Manchester Homeopathic Clinic
  v Manchester Corpn. 257, 259
Mancini *v* Coventry City Council (1984) 270 EG 419; [1984]
  1 EGLR 178 68
Maori Trustee *v* Ministry of Works [1959] AC 1. 197
Marchant *v* Secretary of State for Transport (1979) 250 EG 559; [1979]
  1 EGLR 194 . . . . 386, 388
Margate Corporation *v* Devotwill Investments [1970] 3 All ER 864;
  22 P&CR 328, (1970) 218 EG 559 reversing [1969] 2 All ER 97;
  20 P&CR 150; affirming 19 P&CR 458. . . . . 204, 205
Markland *v* Cannock Rural District Council (1973) 227 EG 1173. 426
Marquis of Salisbury *v* Great Northern Railway (1852) 17 QB 840 86
Marsh *v* Powys County Council [1997] 2 EGLR 177 381
Marshall *v* Basildon Development Corpn [1970] RVR 39 141
Marson *v* Hasley (1975) 233 EG 1183; [1975] 1 EGLR 157 144
Marson *v* London, Chatham & Dover Railway [1868] 113
Masters and Great Western Rly Co Re [1901] 2 KB 84; 70 LJKB 516;
  84 LT 515; 65 JP 420; 49 WR 499. 371
Marten *v* Flight Refuelling Ltd [1961] 2 All ER 696; [1962] Ch 115;
  [1961] 2 WLR 1018; 13 P&CR 389; [1962] JPL 523 . . . . . . 82, 108, 117, 118
Marylebone (Stingo Lane) Improvement Act, Re *ex parte* Edwards
  (1871) LR 12 EQ 389; 25 LT 149 . . . . 89, 92, 172

Marzell *v* Great London Council (1975) 234 EG 621; [1975]
    1 EGLR 179 87
Matthews *v* Environment Agency (unreported: 24 April 2002) 296
Matthews *v* Lewisham London Borough Council (1982) 263 EG 266;
    [1982] 2 EGLR 180. 128
McDermott *v* Department of Transport (1984) 48 P&CR 351; [1984]
    JPL 596, LT. 66
McEwing *v* Renfrewshire County Council (1959) 11 P&CR 306 286
McKay *v* City of London Corpn (1966) 17 P&CR 264 349
McLaren's Discretionary Trustee *v* Secretary of State for Scotland
    [1987] RVR 159 326
McMillan *v* Strathclyde Regional Council [1983] 1 EGLR 188 112
McTaggart *v* Bristol and West Building Society (1985) 49
    P&CR 184 302
Mears *v* St Pancras Metropolitan Borough Council [1963] EGD 129 . . . 144
Melwood Units Pty Ltd *v* Commissioner of Main Roads [1979] 1 All
    ER 161. . . . . 145, 229, 241, 245
Meravale Builders Ltd *v* Secretary of State for the Environment (1978)
    36 P&CR 87; [1978] JPL 699 54
Mercer *v* Liverpool, St Helens, and South Lancashire Rly Co [1904]
    AC 461; 73 LJKB 960; 91 LT 605; 20 TLR 673; 68 JP 533; 53 WR 241
    . . . . 89, 93
Mercury Communications Ltd *v* London & India Dock Investments
    Ltd [1995] 69 P&CR 135; [1994] 1 EGLR 229. . . . . 132, 430
Methodist Church Purposes Trustees *v* North Tyneside Metropolitan
    Borough Council (1979) 38 P&CR 665; 250 EG 647; [1979] 1 EGLR
    33 . . . . 89, 97, 384
Metropolitan Board of Works *v* Howard (1889) 5 TLR 732. 379
Metropolitan Board of Works *v* McCarthy (1874) LR 7 HL 243;
    31 LT 182 . . . . 370 *et seq*
Mills & Allen Ltd *v* Commission for New Towns [2001] RVR 114. 302
Mills *v* East London Union (1872) LR 8 CP 79 . . . . 106, 279
Milnes Re (1875) 1 ChD 28; 24 WR 98; 34 LT 46, CA. 130
Minister of Transport *v* Pettit (1969) 20 P&CR 344; [1969] EGD 69
    . . . . 290, 314, 335, 336
Mizen Bros *v* Mitcham Urban District Council [1929] EGD 258,
    reprinted (1941) 137 EG 102 . . . . 266, 267
Mobil Oil Co *v* Secretary of State [1991] JPL 353 17
Mooney *v* West Lindsay District Council [2000] RVR 225 413
Moore *v* Great Southern and Western Rly Co Re (1858) 10 ICLR 46
    (Irish) 373
Morgan and London and North West Rly Co Re [1896] 2 QB 469; 75
    LT 226. 320
Morgan *v* Metropolitan Railway (1867) LR 3 CP 553; affirming (1868)
    LR 4 CP 77. 128

Morris & Jacobs Ltd *v* Birmingham District Council (1976) 31 P&CR
    305; 235 EG 679; on appeal City of Birmingham District Council *v*
    Morris & Jacobs Ltd (1976) 33 P&CR 27; 240 EG 539; [1975] 2
    EGLR 173; [1976] 2 EGLR 143 228
Munton *v* Greater London Council [1976] 1 WLR 649; [1976] 2 All
    ER 815; 32 P&CR 269; 239 EG 43 . . . . 78, 94, 177
Murray Bookmakers Ltd *v* Glasgow District Council [1979] RVR 254
    . . . . 172, 320
Myers *v* Milton Keynes Development Corpn [1974] 1 WLR 696; [1974]
    2 All ER 1096; 27 P&CR 518; 230 EG 1275 . . . . 150, 201, 221, 231, 324

N
National Carriers Ltd *v* Secretary of State for Transport (1978) 35
    P&CR 245 351
National Provident Institution *v* Avon County Council [1992]
    EGCS 56. 127
Nature Conservancy Council *v* Deller [1992] 2 EGLR 11 334
Naylor *v* British Railways Board (1983) (Unreported) 82
Neeson *v* Department of NI [1985] RVR 118 90
Nelungaloo Proprietary Ltd *v* The Commonwealth [1948] 75
    CLR 495 158
Nesbitt *v* National Assembly for Wales, (unreported: 26 April 2002) . . 388
Newcastle under Lyme Corpn *v* Wolstanton Ltd [1947] 1 Ch 92 422
Newham London Borough Council *v* Benjamin [1968] 1 WLR 694;
    [1968] EGD 115, *sub nom* Benjamin *v* Newham London Borough
    Council (1968) 19 P&CR 365. . . . . 88, 312, 313
Nicholls *v* Highways Agency [2000] 2 EGLR 81 138
Nolan *v* Sheffield Metropolitan District Council (1979) 251 EG 1179;
    [1979] 2 EGLR 178. 303
Norman *v* Department of Transport (1996) 72 P&CR 210; [1996] 1
    EGLR 190. 65
Nuttal *v* Leeds City Council (1982) 262 EG 349; [1982] 1 EGLR 193
    . . . . 137, 286

O
Old England Properties Ltd *v* Telford & Wrekin Council [2000] 3 EGLR
    153; [2001] RVR 175 203
Oppenheimer *v* Minister of Transport [1942] KB 242; [1941] 3 All
    ER 485 . . . . 87, 105, 235, 236
Ossalinsky (Countess) *v* Manchester Corpn (1883) unreported but
    judgment printed in Balfour and Brown, *The Law of Compensation*,
    2nd edition at p659 . . . . 161, 167, 188
Ozanne *v* Hertfordshire County Council [1992] 2 EGLR 201, LT, on
    remission from *sub nom* Hertfordshire County Council *v* Ozanne
    [1991] 1 EGLR 34 HL; on appeal from [1989] 2 EGLR 18, CA; and

on appeal from [1988] 2 EGLR 213; [1988] RVR 133, LT . . . 188, 195, 227

P

Padfield *v* Eastern Electricity Board [1972] RVR 105; (1972) 22
EG 735 434
Palatine Graphic Arts Co *v* Liverpool City Council [1986] QB 335;
[1986] 1 All ER 366; (1986) 52 P&CR 308; [1986] 1 EGLR 19 280
Pandit *v* Leicester City Council (1989) 58 P&CR 305; (1990) 30
RVR 127 . . . . 123, 124
Parker *v* Secretary of State for the Environment (1981) 257 EG 718;
[1981] 1 EGLR 11, CA 54
Parker *v* West Midlands County Council [1979] JPL 178 68
Pastoral Finance Association Ltd *v* The Minister [1914] AC 1083 287
Paul *v* Newham London Borough Council (1991) 30 RVR 64 . . . . . . 92, 315
Pearce *v* Augton (1973) 26 P&CR 357 209
Pearce *v* Bristol Corpn (1949) 1 P&CR 367 338
Pennine Raceway Ltd *v* Kirklees Metropolitan Borough Council (No 1)
[1983] QB 382; [1982] 3 All ER 628; (1982) 45 P&CR 313 407
Pennine Raceway Ltd *v* Kirklees Metropolitan Borough Council (No 2)
[1989] 1 EGLR 30, CA, on appeal from the Lands Tribunal 358
Pennsylvania Coal Co *v* Mahon 260 US 393 (United States Supreme
Court). 402
Penny *v* Penny (1868) LR 5 EQ 277, 18 LT 13 . . . . 90, 159, 175
Penny and South Eastern Rly Co, Re (1857) 7 E&B 660, *sub nom*
R *v* South Eastern Rly Co 29 LTOS 124 372
Penty *v* Greater London Council (1982) 263 EG 893; [1982] 2 EGLR 196
. . . . 424
Pepys *v* London Transport Executive [1975] 1 WLR 234; [1975] 1 All
ER 748; 29 P&CR 248; [1975] EGD 462; [1975] 1 EGLR 20 139
Perkins *v* West Wiltshire District Council (1976) 31 P&CR 427; 237
EG 661; [1976] 1 EGLR 182 66,69
Perry *v* Clissold [1907] AC 73 87
Phipps *v* Wiltshire County Council (1983) 265 EG 393; [1983] 1
EGLR 181 . . . . 139, 297
Pine Valley Developments Ltd *v* Ireland (1991) 14 EHRR 319 440
Pointe Gourde Quarrying and Transport Co Ltd *v* Sub-Intendent of
Crown Lands [1947] AC 565 . . . . 164, 165, 167, 178, 179, 182, 187,
. . . . 220 *et seq*, 241, 244, 245
Pollard *v* Middlesex County Council (1906) 95 LT 870 . . . . 78, 94
Polivitte Ltd *v* Commercial Union Assurance Co plc [1987] 1 Lloyds
Rep 379 148
Porter *v* Secretary of State for Transport [1995] 2 EGLR 175; [1995]
1 PLR 103, LT; [1996] 1 EGLR 10, CA 208, 242
Portsmouth Roman Catholic Diocesan Trustees *v* Hampshire County
Council (1980) 253 EG 1236; [1980] 1 EGLR 150 . . . . 211, 251

Powner & Powner *v* Leeds Corpn (1953) 4 P&CR 167 290
Prasad *v* Wolverhampton Borough Council [1983] Ch 333; (1983) 265
    EG 1073; [1983] 2 All ER 140; [1983] 1 EGLR 10 . . . . . . 273, 275, 276, 304
Preseli Pembrokeshire District Council *v* Greens Motors [1991]
    1 EGLR 211 317
Prest *v* Secretary of State for Wales (1983) 266 EG 527; [1983]
    1 EGLR 17 . . . . 44, 47, 51
Proctor & Gamble Ltd *v* Secretary of State for the Environment [1992]
    1 EGLR 265 51
Provincial Building Society *v* Hammersmith and Fulham London
    Borough Council [1982] RVR 36; [1982] 1 EGLR 183 . . . . 173, 352
Provincial Properties (London) Ltd *v* Caterham and Warlingham
    Urban District Council [1972] 1 QB 453; [1972] 1 All ER 60; 23
    P&CR 8; [1972] JPL 640 204
Purbeck District Council *v* Secretary of State for the Environment
    (1982) 263 EG 261 59
Purfleet Farms Ltd *v* Secretary of State for Transport [2003] 02
    EG 105 139
Pyrah (Doddington) Ltd *v* Northampton County Council (1982) 263
    EG 729; [1982] 2 EGLR 195 . . . . 91, 315, 328

R
RA Vine (Engineering) Ltd *v* Havant Borough Council [1989]
    2 EGLR 15 239
Raja Vyricherla Narayana Gajapatiraju *v* Revenue Divisional Officer,
    Vizagapatam [1939] AC 302 . . . . 184, 185, 193, 228, 426
Ramsden *v* Manchester etc Rly Co (1848) 1 Ex 723 105
Range *v* Buckinghamshire County Council (1985) RVR 54 LT 316
Rathgar Property Co Ltd *v* Haringey London Borough Council [1978]
    RVR 44; 248 EG 693 . . . . 190, 238
Ravenseft Properties *v* Hillingdon London Borough Council (1968)
    20 P&CR 483; [1968] EGD 315 . . . . 90, 93, 111, 171
R *v* Bristol Corporation, *ex parte* Hendy [1974] 1 WLR 498; [1974]
    1 All ER 1047; (1973) 27 P&CR 180 305
R *v* Brown (1867) LR2 QB 630; 16 LT 827 160
R *v* Camden London Borough Council *ex parte* Comyn Ching and
    Co Ltd [1984] JPL 661 50
R *v* Carmarthen District Council, *ex parte* Blewin Trust [1990] 1
    EGLR 29; (1989) 59 P&CR 379 . . . . 55, 98
R *v* City of London Corpn, *ex parte* Mystery of Barbers [1996] 2 EGLR
    128; (1996) 73 P&CR 59 . . . . 74, 75, 119
R *v* Commission for New Towns, *ex parte* Tomkins [1989] 12 EG 59;
    [1989] 1 EGLR 24 81
R *v* Corby District Council, *ex parte* McLean [1975] 1 WLR 735; [1975]
    2 All ER 568; [1975] 2 EGLR 40 298

R *v* Department of Trade and Industry, *ex parte* Healaugh Farms
 [1995] EGCS 203; The Times, December 27 1994 QBD 433
R *v* Essex County Council, ex parte Clearbrook Contractors Ltd [1981]
 (Unreported: 3 April 1981). 81
R *v* Great Northern Rly (1876) 2 QBD 151 313
R *v* Hackney London Borough Council, *ex parte* Structadene Ltd
 [2001] 1 EGLR 15. 81
R (Lemon Land Ltd) *v* Hacney London Borough Council [2002]
 1 EGLR 81 81
R *v* High Bailiff for Westminster, ex parte London County Council
 [1903] 2 KB 189 141
R *v* Islington London Borough Council [1984] 1 All ER 154 301
R *v* Lancashire County Council, *ex parte* Telegraph Service Stations
 Ltd [1988] EGCS 96. 81
R *v* Lands Tribunal, *ex parte* City of London Corpn [1982] 1 All ER
 892, CA 150
R *v* Leeds City Council, *ex parte* Leeds Industrial Co-op Society
 (1996) 73 P&CR 70 120
R *v* Minister of Housing and Local Government, *ex parte* Chichester
 Rural District Council [1960] 1 WLR 587; [1960] 2 All ER 407; [1960]
 EGD 208. 58
R *v* Northumbrian Water, *ex parte* Able UK Ltd [1996] 2 EGLR 15. . . 96, 97
R *v* Parliamentary Commissioner for Administration, *ex parte* Balchin
 [1997] 3 PLR; [1996] EGCS 166. 397
R *v* Secretary of State for Defence, *ex parte* Wilkins [2000] 3 EGLR 11 . . . 80
R *v* Secretary of State for the Environment, *ex parte* Bournemouth
 Borough Council (1987) 281 EG 539; [1987] 1 EGLR 198; [1987]
 JPL 357 . . . . 66, 69
R *v* Secretary of State for the Environment, *ex parte* Kensington and
 Chelsea Royal Borough Council [1987] JPL 567. 36
R *v* Secretary of State for the Environment, *ex parte* Leicester City
 Council (1987) 55 P&CR 344 55
R *v* Secretary of State for the Environment, *ex parte* Melton Borough
 Council [1986] JPL 191 55
R *v* Secretary of State for the Environment, *ex parte* Ostler [1977]
 QB 122; [1976] 3 All ER 90; 32 P&CR 166; 238 EG 971; [1976]
 1 EGLR 11 49
R *v* Secretary of State for the Environment, Transport and Regions,
 ex parte Plymouth City Airport Ltd [2001] 82 P&CR 265. 391
R *v* Secretary of State for the Environment, *ex parte* Rose Theatre
 Trust Co (No 2) [1989] EGCS 107 55
R *v* Secretary of State for the Environment, *ex parte* Ward [1995]
 JPL B39. 209
R *v* Secretary of State for the Environment, *ex parte* Wheeler [2000]
 3 EGLR 63 80

R *v* Secretary of State for Transport, *ex parte* Blackett [1992] JPL 1041 . . . 87
R *v* Secretary of State for Transport, *ex parte* Owen [1995] RVR 223;
    [1995] 2 EGLR 213; [1995] NPC 168 396
R *v* Secretary of State for Trade and Industry, *ex parte* Wolf (1997)
    79 P&CR 299 432
R *v* Stone (1866) LR 1 QB 529; 7 B&S 769; 35 LJMC 208; 14 LT 552;
    30 JP 488; 14 WR 791 313
R *v* Trent Regional Health Authority, *ex parte* Westerman (1995) EGCS
    175; 72 P&CR 448 80
Rank Leisure *v* Castle Vale Housing Action Trust [2001] RVR 301 221
Reed Employment Ltd *v* London Transport Executive [1978]
    1 EGLR 166 286
Reside *v* Ayreshire Council [2000] 3 PLR 86 59
Reynolds *v* Manchester City Council (1981) 257 EG 939; [1981]
    1 EGLR 167 282
Reynolds *v* Phoenix Assurance Co Ltd [1978] 2 Lloyd's Rep 442 169
Richard *v* Great Western Rly; Re [1905] 1 KB 68 132
Richards *v* Swansea Improvement and Tramways Co (1878) 9 ChD
    425; 38 LT 833 111
Richmond Gateway *v* Richmond London Borough Council [1989]
    2 EGLR 182 143
Ricket *v* Metropolitan Rly Co (1867) LR 2 HL 175; 16 LT 542; on
    appeal from (1865) 34 LJ (QB) 257 . . . . 157, 160, 374
Riddle *v* Secretary of State for the Environment (1988) 42 EG 120;
    [1988] 2 EGLR 17 52
Rigby *v* Secretary of State for Transport (1978) 247 EG 473 388
Rivers *v* Dorset County Council [1995] 35 RVR 177 302
Robert Barnes & Co Ltd *v* Malvern Hills District Council [1985]
    1 EGLR 189 415
Roberts *v* Bristol Corpn (1960) 11 P&CR 205 313
Roberts *v* Coventry Corpn [1947] 1 All ER 308 269
Roberts *v* South Gloucestershire District Council [2003] 18 EG 114 201
Rockingham Sisters of Charity *v* R [1922] AC 315 242
Rothera *v* Nottingham City Council (1980) 39 P&CR 613 236
Royal Bank of Scotland *v* Clydebank District Council [1995]
    1 EGLR 229 . . . . 101, 132, 133
Royal Life Insurance *v* Secretary of State for the Environment [1992]
    2 EGLR 23 46
Rugby Joint Water Board *v* Foottit, same *v* Shaw Fox [1973] AC 202;
    [1972] 1 All ER 1057; 24 P&CR 256; [1972] EGD 356 . . . . 90, 179, 224,
    . . . . 228, 315, 328
Runcorn Association Football Club *v* Warrington & Runcorn
    Development Corpn (1982) 264 EG 627; 45 P&CR 183; [1982]
    2 EGLR 216 . . . . 172, 256, 260, 310

Ryde International plc *v* London Regional Transport [2001]
1 EGLR 101 269

S

S *v* United Kingdom (1984) 41 DR 226 439
SJC Construction Co Ltd's Application, Re (1974) 28 P&CR 200;
affirmed *sub nom* SJC Construction Co *v* Sutton London Borough
Council (1975) 29 P&CR 322; 234 EG 363; [1975] 1 EGLR 105, LT . . . 379
St Helens Smelting Co *v* Tipping (1865) 11 HL Cas 642 367
St John's College, Oxford *v* Thames Water Authority [1990]
1 EGLR 229. . . . . 239, 426, 435
St John's Wood Working Men's Club *v* LCC (1947) 150 EG 213 257
Sadik and Sadik *v* Haringey London Borough Council [1978] JPL 778;
244 EG 643 290
Salisbury (Marquis) *v* Great Northern Railway (1852) 17 QB 840 86
Salop County Council *v* Craddock [1970] EGD 87 . . . . 195, 241
Sample (J) (Warkworth) Ltd *v* Alnwick District Council (1984) 271
EG 204; [1984] 2 EGLR 191. 414
Save Britain's Heritage *v* No 1 Poultry [1990] 3 PLR 50; 60 P&CR 539 . . 44
Sceneout Ltd *v* Central Manchester Development Corpn [1995] 34
EG 77; [1995] 2 EGLR 179; [1995] RVR 200; LT 283
Schwinge *v* London & Blackwell Railway Co (1855) 24 LJ Ch 405 113
Seddon Properties Ltd *v* Secretary of State for the Environment [1978]
JPL 835; 248 EG 951 48
Segama *v* Penny Le Roy Ltd (1984) 269 EG 322. 145
Selborne (Gowns) Ltd *v* Ilford Corpn (1962) 13 P&CR 350; [1962]
EGD 149. . . . . 214, 301, 302, 320, 321
Senate Electricial Wholesalers Ltd *v* Acatel Submarine Networks
Ltd [1999] 2 Lloyd's Rep 423 283
Service Welding Ltd *v* Tyne and Wear County Council (1979) 250
EG 1291; [1979] 1 EGLR 36. . . . . 273, 277, 289, 191
Sheffield Development Corpn *v* Glossop Sectional Buildings Ltd
[1994] 2 EGLR 29 282
Shepherd & Shepherd *v* Lancashire County Council (1977) 33
P&CR 296 386
Shevlin *v* Trafford Park Development Corpn [1998] 1 EGLR 115. 140
Shewu *v* Hackney London Borough Council [1999] 3 EGLR 1. 352
Shimizu (UK) Ltd *v* Westminster City Council [1995] 1 EGLR 167;
[1996] 3 PLR 410
Shraff Tipp Ltd *v* Highways Agency [1999] 2 EGLR 205 132
Simeon and the Isle of Wight Rural District Council, Re [1937] Ch 525;
106 LJ Ch 335; 157 LT 473; 53 TLR 854; 101 JP 447; 81 SJ 625; 3 All
ER 149; 35 LGR 402. 376
Simmonds *v* Kent County Council [1990] 1 EGLR 227 . . 123, 124, 132, 306

Simpsons Motor Sales (London) Ltd *v* Hendon Corpn [1964] AC 1088;
    [1963] 2 All ER 48; 14 P&CR 386; [1964] EGD 134 . . . . 50, 55, 95
Simpson *v* Stoke-on-Trent City Council (1982) 262 EG 673; [1982]
    1 EGLR 195; [1982] JPL 454. . . . . 128, 291
Sinclair *v* Department of Transport [1997] 34 EG 92 68
Singh *v* Rochdale Metropolitan Borough Council (1992) 65 P&CR 75. . 306
Slipper *v* Tottenham and Hampstead Junction Railway Co (1867)
    LR 4 Eq 112, 36 LJ Ch 841, 15 WR 861, 16 LT 446. . . . . 106, 309
Slot *v* Guildford Borough Council [1993] 1 EGLR 213 406
Smart & Courtney Dale Ltd *v* Dover Rural District Council (1972) 23
    P&CR 408 58
Smith *v* Birmingham Corpn (1974) 29 P&CR 265 LT. 277, 289
Smith *v* Kent County Council [1995] 2 EGLR 196 . . . . 70, 111
Smith *v* Strathclyde Regional Council (1981) 42 P&CR 397 275
Smith & Waverley Tailoring *v* Edinburgh District Council (1976) 31
    P&CR 484 302
Soper & Soper *v* Doncaster Corpn (1964) 16 P&CR 53; [1964] EGD 201
    311
South Eastern Rly Co and LCC's Contract, Re, South Eastern Railway
    Co *v* LCC [1915] 2 Ch 252; 113 LT 392 . . . . 163, 167, 239, 241, 249
Sovmots Investments Ltd *v* Secretary of State for the Environment
    [1977] QB 411; [1976] 2 WLR 73; [1976] 1 All ER 178; 31 P&CR 59;
    on appeal, [1977] QB 445; [1976] 3 All ER 720; appeal reversed in
    House of Lords [1977] 2 WLR 951; [1977] 2 All ER 385; 243 EG
    995; [1977] 2 EGLR 22 . . . . 51, 104, 108
Sparks *v* Leeds City Council [1977] 2 EGLR 163; (1977) 244 EG 66
    . . . . 256, 258
Sporrong & Lönnroth *v* Sweden (1982) 5 EHRR 35 . . . . 439, 440
Sprinz *v* Kingston-upon-Hull City Council (1975) 30 P&CR 273;
    [1975] EGD 517. . . . . 220, 223
Stanford Marsh Ltd *v* Secretary of State for the Environment [1997]
    1 EGLR 178. 141
Stebbing *v* Metropolitan Board of Works (1870) LR 6 QB 37 160
Stoke-on-Trent City Council *v* Wood Mitchell (1978) 248 EG 870, on
    appeal from LT, (1977) 241 EG 856; [1977] 1 EGLR 156 . . . . 356, 358
Stokes *v* Cambridge Corpn (1961) 13 P&CR 77; [1961] EGD 207
    . . . . 196, 426, 435, 438
Stourcliffe Estate Co Ltd *v* Bournemouth Corpn [1910] 2 Ch 12 74
Streak & Streak *v* Berkshire County Council (1976) 32 P&CR 435 149
Stirling Plant *v* Central Regional Council [1995] The Times 9
    February 1995 52
Surrey County Council *v* Bredero [1993] 1 EGLR 159 379
Sutton London Borough Council *v* Bolton [1993] 2 EGLR 181 . . . . . 82, 119
Sutton *v* Secretary of State for the Environment (1984) 270 EG 144 211

Sydney Municipal Council *v* Campbell [1925] AC 338; 133 LT 63 52
Syers *v* Metropolitan Board of Works (1877) 36 LT 277 320

T

Tamplin's Brewery Ltd *v* County Borough of Brighton (1971) 22
   P&CR 746; [1970] EGD 801; on appeal (1972) 222 EG 1587 288
Taqueu *v* Lancaster City Council [1999] 2 EGLR 103 140
Taylor *v* Oldham Corpn (1876) 2 Ch D 395 422
Taylor *v* O'Connor [1971] AC 115 358
Telegraph Service Stations Ltd *v* Trafford Borough Council [2000]
   RVR 356 198
Texas Homecare Ltd *v* Lewes District Council [1986] 1 EGLR 205 414
T G O'Fee Ltd *v* Highways Agency (unreported: 17 August 1999) 272
Thames Water Utilities *v* Oxford City Council [1999] 1 EGLR 167
   . . . . 108, 119
Thameside *v* Greater London Council [1979] 1 EGLR 167 135
Thomas & Son Ltd *v* Greater London Council (1982) 262 EG 991
   . . . . 292, 296
Thornton *v* Wakefield Metropolitan District Council [1991]
   2 EGLR 215 223
Thurrock, Grays and Tilbury Joint Sewerage Board *v* Thames Land
   Co (1925) 90 JP 1; 23 LGR 648 . . . . 105, 422, 434
Tomkins *v* Commission for New Towns see R *v* Commission for New
   Towns, *ex parte* Tomkins [1989] 12 EG 59; [1989] 1 EGLR 24 81
Toye *v* Kensington and Chelsea Royal London Borough Council
   [1994] 1 EGLR 204; [1994] RVR 16; [1994] 09 EG 186; [1994]
   1 EGLR 204 . . . . 140, 141
Tozer Kemsley & Millbourne Estates plc *v* Secretary of State for
   Transport [1996] EGCS 7 80
Trocette Property Co Ltd *v* Greater London Council and Southwark
   London Borough Council (1973) 27 P&CR 256; [1973] EGD 661;
   on appeal (1974) 28 P&CR 408 . . . . 185, 194, 222, 311
Trustees for Methodist Church Purposes *v* North Tyneside
   Metropolitan Borough Council (1979) 38 P&CR 665; [1979]
   JPL 381; 250 EG 647; [1979] 1 EGLR 33 . . . . 89, 97
Trustees of the Manchester Homeopathic Clinic *v* Manchester Corpn
   (1970) 22 P&CR 241 257
Tudor Properties Ltd *v* Bolton Metropolitan Borough Council [2000]
   40 RVR 94 143
Tull's Personal Representatives *v* Secretary for Air [1957] 1 QB 523;
   1 All ER 480 . . . . 269, 273
Turner *v* Secretary of State for the Environment (1973) 28 P&CR 123;
   (1973) EGD 1094 49
Turris Investments Ltd *v* CEGB (1981) 258 EG 1303 . . . . 238, 241, 247

U

Ullah *v* Leicester City Council [1996] 1 EGLR 244 . . . . 191, 200, 280
Uttley *v* Todmorden Local Board of Health (1874) 44 LJCP 19; 31
  LT 445; 39 JP 56 372

V

Valentine *v* Skelmersdale Development Corpn (1965) 195 EG 489 327
Venables *v* Department of Agriculture for Scotland (1932) Sessions
  cases 573. . . . . 273, 275
Venrich *v* Secretary of State for the Environment [1990] 1 EGLR 245 . . . 55
Vincent *v* Thames Conservancy (1953) 4 P&CR 66 133
Vine (RA) Ltd *v* Havant Borough Council [1989] 2 EGLR 15 150
Vyricherla Narayana Gajapativaju *v* The Revenue District Officer,
  Vizagapatan [1939] AC 302, see also Raja Vyricherla Narayana
  Gajapatiraju *v* Revenue Divisional Officer, Vizagapatam [1939]
  AC 302 . . . . 184, 185, 193, 228, 426

W

W & S (Long Eaton) Ltd *v* Derbyshire County Council (1976)
  31 P&CR 99; 236 EG 726; [1975] 1 EGLR 160; (CA) [1975] 2
  EGLR 19. 178
Wadham *v* North Eastern Ry Co (1884) LR XIV QBD 747 379
Wagstaff *v* Department of the Environment, Transport and the
  Regions [1999] 1 EGLR 108. . . . . 370, 376, 379, 388
Wain *v* Secretary of State for the Environment (1982) 262 EG 857;
  [1982] 1 EGLR 170. 58
Wakerley *v* St Edmundsbury Borough Council (1977) 33 P&CR 497;
  249 EG 639; [1979] 1 EGLR 19. 319, 334, 335, 339
Waltham Forest London Borough Council *v* Secretary of State for the
  Environment [1993] NPC 31 39
Walton-on-Thames Charities *v* Walton and Weybridge Urban District
  Council (1968) 20 P&CR 250 204
Walton's Executors *v* Commissioners of Inland Revenue [1996]
  1 EGLR 159, on appeal from [1994] 2 EGLR 217 . . . . 314, 334
Ward *v* Wychavon District Council [1986] 2 EGLR 205. 416
Waring *v* Foden [1932] 1 Ch 276 348
Waters *v* Welsh Development Agency [2002] 2 EGLR 107, on appeal
  from [2001] 1 EGLR 185 LT 188, 228
Waterworth *v* Bolton Metropolitan Borough Council (see Bolton
  Metropolitan Borough Council *v* Waterworth). 195, 237, 243
Watson *v* Secretary of State for Air [1954] 3 All ER 582; 5 P&CR 13
  . . . . 287, 314, 326, 327, 337
Watts *v* Watts (1874) LR 17 Eq 217 94
Webb *v* Minister of Housing and Local Government [1965] 1 WLR
  755; [1965] 2 All ER 193 . . . . 47, 51

Welsh Water Development Authority *v* Burgess (1974) 28 P&CR 378 . . 372
West Midlands Joint Electricity Authority *v* Pitt [1932] 2 KB 1 433
West Suffolk County Council *v* W Rought Ltd [1957] AC 403; [1956]
    3 All ER 216; 6 P&CR 362. 357
Westminster Bank Ltd *v* Minister of Housing and Local Government
    [1971] AC 508; [1970] 1 All ER 734; 21 P&CR 379; [1970] EGD 194
    . . . . 403, 418
Westminster City Council *v* Great Portland Estates [1984] 3 All
    ER 744 44
Westminster City Council *v* Quereshi [1991] 1 EGLR 256. . . . . 85, 98
Wharvesto Ltd *v* Cheshire County Council (1984) 270 EG 149; [1984]
    1 EGLR 191. 271
White JD Ltd *v* Secretary of State for the Environment [1982]
    JPL 506 208
Whitehead *v* Leeds Bradford International Airport [1999] 39
    RVR 241 388
Whitehouse *v* Jordan [1981] 1 WLR 246 148
Wiberg *v* Swansea City Council [2002] RVR 143 134
Wickham Growers Ltd *v* Southern Water plc [1997] 1 EGLR 175 146
Wildtree Hotels Ltd *v* Harrow London Borough Council [2000] 3 All
    ER 289; [2000] 3 WLR 165; [2000] 31 EG 85; [2000] 2 EGLR 5 on
    appeal from [1999] QB 634; [1998] 3 All ER 638; [1998] 3 EGLR 133
    . . . . 373, 375, 377, 378
Wilkinson *v* Middlesbrough Borough Council (1982) 261 EG 673;
    on appeal from (1979) 250 EG 867; [1982] 1 EGLR 23. 257
Willett *v* Inland Revenue Commissioners [1982] 2 EGLR 234 334
Williams *v* Blaenau Gwent Borough Council (1994) 67 P&CR 393;
    [1994] 2 EGLR 201 . . . . 97, 132, 134
Williams *v* Blaenau Gwent Borough Council (No 2) [1999]
    2 EGLR 195 134
Williams *v* Secretary of State for the Environment (1976) 240 EG 876;
    [1976] 2 EGLR 181 . . . . 78, 94
Williamson *v* Cambridgeshire County Council [1977] 1 EGLR 165;
    [1977] JPL 529 206
Williamson *v* Cumbria County Council (1994) 68 P&CR 367; [1994]
    2 EGLR 206 382
Wilson *v* Liverpool City Council [1971] 1 WLR 302; [1971] 1 All ER
    628; 22 P&CR 282; [1971] EGD 144; *sub nom* Wilson and Wilson
    v Liverpool County Borough Council (1970) 21 P&CR 452 . . . . 225, 226
Wilson *v* Minister of Transport (1980) 254 EG 875; [1980] 1 EGLR 162
    . . . . 112, 290, 235, 345, 353
Wimpey & Co Ltd *v* Middlesex County Council [1938] 3 All
    ER 781 286
Windward Properties Ltd *v* Government of Saint Vincent and the
    Grenadines [1996] 1 WLR 279 . . . . 143, 274

Wombwell Foundry and Engineering Ltd *v* National Coal Board
[1979] RVR 13 424
Woolfson *v* Strathclyde Regional Council (1978) 248 EG 777;
[1978] 2 EGLR 19. . . . . 270, 271
Worlock *v* Sudbury Rural District Council (1961) 12 P&CR 315; [1961]
EGD 156 . . . . 314, 335, 336
Wright *v* Municipal Council of Sidney [1916] XIV NSW 348 278
Wrexham Maelor Borough Council *v* MacDougall [1993] 2 EGLR 23
. . . . 174, 269, 270, 271, 274, 293, 297, 301, 303, 304, 318
Wrotham Park Settled Estates *v* Hertsmere Borough Council [1993]
2 EGLR 15 378
Wrotham Park Estates Co *v* Parkside Homes [1974] 1 WLR 798 379

Y
Yarrow *v* United Kingdom (1983) 30 DR 155 439
Yates *v* Yates The Times 2 March 1993 39

Z
Zoar Independent Church Trustees *v* Rochester Corpn [1975] QB 246;
[1974] 3 All ER 5; 29 P&CR 145; [1974] EGD 799 . . . . 256, 257, 258

Table of Statutes

Page

Acquisition of Land Act 1981 . . . . 27, 28, 29, 100, 102, 170, 428, 433
   s. 4. . . . . 2, 3, 25, 89, 179
      7 (1) 29
      9 . . . . 100, 129
      11 (2). 29
      12 (1). 29
      13 (1). 35, 37, 41
      13 (2). 32, 33, 41
      13 (4). 33
      14 37
      15 37
      16 . . . . 38, 350
      17 38
      18 . . . . 24, 38, 40
      19. . . . . 24, 38, 39, 40
      19 (1). 39
      19 (2). 39
      23. . . . . 40, 54, 55, 443
      25 50
      26 94
    Sch. 1 28
          2. . . . . 105, 347, 348
          3 428
Acquisition of Land (Assessment of Compensation) Act 1919 . . . 168, 171,
. . . . 265, 294
Act for the Rebuilding of London 1667. . . . . 163, 247
Acquisition of Land (Authorisation Procedure) Act 1946. 27
Admiralty (Signal Stations) Act 1815 21
Agriculture (Miscellaneous Provisions) Act 1963
   s. 22 337
Agriculture (Miscellaneous Provisions) Act 1968
   s. 12. . . . . 336, 341, 342
     15 333
Agricultural Holdings Act 1986 . . . . 328, 329, 342, 343
   s. 25 330

60 330
60 (4) 331, 336, 341
Case B 330, 333
Agricultural Tenancies Act 1995 . . . . 330, 341
   s. 5–7 340
Ancient Monuments and Archaeological Areas Act 1979 307
   s. 1 . . . . 410, 411
      2 411
      7 412
      7 (3) 412
      27 412
Arbitration Act 1950 134
   s. 29 142
Arbitration Act 1996
   s. 47 138
      49 . . . . 138, 142
      57 (3)–(7) 138

Building Act 1984 308

Channel Tunnel Act 1987 . . . . 21, 156
Civil Aviation Act 1982 393
   s. 76 368
      79 395
Civil Evidence Act 1995 . . . . 137, 147
Coal Mining (Subsidence) Act 1957
   s. 13 (2) 423
Coal Mining (Subsidence) Act 1991
   s. 7 423
      8–11 423
      22 423
      26–28 423
      40 424
      40 (2) 424
Coast Protection Act 1949 . . . . 47, 51
Commonable Rights Compensation Act 1882 350
Commons Registration Act 1965 . . . . 348, 349
Community Land Act 1975 274
Compulsory Purchase Act 1965 . . 25, 76, 79, 84, 122, 171, 306,321, 330, 331
   s. 2 129
      3 . . . . 77, 78, 156, 290
      4 . . . . 37, 85, 94, 98
      5 86
      5 (2B) 95
      5 (2C) 95

6 . . . . 93, 133

7 . . . . 25, 76, 133, 134, 146, 157, 170, 172, 234 *et seq*, 256, 312, 376,
. . . . 378, 380, 389, 428, 429, 433, 438

8 . . . . 112, 123, 132, 344, 429

8 (1) 110, 112

(2) 112

(3) 112

10 . . . . 76, 88, 107, 117, 133, 134, 173, 307, 360, 365, 370, 371,
. . . . 378, 379, 417,419

(1) 370

(2) 370

11 . . . . 92, 125, 309, 312, 353

11 (1) 80, 123, 124, 126

(3) 122

(4) 123

12 . . . . 126, 127

13 128

14 352

15 352

16 352

17 352

19 312

20 . . . . . . 106, 172, 256, 309, 310, 312, 313, 314, 319, 320, 332, 335, 341

(2) 315, 335

(4) 313

22 . . . . 120, 127, 353

23 295

Sch 1 . . . . 129, 130

para 2 130

4 130

6 130

2 128

3 124

4 . . . . 349, 350

Compulsory Purchase (Vesting Declarations) Act 1981 . . . . 98, 115

s. 3 99

4 99

5 99

6 99

7 (1) 100

(3) 100

8 . . . . 125, 178

8 (1) 100

9 100

10 . . . . 101, 132, 306

    10 (3) 133
    Sch. 1 . . . . 101, 110, 113, 114

Defence Act 1842. . . . . 21, 158
Defence of the Realm (Acquisition of Land) Act 1916
    s. 5 (3). 82
Education Act 1944. 381
Electricity Act 1989
    s. 10 431
        Sch. 3 . . . . 431, 432, 433,

Finance Act 1894
    s. 7 (5) 145, 197
Finance Act 1910. 182
Finance Act 1975
    s. 38 . . . . 333, 334
Forestry Act 1967 . . . . 28, 413
    s. 40 28

Gas Act 1986 427
    s. 9 427
        Sch. 3. . . . . 427, 429
Gulf Oil Refining Act 1965. . . . . 20, 368

Health and Safety at Work Act 1974 191
Highways Act 1959
    s. 72 403
Highways Act 1980 . . . . 17, 22, 25, 28, 34, 64, 122, 308, 371
    s. 16 28
        28 . . . . 416, 417
        45 417
        66 418
        70 418
        72 403
        73 418
        74 418
        97 419
            (3) 392
        116–120. 416
        124–125. 416
        126 416
        246. . . . . 396, 398
            (2) 397
            (2A) 397
            (3). 397

　　　　(4). 397
　　　　(6). 397
　　　247(6) 76
　　　250 108
　　　252. . . . . 109, 110
　　　258 32
　　　261. . . . . 247, 250, 251, 252
　　　282 398
　　　307 419
　　　308 420
Housing Act 1957 . . . . 44, 104
Housing Act 1985 . . . . 4, 64, 348
　s.　17 104
　　　284 61
　　　287 61
　　　290. . . . . 28, 37, 63
　　　294 416
　　　295. . . . . 108, 416
　　　583 124
　　　584 124
　　　585 261
　　Schedule 2 298
　　Schedule 22 28
Housing Act 1988 31
Human Rights Act 1998. 6, 11, 157, 269, 403, 437
　s.　3 437
　s.　4 437
　　　6 438

Inclosure Acts 1852–54. 350
Interpretation Act 1978
　Sch. 1 104

Land Charges Act 1972 93
Land Compensation Act 1961 . . . . 171, 262, 313, 422
　s.　1. . . . . 132, 133, 135, 434
　　　2–4 433
　　　4. . . . . 88, 138, 139, 140, 141
　　　4　(1) 139, 141
　　　4　(1)(b) 96, 97
　　　4　(3) 140
　　　5 . . . . 77, 182, 313, 408, 409, 410, 412
　　　rule　(1) 182, 419,426, 438
　　　　　　(2) 168, 176, 181, 182, 185, 211, 217, 239, 263, 265, 268, 282,
　　　　　. . . 292, 294, 323, 325, 326, 338, 344, 357, 358, 386, 419, 426, 438

(3) 187,188, 189, 190, 195, 231, 344, 386, 419
(4) 191, 260, 344, 351, 386, 419
(5) 137, 173, 175, 176, 255, 251, 258, 259, 260, 263,
. . . . 307, 312, 351
(6) 263, 265, 268, 269, 270, 275, 282, 293, 294, 296,
. . . . 297, 307, 318, 358, 361, 438
6 . . . . 182, 218, 221, 224, 250, 252, 398
6 (3) 220
7 . . . . 215, 247, 249, 252, 253, 389
8. . . . . 233, 247, 252
8 (5) 250
9 . . . . 182, 217, 221, 222, 223, 231
10A 269, 274, 318
14. . . . . 199, 231, 241
(2). 200
(3). 199
(3A) 192, 200, 207
(6). 200
15 . . . . 231, 241
(1) 201
(3) 202
(5) 206
16 . . . . 231, 241
(1). 204
(2). 204
(3). 205
(4). 205
(7) 205
17 . . . . 77, 200, 206, 211, 231, 241
(1) 206, 207
(3) 207
(4) 208, 210
(5) 208
(6) 208
(7). 209, 210
(9A) 209, 274, 296
18 209
22 . . . . 77, 78
(2) 206
(2)(a) 210
23. . . . . 212, 213, 214, 215
(3) 213
(4) 213
(5) 213
24 . . . . 213, 214

24 (4) 213
25 (2) 214
   (3) 214
   (4) 214
26 214
29 211
29 (1) 213
31 . . . . 61, 89, 97, 132
31 (1) 96
   (2) 97
   (3) 97
39 (1) 204, 434
Sch. 1 . . . . 218, 231, 250, 253, 398, 398
       3 215
       para 1 215
       para 2 215
       para 3 215
Land Compensation Act 1973 . . . . . 35, 64, 110, 132, 144, 295, 307, 360, 419
s. 1 381
  1 (6) 381
  2 382
  3 384
    (3) 385
    (5). 296, 391
  4 389
  5 . . . . 387, 389
  6 387
  8 389
  8 (2) 114
  9 . . . . 390, 391
10 383
11 383
12 383
17 392
19 (2A) 134, 384, 392
20 394
20A 395
26 398
26 (2A) 398
27 398
28 398
29 198
29 (1) 297
   (2) 298
   (3) 298

29 (4) 299
   (5) 298
29 A 299
29–32 297
30 (1) 300
   (2) 300
32 (2B) 300
32 (3) 299
   (3A) 299
   (5) 299
   (7) 301
   (7A) 300
34 342
   (3). 342
34–36 342
35 343
36 344
   (4) 344
37 . . . . 172, 174, 270, 271, 274, 275, 301, 320
   (1)(a) 302
   (1)(c) 303
   (2) 174, 301
   (5) 305
   (6) 307
   (7) 303
38 . . . . 301, 303
39 . . . . 177, 305, 434
41 305
43 . . . . 306, 328
44 245
45 260
46 282
47 . . . . 256, 319
48 . . . . 90, 92, 332, 333, 335, 337, 339, 340, 341
   (5) 336
   (6) 337
50 92
   (2) 177
51 220
52 . . . . 97, 123, 125, 134, 140, 362
52 (4A) 126, 307
52 A 126
52 A(1) 307
53 . . . . 114, 116, 345
54 . . . . 114, 115, 345

    (3) 115
    (5) 115
    (6) 116
  55 .... 114, 116, 345
  56 .... 114, 116, 345
    (2).. 116
  57 .... 114, 345
  58 111
  59 .... 331, 339, 340
  63 .... 307, 377
Land Drainage Act 1930
  s. 34 (3) 133
Land Drainage Act 1991............................ 27, 307, 424
  s. 14 (5)... 424
Landlord and Tenant Act 1927 321
  s. 18 (1) 317
Landlord and Tenant Act 1954........................... 256, 310
  s. 24 .... 302, 314, 320, 321
    37 .... 302, 303
    (4) 302
    39 (2) 319
Landlord and Tenant Act 1987 4,12
Landlord and Tenant (Covenants) Act 1995.................. 316
Lands Clauses (Consolidation) Act 1845 .... 24, 84, 117, 158, 163,
.... 171, 265, 267
  s. 63 .... 157, 159, 160, 170, 389
    68 370
    121 312
    128 82
Lands Tribunal Act 1949 131
  s. 1 (3) 132, 133
    3 (4) 150
    (6)(a)(ii) 134
Law of Property Act 1925
  s. 40 .... 78, 94
    42 (7) 130
    84 186
    193 349
Law of Property (Miscellaneous Provisions) Act 1989
  s. 2 .... 75, 78, 94
Leasehold Reform Act 1967.................. 4, 11, 12, 13, 383, 441, 442
  s. 5 311
Leasehold Reform, Housing and Urban Development Act 1993..... 4, 12,
.... 357, 403
Light Railways Act 1896 22

Limitation Act 1939
  s. 27 (6) 134
Limitation Act 1980
  s. 9 . . . . 134, 384, 392
     34 134
Local Government Act 1972
  s. 120 . . . . 75, 107
       (3) 76
     122. . . . . 119, 120
     123 . . . . 80, 81
     128(2). 81
Local Government Act 1988
  Sch 5. 80
Local Government and Housing Act 1989 261
  s. 92 63
Local Government (Miscellaneous Provisions) Act 1976. . . . . 104, 107
  s. 13 . . . . 31, 108, 110, 246
     14 107
     15 121
       (5). 122
       (6). 122
       (7). 122
       (8). 122
     29 128
  Sch. 1. 110
Local Government, Planning and Land Act 1980 80
  s. 142 212
     143 212
London County Council (Improvements) Act 1897. 247
London Transport Act 1969. . . . . 20,21, 105

Metropolitan Paving Act 1817. 21
Mines (Working Facilities and Support) Act 1966 422

National Trust 1907
  s. 21 129
National Trust Act 1939
  s. 8 129
New Towns Act 1965
  s. 11 271
New Towns Act 1981 . . . . 28, 80, 104, 213
  s. 1 63

Okehampton Bypass (Confirmation of Orders) Act 1985 40
Open Spaces Act 1906. . . . . 18, 73

Petroleum (Production) Act 1934 422
  s. 3 (2)(b) 423
Pipe-lines Act 1962 .... 28, 109, 421, 434
  s. 11 434
     (5)... 434
    12 434
    13 434
  Sch. 2... 434
    3... 434
Planning (Listed Buildings and Conservation Areas) Act 1990..... 4, 213,
                                                  308
  s. 1 409
    3 411
    27 410
    28 410
    29 411
    31 401
    32 60
    48 262
    50 262
    51 261
Planning and Compensation Act 1991 .... 315, 335, 404
  s. 31 410
    65 206
    66 (2)... 212
    67 .... 71, 86, 95
    70 .... 187, 189
  Sch. 18 307
Public Health Act 1875................................... 433
Public Health Act 1936
  s. 15 .... 105, 109
    278 109

Railway Clauses (Consolidation) Act 1845
  s. 77 347
    78–85... 105, 347
Rent Act 1977................................... 31, 301, 314, 321
  s. 3 302
Rent (Agriculture) Act 1976................................. 31

Statutory Orders (Special Procedure) Acts 1945–69............... 23, 38

Taxation of Chargeable Gains Act 1992
  s. 42 355
    243 356

245 56
246 356
247 356
Telecommunications Act 1984 132
   Sch. 2 429
Town and Country Planning Act 1947 . . . . 166, 202, 404, 405, 417
Town and Country Planning Act 1959 167
Town and Country Planning Act 1971
  s. 127 416
    112(1) 55
Town and Country Planning Act 1990 . . . . 104, 122, 271, 308, 347, 387
  s. 56 415
    97 406
    102. . . . . 57, 406, 409
    107 407
    108 406
    115 408
    116 409
    117 409
    137 . . . . 57, 58
      (3) 58,
    138 59
    140 59
    141 59
    142 . . . . 59, 60
    143 . . . . 60, 61
      (2) 60
      (8) 61
    145–147. 61
    149 65
      (2) 397
    150–152. 65
    150 65
    151 67
      (6) 68
    152 68
      (2) 69
    153 69
    154 69
    155 68
    156 71
    159 71
    158–160. 70
    161 65
    166. 111

168 65
171B 191
184 414
185 414
186(5) 415
191 200
198 412
203 . . . . 412, 413
204 412
220 414
223 414
226 . . . . 82, 118, 441
227 . . . . 76, 118
233 81
237 . . . . 74, 82, 108, 118, 119
   (1) 119, 120
   (2) 118
   (4) 118, 120
249 419
280 351
281 351
Sch. 3 . . . . 58, 344, 407
      para 1 . . . . 202, 203
      para 2 202
      5, 9, 11 409
      10 . . . . 202, 203
      13 . . . . 62, 66, 67, 68, 70, 189
Town and Country Planning (Minerals) Act 1981 409
Town Development Act 1952 249
Transport and Works Act 1992 64
 s. 1 23
   3 3
   5 23
  11 24
  13 24
  20 23
  22 . . . . 24, 40
  Sch. 1 23
Tribunals and Inquiries Act 1992 . . . . 24, 40

Value Added Tax Act 1994
 s. 33 361
  Schedule 10 359

Wandsworth to Croydon Railway Act 1801 20

War Damage Act 1965 20
Water Act 1989 132
Water Industry Act 1991 . . . . 12, 27, 132, 308, 425
    s. 156 82
        158(7) 425
        159. . . . . 15, 105, 109, 425, 442,443
        180 15
        185 12
        Sch. 12. . . . . 15, 425
Works Act 1974. 191

Table of Statutory Instruments

CPR Practice Directions
PD 21.9. 150
Part 54 55
Part 54.2. 129
Compulsory Purchase by Ministers (Inquiry Procedure) Rules 1994 . . . 34
Compulsory Purchase by Non-Ministerial Acquiring Authorities
    (Inquiries Procedure) Rules 1990. . . . . 34, 42
    r 4 34
    6 34
    7(1) 35
    11(1) 35
    11(2) 35
    13 35
    15. . . . . 35, 36
    16 36
    17(1) 36
    17(4) 36
Compulsory Purchase of Land Regulations 1994 . . . . 29, 99
Control of Advertisement Regulations 1992 . . . .
Highways (Inquiry Procedure) Rules 1994 34
Lands Tribunal Rules 1996
    r 6 142
    10. 135
    27. 138
    28. . . . . 137, 149
    28(1) 137
    28(11) 138, 139
    32. . . . . 134, 138, 308
    33(1) 137
    34. 134
    37. 138
    38 . . . . 135, 307
    39. . . . . 135, 136
    42. 136
    43. . . . . 135, 137
    50. . . . . 138, 140

Noise Insulation Regulations 1975 394
    r 3 395
    13. 395
Town and Country Planning (Blight Provisions) Order 2000. 65
Town and Country Planning (Compensation for Restrictions on
    Mineral Working and Mineral Waste Depositing) Regulations
    1997 409
Town and Country Planning (Control of Advertisements)
    Regulations 1992. 412
Town and Country Planning (General Permitted Development)
    Order 1995 . . . . 200, 202, 406, 407
Town and Country Planning (Trees) Regulations 1999 413
Transport and Works (Application and Objection) Rules 1992. . . . . . 23, 41
Transport and Works (Inquiries Procedure) Rules 1992 . . . . 24, 41

CIRCULARS

Awards of Costs incurred in Planning and Compulsory Purchase
    Order Proceedings 8/93. 37
Compulsory Purchase Orders: Procedures 14/94 31
Crichel Down Rules Circular 6/93 80
Purchase Notices 13/1983 . . . . 57, 59

PART I

THE POWER TO COMPULSORILY PURCHASE LAND

Chapter 1

Introduction

The use of compulsory acquisition powers
Compensation and compulsory acquisition
Compulsory acquisition and the law
Human rights
Law reform

1.1 The use of compulsory acquisition powers

Most people think of compulsory acquisition as part of the power of the State to expropriate private land for some public purpose. While it is the State, through the parliamentary process, which provides powers of compulsory acquisition, the powers which are available in this country are wide, and go far beyond the taking of land for public projects.

(a) Public projects

Taking land compulsorily for public projects, such as roads and airports, is understood and accepted as a proper use of powers of acquisition. This book is primarily about this use of the compulsory acquisition power. However, there are increasing signs of tension in this country arising from the use of such powers by privatised undertakings, such as the water and electricity industries. There is resistance to the use of these powers where a private undertaking is able to profit from the taking of land at a price which disregards the value of the land to the project.

(b) Land reform

Land reform policies usually proceed on the basis that the ownership of land is unequal or not fairly distributed, and this produces economic inefficiencies or social tension. One immediately thinks of landless agricultural peasants in a Third World country.

3

However, we do have land reform policies in this country, although they are not so called. Under the Leasehold Reform Act 1967 the owners of long leases are entitled to enfranchise the freehold. It is said that this policy is justified because the long leasehold system is inefficient; in certain areas a monopoly landlord owned all the freehold. Freeholds were therefore not freely marketable and this produces economic inefficiencies. It is also said there is unfairness because the leaseholder pays for the building, but loses it at the end of the lease.

There are more recent examples of what might be called land reform acquisition powers in the Landlord and Tenant Act 1987 and the Leasehold Reform, Housing and Local Government Act 1993. All these statutes contain powers of acquisition available to individuals to take private land and redistribute land ownership. Save for certain points of comparison, this use of powers of acquisition is not dealt with in this book.

(c) Sanction

Sometimes the State will obtain powers of compulsory acquisition to use as an ultimate sanction to encourage or discourage certain behaviour. Thus the Housing Act 1985 contains powers to take houses that have fallen into disrepair, and there are powers in the Planning (Listed Buildings and Conservation Areas) Act 1990 to acquire listed buildings where an owner fails to comply with obligations to keep in repair. The sanction use of powers of acquisition is dealt with in this book because the effect of the sanctions generally lies in some restricted entitlement to compensation.

(d) Regulation

Planning and pollution control legislation plainly prevents owners from using their property as they might choose. In that regard it is arguable that part of the bundle of rights that makes up the concept of legal ownership is taken away. Where compensation is payable for certain of the regulatory controls over property, this is considered in this book.

1.2 Compensation and compulsory acquisition

It is too simple to say that whenever land is taken compulsorily fair compensation should be paid. The measure of compensation must be interrelated with the policy behind the acquisition power. Thus there may be little point in having a compulsory power as a sanction if the defaulting owner is fully compensated. There is a rather crude relation in this country between the measure of compensation (if any) and the use of the powers. That was recognised by the European Court of Human Rights in *James* v *United Kingdom Government* [1986]. Thus compensation is only paid in very limited circumstances where land is the subject of the regulation power considered above.

1.3 Compulsory acquisition and the law

This book is divided into four principal parts appropriate, it is submitted, to four different aspects of the law of compulsory purchase and compensation. Part I considers the need for powers to compulsorily purchase land. Today, these powers are almost entirely statutory and they are set out only in sufficient detail to enable the valuer or surveyor to understand the background to the exercise of compulsory purchase. Part II is concerned with the procedures that follow the obtaining of compulsory purchase powers, and the steps that have to be taken to exercise those powers and take possession of land. The rules, both statutory and judicial, for determining the amount of compensation payable for a compulsory purchase of land are the subject of Part III. There are circumstances where, although no land is compulsorily purchased, an owner may claim compensation for some injury or damage to his land, or a depreciation in its value, caused by the activities or decisions of public authorities; the circumstances are outlined in Part IV.

Although modern compulsory purchase and the associated rules of compensation are statutory in origin, the interpretation of the relevant statutes has been the subject of a considerable amount of litigation, and the resulting case law is important. Since most readers of this book will not have ready access to the volumes of reported cases, a rather fuller treatment of the important cases will be found than is usual in a textbook. For much the same reason there are no footnotes and all references to statutes, orders, regulations and law cases are incorporated in the text. Following each case name will be found the year it is reported, e.g. [1979], and, occasionally, the court concerned – LT for Lands Tribunal, QBD for Queens Bench Division, CA for Court of Appeal and HL for House of Lords. Consultation of the Table of Cases will give what is called the citation, which enables the case to be found in the law reports.

The purpose of this book is to provide an outline of the subject, particularly for students taking examinations in estate management, surveying, valuations and planning, and for practitioners in these disciplines. The text needs to be of a manageable length, concentrating on principles, yet illustrating the practical application of the principles with suitable cases. Here a warning must be given. The non-lawyer generally assumes that law is certain and, if applied to a given set of facts, a definitive answer can be given, upon which reliance may be placed. Nothing could be further from the truth. One can never be absolutely certain what the law is until a court (or the Lands Tribunal) has decided a case; one then knows the answer, but only for that case. Of course one can predict what a court might decide where a set of facts closely follows the facts in a previously decided case, or is clearly within the words of a statute; this is what a lawyer does in advising a client, and this is what the author has done in the following pages when making statements or propositions of what the law is. Sometimes the law is so doubtful that this is not possible; then the author has either left that doubt unresolved, or expressed his view as to what the law ought to be.

The Lands Tribunal has jurisdiction to determine the amount of compensation payable in most circumstances of compulsory purchase. Its decisions are nearly always decisions on the evidence before it in any particular case and are therefore not precedents binding on itself in later references.

1.4 Human rights

The Human Rights Act 1998 gives effect to the rights and freedoms under the European Convention on Human Rights. The effect of the Act and the application of the Convention on the compulsory taking of land are, as yet, uncertain. Human rights are considered in Chapter 27 below.

1.5 Law reform

The last two years has seen much activity directed to the reform of the law relating to compulsory acquisition. In July 2000 the Department of the Environment, Transport and Regions published its final report – *Fundamental review of the laws and procedures relating to compulsory purchase and compensation*. That review set out a number of recommendations that arose out of the deliberations of an advisory group. The Government followed this with its own proposals in *Compulsory Purchase and Compensation: Delivering a fundamental change.* At about the same time, the Law Commission took an interest in the reform of the law relating to compulsory purchase and compensation. The Commission published a scoping paper in March 2001, and then followed this with two consultation papers – *Towards a compulsory purchase code: (1) compensation* (Consultation Paper No 165) and *(2) procedure* (Consultation Paper No 169).

Any student of this subject will wish to consult the Law Commission consultation papers. As always, they are extremely well researched and provide an illuminating background to understanding the law relating to compensation and procedure. Whether the Government will find time to bring forward legislation to reform the law, and what shape that law reform will take, remains to be seen. As the student will see, in passing through this book, the statutory structure of the law is spread over a number of different enactments that commence in 1845, until the present time. Some consolidation would be desirable. The fundamental changes in the nature of planning and development plans over the last 30 years has left parts of the compensation legislation behind. Especially that concerning the assumptions that can be made as to the planning status of land being compulsorily acquired. However the central corpus of compensation law has developed through a number of decisions in the courts and in the Lands Tribunal over a considerable period of time. If a fundamental reform of that central corpus had the effect of throwing away the valuable guidance in those decisions, that would be unfortunate. It does not assist either acquiring bodies or claimants if they are faced with new rules untested and unguided by decisions in the courts and the Tribunal.

Meanwhile the government introduced the Planning and Compensation Bill in late 2002. This will widen and clarify powers of compulsory acquisition under The Town and Country Planning Act 1990. It will introduce a loss payment to make some allowance for the upset, discomfort and inconvenience in being compulsorily acquired.

Chapter 2

The Need for Statutory Powers

How can land be expropriated?
Public benefit and compensation
Compulsory purchase outlined
Acquisition of rights other than full ownership
The need for statutory powers
Purchase by agreement

2.1 How can land be expropriated?

This chapter is intended for the student or layman whose knowledge and experience of law, and of what laws are for, is limited. If the rest of the book is to have any meaning or purpose, the reader should have some idea why laws of compulsory purchase are necessary and what those laws seek to do.

Let us start with the essence of the problem: one person (or some public authority) wishes to acquire the land of another, if necessary, without his consent. Perhaps an example will focus our minds on the problem and the possible solutions.

If Marigold has the exclusive use and enjoyment of Herbaceous Border, and Clover desires it for himself to the exclusion of Marigold, Clover can set about satisfying his designs in a number of ways. Clover can use force, or the threat of it, and dispossess Marigold – the force approach. The method is not unknown in certain countries today, and it has some advantages – no notices, no objections and no compensation. It was even used in this country before Henry II restored order. However, if Clover is uncertain about his strength, or legal or moral rules prevent the use of force, he may attempt to become owner of Herbaceous Border by purchase. He either waits until the property is put on the market, or he will offer a price to Marigold. Depending on her attachment to the land and her willingness or otherwise to sell, the two may reach an agreement whereby Clover will become owner – this can be called the agreement approach. If Marigold is not initially a willing seller, Clover may have to offer a substantial price to turn unwillingness into willingness and to persuade Marigold to sell Herbaceous Border.

If the force approach is ruled out, because it is immoral or illegal, and the agreement approach is unsuccessful, because Marigold does not want to sell, there is no way which will enable Clover to become the owner of Herbaceous Border without its owner's consent under either of these approaches.

If Marigold and Clover live in a country with a developed legal system, that system may contain laws acknowledging the idea of private property and providing rules for its protection. Although this would prevent Clover using the force approach, he might be able to persuade the law-makers to pass a law to legalise force or to compel Marigold to make an agreement: we can call this the compulsory purchase approach. We will examine the full implications of this approach a little further on. Meanwhile some other possibilities must be considered.

If the legal system of a particular country does not acknowledge the idea of private ownership of land, none of the approaches so far considered will be appropriate; who may use Herbaceous Border becomes a matter for the community, State authority or government concerned: the individual will have no 'rights'.

In the United Kingdom we retain a monarchy and, under that institution, the Crown may have powers. The exercise of such powers is known as royal prerogative. In certain areas of government activity royal prerogative remains important, but in the field of land acquisition, Parliament has severely curtailed the use of prerogative powers. Although in the past, the Crown had undoubted prerogative to take land without its owner's consent, particularly in time of war, it is doubtful whether the Crown can take land under this method today, except in the most exceptional circumstances: see next chapter.

Finally, the position in the United States of America must be mentioned. There the legislatures have power to take private property for public use without the owner's consent: this is by virtue of the doctrine of eminent domain. If a public purpose will be served by taking of property, the owner's rights are subject to the general good; the government, as representing that general good, may exercise this power through the legislature. The safeguard for the individual lies in the Constitution of the United States that private property shall not be taken for public use without just compensation.

The origin of the doctrine of eminent domain is unclear, though certainly it reflects the supremacy of the State over the people and their private property, and is therefore similar to the power of a monarch. This power is reflected in the doctrine of eminent domain in the United States and the royal prerogative in the United Kingdom; but, whereas the doctrine supports the legislative power to take private property, the royal prerogative is practically defunct in land acquisition.

2.2 Public benefit and compensation

It has already been suggested that the power to take land compulsorily, such as under the compulsory purchase approach, is granted by the legislature. This is true of a number of countries including the United Kingdom and the United States of America. In the United States, the power of the legislature to grant powers of compulsory purchase is limited by the constitution; the fifth amendment directs that private property shall not be taken for public use without just compensation. Although there is no written constitution in the United Kingdom, it seems unlikely that Parliament would grant powers of compulsory purchase unless it was satisfied that the powers were required for some public benefit and, where private property was to be taken, the expropriated owners would receive compensation. The expressions 'public benefit' and 'compensation' demand some consideration. It is beyond the scope of this work to fully develop critical arguments about these two expressions, but some brief ideas are put forward for readers to think about. Now that the Human Rights Act 1998 is in force, the Convention rights, that embrace these ideas, are dealt with in Chapter 27.

1. Public benefit

In England Parliament has authorised the use of compulsory powers to take or affect private property for a variety of purposes. Powers granted to planning authorities under the town and country planning legislation have significantly affected the right of private landowners to use or develop their land as they so wish. When Parliament enacted the Leasehold Reform Act 1967, powers of compulsory purchase were given to private individuals, a class of residential tenants. Under these powers an eligible tenant is entitled to compel his landlord to grant either the freehold interest or an extension to the tenant's lease. More recently, under the Landlord and Tenant Act 1987, tenants of flats were given powers, exercisable in specified circumstances, to acquire the freehold of their respective block of flats. There are now increased powers in the Leasehold Reform, Housing and Urban Development Act 1993. Following privatisation, powers of compulsory purchase and the right to lay sewers through private property have been granted to the new companies: see, for example, the Water Industry Act 1991. Normally one thinks of Parliament authorising compulsory purchase for the purposes of making or improving public highways or for other more obvious public purposes. But the examples just given show the extremes of what Parliament has appeared to accept are valid uses of the compulsory purchase power.

Legislation in this country follows preliminary consultations initiated by the government departments and the democratic processes associated with Parliament. Certainly, many people may object to the enactment of these rather extreme examples of compulsory purchase, but one must assume that Parliament accepts them as being for the public benefit. Parliament will amend a bill if it sees a disparity between the benefit to the expropriator and the harm to the expropriatee. Thus section 185 of the Water Industry Act 1991 was introduced to permit landowners to compel water companies to remove laid mains and sewers in certain circumstances. The United Kingdom is a signatory to the European Convention for the Protection of Human Rights and Fundamental Freedoms and under that convention there are articles protective of private possessions. In the case of *James* v *United Kingdom Government* [1986], the trustees for the Duke of Westminster sought to challenge the Leasehold Reform Act 1967 as being a breach of the treaty that protects private property being taken unless for the 'public interest'. The European Court of Human Rights rejected the claim on the basis that every legislature enjoys a wide margin of appreciation in implementing social and economic policies and Parliament was entitled to conclude that there were social injustices which needed to be put right by the 1967 Act. All this shows that the expression 'public benefit' is a very wide one and that broadly it is for Parliament to decide the purposes for which compulsory purchase powers may be granted.

2. Compensation

It has been suggested that the legislature, in our case, Parliament, would not authorise the use of compulsory powers to take private property without the payment of compensation. Many readers will suppose that the expression 'compensation' means the financial equivalent expressed in pounds sterling of property taken. It is clear from many of the examples of compulsory purchase that this expression has a wider meaning. Taxation is a power that is closely analogous to compulsory purchase of land: both involve the compulsory taking of private property. John Locke, in his *Essay on Government*, argued that taxation and the compulsory acquisition of land were merely exercises of the same basic power. Clearly, where a person's wealth is taxed there is no direct provision of compensation in the sense of a financial equivalent in money; arguably there is compensation in being a member of a State and being entitled to its protection and the other benefits of government that are paid for out of taxation.

The example of the Leasehold Reform Act 1967 has already been considered in relation to the meaning of public benefit. Under this Act, the price an enfranchising tenant pays for the compulsory purchase of the freehold to his property is statutorily defined and is in most cases less than the open market value. In the *James* case, the trustees' argument, that under this legislation the freeholder was not being properly compensated, was rejected. The European Court said that if full monetary compensation were payable the purpose of the 1967 Act, to remove certain social injustices, would not be achieved. Obviously if an enfranchising tenant was obliged to pay the full market value of the freehold interest, there would be little point in the Act for two reasons. First, the primary purpose of the Act is the recognition that some part of the value of the freehold is attributable to the value of the building on it and this belongs to the tenant. Second, if the compensation were to be at market value a tenant would not need powers of enfranchisement as he could purchase any property for the same price in the market-place. This last point is not always strictly true in practice because in many parts of the country there are monopoly suppliers of freehold interests in land.

These are rather extreme examples where compensation may not be the full financial equivalent of the property taken. They show that it must not be assumed that Parliament always intends that compensation should be measured in purely financial terms. Parliament may well intend that in some cases compensation should be less than financial equivalence or perhaps be in some other form of satisfaction other than money, and taking private property by taxation is an obvious case. However, most of this book is concerned with the compulsory purchase of land for which the normal rule is that compensation, defined in some way, is very broadly the financial equivalent of what is taken.

2.3 Compulsory purchase outlined

An outline of the compulsory purchase approach can now be given. The authority or body requiring land must first obtain legislative powers to legalise the compulsory purchase.

The community is consenting to the compulsory purchase through its elected representatives in Parliament. That consent is likely to be given if the property is to be taken for some purpose of public benefit and compensation is to be paid to those who will lose. It is assumed that Parliament would not consent to the enactment of compulsory purchase powers unless these two criteria are satisfied.

The Act of Parliament will usually authorise a named authority, or body, to compulsorily purchase certain land for stated purposes. Compulsory purchase is analogous to an ordinary private purchase of land in that the expropriated owner or 'vendor' conveys his legal title to the 'acquiring authority'. The only difference between a compulsory purchase and a private transaction, that needs pointing out at this stage, is that if the owner refuses to convey, the acquiring authority may prepare the deed of conveyance themselves; this will effectively pass title to them and, if the authority wishes to take possession, there is a right to do so against the owner's will, after giving notice. However, there is a procedure under which a conveyance is dispensed with and an acquiring authority becomes owner of the land on a certain date following a declaration that title in the land shall vest with them. The analogy with a private purchase does not seem valid when this procedure applies, and although it can be called compulsory acquisition, it is difficult to call it compulsory purchase: see Chapter 7. Apart from this, for all practical purposes, the terms compulsory purchase and compulsory acquisition can be regarded by the reader as interchangeable.

If a compulsory purchase is analogous to a private purchase, it follows that the acquiring authority will acquire, in the conveyance, whatever title, freehold or leasehold the original owner possessed. However, any incumbrances, such as easements, restrictive covenants or equitable interests, will not prevail against an acquiring authority acting under statutory powers; any person who has the benefit of such interests will, if they are interfered with, be entitled to compensation: see Chapter 23.

An acquiring authority, which purchases a reversionary interest, will be bound by leases which affected the previous owner, but is not bound by statutory security of tenure.

2.4 Acquisition of rights other than full ownership

So far, in this introductory discussion, it has been assumed that an acquiring authority needs ownership and possession of the land for its purposes and that the expropriated owner will be fully displaced. Very often the requirements of an authority can be satisfied by the creation, in its favour, of a right over land which is less than full ownership. Requisition in time of war is a good example: ownership is not expropriated but possession is taken for a time and then returned to the owner.

If some right over land which is less than full ownership of the freehold interests is required by an authority, it may only obtain this, compulsorily, by statutory powers. Such a right may be in the nature of an easement, e.g. to lay pipes or cables, in which case the right is granted by the owner, or exercised compulsorily if necessary, and there is an analogy with a grant of an easement in a private transaction.

However, the unique nature of pipes required as sewers or water mains needs mentioning. A public sewer may run through private property, but it and the space through the soil it occupies, and the manholes connected to it, are owned in fee simple by the water authority. The right to construct a public sewer through private property and acquire this freehold interest is obtained merely by serving reasonable notice on the owners concerned; they have no rights to object, though they are entitled to compensation: Water Industry Act 1991, sections 159 and 180, and Schedule 12. This is different in nature from compulsory purchase.

2.5 The need for statutory powers

A private individual in this country is free to purchase land or, within certain limitations now to be considered, use land in any way he chooses. A company is in the same position provided its memorandum contains appropriately wide powers (a memorandum of association is a document signed by persons who wish to incorporate a company which contains, among other things, the powers of the company); however, both will need legislative authority to do some act which would otherwise be contrary to the law. The law of nuisance prevents a landowner from causing such effects as smoke, noise and vibration on his land which will unreasonably affect the use and enjoyment of his neighbour's land. If he wishes to run a railway which may cause a nuisance he must seek Parliamentary approval to legalise what would otherwise be unlawful. Therefore, statutory powers will be required for many activities that would otherwise be unlawful: motorways and aerodromes because of noise nuisance, refuse tips and sewerage works because of smells and so on.

However, the typical acquiring authority today is more likely to be a local or public authority set up by statute, or a ministry or a department of State or central government. The Acts of an authority created by Parliament must be within the powers granted to it by the legislation; an Act which exceeds those powers is *ultra vires* and can be restrained by the courts: see the cases on this subject in Chapter 4. Accordingly, such an authority needs statutory powers to purchase land and to build on it, or construct works, or carry out activities; an individual or a company would need no such statutory powers. The position of a government department is slightly different because ministers exercise, on behalf of the Crown, the residue of prerogative powers in domestic affairs. However, as already explained, royal prerogative has probably been abolished with regard to land acquisition and today a minister always obtains statutory powers to acquire land and to use it for the purposes he has in mind. A minister is also subject to the *ultra vires* rule; he may only act within the statutory powers; and, where those powers are discretionary, he must not abuse that power or frustrate the purposes of the Act concerned: see further in Chapter 4.

We have already seen at 2.3 above that the essential characteristic of the compulsory purchase approach is that the owner's free consent to sell is dispensed with. A final reason for statutory powers is to give effect to that and to provide the acquiring authority with powers to enter and take land, acts which would otherwise be unlawful in the absence of legislation.

Statutory powers are therefore needed for three purposes:

1. To authorise the compulsory purchase approach; in effect to make legal an act which would otherwise be a trespass;
2. To legalise an activity that would otherwise be unlawful and could be restrained by the courts, e.g. a nuisance;
3. To give power to authorities of statutory creation, e.g. local

authorities, or to government departments, to carry out a particular activity.

These three aspects may be covered in one statute: for example the Highways Act 1980 authorises highway authorities (county councils and the Department of Transport) to construct and improve roads, and to acquire land by agreement, or compulsorily, for such purposes. The use of public works of this nature may amount to a nuisance; this is legalised by the words in the statute conferring immunity (see Chapter 23 for the immunity in respect of an aerodrome); or, it is legalised by necessary implication. In *Hammersmith City Rly Co* v *Brand* [1869] HL, it was held that if Parliament, by statute, authorises an activity, such as building and running a railway, it is implicit that it also authorises any necessary nuisance that activity causes. A modern problem is to be found in *Allen* v *Gulf Oil Refining Ltd* [1981] HL: the Gulf Oil Refining Act 1965 authorised the acquisition of land but did not expressly authorise the construction of a particular refinery (which would therefore need planning permission). A local inhabitant claimed damages or compensation against Gulf Oil, and alleged that the use of the refinery was causing a nuisance or there had been negligence in its construction or operation. The House of Lords decided that the 1965 Act showed that a refinery would be built, and that was authority, express or implied, to operate it. Gulf Oil therefore enjoyed statutory immunity to any claim in nuisance based on the inevitable consequences of operating the refinery. The immunity did not extend to any nuisance that was not the inevitable cause of running a refinery, nor did it extend to negligence.

In *Mobil Oil Co* v *Secretary of State for the Environment* [1991] it was held that the power to construct a motorway service area was necessarily implicit in the power to acquire land for the purpose.

2.6 Purchase by agreement

Returning to our example at the beginning of this chapter one of the approaches available to Clover, to obtain Herbaceous Border for himself, is the agreement approach, whereby Marigold freely consents to sell her land to him; in practice this approach is frequently used in this country.

Authorities of statutory creation will need statutory powers to acquire land by agreement even though the owner is willing to sell and compulsory purchase powers are unnecessary; to acquire land for a purpose without such powers is *ultra vires* and unlawful.

All statutes authorising the use of powers of compulsory purchase also permit the acquiring authority to purchase by agreement where the owner consents and certain statutes, for example the Open Spaces Act 1906, only permit a purchase by agreement and contain no powers of compulsory purchase: see further at Chapter 6.

Chapter 3

The Sources of Compulsory Purchase Powers

Introduction
Royal prerogative
Private Act of Parliament
Public General Act of Parliament
Public General Act of Parliament and provisional order
Public General Act of Parliament and compulsory purchase order
Transport and Works Act 1992 and works order
Common acquisition and compensation procedures
Summary

3.1 Introduction

The need for statutory powers was explained in Chapter 2. One of the reasons for obtaining statutory powers is to legalise compulsory purchase: a landowner need not sell his land against his will unless compelled to do so by the law, though, in practice the knowledge of the existence of compulsory purchase powers in the background is sufficient to persuade most owners to sell to an acquiring authority without the need for the ultimate sanctions of the law to be applied. This chapter outlines the various sources of compulsory purchase powers; apart from royal prerogative, they are all statutory in origin.

3.2 Royal prerogative

The prerogative is the residue of powers in the hands of the Crown. Once the Crown had substantial powers, but from the time of William and Mary the prerogative power of the Crown has been exercised by the Crown's ministers; it is a discretionary power exercised for the public good in certain spheres of activity for which Parliament has made no provision by statute. In certain areas of government prerogative powers are still important, but they probably no longer exist in the field of land acquisition. It is possible that in the time of war the Crown may exercise the prerogative by expropriating property for the defence of the realm; although in *Burmah Oil Co Ltd* v *Lord Advocate* [1964], the House of Lords decided that this war prerogative could not be exercised without paying compensation to expropriated owners. This decision was altered by the retrospective War Damage Act 1965 denying such compensation.

As this power is only available to the Crown and not to other public or local authorities and as even the Crown prefers to expropriate or requisition land under the authority of statute in time of war, the royal prerogative, as a source of compulsory purchase powers, is of no practical significance today. In any event, where both the royal prerogative and a statute cover the same activity, the Crown may only proceed under the statute: *A-G* v *De Keyser's Royal Hotel* [1920] HL.

3.3 Private Act of Parliament

This was once the only way of obtaining powers of compulsory purchase; it is now less important, though it is still used for certain cases where no other powers exist. The Gulf Oil Refining Act 1965 (mentioned on p17) is an example; it authorised the company to compulsorily purchase land to build an oil refinery at Milford Haven.

A private (or local) Bill is presented to Parliament, seeking authority to compulsory purchase specified land for a stated purpose. The land is particularised in a schedule to the Bill and reference is made to deposited plans. The Bill is subject to certain formalities, in addition to the usual procedures for considering a Bill before Parliament; the persons affected are notified and may make objections by way of a petition, and these petitions are heard before a select committee of each House.

The Wandsworth to Croydon Railway Act 1801 (Surrey Iron Railway) is the earliest Act authorising the compulsory purchase of specified land for constructing a railway. Not only did it authorise the taking of land but it set out the procedures for acquiring ownership and possession, and for settling compensation. Today the acquisition and compensation procedures have been standardised and are contained in separate statutes: see section 3.8 below. A modern private or local Act, such as the London Transport Act

1969, which authorised the compulsory purchase of land for a further underground line, incorporates those standard procedures by reference, rather than setting them out in full in the Act itself.

The Channel Tunnel Act 1987 is a recent example of an Act in which powers for compulsory purchase of specified land for a particular project were authorised. The Act gave rise to two interesting controversies. Once the Bill had received its second hearing, the principles of the Bill had been approved by Parliament. Petitioners who appeared before the committee stage were limited to presenting objections of a technical nature and could not argue against the principles of a channel tunnel. There was also no certainty that every petitioner who wished to be heard would be given that opportunity. The select committee kept to a strict timetable and many petitioners were disappointed.

The second controversy concerned the compensation provision in the Act. The Act incorporates the standard compensation provisions of the Land Compensation Act 1961. Under these an expropriated owner is entitled to compensation based on the market value of his land had there been no project or scheme of the acquiring authority. Some of the land taken under the Act was to be used for commercial activities in the hands of commercial companies; desirable for the success of the tunnel but not strictly essential for its construction. Many of the affected landowners considered that their compensation should, contrary to the normal rule, reflect the value of their lands to the strictly commercial aspects of the project.

3.4 Public General Act of Parliament

A public general Act is a statute which has general applicability and makes no reference to a particular locality or to named persons or specified land. Such an Act will authorise a named acquiring authority to compulsory purchase any land for its purposes without any further authorisation.

This source of compulsory purchase powers is very unusual; the Admiralty (Signals Stations) Act 1815 and the Defence Act 1842 (which authorises the taking of land for the defence of the realm, and is anyway in abeyance during peace time) are two examples. An Act of a similar nature, in that it gives general authority to acquire land without further authorisation, though only of local effect, and therefore, strictly, a local Act, is the Metropolitan Paving Act 1817 (Michael Angelo's Act), which permits land to be taken for street widening and improvement in the metropolis of London.

3.5 Public General Act of Parliament and provisional order

Under this arrangement there are two stages to the authorisation of compulsory purchase. First, there is a public general Act, which, as in the preceding case, has general applicability, making no reference to a particular locality, to named persons or to specified land. This Act settles the principle of compulsory purchase: Parliament has, in effect, said that such powers may be used to achieve the purposes set out in the Act. The second stage of the procedure relates to a particular scheme: a provisional order is made which specifies the required land; this order will have to be confirmed by the appropriate minister, and then it is submitted to Parliament in the form of a provisional order confirmation Bill, which, if approved as an Act, authorises the taking of specified land.

Although once the more usual way for local authorities to obtain compulsory purchase powers, it is a somewhat cumbersome process and has been almost entirely superseded by the procedure described in the next section. One of the few remaining Acts incorporating this procedure is the Light Railways Act 1896, which authorises the taking of land for light railways.

3.6 Public General Act of Parliament and compulsory purchase order

As in the procedure described in the preceding section, there are two stages, a public general Act, which authorises the use of compulsory purchase powers to take land for a particular purpose, and a second stage which specifies the land needed for a particular scheme. For this second stage, a compulsory purchase order specifies the land required, but, instead of the order being confirmed by the minister and Parliament, it is confirmed only by the minister. If there are objections to the order which are not withdrawn the minister will hold a public inquiry.

Today most acquisitions by local and public authorities, including government departments, are made under Acts incorporating this procedure. Examples are too numerous to cite, but the Highways Act 1980, which authorises the use of compulsory purchase powers to take land needed for the construction and improvement of highways, is notorious. Although the public general Act contains the power to acquire land compulsorily, the second stage procedure, the making and confirmation of the compulsory purchase order is, in most cases, governed by the Acquisition of Land Act 1981.

In a few cases, to be considered in the next chapter, a compulsory purchase order is the subject of 'special parliamentary procedure'. This procedure, which follows the standard procedure up to the minister's confirmation of the order, is the subject of the Statutory Orders (Special Procedure) Act 1945; Parliament has the opportunity of considering the order and any petition against it in a manner examined in Chapter 4.

3.7 Transport and Works Act 1992 and works order

Until the Transport and Works Act 1992 came into force, the promoter of any enterprise involving such works as railways and light tramways obtained powers of compulsory purchase, and other necessary statutory powers, by promoting a Bill in Parliament. Parliamentary procedure has been found inappropriate to examine effectively what is usually a local project in respect of which there may be many local objectors.

The Transport and Works Act 1992 provides a new procedure for obtaining authority to construct transport and other works and for any necessary compulsory purchase of land. Under sections 1 and 3 of the 1992 Act a works order may be made by statutory instrument by the Secretary of State for Transport. Orders may be made relating the construction or operation of railways, tramways, trolley vehicle systems, and certain other systems of guided transport, the construction or operation of inland waterways, and certain other works which may affect or interfere with rights of navigation in territorial waters.

By section 5 of and Schedule 1 to the 1992 Act a works order may provide for the compulsory acquisition of land and rights in land, the extinguishment of rights over land, the alteration of agreements relating to land as well as other necessary and ancillary matters. A works order may apply, modify or exclude other statutory provisions.

By section 20 of the 1992 Act any person or body which has power to promote a Bill in Parliament may apply for a works order. This would include an individual, a company and most statutory bodies. The Secretary of State has made rules providing for the steps to be taken prior to an application for a works order: see the Transport and Works (Application and Objection) Rules 1992. An application must be advertised in the *London Gazette* and a local newspaper, site notices must be posted and notice must be served on all owners, lessees and occupiers of land proposed to be compulsorily acquired.

The rules make provision for the making of objections within a prescribed period. The Secretary of State must hold a hearing or a public local inquiry if this is required by an objector, and that objector is the local authority for the area, or is an owner or occupier of land to be compulsorily acquired: see section 11 of the 1992 Act. The Secretary of State may disregard objections concerned only with compensation.

Rules have been made under section 9 of the Tribunals and Inquiries Act 1992 for public inquiries into works orders: see the Transport and Works (Inquiries Procedure) Rules 1992.

The Secretary of State has power to make a works order with or without modifications: see section 13. By section 22 of the 1992 Act any person aggrieved by a works order may challenge it by an application in the High Court within six weeks of the publication of the Secretary of State's notice of its making on the grounds that the order is not within the power of the Act or that there has been a failure to comply with some procedural requirement.

A works order will be subject to special Parliamentary procedure in the circumstances where a compulsory purchase order is subject to that procedure by virtue of section 18 or 19 of the Acquisition of Land Act 1981: see p38.

3.8 Common acquisition and compensation procedures

Certain matters are common to every compulsory purchase; conveyance of title, untraced owners, refusal of an owner to sell or give possession, the possible need of the acquiring authority to enter before conveyance, amount of compensation, resolving compensation disputes, etc. These and many other problems need to be resolved and contained in statutory powers. Because of the inconvenience of setting out all these matters in each Act authorising compulsory purchase, the Lands Clauses Consolidation Act 1845 was passed to provide, in common form, standard powers covering the acquisition and compensation procedures. The 1845 Act could then be incorporated, by a simple and short form of words, in any subsequent Act authorising powers of compulsory purchase.

Although the 1845 Act is still applicable to some Acts containing compulsory purchase powers today, certain provisions of that Act have been consolidated in the Compulsory Purchase Act 1965, and it is the 1965 Act which governs the acquisition procedures in most cases now: see Chapters 7–9 in Part II.

Section 7 of the 1965 Act contains the right to compensation when land is taken, although the rules for the assessment of compensation in respect of any compulsory acquisition are found, principally, in the Land Compensation Act 1961, and in many judicial decisions: section 7 of the 1965 Act was originally enacted as section 63 of the 1845 Act: see Part III.

The terms 'special Act' or 'enabling Act' are often used where these standard acquisition and compensation procedures apply: the terms refer to the Act which authorises the use of compulsory powers and to which the standard procedures will apply if incorporated by reference. Where a compulsory purchase order has to be used, that, together with the enabling Act, are referred to as the 'special Act'.

3.9 Summary

The various statutory powers, in the more usual cases of a private Act, or a public general Act, may be related to the stages of a compulsory purchase and summarised as follows:

	Public General Acts	*Private Act*
Stage 1		
(a) General power of compulsory purchase	e.g. Highways Act 1980	contained in the private Act
(b) Power to compulsorily purchase specified land	compulsory purchase order – (procedure in Acquisition of Land Act 1981)	contained in the private Act
Stage 2		
Power to acquire title, take possession and pay compensation	Compulsory Purchase Act 1965	the private Act may incorporate the Compulsory Purchase Act 1965 by reference
Stage 3		
Rules for the assessment of compensation	Land Compensation Act 1961	Land Compensation Act 1961

Each of these three stages is reflected in the first three parts of this book.

Chapter 4

Compulsory Purchase and Works Orders

Introduction
Preparation and making of an order
Objections and confirmation of an order
Special kinds of land
Special Parliamentary procedure
Works orders
The role of the confirming minister
Challenging an order in the High Court

4.1 Introduction

Apart from the private or local Act of Parliament, which both authorises the taking of land and specifies the particular land to be taken for a scheme, the most usual source of compulsory purchase powers is the public general Act (the 'enabling Act') and the compulsory purchase order ('the order' or 'CPO') made by the acquiring authority and confirmed by the appropriate minister or Secretary of State (see section 3.6 in the preceding chapter).

The Acquisition of Land Act 1981 consolidates the Acquisition of Land (Authorisation Procedure) Act 1946 and sets out the procedure to be followed in the preparation, making and confirmation of a CPO. The 1981 Act applies to all enabling Acts passed before the 1946 Act, which authorised compulsory purchase of land by local authorities; through a reference to the 1946 Act, its provisions have been incorporated in most enabling Acts passed since 1946 which authorise the compulsory purchase of land by local and public authorities and by government departments. Similarly, the 1981 Act will apply to all enabling Acts passed since 1981 which incorporate its procedures. It applies to compulsory purchase under the Water Industry Act 1991 and Land Drainage Act 1991.

There are just a few enabling Acts which authorise local authorities to take land by compulsory purchase order which do not incorporate the 1981 Act: section 290 of the Housing Act 1985 (slum clearance) and the New Towns Act 1981 are examples. The procedure for the making and confirmation of a CPO under section 290 of the Housing Act 1985 is set out in Schedule 22 to that Act. Because the principles behind these other procedures are much the same as the procedure in the 1981 Act, it is not intended to describe them separately: it must be appreciated that there are certain differences of detail. A number of Acts which contain powers of acquisition for the defence of the realm and other defence purposes are not governed by the 1981 Act, nor is the Forestry Act 1967, section 40, or the Pipe-lines Act 1962, sections 11–14.

The term 'minister' has been used in this chapter to describe a minister of the Crown or a Secretary of State. It should be remembered that the minister responsible for confirming most CPOs is either the Deputy Prime Minister or the Secretary of State for Transport.

In some cases certain preliminary procedures are necessary before commencing the steps for making a compulsory purchase order. Thus, the line of a new public highway can be established by a scheme under section 16 of the Highways Act 1980. The scheme is published, objections are invited and a public local inquiry is usually held. If the scheme is approved by the Secretary of State, the procedure for making a compulsory purchase order will follow. In many cases involving the improvement of existing public highways, the necessary orders under the Highway Act 1980 are published at the same time as the CPO and objections to all the orders may be heard at one public local inquiry.

In all cases the acquiring authority will consider whether it needs the whole freehold title to the land, or whether some lesser right, such as an easement, will suffice: see Chapter 8. Thus, in connection with highways, a right to drain onto adjoining land may be required.

4.2 Preparation and making of an order

1. *Preparation*

Part II of the Acquisition of Land Act 1981 sets out the procedure for making an order for purchases by a local authority (a procedure usually applicable to other acquiring authorities) and Schedule 1 to the 1981 Act sets out the procedure when a purchase is to be made by a minister of a government department. The procedure to be followed by local or other acquiring authorities will be described; that used when a government department is seeking an order is very similar. A compulsory purchase order must be in a form currently prescribed by the Compulsory Purchase of Land Regulations 1994, there is an example on p30.

2. *Notification and publicity*

Before the acquiring authority submit the order to the appropriate minister for confirmation, certain persons must be notified, and certain publicity must be given of the making of the order so as to enable any person to make an objection. As we shall see, these objections will be considered by the minister before he decides whether to confirm the order or not.

Part II of the 1981 Act prescribes the following requirements as to notification and publicity:

(a) A notice must be published for two successive weeks in one or more local newspapers circulating in the locality that an order has been made and will be submitted for confirmation; the notice must describe the land and state the purpose for which the land is required, a place in the locality where a copy of the order and map can be inspected, and specify the time (at least 21 days from the first publication of the notice) within which objections can be made to the appropriate minister (referred to as 'the confirming authority'): section 11(2);

(b) A notice must be served on every owner, lessee and occupier (except tenants for a month or any period less than a month) of any land covered by the order, explaining the effect of the order, that it is about to be submitted to the minister, and, as in (a) above, specifying the time (at least 21 days from the service of the notice) within which objections can be made: section 12(1).

Under the 1981 Act, 'owner' means a person other than a mortgagee not in possession, who is for the time being entitled to dispose of the fee simple and includes a tenant with an unexpired term exceeding three years; 'land' includes messuages, tenements and hereditaments and anything falling within the definition of land in the Act authorising compulsory purchase: section 7(1).

Although an easement may be land, owners of the benefit of easements affecting any of the land covered by the CPO are not

Example

Compulsory Purchase Order
The Highways Act 1980 and the Acquisition of Land Act 1981

The Blankshire County Council hereby make the following order:

1. Subject to the provisions of this order, the said Blankshire County Council are, under section 239 of the Highways Act 1980, hereby authorised to purchase compulsorily for the purpose of widening the highway known as Lover's Lane, Blanktown the land which is described in the Schedule hereto and is delineated and shown coloured pink on the map prepared in duplicate, sealed with the common seal of the said Blankshire County Council and marked 'Map referred to in the Blankshire County Council (Lover's Lane) Compulsory Purchase Order 1993'. One duplicate of the map is deposited in the offices of the said Blankshire County Council and the other is deposited in the offices of the Department of Transport.
2. Section 27 of the Compulsory Purchase Act 1965 shall not apply in relation to the purchase of land authorised by this order.[1]
3. Part[s] II [and III] of Schedule 2 to the Acquisition of Land Act 1981 [is] [are] hereby incorporated with the enactment under which the said purchase is authorised, subject to the modification that ...[2]
4. This order may be cited as the Blankshire County Council (Lover's Lane) Compulsory Purchase Order 1993

Schedule

Number on Map	Extent, description and situation of land	Lover's Lane Owners or reputed owners	Lessees or reputed lessees	Occupiers (other than licensees or tenants for a month or less)
1	0.1 hectare forming front garden of 21	Albert Oldcastle	none	Albert Oldcastle

[The order includes land falling within special categories to which Part III of the Acquisition of Land Act 1981 applies, namely[3] –

Number on map   special category

Note
1. This clause is optional, where it is inserted, the obligation imposed by section 27 of the Compulsory Purchase Act 1965 on an acquiring authority to make good any deficiency of rates on the acquired land is suspended.
2. If the acquiring authority wish to avoid the expense of paying compensation for minerals lying under the land, the 'mining code' may be incorporated in the order and the minerals will not be compulsorily acquired. [This code is more fully considered in Chapters 8 and 21.]
3. The compulsory acquisition of land of a local authority, land held by a statutory undertaker for its purposes, land held inalienably by the National Trust, land forming part of a common, open space, or fuel or garden allotment, or an ancient monument or archaeological area, may be the subject of the special provisions of sections 17 to 20 of the Acquisition of Land Act 1981 and the order may have to be the subject of special parliamentary procedure.

    The order is 'made', in the case of a local authority, by a resolution in accordance with the standing orders and other procedures of the authority, and, in the case of a minister exercising powers of compulsory purchase, by the preparation of the order as a draft. The order is sealed and dated.

owners of land covered by the CPO and are therefore not entitled to be served with a notice under (a) above: *Grimley* v *Minister of Housing and Local Government* [1971]. But where an authority wants to acquire rights over land, such as easements to drain or of support, these rights must be specified in the order and the affected owners notified: section 13 of the Local Government (Miscellaneous Provisions) Act 1976.

A statutory tenant under the Rent Act 1977 or the Rent (Agriculture) Act 1976, or a licensee under an assured agricultural occupancy under Part I of the Housing Act 1988 need not be served with this notice (section 12(2)). See also *EON Motors Ltd* v *Secretary of State for the Environment* [1981] where it was held that a weekly tenant was not entitled to a notice. A wife, who was the joint owner of a house with her husband, does not have to be served with a notice if her husband was served: see *George* v *Secretary of State for the Environment* [1979].

> (c) in cases where the ownership of land cannot be traced, and it is not practicable to ascertain the name or address of an owner, lessee or occupier, a notice, containing the information set out in (b) above, may be sent to the 'owner', 'lessee' or 'occupier' and delivered to the premises, or, if it is unoccupied it must be affixed to a conspicuous object on the land concerned.

3. *Statement of reasons*

Circular 14/94 – *Compulsory Purchase Orders: Procedures* – which contains general advice on the preparation of orders, recommends that a statement of reasons for making the order should be served with the personal notices. This statement will be required before any public local inquiry and is further explained at p35 below.

4. *Submission to the minister*

When the requirements as to publicity and notification have been carried out by the acquiring authority, the order is submitted to the minister for his consideration together with certificates that the publicity and notification procedures have been carried out. Where the order includes a listed building, or contains land in a conservation area, the minister must be informed.

4.3 Objections and confirmation of an order

1. Objections

Any person can make an objection in writing to an order. An objection must be sent to the appropriate minister within the time-limit specified in the notices published in the local newspapers or in the personal notices sent to the affected owners, lessees and occupiers. If any objection which is duly made is not withdrawn, the minister shall hold a public local inquiry or otherwise arrange for the person making the objection to be heard by an inspector: section 13(2).

Objections fall into three groups. First, there may be objections from persons, often the owners, lessees or occupiers affected, but also others living or working near the area of acquisition, who seek some modification of the land required for the purposes of the acquisition, or a change in the detail of the development proposed by the acquiring authority. These objections may secure changes in the proposals which can reduce the visual or noise intrusion of a scheme, or alter the land requirements to minimize inconvenience to adjoining landowners, or provide bridges, tunnels or other solutions to the problems of owners whose land may be severed by the acquisition.

The second group of objections are those who, while accepting the acquiring authority's scheme, seek an alternative site, or, in the case of a new road, an alternative route. In the case of an alternative route for a new road, the objector making the proposal, is required by the Highways Act 1980 (section 258) to send to the minister at least 14 days before any inquiry sufficient information about the alternative route to enable it to be identified.

The third group of objections will be from persons who seek to prevent the acquiring authority's proposals from being carried out at all. These objectors see the right to object and the subsequent public inquiry as the public participation process for deciding the principle of the scheme behind the proposal to acquire land. In connection with the schemes and proposals of local authorities, the principle of a scheme, and the balancing of its advantages and disadvantages, will be considered through the democratic decision-making process of the appropriate committee and council meetings; in theory the normal democratic techniques of lobbying etc can be used at this stage, and the later inquiry stage can be used to seek modifications of detail for which it is best suited. In practice, matters do not always work out in this way and the public may only learn and fully appreciate the consequences of a scheme after the local authority has reached a decision. In any event, where a minister is the acquiring authority, and he is putting forward a scheme, there is no first stage of democratic decision-making. Trunk road and motorway proposals of the Secretary of State for Transport are notorious in this regard. Here, the objectors see an inquiry as the only forum for public debate about the principle of the scheme, even when there has been an earlier highways scheme order and public inquiry. Unfortunately, the inquiry process is ill-suited to this purpose; apart from the problems of an unsatisfactory procedure, the ultimate decision is taken by the appropriate minister who regards it as a policy decision for which he is answerable to Parliament (but Parliament has no time to debate each and every scheme). In the past objectors were often frustrated where a motorway scheme was put forward in stages and contained in several compulsory purchase orders which were confirmed at different dates; where part of the route of a motorway has already been fixed by the earlier highway scheme or line order, it becomes extremely difficult to object to the principle or need for a motorway if the later order concerned covers but one stage of the whole route.

The present procedures seek to adopt a more flexible, less adversarial stance at highway inquiries, with much more assistance to objectors in the conduct of their cases, though the policy for trunk roads and motorways will remain a ministerial matter subject to more Parliamentary debate. The House of Lords has stated the criteria to be fulfilled before a highway scheme can be successfully challenged in the courts after it has been confirmed by the minister: *Bushell* v *Secretary of State for the Environment* [1981] HL. All the technical and factual knowledge of a government department's civil servants is the knowledge of the minister, therefore the advice he receives internally need not be disclosed to objectors.

The minister is entitled to require an objector to state in writing the grounds of his objection and may disregard any objection if it concerns a matter, such as compensation, which can be dealt with by the Lands Tribunal: section 13(4), 1981 Act.

2. *Public local inquiries*

The 1981 Act directs that if any objection is made to an order by a person served with a personal notice, and is not withdrawn, the appropriate minister must either hold a public local inquiry or a hearing: section 13(2). A hearing is supposed to be a less formal affair, though the same procedural rules apply, there is no public notice that it is to take place. There are certain advantages of a public local inquiry where evidence can be given on oath and witnesses compelled to attend or produce documents; a hearing is therefore uncommon, but it might be used to hear a single objector. Persons who are not affected owners or occupiers may object to the order, but the minister is not bound to hold an inquiry to hear their objections. The inquiry is held before an inspector appointed by the minister, or in connection with highway schemes of the Department of Transport, appointed by the Lord Chancellor from a panel of independent persons. This latter arrangement brings a degree of independence to the process.

The conduct of most inquiries under the 1981 Act is subject to statutory rules of procedure. For compulsory purchase orders of local and other acquiring authorities, the Compulsory Purchase by Non-Ministerial Acquiring Authorities (Inquiries Procedure) Rules 1990 apply. A similar set of rules apply where a minister is the acquiring authority: Compulsory Purchase by Ministers (Inquiries Procedure) Rules 1994. Where a highway scheme is the subject of the compulsory purchase order, an inquiry may also be required for that scheme under the Highways Act 1980, but the two inquiries can be held concurrently as one inquiry. Highway scheme inquiries are subject to the Highways (Inquiries Procedure) Rules 1994.

The inquiry procedure is also subject to the rules of natural justice. These rules, developed by the courts, provide that there must be fairness in the conduct of an administrative process and, in particular, each side must have a fair opportunity to be heard and to hear and to question the case against them. As we shall see, an order can be challenged if there has been a breach of either the rules of natural justice or the statutory rules of procedure.

The 1990 rules provide for the procedure before the inquiry, and the manner in which the inspector and minister proceed after the inquiry:

(a) *Procedure before the inquiry*

The minister must notify the acquiring authority and each statutory objector that he intends to hold an inquiry (the date of this notice is 'the relevant date' for the subsequent time table) and must notify the acquiring authority of the substance of each objection from a statutory objector and, so far as possible, the substance of other objections: rule 4. The minister may cause a pre-inquiry meeting to be held: rule 6.

Normally the inquiry must be held within 22 weeks of the relevant date or eight weeks after a pre-inquiry meeting: rule 11(1). But the minister must give at least 42 days' notice to the statutory objectors and the acquiring authority of the date and place of the inquiry: rule 11(2). The acquiring authority must give each statutory objector and the minister a written statement of its case at least 28 days before the inquiry date and not later than six weeks after the relevant date: rule 7(1).

A statutory objector is any owner, lessee or occupier of affected land (and with highway schemes it includes any person entitled to claim compensation under the Land Compensation Act 1973 because of the noise or other 'physical factors'); such a person is entitled to be notified of the inquiry date, to receive the acquiring authority's reasons and to appear at the inquiry: see section 13 of the 1981 Act. Other objectors learn of the inquiry by public advertisement and may appear at the inquiry at the discretion of the inspector; in practice this is invariably exercised in favour of any person who wishes to appear.

Copies of statements of evidence should be sent to the inspector, and in the case of the acquiring authority, to other parties, not less than three weeks before the inquiry.

(b) Procedure at the inquiry

Normally the acquiring authority begins with their case, and they usually have the final right of reply. The acquiring authority and the statutory objectors are entitled to call evidence and to cross-examine persons giving evidence; other persons may only do so if the inspector consents: rule 15. If a government department has expressed a view in support of the order, it shall make available a departmental representative; he may be cross-examined in the usual way, although questions directed to the merits of government policy should be disallowed by the inspector: rule 13.

While the inspector may allow the acquiring authority to alter or add to their written statement of reasons he shall adjourn the inquiry or otherwise give every statutory objector adequate opportunity of considering any fresh reasons or documents: rule 15.

The inspector may take into account any written representations received from persons not attending the inquiry: he is required to disclose this to the inquiry: rule 15. Inspectors are usually fairly relaxed about the relevance of evidence, but in *R v Secretary of State for the Environment, ex parte Royal Borough of Kensington and Chelsea* [1987], the inspector wrongly ruled that evidence could not be adduced of harassment and intimidation of tenants by or on behalf of the landlord of the subject property. It was decided that as the reason for making the order in the first place was that the tenants, by reason of the harassment and intimidation, were in need of proper housing accommodation, and as this was a proper use of the power to acquire land compulsorily under Part II of the Housing Act 1985, the inspector had erred in his ruling. Taylor J, in the same case, decided that a court could only intervene during a public inquiry on an application for judicial review in the most exceptional circumstances.

The inspector is entitled to make an unaccompanied site inspection before or during the inquiry. He may, and if requested must, make a site inspection at the close of the inquiry and the acquiring authority's representative and any statutory objector are entitled to accompany him on that visit: rule 16.

(c) Procedure after the inquiry

After the close of the inquiry the inspector makes a report in writing which contains his findings of fact and his recommendations: rule 17(1). The report is then considered by the minister who is free to make whatever decision he thinks, as a matter of policy, is right. However, he is bound by certain rules if he disagrees with any finding of fact in the inspector's report or he takes into consideration any new evidence (other than government policy) or any new issue of fact not raised at the inquiry, and in either case does not accept a recommendation of the inspector. In such a situation he must, before he makes a decision, notify the acquiring authority and any statutory objector giving them an opportunity of making written representations or, where he takes into consideration any new evidence or new issue of fact, of seeking a reopening of the inquiry: rule 17(4).

When the minister has reached his decision he is required to notify, in writing, the acquiring authority, the statutory objectors, and any other person who appeared at the inquiry and asked to be notified. A copy of the inspector's report or a summary of it is sent with the minister's decision letter: rule 18.

3. Costs

Circular 8/93 – *Awards of Costs incurred in Planning and Compulsory Purchase Order Proceedings* – advises that a statutory objector, who is successful, should be awarded costs unless there are exceptional reasons for not doing so. The claimant for costs must have made a formal objection to the order; the order was the subject of a local inquiry which the objector attended (or was represented at) and the claimant was heard as a statutory objector. The claimant's objection must have been sustained to the extent that the order was not confirmed or his land was wholly or partly excluded from the order.

No specific application for costs need be made, as the Secretary of State will write to the parties concerned. Costs are awarded against the authority making the order. In the case of owners objecting to an order under section 290 of the Housing Act 1985 – clearance areas, then even an unsuccessful objector is entitled to some expenses.

4. Confirmation of an order

If no objection is made by any owner, lessee or occupier or if all objections made by such persons are withdrawn, the minister may confirm the order with or without modifications: section 13(1), 1981 Act. If objections have been made and the minister has held an inquiry, his decision letter will state whether he intends to confirm the order and what, if any, modifications he incorporates. The minister can omit land from an order, but may only add land with the consent of the affected owners, occupiers and lessees: see section 14 of the 1981 Act.

As soon as the minister has formally confirmed an order, the acquiring authority must publicise the fact in one or more local newspapers, and notify the owners, lessees and occupiers of the land covered by the order: section 15 of the 1981 Act.

The date of the publication of the minister's confirmation of an order is important: the acquiring authority then has three years within which to exercise the powers of compulsory purchase: section 4 of the Compulsory Purchase Act 1965. It seems also clear that, for certain compensation purposes, there is no duty on an owner whose land is covered by an order to take steps to mitigate his likely losses, such as by looking for suitable alternative premises until the order has been confirmed: see *Lindon Print Ltd* v *West Midlands County Council* [1987]. The 1981 Act gives a minister a discretion in the exercise of his powers of confirmation. The minister's obligation to exercise this discretion lawfully is considered below in section **4.7** of this chapter.

4.4 Special kinds of land

Certain classes of land are given special protection from compulsory purchase. Land belonging to statutory undertakers may be excluded in certain circumstances unless the minister certifies otherwise: see section 16 of the 1981 Act.

Other special kinds of land may be subject to special parliamentary procedure: see **4.5** below.

4.5 Special Parliamentary procedure

1. *Special descriptions of land*

In so far as a compulsory purchase order authorises the purchase of the following descriptions of land:

- (a) land belonging to local authorities and land belonging to statutory undertakers for the purposes of their undertaking: section 17;
- (b) National Trust land held by the Trust inalienably, where an objection to the order has been made by the Trust and has not been withdrawn: section 18;
- (c) Subject to the exceptions considered below, land forming part of a common, open space or fuel or field garden allotment: section 19

the order, with some exceptions, is subject to special parliamentary procedure. The order is made in the manner so far described in this chapter, an inquiry is held into any objection, and the minister confirms the order in the usual way. However, it is at this stage that such an order is subject to a procedure prescribed by the Statutory Orders (Special Procedure) Act 1945 and the order must be confirmed by Parliament.

In respect of land forming part of a common etc. (see (c) above) there are three exceptions to the requirement that an order covering such land is subject to special parliamentary procedure. First, if the minister certifies that there has been or will be given exchange land of equal benefit to the persons entitled to rights of common or other rights, and to the public: section 19(l)(a). Second, that the land being purchased is required in order to secure its preservation or improve its management: section 19(1)(a). Third, that the land required does not exceed 250 sq yds in extent or it is required for widening or drainage of a highway and the minister certifies that exchange land is unnecessary having regard to the interests of the commoners and the public. In these cases the minister must first seek the views of the commoners and other affected persons and, depending on their representations and objections, he may have to hold a public inquiry: section 19(2). It is not necessarily unreasonable for the minister to refuse to hold a public local inquiry before issuing a certificate under section 19: see *Waltham Forest London Borough Council* v *Secretary of State for the Environment* [1993].

The Secretary of State is entitled to consider the planned or likely development which might affect the acquired land or the exchange land in deciding whether or not to issue a certificate under section 19: see *Greenwich London Borough Council* v *Secretary of State for the Environment; Yates* v *Yates* [1993].

2. Procedure

The order is laid before Parliament and petitions against the order may be presented within 21 days. Petitions are categorised as 'petitions of amendment' (those seeking amendments of the confirmed order) and 'petitions of general objection' (those seeking that the order should not be validated). Petitions are like objections and any person is entitled to submit a petition, in the proper form, to the Private Bill Office at the Houses of Parliament. A report of the petitions is laid before both Houses and if neither House passes a resolution to annul the order within 21 days, the petitions are referred to a joint committee of both Houses. If no petitions have been received and, during the 21-day period, no resolution is passed to annul the order, the order comes into operation at the end of that period.

The petitions will be considered by the joint committee of the two Houses; it may report that the order be approved, with or without amendments, or, if there are petitions of general objection, it may report that the order should not be approved. If the Committee report the order without amendments, it comes into operation when the report is laid before Parliament. Where there are amendments, it will come into operation on a date determined by the minister. However, if the minister does not accept the amendments or the Committee report that the order should not be approved, the order cannot take affect unless confirmed as an Act of Parliament.

The best example of the use of this procedure arose in the case of the Okehampton bypass where, because of certain opposition, and the possibility that some of the affected land might have been open space, the order had to be confirmed by the Okehampton Bypass (Confirmation of Orders) Act 1985.

4.6 Works orders

Under the Transport and Works Act 1992 a works order may be made by statutory instrument by the Secretary of State following an application from any person entitled to promote a private Bill in Parliament. Works orders are made for projects, such as railways and light tramways, for which there is no other specific statutory authority. An outline of the procedure is given in Chapter 3 at p23 above.

Many of the principles in this chapter will, however, have application to works orders. Rules governing the conduct of public local inquiries into a works order have been made under the Tribunals and Inquiries Act 1992. Although there are certain differences, the conduct of a public local inquiry into a works order is likely to be similar to that into a compulsory purchase order and as considered at **4.3** above.

Works orders may be subject to special Parliamentary procedure in circumstances where a compulsory purchase order would be so subject under sections 18 and 19 of the Acquisition of Land Act 1981: see **4.5** above. The role of the Secretary of State in confirming a works order is likely to be the same as the role of the minister in confirming a compulsory purchase order and is considered below at **4.7**.

By section 22 of the Transport and Works Act 1992 any person aggrieved may challenge an order within six weeks of its confirmation in the High Court on the same grounds as those which are found in section 23 of the Acquisition of Land Act 1981. Accordingly, the considerations under **4.8** below in challenging a compulsory purchase order in the High Court will also apply.

See further the Transport and Works (Applications and Objections) Rules 1992 and Transport and Works (Inquiries Procedure) Rules 1992.

4.7 The role of the confirming minister

1. *The exercise of discretion*

The Acquisition of Land Act 1981 grants to the appropriate minister the power to confirm a compulsory purchase order submitted in accordance with the Act. Where no objection has been made to an order, the minister 'may, if [he] thinks fit, confirm the order with or without modifications': section 13(1). However, if any objection has been made, and a public local inquiry has been held or an objector otherwise heard, the minister 'after considering the objection and the report of the person who held the inquiry . . ., may confirm the order either with or without modifications': section 13(2). Although these bland statutory powers shed little light on the responsibility of a minister in deciding whether to confirm an order, case law shows the possible legal constraints within which a minister must exercise his powers.

Usually there are objections to an order and the minister will therefore have the benefit of his inspector's report. In the decision of *Bushell* v *Secretary of State for the Environment* [1981], Lord Diplock explained what he thought was the purpose of the public inquiry process as a consequence of which an inspector produces his report. He said at p612E:

> The subject matter of the inquiry is the objections to the proposed scheme that have been received by the minister from local authorities and from private persons in the vicinity...whose interests may be adversely affected...The purpose of the inquiry is to provide the minister with as much information about those objections as will ensure that in reaching his decision he will have weighed the harm to local interests and private persons who may be adversely affected by the scheme against the public benefit which the scheme is likely to achieve and will not have failed to take into consideration any matters which he ought to have taken into consideration.

Lord Diplock is making clear that the inspector is gathering facts about the objections that have been made, giving appropriate weight to these objections in relation to the proposed scheme and its purposes and reporting his conclusions for the minister to consider. An early problem before the courts was whether a minister, in making his decision to confirm an order, was restricted to matters that formed the subject-matter of the inquiry and his inspector's report. In *B Johnson & Co (Builders) Ltd v Minister of Health* [1947], Lord Greene MR explained that the procedure for the making and approval of an order was not simply a contentious matter between acquiring authority and objectors; it did not resemble ordinary litigation. He said:

> There is a third party who is not present viz., the public, and it is the function of the minister to consider the rights and interests of the public. That by itself shows that it is completely wrong to treat the controversy between objector and local authority as a controversy which covers the whole of the ground. It is in respect of the public interest that the discretion that parliament has given to the minister comes into operation. It may well be that, on considering the objections, the minister may find that they are reasonable and that the facts alleged in them are true, but, nevertheless, he may decide that he will overrule them. His action in so deciding is a purely administrative action, based on his conceptions as to what public policy demands ...

The minister is therefore entitled to have his own policy; a policy which he believes to be in the wider public interest and which he may take into account as a factor additional to the information derived directly from the inquiry and the inspector's report.

In the *Bushell* case, which involved the route of a proposed motorway, Lord Diplock said (at p613) that if a minister was to give proper consideration to objectors, fairness required that the objectors should have an opportunity of putting to the minister the reasons for their objections to the scheme and the facts on which they are based. Fairness also requires that objectors should be given sufficient information about the reasons relied on by the authority as justifying the scheme to enable the objectors to challenge the accuracy of any facts and the validity of any arguments on which the authority's reasons are based. The obligation to provide a written statement of case is satisfied by rule 7 of the Compulsory Purchase by Non-ministerial Acquiring Authorities (Inquiries Procedure) Rules 1990.

The analysis of Lord Greene MR in *B Johnson & Co v Minister of Health*, as to the functions of a minister in confirming an order, was approved in the *Bushell* case. Lord Diplock pointed out that although a minister has imposed upon him a quasi-judicial role, namely when he is considering the respective representations of the promoting authority and of the objections made at the local inquiry and the report of the inspector on them, and this role requires him to act fairly in that after the inquiry has closed he must not hear one side without letting the other know nor accept from third parties fresh evidence which supports one side's case without giving the other side an opportunity to answer it, this role ceases when he comes to make his ultimate decision. On the substantive matter, namely whether the order should be confirmed or not, the interests of the general public, who are not represented at the inquiry, are interests which the minister has a duty to treat as paramount. It follows from this that a minister is entitled, as part of his decision-making process, to consult with officials in his own department and obtain advice to enable him to form a balanced judgment on the strength of the objections and the merits of the scheme.

Against the background of that law, readers may appreciate that a minister may be entitled to reach a decision contrary to the recommendations and conclusions of his inspector. The minister is entitled to take into account wider considerations, such as public policy, and to make use of any information held within his own department: see the *Bushell* case. However, there are certain safeguards in rule 17 of the Inquiries Procedure Rules 1990 where a minister is proposing to differ from the inspector on a finding of fact or to take into consideration some new evidence not raised at the inquiry (see p36 above).

2. The duty to give reasons

The Tribunals and Inquiries Act 1992 places a duty on a minister, in notifying his decision following a public local inquiry, to give reasons for that decision. In *Ashbridge Investments Ltd* v *Minister of Housing and Local Government* [1965], Lord Denning MR said that: '...the court can interfere with the minister's decision if he has acted on no evidence; or if he has come to a conclusion to which on the evidence he could not reasonably come ...'. In that case a building was included in a slum clearance area; the owner of the building challenged the compulsory purchase order on the ground that the building was either not a house, or if it were, it was not unfit for human habitation. As there had been an inquiry and an inspector had set out the facts which gave to the minister the necessary evidence upon which he made his decision, the challenge failed. However, in *Coleen Properties Ltd* v *Minister of Housing and Local Government* [1971], a case also concerning a clearance area, the issue was whether the minister, in confirming the order and including a

house which was not itself unfit for human habitation, had
evidence to make his decision. It was a requirement of the Housing
Act 1957 that land could be included in a compulsory purchase
order if 'the acquisition of which is reasonably necessary for the
satisfactory development ... of the area'. It was held that the
minister, in disagreeing with the inspector's recommendation to
exclude the house in question, had no evidence which justified the
minister in overruling the inspector's conclusion that the
acquisition of the property was not reasonably necessary. The test
of 'reasonably necessary', a requirement of the statute, did not
involve a matter of policy, but an inference of fact. The minister was
entitled to decide questions of policy, but he could not overrule the
inspector's recommendation in relation to an inference of fact
unless there was material sufficient for the purpose.

In *Landau* v *Secretary of State for the Environment* [1991], it was
held (1) that a decision under rule 10 of the Compulsory Purchase
by Public Authorities (Inquiries Procedure) Rules 1976 to confirm a
compulsory purchase order required reasons to be given which
were proper, intelligible and adequate (see *Westminster City Council*
v *Great Portland Estates* [1984]); and (2) an alleged deficiency of
reasons is a ground of challenge if the interests of the applicant has
been substantially prejudiced: see *Save Britain's Heritage* v *No 1
Poultry* [1990].

3. *Alternative schemes*

In presenting a case, objectors may well suggest alternative schemes
or sites for a project. In *Prest* v *Secretary of State for Wales* [1983], Lord
Denning MR was dealing with a case where an affected landowner
had offered to convey one or other of alternative sites to the
promoting authority. He referred to *Brown* v *Secretary of State for the
Environment* [1978] where Forbes J said that where other land was
suitable for the purpose of a project 'no reasonable Secretary of
State faced with that fact could come to the conclusion that it was
necessary for the authority to acquire other land compulsorily for
precisely the same purpose'. In the *Prest* case the Court of Appeal
said that in reaching his decision it would be wrong for a minister
to exclude from his decision-making process relevant facts known
and established at the time his decision is being made. In the case,
the speculative possibility that the land, the subject of the order,
would get planning permission for industrial development
purposes had turned into a probability, thus considerably

increasing the possible land acquisition costs of the project. There was also fresh evidence that the scheme of the authority, a sewerage works, might need less land because of modern methods of treatment. As the objecting landowner was prepared to make an alternative site available at existing use value, Lord Denning MR said that a minister ought to see that an acquiring authority, using taxpayers' money, will not be paying too much for the land especially where there is an alternative site which can be acquired at a much lower price. The minister's failure to consider this matter was a failure to consider a relevant consideration and the minister's confirmation of the order was quashed.

It must not be assumed from the Prest case that the question of the land costs or other financial matters will always be material considerations which the confirming minister must take into account. In *Green* v *Secretary of State for the Environment* [1984] an order was challenged on the grounds that the costs of compensating the objector for his land would not leave sufficient financial benefit in the scheme. That challenge was dismissed as it was said that an acquiring authority is entitled to proceed with a scheme on wider considerations than the direct costs and benefits in the scheme. Later, in *Burton* v *Secretary of State for Transport* [1988] the Court of Appeal, in judgments critical of the procedural requirements that allow objectors to challenge and hold up orders without sufficient cause, decided that although the minister had not shown that he had expressly considered the costs of accommodation works, he had not failed to consider a relevant consideration as the costs of the works were unknown and likely to be a very small component of the large cost of the whole scheme.

In *de Rothschild* v *Secretary of State for Transport* [1989], the affected landowners had objected to a compulsory purchase order and had put forward at the public inquiry alternative schemes on land they owned, arguing that they were superior on a variety of grounds. They were prepared to sell the alternative land at valuation. The minister's decision confirming the order, and rejecting the suggested alternatives as he did not believe they had sufficient advantages or benefits over the proposed scheme, was challenged by the landowners. In the Court of Appeal, the landowners contended that there were special rules for compulsory purchase orders as a taking of private property was involved. They mentioned that the protection of private property was the subject of Magna Carta and, more recently, the European Convention on Human Rights. Once more the Court of Appeal emphasized that a confirming minister has a variety of considerations that he must take into account in deciding whether to confirm an order and the proceedings are not on the basis of an action as between objectors and acquiring authority – a *lis inter partes*. The test was not as to whether there was a compelling case for an order with any doubt being resolved in favour of the landowner; rather it was based on what are called the *Wednesbury* principles (see below) and there had been no breach of these principles.

4. Financial viability

Provided the Secretary of State has compelling reasons for the compulsory purchase order, lack of viability of the underlying scheme is not a ground of challenge: see *Royal Life Insurance* v *Secretary of State for the Environment* [1992]. In *Landau* v *Secretary of State for the Environment* [1991] financial and non-financial objections were advanced by the affected owner who contended that his scheme could be carried out without a grant, whereas the acquiring authority's scheme depended on a grant which was not assured. The inspector rejected the non-financial objections, and in so doing rejected the financial ones.

5. The Wednesbury principles

Lord Greene MR in *Associated Provincial Picture Houses* v *Wednesbury Corpn* [1948] CA restated certain principles which are now known as the *Wednesbury* principles. Although applied to a local authority's alleged misuse of power, they are equally applicable to a minister's use of power in making his decision on a compulsory purchase order.

The *Wednesbury* principles can be stated as follows:

(i) the minister (or a local authority) exercising a discretionary power must not refuse to take into account matters which he ought to take into account, and conversely, he must not take into account matters which he ought not take into account;

(ii) even if the first principle has been complied with, the decision must not be so unreasonable that no reasonable minister (or authority) would have made it.

In *Ashbridge Investments* v *Minister of Housing and Local Government* [1965] CA, a case in which a compulsory purchase order was specifically in issue, Lord Denning MR in an often cited passage, said:

> The Court can only interfere on the ground that the Minister has gone outside the powers of the Act or that any requirement of the Act has not been complied with ... it seems to me that the Court can interfere with the Minister's decision if he has acted on no evidence; or if he has come to a conclusion to which on the evidence he could not reasonably come; or if he has given a wrong interpretation to the words of the statute; or if he has taken into consideration matters which he ought not to have taken into account, or vice versa; or he has otherwise gone wrong in law ... the Court should look at the material which the inspector and the Minister laid before them, ... and see whether on that material the Minister has gone wrong in law.

These principles have been applied to the exercise of many aspects of central government and local authority powers. However, the question has arisen from time to time whether the exercise of the power of compulsory purchase, a power that results in the compulsory taking of private property, is the subject of more stringent rules. In many compulsory purchase cases expressions protective of private property are to be found. For example in *Coleen Properties Ltd* v *Minister of Housing and Local Government* [1971], Lord Denning MR said: 'when seeking to deprive a subject of his property and cause him to move himself, his belongings and perhaps his business to another area, the onus lies squarely on the local authority to show by clear and unambiguous evidence that the order sought for should be granted'. In the *Prest* case, Lord Denning MR said: 'I regard it as a principle of our constitutional law that no citizen is to be deprived of his land by any public authority against his will, unless it is expressly authorised by Parliament and the public interest decisively so demands...'. However, this principle has never in practice been anything more than a presumption of statutory interpretation. Thus, in *Webb* v *Minister of Housing and Local Government* [1965], where a compulsory purchase order was made under the Coast Protection Act 1949, it was said that land could not be taken under the order for purposes outside the powers of the Act, namely to make a promenade: 'these were purposes outside the powers of the Act. Landowners are entitled to have their land taken from them only for purposes lawfully authorised and not to have them taken for ulterior or political reasons'.

In the *de Rothschild* case, Slade LJ reviewed the earlier decisions and decided that even the judgment of Lord Denning MR, in the *Prest* case 'was ultimately founded on the grounds of unreasonableness and of failure to take into account a material consideration'. Slade LJ understood the earlier cases as showing that they give a warning 'that in cases where a compulsory purchase order is under challenge, the draconian nature of the order will itself render it more vulnerable to successful challenge on *Wednesbury/Ashbridge* grounds unless sufficient reasons are adduced affirmatively to justify on its merits'. However, the Court of Appeal decided in the *de Rothschild* case that the minister had taken into account all relevant considerations. The *de Rothschild* case, decided on the basis that the minister can confirm an order if he is persuaded there is sufficient justification on the merits, does conflict with the *Prest* case. The test, for the valid use of confirming powers, in the *Prest* case is that where the scales are evenly balanced – for and against compulsory acquisition – the decision should come down against compulsory acquisition. At some time in the near future the House of Lords may have to reconsider the appropriate tests. Even if both cases are treated as applications of *Wednesbury* principles, the cases show conflicting notions of the tests of unreasonableness.

In *Bolton MBC* v *Secretary of State for the Environment and Greater Manchester Waste Disposal Authority* [1990] Glidewell J stated certain principles in relation to the confirmation of compulsory purchase orders:

(a) The formulation of the principle that the decision-maker must not fail to take into account a relevant matter has the same meaning in the *Wednesbury* case, the *Ashbridge* case and as expressed by Forbes J in *Seddon Properties Ltd* v *Secretary of State for the Environment* [1978];

(b) The decision-maker ought to take into account any matter which might cause him to reach a different conclusion to that he would reach if he failed to take into account the matter;

(c) If a matter is trivial and there is no real possibility that it would make a difference to his decision, the decision-maker need not take it into account;

(d) A distinction must be made between matters which the decision-maker is obliged by statute to take into account and those implied from the nature of the decision;

(e) It is for the court to decide which matters fall within the second category in (d) above where the decision is challenged;

(f) If the court decides that a matter was fundamental to the decision, or there was a real possibility that the consideration of the matter would have made a difference to the decision, the court may hold the decision was not validly made. But if the court is uncertain, it does not have before it any material to hold the decision was invalid;

(g) Even if the court finds the decision was invalidly made, it has discretion in exceptional circumstances to refuse relief.

4.8 Challenging an order in the High Court

Section 23 of the 1981 Act, contains the right of 'any person aggrieved' to question the validity of a compulsory purchase order in the High Court on the following grounds:

(a) there is no power in the 1981 Act, or the enabling Act, to authorise the order; or,

(b) the requirements (mainly procedural) of the appropriate Acts and regulations (including the Inquiries Procedure Rules) have not been complied with and the interests of the person applying to the High Court have been substantially prejudiced.

A 'person aggrieved' will include any person with an interest in the land covered by the order. There is considerable doubt whether an amenity objector or a neighbour who will lose no land can be regarded as such a person. In *Turner* v *Secretary of State for the Environment* [1973], Ackner J decided that a person permitted to appear at a public local inquiry (into a planning matter) was a person aggrieved and could challenge a minister's decision. It is to be hoped that this more flexible approach to what is called the problem of *locus standi* will in future prevail. Decisions that do not amount to a challenge of an order may be challenged by way of judicial review. This is considered at the end of this chapter.

The final hurdle, in what some people regard as an unnecessarily limited right to challenge an order, is that the application to the court must be made within a six-week window commencing on the date that the confirmation of the order is first published. An application under section 23 made after the minister has confirmed the order, but before the notice of confirmation, was invalid in *Enterprise Inns plc* v *Secretary of State for the Environment, Transport and Regions* [2001]. In *R* v *Secretary of State for the Environment, ex parte Ostler* [1976] CA, in which the party challenging the order did not become aware of a secret assurance given by the Department of the Environment to a neighbour about a certain aspect of a road scheme until long after the period of six weeks, the court decided that it could not consider an application to challenge outside that period. Although the secret assurance prejudiced the position of Ostler, the challenger, and had he been aware of it in time it might have been a ground for challenging the order, the Court of Appeal were bound by the statutory time-limit. There must be some time-limit as the acquiring authority must be satisfied that taking property and commencing works will not turn out to be unlawful. In a few cases this time-limit may deprive a person of a right to challenge if he is unaware of a matter that could give rise to a challenge until it is too late.

Section 25 of the 1981 Act states that a compulsory purchase order cannot be questioned in any legal proceedings whatsoever except in the manner described above. But this would not preclude a court from quashing a resolution of a local authority to make a compulsory purchase order which was invalid: see *R* v *Camden London Borough Council, ex parte Comyn Ching Co Ltd* [1984].

Nor does it preclude a court from allowing judicial review of a decision to act on a notice to treat or a general vesting declaration where there is 'bad conscience' on the part of the acquiring authority, such as unreasonable delay, bad faith, misconduct or abuse of powers; see *Simpsons Motor Sales* v *Hendon Corporation* [1964].

1. The grounds for challenging an order

The grounds contained in the 1981 Act are set out above and reference should be made to the previous section on 'the role of the confirming minister'. They amount to a decision not within the statutory powers, usually referred to as an *ultra vires* decision, or failure to comply with a relevant requirement of the legislation. *Ultra vires* can be said to include three matters: the use of compulsory purchase powers outside the statutory wording of the legislation; the misuse of the powers – see the *Wednesbury* principles; or a breach of the rules of natural justice – these rules require impartiality by the decision-maker and the right to hear and be heard in a matter affecting a person's interest. Gross procedural irregularity would be *ultra vires*, but a failure to comply with relevant requirements of the legislation suggests some less serious procedural irregularity, and substantial prejudice must be established. There follow some examples of each:

(a) *Ultra vires*

    (i) Compulsory powers cannot be used for a purpose not within the enabling Act:

    Webb v *Minister of Housing and Local Government* [1965] CA: a compulsory purchase order was made under the Coast Protection Act 1949, ostensibly for coast protection work, although in fact some of the land was required for making a promenade. There was no power under the 1949 Act to acquire land for any purpose other than coast protection, and the order was quashed. *Sovmots Ltd* v *Secretary of State for the Environment* [1976]: no power to acquire the grant of rights not already created. See also *Proctor & Gamble Ltd* v *Secretary of State for the Environment* [1991].

    (ii) The minister should bear in mind the *Wednesbury* principles and must consider every relevant matter, and, although he is entitled to disregard trivial or insubstantial points raised at the inquiry (as indeed may the inspector), it must be clear from his decision letter that he has had regard to the relevant matters.

    London Welsh Association Ltd v *Secretary of State for the Environment* [1979] QBD: at the inquiry, the association put forward their own schemes for the development of the homes which were the subject of a compulsory purchase order; one of these schemes, the acquiring authority conceded, might have been an acceptable alternative to compulsory purchase. The inspector referred to the schemes in her report, but the minister failed to mention the scheme that had some acceptance to the authority. The order was quashed as it was unreasonable for the minister to disregard that scheme in coming to his decision. The Court of Appeal has since allowed an appeal by the Secretary of State on the ground that a general reference in his decision letter to the matters in the inspector's report could be sufficient reference to a material consideration.

    Sovmots Ltd v *Secretary of State for the Environment* [1976] QBD: the question of the cost of acquiring certain flats was one of the issues at the public inquiry. Forbes J stated that the costs of development by the acquiring authority could, in appropriate cases, be a consideration which the minister has a duty to take into account.

    Prest v *Secretary of State for Wales* [1983] CA: the owner of an agricultural estate, part of which was the subject of a compulsory purchase order for the purpose of a sewerage disposal scheme, offered to sell to the water authority one of two alternative sites at agricultural values in place of the land the authority wanted which had a development value. Although the construction costs of the alternative sites would have been higher, the lower land acquisition costs might have reduced the total costs. The minister failed to take into account the land acquisition costs of the alternative sites; these were relevant considerations and because they were ignored, the order was quashed.

de Rothschild v *Secretary of State for Transport* [1989]: alternative schemes put forward by objecting landowner; minister entitled to confirm original order where suggested alternatives had no sufficient advantages or benefits justifying their adoption.

Stirling Plant v *Central Regional Council* [1995]: an acquiring authority is entitled to refuse an offer of a long lease and make a compulsory purchase order instead.

The minister must not take into account irrelevant considerations in reaching his decision:

Hanks v *Minister of Housing and Local Government* [1963] QBD: in confirming an order under the Housing Acts for housing purposes, the minister took into account certain 'planning matters'. These were held not to be irrelevant considerations.

Sydney Municipal Council v *Campbell* [1925] PC: in deciding to acquire land under an Act enabling land to be taken for constructing highways, the acquiring authority had been motivated by the desire to acquire land and recoup betterment values rather than construct streets. This was held by the Privy Council to be an irrelevant consideration in reaching the decision. (This case could also be considered under (i) above.)

Riddle v *Secretary of State for the Environment* [1988]: A compulsory purchase order was validly made even though the purpose of making the order was to coerce the owner of a house into carrying out repairs which, if done, would result in the order being withdrawn.

Leggatt v *Secretary of State for the Environment* [1991]: land, which was compulsorily purchased for a motorway service area, was subject to an option in favour of a petroleum company. The minister did not have as an ulterior motive the obtaining of a large premium in granting a lease to the company; the reason for compulsory purchase was to implement a standard policy for the development of service areas. Accordingly, the minister was entitled to confirm the order.

(iii) The rules of natural justice must be complied with:

Fairmont Investments Ltd v *Secretary of State for the Environment* [1976] HL: at the conclusion of the inquiry, the inspector on his site visit observed some broken glass 'tell-tales' on the houses, the subject of the order. He concluded from this observation that the foundations of these houses were inadequate and the houses could not be rehabilitated because of a lack of stability: the minister, as a result, confirmed the compulsory purchase order. It was held there had been a breach of the rules of natural justice because the instability of the houses due to inadequate foundations had not been an issue at the inquiry and the owner had not been able to counter the 'evidence', obtained by the inspector, with any evidence of his own that the foundations were not inadequate.

Bushell v *Secretary of State for the Environment* [1981] HL: in this case it was held there is no breach of the rules of natural justice if an inspector at a highway inquiry exercises his discretion to refuse cross-examination of the Department's experts by objectors seeking to challenge the methods they used to establish traffic predictions. (A decision to construct a motorway was held, anyway, to be an administrative decision and government policy and not open to question at a public local inquiry.)

If an objector unreasonably believes that an inquiry into a compulsory purchase order is not to proceed on a certain date, he has only himself to blame if it does proceed on that date, and he absents himself: *Ackerman* v *Secretary of State for the Environment* [1981] CA. He cannot argue that there has been a breach of the rules of natural justice.

Bolton Metropolitan Borough Council v *Secretary of State for the Environment* [1990] CA: the court considered the relevant principles to be taken into account when some new matter of objection arises after the close of any public inquiry.

(b) *Failure to comply with a relevant requirement of the legislation*

Unless there is a breach of the rules of natural justice, a person who challenges an order on the ground of a procedural irregularity must show that he has been substantially prejudiced: 1981 Act, section 23:

Meravale Builders Ltd v *Secretary of State for the Environment* [1978]: there had been a failure to comply with the inquiry rules in that the Secretary of State had differed from his inspector on a finding of fact, and had failed to re-open the inquiry; there had been substantial prejudice to the applicants.

George v *Secretary of State for the Environment* [1979] CA: Mr and Mrs George owned a house included in a compulsory purchase order. Mr George, but not his wife, was served with a notice of intention to make such an order; under the statutory requirements, Mrs George should also have received such a notice, but she did hear of the intention of the acquiring authority informally through her husband. It was held that Mrs George had not been 'substantially prejudiced'; her husband had looked after her interests as well as his own. A further point was taken that even if the order could not be challenged on the ground of procedural irregularity, it might be *ultra vires* (see (a) above) by reason of a breach of the rules of natural justice. The court accepted that a breach of the rules of natural justice could be a ground for quashing an order as being *ultra vires*, but for a breach of these rules the person concerned must show that there had been actual injustice or a real risk of substantial prejudice or injustice: this, Mrs George had failed to show.

Finally, Lord Denning MR, has said that 'it would be a mistake to go through an inspector's report, or a [minister's] decision letter, as if one were going through a statute to see if one can find a hole in it. These inquiries are conducted by laymen – experienced, good laymen – and they set out their reasons for coming to a decision. As long as it is broadly correct, and no injustice has been done, then the order should not be upset by the courts': *Parker* v *Secretary of State for the Environment* [1981] CA.

There is no prejudice where an inquiry is re-opened, and the minister considers the reports of both inspectors, not withstanding that an objector, who did not have an interest with affected land until a later date did not appear at the first inquiry. He had ample opportunity of being heard: see *Venrich* v *Secretary of State for the Environment* [1990].

2. Judicial review

Although a compulsory purchase order may be challenged in the High Court under section 23 of the 1981 Act, a decision to make an order, or a decision by a confirming minister not to confirm an order, may be the subject of judicial review under Part 54 of the Civil Procedure Rules: see *Islington London Borough Council* v *Secretary of State for the Environment* [1980]. Judicial review may also be used to challenge a decision by an acquiring authority to act on a notice to treat or general vesting declaration: see *Simpsons Motor Sales* v *Hendon Corporation* [1964].

In *R* v *Secretary of State for the Environment, ex parte Melton Borough Council* [1986], the local authority failed in its application for judicial review to quash a minister's decision to refuse to confirm an order for a road; the minister had not been convinced that an alternative route was not more suitable, a decision he was entitled to reach: see also *Glasgow City* v *Secretary of State for Scotland* [1990]. The minister's decision to refuse to confirm an order was also upheld in *R* v *Secretary of State for the Environment, ex parte Leicester City Council* [1987]. In this case the council had made an order under section 112(l)(a) of the Town and Country Planning Act 1971 for land 'required' for development; the council had undertaken not to enforce the order if the owners withdrew their objections and made a financial contribution towards its development. The minister was not in error in refusing to confirm the order on the grounds that he believed the land was not 'required' by the council and that it was improper to use an order as a means of persuading owners to make financial contributions.

In *R* v *Secretary of State for the Environment, ex parte Rose Theatre Trust Co (No 2)* [1989], the judge decided that as a person must have 'a sufficient interest' in the matter to bring judicial review proceedings, there were limitations on those who had the necessary *locus standi*.

However, in *R* v *Carmarthen District Council, ex parte Blewin Trust* [1990], where the owners of an hotel sought relief restraining the acquiring authority from executing a general vesting declaration on the ground that the authority had changed its proposals for the use of the land, the relief was refused on the ground that there had not been 'bad conscience' on the part of the authority as considered in *Simpsons Motor Sales* v *Hendon Corporation* [1964].

Chapter 5

Purchase and Blight Notices

Introduction
Purchase notices under the planning Acts
Purchase notices under the housing Acts
Blight notices

5.1 Introduction

This chapter concerns two forms of what might be called compulsory purchase in reverse: two situations when an owner can compel a local authority to purchase land from him. Here the initiative is with the individual and it may be used as a consequence of certain decisions under the planning or housing Acts that affect the saleability of land in the hands of certain owners. Circular 13/83 contains useful advice on purchase notices.

5.2 Purchase notices under the planning Acts

1. The right to serve a purchase notice on the refusal or conditional grant of planning permission: section 137 of the Town and Country Planning Act 1990.

Any owner of land (and where (b) below applies any person with an interest in the affected land) may serve a purchase notice on the district council or London borough council requiring them to purchase his interest in the land where:

- (a) Planning permission has been refused, or granted subject to conditions; or
- (b) A planning permission is revoked or modified; or
- (c) A discontinuance order has been made under section 102 of the 1990 Act; and
- (d) The land has become incapable of reasonable beneficial use in its existing state (or if planning permission was granted

subject to conditions, the land cannot be rendered capable of reasonable beneficial use because of these conditions); and,

(e) The land cannot be rendered capable of reasonable beneficial use by making use of any existing planning permission or any permission which the local authority or Secretary of State has undertaken to grant.

To put it more shortly, if planning permission is refused and the land cannot be put to any reasonably beneficial use, the owner can serve his purchase notice.

A purchase notice served under section 137(2)(a) must relate to the whole of the land the subject of a refusal or conditional grant of planning permission. Such a notice cannot be served in respect of part only of that land: see *Cook v Winchester City Council* [1995]. Further the claimant must own the whole of the land: see *Smart & Courtney Dale Ltd v Dover Rural District Council* [1972].

Incapable of reasonable beneficial use

The important requirement is that the land has become incapable of reasonable beneficial use: see section 137(3). Reasonable beneficial use does not necessarily mean profitable use (although profitability is often relevant), nor does it mean that the land is less useful to the owner in its present state than if developed: see *R v Minister of Housing and Local Government, ex parte Chichester Rural District Council* [1960] QBD. In *Colley v Secretary of State for the Environment* [1998] it was said that the word 'use' in the expression in section 137(3) 'incapable of reasonably beneficial use' was concerned with use rather than the value of land.

If only part of the land is incapable of reasonable beneficial use, and part is capable of such use, then the owner can only serve a notice in respect of the part that is incapable of reasonable beneficial use: *Wain v Secretary of State for the Environment* [1982] CA. 'Land' includes a building: section 336(1).

In deciding whether land has any reasonable beneficial use, one first considers if there is any existing use that is beneficial (waste land that was partly used as a sports ground and could, in part, be let for grazing, had a beneficial use: *General Estates Company Ltd v Minister of Housing and Local Government* [1965]). If there is no existing use that is beneficial, the next question is whether there are any other uses that could be reasonably beneficial; any use in Part I of Schedule 3 to the 1990 Act can be considered provided the development can be carried without an express grant of planning permission. A use which is 'new development' ('new development' is any development not in Schedule 3) must not be considered. Whether any use is or is not reasonably beneficial will be a question of fact and degree, and for the minister to decide: *Brookdene Investments* v *Minister of Housing and Local Government* [1970] QBD. Any unauthorised prospective use is to be disregarded: see section 138 of the 1990 Act.

In *Colley* v *Secretary of State for the Environment* [1998] it was held that some woodland could still be capable of reasonable beneficial use as commercial woodland even though it was protected by a tree preservation order.

The expression 'has become' suggests that its state of incapability of reasonable beneficial use is a new state and is attributable to the planning decision. This interpretation is not accepted by the minister (see para 13 of Circular 13/83), who is prepared to accept that the criteria includes the physical state of the land. In *Purbeck District Council* v *Secretary of State for the Environment* [1982] the Secretary of State's confirmation of a purchase notice was quashed on the ground that the minister had failed to consider that the reason for the state of the land was an unauthorised activity. That case was distinguished in *Balco Transport Services Ltd* v *Secretary of State for the Environment* [1985] where the Court of Appeal decided that if an unauthorised activity could be the subject of an enforcement notice, and so made reasonably beneficial of use, the owner could not serve a valid purchase notice: if the unauthorised activity was immune from enforcement, then he could serve a valid purchase notice.

Where planning permission has been granted for an area of land and a condition imposed restricting the use of a small part of that area, e.g. open space or play area in a residential estate, then a purchase notice cannot be used if planning permission is subsequently refused to develop that area of restricted use: see section 142 of the 1990 Act.

2. *The procedure: sections 139–141 of the 1990 Act*

The purchase notice is served on the district council (or London borough) within 12 months of the decision concerned. The procedural requirements, and time-limit, are found in the Town and Country Planning General Regulations 1992. In the Scottish case of *Reside* v *North Ayreshire Council* [2000], it was decided that the start date of the 12-month time-limit, where there is an appeal, was the date of an inspector's decision. Within three months of the service of the purchase notice, the council must serve a response notice stating that:

(a) the council is willing to comply and to purchase the land; or
(b) another specified authority is willing to purchase; or
(c) neither the council nor any other authority are willing to accept the purchase notice, and that a copy has been sent to the Secretary of State with reasons for not complying with the notice.

If (c) applies, the Secretary of State invites representations from the owner, the council and the county planning authority. And if he has in mind substituting any other authority for the council as being required to comply with the purchase notice, he seeks their views as well. If required to, the Secretary of State holds a hearing or public local inquiry; he may then confirm the purchase notice, substitute another authority for the council, refuse to confirm the purchase notice and grant planning permission or vary any conditions; he may also in lieu of confirming the purchase notice, direct that planning permission shall be granted for some form of development other than that applied for.

The Secretary of State need not confirm a purchase notice covering land which includes some land the subject of restrictions against development imposed by a planning condition or was clearly intended as amenity land in a planning application: section 142 of the 1990 Act.

Unless there is an appeal against the planning decision before the Secretary of State, the purchase notice is deemed confirmed if the Secretary of State fails to make a decision before the end of the relevant period: see section 143(2) of the 1990 Act. The relevant period is nine months from the service of the purchase notice or, if earlier, six months from the date on which a copy of the notice was transmitted to the Secretary of State: section 143 of the 1990 Act.

3. *Listed buildings*

Section 32 of the Planning (Listed Buildings and Conservation Areas) Act 1990 makes stricter provision for the service of a purchase notice where listed buildings consent is refused, granted subject to conditions or is revoked or modified. The procedure and conditions for service are stricter than under the Town and Country Planning Act 1990.

4. Deemed compulsory purchase

If a purchase notice is accepted by the council or some other authority, or confirmed by the Secretary of State, the authority acquiring is deemed to have served a notice to treat: section 143(1) of the 1990 Act. A notice to treat is the first step in the use of the acquisition powers in the more usual compulsory purchase order situation. Notices to treat are therefore considered in Part II of this book. However, by section 67 of the Planning and Compensation Act 1991, a deemed notice to treat will cease to have effect after three years where the planning decision which founded the purchase notice was made after September 25 1991. The point is that once a purchase notice is accepted, the authority is deemed to be compulsorily purchasing the land, and the rules and basis of compensation for a compulsory purchase should apply. Once a purchase notice is accepted or confirmed, as a deemed notice to treat it cannot be withdrawn under section 31 of the Land Compensation Act 1961: see section 143(8) of the 1990 Act. But there appears to be no prohibition on the withdrawal of a purchase notice before it is accepted or confirmed.

Where a purchase notice has been accepted or confirmed, a claim for damages may be brought against the authority if it fails to negotiate with the owner in good faith: *Bremer* v *Haringey London Borough Council* [1983].

5. Agricultural land

There are special provisions where part of an agricultural unit is subject to a deemed notice to treat following the service of a purchase notice and the remainder of the unit is not economically viable: see sections 145–147 of the 1990 Act.

5.3 Purchase notices under the housing Acts

Under section 284 of the Housing Act 1985, the housing authority may make an obstructive building order in respect of a building which is so obstructive to other buildings as to render them dangerous or injurious to health. Such a building will have to be demolished but the owner of any interest in the building may 'make to the local authority an offer for the sale of his interest'; the authority shall accept the offer and must then carry out the demolition as soon as possible after obtaining possession: see section 287.

5.4 Blight notices

Certain owners can serve a blight notice to compel an authority to acquire their 'blighted' properties. 'Blight' in the legal sense is not the generalised description adopted by lay people in their reference to a state of affairs where property values are affected by local authority planning decisions or other activities, although such a state of affairs may include circumstances in which a blight notice can be served. Blight has a specific meaning and the circumstances are specified in the Town and Country Planning Act 1990. The right to serve a blight notice is limited to certain categories of owner occupiers. Broadly, the purpose of blight notices is to compel authorities to purchase land in advance of their compulsory purchase needs in order to mitigate hardship.

Where land is not blighted in the legal sense, discussed below, there are some circumstances where highway and other authorities have a discretionary power to acquire affected properties. This is considered in Chapter 24 below.

1. The classes of blighted land are specified in Schedule 13 to the 1990 Act

Land designated for public authority functions in development plans etc.

1. Land indicated in a structure plan (including a plan submitted to the Secretary of State for approval or consideration of alterations, or the Secretary of State's modifications to a plan) as land which may be required for the purpose of the functions of public authorities (including a telecommunications operator) or as land which may be included in an action area; or

2. Land allocated for the purposes or functions of public authorities by a local plan (including a local plan still subject to the public inquiry before its approval, proposals for alteration of a local plan and proposed modifications of a local plan before its approval) or defined in such a plan as a site for public authority development (land that is designated for housing is not blighted unless it is clearly to be developed by a local authority: *Bolton Corpn* v *Owen* [1962]; see also *Elcock* v *Newham London Borough Council* [1996]) LT;

3. Land indicated in a unitary development plan as land

required for public authority functions or as land to be included in an action area;

4. Land allocated by a unitary development plan for the functions of public authorities.

5. Land indicated in a plan (other than a development plan) approved by resolution of a local planning authority as land which may be required for the purposes of paragraph 1 above other than an action area.

6. Land indicated in a plan, which is not a development plan, but which is approved by the local planning authority for the purpose of 'safe-guarding' when exercising development control powers because the land is required for the purposes of a public authority. If land is required for a public authority purpose, that fact may not necessarily be indicated in the development plan (see 1 above); the planning authority may refuse permission to develop that land to safeguard it for the intended purpose.

New towns and urban development areas

7. Land within an area described as the site of a proposed new town in a draft order.

8. Land designated as a site of a new town in an order in operation under section 1 of the New Towns Act 1981.

9. Land which is intended or has been designated as an urban development area.

Clearance and renewal areas

10. Land declared to be clearance area by resolution under the Housing Act 1985.

11. Land surrounded by or adjoining an area declared to be a clearance area and land the authority has resolved to purchase under section 290 of the 1985 Act.

12. Land indicated by information under section 92 of the Local Government and Housing Act 1989 as land to be acquired as a renewal area.

Highways

13. Land indicated on a development plan as land proposed for a highway or a highway improvement or alteration; or

14. Land on or adjacent to the line of a highway in an order or scheme for a new highway or a highway improvement made under the Highways Act 1980, including land in any proposed order or scheme which has been submitted to the Secretary of State for confirmation, and land required under the Land Compensation Act 1973 for works of mitigation;

15. Land shown on a plan approved by resolutions of a local highway authority as land for a new highway or highway improvements;

16. Land included on a plan published by the Secretary of State as land for a public highway improvement area and notified to the local planning authority;

17. Land shown on plans resolved by the local highway authority for acquisition for mitigation purposes.

18. Land shown in a written notice by the Secretary of State to be acquired for mitigation purposes.

19. Land within the outer lines laid down in a new streets order, prescribing the minimum width of new streets, and upon which there is a dwelling erected before the making of the order (an owner may find his property is unsaleable because such an order may be made long before the street widening takes place).

General improvement area

20. Land in general improvement area (Part VIII of the Housing Act 1985) or indicated in a notice published for that purpose;

Compulsory purchase

21. Land authorised to be acquired by a private Act or within limits of deviation permitted by such an Act;

22. Land within a compulsory purchase order, including an order authorising the acquisition of rights (in respect of which the appropriate acquiring authority has not yet served a notice to treat), a compulsory purchase order submitted to the minister for confirmation or, where a minister is the acquiring authority, a draft compulsory purchase order (a resolution to make an order, but where no other steps are taken to make an order, is not within this paragraph);

23. Land proposed in an application for, in a draft order under, within limits of deviation or authorised to be acquired by, an order under the Transport and Works Act 1992.

2. The persons entitled to serve a blight notice: section 149 of the 1990 Act

Only certain persons may serve a blight notice; essentially those to whom having blighted land is an especial hardship:

(a) Owner-occupiers of any hereditament, of which the net annual value for rating purposes does not exceed a prescribed limit (at present £24,600 – see the Town and Country Planning (Blight Provisions) Order 2000). This would include the owners of small business premises or shops.
(b) Residential owner-occupiers of a private dwelling.
(c) Owner-occupiers of agricultural units.

An owner-occupier is the owner of the freehold or a lease with at least three years unexpired who has been in occupation of the whole or a substantial part of the hereditament for the six months preceding the service of a blight notice, or a period of six months ending not more than 12 months before the blight notice; and if the latter, the hereditament or dwelling must have been unoccupied since the owner-occupier vacated: section 168.

Where the subsoil under an adjoining public highway is presumed to be owned with the adjoining land, and highway improvements are proposed which will affect the subsoil, it was held by the Lands Tribunal in *Norman* v *Department of Transport* [1996] that the subsoil is part of the hereditament for the purposes of serving a blight notice. At the time of writing this case is being appealed.

The 1990 Act also permits a mortgagee the right to serve a blight notice where he is entitled to exercise his powers of sale, can give immediate vacant possession and has been unable to sell the interest concerned except at a price substantially lower than he might reasonably have been expected to obtain had the land not been within the circumstances of blight: section 161. A personal representative of a deceased owner-occupier has a similar right to serve a blight notice and must also show he has been unable to sell except at a substantially lower price: section 161 of the 1990 Act.

3. Procedure: sections 150–152 of the 1990 Act

A person who qualifies under 2 above and has land within one of the circumstances of planning blight outlined in 1 above may serve a blight notice on the appropriate authority. It is not good enough that the claimant's land is blighted and difficult to sell because it will be close to a proposed highway: hardship alone will not found a blight notice; the land must be land that will be needed: *McDermott v Department of Transport* [1984]. In some circumstances land may be blighted under more than one of the categories of blight and more than one authority may be the 'appropriate' authority. In *R v Secretary of State for the Environment, ex parte Bournemouth Borough Council* [1987] where land was blighted by a development plan indication of a proposed highway, it was decided that both the local planning authority and the highway authority were each the 'appropriate' authority, and the Secretary of State had no power to make a selection.

Except where the land falls within para 21 or 22 of Schedule 13 (see p64 above) and the powers of compulsory acquisition remain exercisable, the claimant must, before serving a blight notice, have made reasonable endeavours to sell his interest and in consequence of the blight has been unable to do so, or unable to do so except at a price substantially lower than he would have expected in the absence of blight. It would seem that in a case within para 23 of Schedule 13 – a transport and works order – there is no exception to this rule. It may be possible to argue that such an order is a 'special enactment' and therefore falls within paras 21 or 22 to which the exception does apply. Individual circumstances will dictate what is a reasonable endeavour to sell. It may include advertising or placing the property with an agent who makes attempts to seek a purchaser: see *Perkins v West Wiltshire District Council* [1976]. It is not sufficient to make no attempt to sell if an agent advises that no purchaser could be found in view of the planning blight. The attempt to sell need not be after a date when the land becomes formally blighted. The costs of any attempt to sell are not recoverable as compensation: see *Budgen v Secretary of State for Wales* [1985].

Where an owner owns the whole of a hereditament or an agricultural unit, a blight notice cannot be served in respect of part only; and where an owner is entitled to an interest only in part of a hereditament or an agricultural unit, a blight notice cannot be served in respect of less than the entirety of the respective part: section 150. But if a blight notice is served in respect of less than the whole of the owner's land, and so in contravention of this provision, the invalidity of the notice must be raised in the authority's counternotice or otherwise, the Lands Tribunal will have no jurisdiction to determine the question: *Binns* v *Secretary of State for Transport* [1986].

This last case, together with the much earlier case of *Lake* v *Cheshire County Council* [1976], illustrates that it is strictly statutorily impossible to serve a valid blight notice in respect of part of a hereditament (as defined in the valuation list) or part of an agricultural unit. Even if a notice is served in respect of the whole property, and the authority are prepared to take part, it may be difficult to compel them to take the whole: *Lake* v *Cheshire County Council* [1976].

5. *Counternotice by appropriate authority*

The appropriate authority may accept the blight notice and proceed to acquire the land: the purchase is then deemed to be a compulsory purchase. Alternatively, the authority may serve a counternotice within two months objecting to the blight notice. The grounds of objection are set out in section 151 of the 1990 Act. They include the following:

(a) that no part of the hereditament or agricultural unit is comprised in blighted land;

(b) that the appropriate authority do not propose to acquire any of the land;

(c) that they only propose to acquire part of the land referred to in the blight notice for their purposes (they can only be made to acquire the whole of a person's property if there would be material detriment to any part not acquired – see Chapter 8);

(d) that in the case of land falling within paras 1, 3 or 13, but not 14, 15 or 16 of Schedule 13 (see p64 above) the authority do not propose to acquire any of the land within the next 15 years, or such longer period as may be specified in the counternotice;

(e) that on the date of the blight notice the person who served the blight notice is not entitled to an interest in any part of the land to which the blight notice relates;

(f) that the interest of the claimant does not qualify (the reasons must be stated in the counternotice);

(g) that the person who served the blight notice has not made reasonable endeavours to sell, or he could only sell at a price that is depreciated by the planning blight.

An authority cannot rely on (d), that in appropriate cases it does not propose acquiring the land within the next 15 years, if ground (b) is appropriate (section 151(6)). Unfortunately, this does not apply if the authority is only proposing to take part of the land under ground (c); it may also serve a counternotice relying on ground (d) that it does not propose acquiring within 15 years (*Parker* v *West Midlands County Council* [1979] LT).

The proper date for considering the validity of an objection that no part of the land is to be acquired is the date of the counternotice, not the date of the blight notice: *Mancini* v *Coventry City* [1984] CA. But if a local authority changes its policy, and abandons a scheme, after the date of the counternotice, the Lands Tribunal cannot consider the abandonment and is constrained to consider the facts as they were at the date of the counternotice: see *Burn* v *North Yorkshire County Council* [1992]. This can mean that an authority is able to change its policy after receiving a blight notice and before it serves the counternotice. As the Court of Appeal observed in the *Mancini* case, the Lands Tribunal has no discretion to deal with the hardship suffered by the owner. Further, the Tribunal can only deal with the grounds in any counternotice, and it is irrelevant that at a later date the requirement for the land in question has ceased because of a new route for a road: see *Entwistle Pearson (Manchester) Ltd* v *Chorley Borough Council* [1993]. However the Court of Appeal in the *Mancini* case left open whether events post the date of any counternotice were relevant. This has been rejected by the Lands Tribunal in *Sinclair* v *Department of Transport* [1997] under ground (a).

Where an authority serves a counternotice on grounds (b) or (d), that either it does not propose to acquire any of the claimant's land or it does not propose to acquire within the next 15 years, and it makes a compulsory purchase order including that land, the order will have no effect in relation to the claimant's land in two circumstances. Either the counternotice objection was referred to the Lands Tribunal and upheld, or no such reference was made within the time-limit (section 155). This provision should deter authorities from improperly making use of objections based on grounds (b) or (d).

Where an authority has served a counternotice objecting to a blight notice in respect of land falling within paras 1, 2, 3, 4 or 14 of Schedule 13 (see pp 62 and 64 above), and the relevant plan, alterations, order or scheme comes into force, the authority may serve a further counternotice specifying different grounds of objection: see section 152. The purpose of this provision is to allow the authority to serve a counternotice containing objections based on the actual order etc. which might have excluded the land in question. The second counternotice must be served within two months of the appropriate plan etc. coming into force: see section 152(2). A second counternotice cannot be served if an objection has been made and withdrawn, or the Lands Tribunal has made a determination.

5. Counternotice objections are referred to the Lands Tribunal: section 153 of the 1990 Act

A person who has received a counternotice containing any of the grounds for objecting to a blight notice set out at 3 above may require the objection to be considered by the Lands Tribunal. Where a blight notice has been served on two 'appropriate' authorities, and each has served a counternotice, the tribunal may review the validity of the objection in each notice and decide if the blight notice or notices can be upheld: *R* v *Secretary of State for the Environment, ex parte Bournemouth Borough Council* [1987]. The Tribunal will review any objection and will uphold it unless it considers it is not well-founded. But the position is different where the objection is that land is not required by the authority (see (b) and (c) above): the Tribunal is then required not to uphold the objection unless it is shown to the satisfaction of the Tribunal that the objection is well-founded. It was said in *Perkins* v *West Wiltshire District Council* [1976] LT that the designation of land as public open space in the development plan was an indication that land was to be acquired. The House of Lords decided in *Essex County Council* v *Essex Congregational Church* [1963] that the authority could not raise an objection at the Lands Tribunal that was not in its counternotice.

If the Tribunal does not uphold an objection, it will declare the blight notice to be valid; or, if it upholds an objection on the ground that the authority only proposes to acquire part of the land covered by the blight notice, it may declare the blight notice valid in respect of that part. Where a blight notice is declared valid in this manner, the authority concerned is deemed to have served a notice to treat and will acquire subject to compulsory purchase procedures and compensation (section 154).

Lands Tribunal examples:

Louisville Investments Ltd v *Basingstoke District Council* [1976]: Land belonging to L was included in a compulsory purchase order submitted to the minister for confirmation. After the service of the blight notice by L, the authority withdrew the compulsory purchase order but not before it had served a counternotice that it had no proposals to acquire the land. In considering all the events up to the date of the decision, the Tribunal was not satisfied that the authority had abandoned its proposals to acquire L's land.

Charman v *Dorset County Council* [1986]: A service road was indicated on a local plan. The county council's objection to a blight notice was not upheld as it could not establish that the road was not required.

Kayworth v *Highways Agency* [1996]: the claimant's land was 'safeguarded' for a proposed road-widening scheme. The Agency refused to accept a blight notice on the ground that it did not intend to acquire any of the land; there had been a change of policy prior to the counternotice, although It was not publicised. The blight notice was upheld as no action had been taken after the material date of the counternotice.

Smith v *Kent County Council* [1995]: a blight notice was upheld in respect of a residential property. Regard was had to the broad issues of loss of privacy due to loss of trees; there would have been a serious effect on the amenity of the property under the scheme.

6. *Agricultural units*

Sections 158–160 of the 1990 Act contain special provisions as to blight notices served by an owner-occupier of agricultural units. It is possible that not all of a farm is within one of the categories of planning blight specified in Schedule 13 to the 1990 Act (see 1 above); an owner-occupier may, none the less, serve a blight notice in respect of the whole farm, or a part of the farm, if the 'unaffected area' (the area not subject to planning blight) is not reasonably capable of being farmed, either by itself or with other land in the same unit (if the blight notice does not cover the whole unit), or with another unit occupied by the person serving the blight notice (and of which he owns the freehold or a lease with at least three years unexpired: section 158).

The council receiving such a blight notice may, by counternotice, object to the inclusion of the 'unaffected area' on the grounds that it can be farmed by itself or with other land occupied by the owner. The question can then be referred to the Lands Tribunal; the Tribunal can declare the original blight notice valid, in which case both affected and unaffected land has to be acquired; or uphold the council's objection and only the affected land is then acquired. The council may make the separate objection that it has no proposal to acquire all the land in the blight notice, but this can only be made if the objection that the unaffected land can be farmed viably is also made: section 159.

7. *Withdrawal of blight notice*

Any person who has served a blight notice may withdraw it at any time before compensation has been determined by the Lands Tribunal (or within six weeks of such determination). A blight notice cannot be withdrawn once the appropriate authority has entered and taken possession: see generally section 156 of the 1990 Act. A blight notice can be deemed to have been withdrawn where a claimant sells the property: see *Carrell* v *London Underground* [1995] and *Bennett* v *Wakefield Metropolitan District Council* [1997].

8. *Deemed compulsory purchase*

Where there is no counternotice to a blight notice, or the Lands Tribunal uphold its validity, the appropriate authority is deemed to have served a notice to treat. By section 67 of the Planning and Compensation Act 1991 such a notice to treat will cease to have effect after three years in cases where the blighted land becomes blighted after September 25 1991.

Chapter 6

Purchase and Disposal by Agreement

Introduction
Contractual rights and the exercise of statutory powers
Purchase by agreement: no compulsory purchase order
Purchase by agreement: compulsory purchase order in the
   background
Disposal of land

6.1 Introduction

Bodies of statutory creation, such as local authorities, need statutory authority to purchase land, whether or not they intend to do so compulsorily. Enactments authorising compulsory purchase invariably authorise the public authorities or government departments concerned to purchase land by agreement as well as with the use of compulsory powers: some Acts, such as the Open Spaces Act 1906, only authorise the purchase of land by agreement.

Where it is known that land is required by an authority, an owner may be prepared to sell his interest to that body in advance of the making of a compulsory purchase order and the service of a notice to treat; this can be called purchase 'under the shadow' of compulsory purchase powers. An authority may decide to purchase land when it is put on the market, either because it is prepared to purchase in advance of its needs or because it is prepared to take any suitable property that becomes available and does not need a particular site for its purposes, e.g. in providing housing accommodation for policemen.

Certain problems can arise when selling land by agreement to an authority with compulsory purchase powers. This chapter considers these and the problem of how an authority should dispose of land that it has purchased with compulsory powers and which becomes surplus to its requirements. The first problem is whether a contract with an authority with statutory powers can be overridden.

6.2 Contractual rights and the exercise of statutory powers

In *Ayr Harbour Trustees* v *Oswald* [1883] (HL) Lord Blackburn said:

> I think that where the legislature confer powers on any body to take lands compulsorily for a particular purpose, it is on the ground that the using of that land for that purpose will be for the public good. Whether that body be one which is seeking to make a profit for shareholders, or, as in the present case, a body of trustees acting solely for the public good, I think in either case the powers conferred on the body empowered to take the land compulsorily are entrusted to them, and their successors, to be used for the furtherance of that object which the legislature has thought sufficiently for the public good to justify it in entrusting them with such powers; and, consequently, that a contract purporting to bind them and their successors not to use those powers is void.

Thus, in *Dowty Boulton Ltd* v *Wolverhampton Corporation* [1971], where a local authority owned an airport which it was bound by covenants with an adjoining factory owner to maintain as an airport, it was held that the local authority was entitled to appropriate the land to planning purposes. In consequence of the appropriation the land could then be used for housing purposes and the owner of the factory building would then become entitled to the payment of compensation for the interference with the benefit of the covenants.

In *R* v *City of London Corporation, ex parte Master Governors and Commonalty of the Mystery of the Barbers of London* [1996] a local planning authority had acquired by compulsory purchase a building site upon which a building was erected. A little while later it covenanted with an adjoining landowner not to interfere with light or air passing through any of the windows of the building on the adjoining landowner's property. Many years later it was proposed to demolish the building on the land owned by the local planning authority and erect another one which would interfere with the passage of light and air to the adjoining landowner's property, and therefore breach the covenants. It was held that the covenants could be overridden under the provisions of section 237 of the Town and Country Planning Act 1990 because the local planning authority's land had been acquired for planning purposes.

However it does not follow from the application of the broad proposition in *Ayr Harbour Trustees* that all contracts with bodies having statutory powers will necessarily be void. In *Stourcliffe Estate Company Ltd* v *Bournemouth Corporation* [1910] a local authority took a conveyance of land subject to restrictive covenants. It was held that where a local authority purchases land by agreement for any of the purposes for which it is authorised, it is not *ultra vires* for the local authority to enter into covenants with the vendor restricting the erection of buildings on the land purchased. That case was applied in *Dowty Boulton Paul Ltd* v *Wolverhampton Corporation* [1971], an earlier stage in the *Dowty Boulton Paul* proceedings, where an injunction was being sought to restrain the local authority from breaching the covenants until the trial of the action. It was held that the factory owner had made out a *prima facie* case that the local authority could not override the covenants.

The apparent conflict between the two decisions involving *Dowty Boulton Paul* can be reconciled. The later decision concerned a new scheme where the local authority had sought to appropriate the land to planning purposes. As in the *Barbers Company* case, statutory powers can override a contract where some new project or scheme is being advanced notwithstanding that covenants introduced under some earlier scheme are, *prima facie*, enforceable and not void.

6.3 Purchase by agreement: no compulsory purchase order

Most modern statutes authorise acquiring authorities to acquire land either by agreement or compulsorily. Section 120 of the Local Government Act 1972 contains a wide power for local authorities to acquire land by agreement for any of their statutory functions, or for 'the benefit, improvement or development of their area'. If an acquiring authority, with the necessary statutory powers, propose to purchase land with the agreement of the vendor without having first made a compulsory purchase order, the transaction is in many respects the same as any private transaction involving the sale of land. The parties first reach agreement, and if that agreement was made 'subject to contract', they then proceed to a contract. As with any private transaction, no contract for the sale of land or any other interest in land is enforceable in the courts unless the requirements of section 2 of the Law of Property (Miscellaneous Provisions) Act 1989 are satisfied. These are that the contract must be in writing and incorporate all the terms in one document, or where there is an exchange, in each. The terms may be incorporated in a document either by being set out in it or by reference to some other document. The document incorporating the terms or, where contracts are exchanged, one of the documents (but not necessarily the same one) must be signed by or on behalf of each party to the contract. Such a contract can be enforced by the decree of specific performance.

In certain cases the provisions of Part I of the Compulsory Purchase Act 1965 will be applicable to a purchase by agreement: see section 120(3) of the Local Government Act 1972 and section 227 of the Town and Country Planning Act 1990 (the provisions of Part I other than sections 4–8, 10 and 31).

However, there are certain problems that landowners need to consider before contracting to sell to acquiring authorities. First, an authority with statutory powers cannot, by a term in a contract, agree not to use any of its statutory powers, e.g. it could not, by a restrictive covenant, agree not to build on land purchased from a vendor if it has statutory powers enabling it to build. See *Ayr Harbour Trustees* v *Oswald* [1883] HL, where the trustees had tried to get away with a lower price for Oswald's land by agreeing that the conveyance to them should restrict their statutory powers to carry out harbour works; it was held that such an agreement would be of no effect. In *Dowty Boulton Ltd* v *Wolverhampton Corporation* [1971] the corporation had granted a right to use an airfield to the company for a period of 99 years. The corporation later decided to appropriate the land for housing and claimed the covenant in favour of the company no longer bound them. It was contended on behalf of the corporation that it could not, by contract, fetter its statutory powers. However, it was decided that where an authority has already exercised a statutory power to grant rights to another party extending over a number of years, the principle that it could not fetter its statutory power did not apply. Although the company succeeded in establishing their contractual right against the corporation, they were not granted any injunctive relief, and so presumably their remedy lay in damages only.

Where land is acquired by agreement by a local authority, Part I of the Compulsory Purchase Act 1965 will apply: *Re Elm Avenue, Milton* [1984]: see section 120(3), Local Government Act 1972. This will mean that if an authority in the exercise of its statutory powers interferes with or injures any interest in the land acquired (such as an easement or restrictive covenant), the owner of that interest will be entitled to compensation under section 10 of the 1965 Act.

However, the provisions of the Compulsory Purchase Act 1965, as to compensation and disturbance, do not always apply to a purchase by agreement. Thus, where land is acquired by agreement for highway purposes, sections 7 and 10 of the Compulsory Purchase Act 1965 will not apply: section 247(6) of the Highways

Act 1980. These two provisions entitle the owner of land taken, and the owner of rights over the land, to compensation. Clearly, the owner of the land taken, as vendor, can bargain for his price in his agreement. The owner of rights over the land is in a more difficult position as he cannot maintain his rights against the use of statutory powers, and has no compensation claim. The provisions of the Land Compensation Act 1961 as to the measure of compensations only apply to a 'compulsory' acquisition (section 5) – again vendors must bargain for a price.

Disturbance represents the expenses and other losses above the value of land; they can be significant. It seems prudent that in any contract to sell by agreement there should be inserted sufficient terms to protect the interest of the vendor. However, by definition, any such sale is by agreement and if the vendor is dissatisfied he cannot be compelled to enter into a contract to sell.

Where land is to be acquired by agreement, a problem may arise as to the assumption to be made as to likely planning permissions. Section 22 of the Land Compensation Act 1961 will not be satisfied, and an application for a certificate of appropriate alternative development cannot be made under section 17 of that Act, unless a notice has been published of a compulsory purchase order, a notice to treat has been served, or an offer in writing by the authority to negotiate for the purchase of the land.

An acquisition by agreement has disadvantages to acquiring authorities as well. If an authority agrees to withdraw a draft compulsory purchase order in return for the landowner's agreement to sell the land, then two things may follow. First, any ambiguities in the sale agreement will be construed in favour of the vendor, for he will have given up his right to object to a compulsory purchase order; and, second, if the contract stipulates a basis of compensation more favourable to the vendor than the statutory basis on a compulsory acquisition, the authority is bound by that favourable basis: see *Alfred Golightly & Sons Ltd* v *Durham County Council* [1981] LT.

A form of agreement as if a notice to treat has been served can be seen in *All Souls College, Oxford* v *Middlesex County Council* [1938].

6.4 Purchase by agreement: compulsory purchase order in the background

Land is commonly purchased by agreement with a confirmed compulsory purchase order in the background. Section 3 of the

Compulsory Purchase Act 1965 makes it lawful for the acquiring authority to agree with the owners of any land subject to compulsory purchase, and with all parties having an estate or interest in any of the land, for the absolute purchase, for a consideration in money. Since September 25 1991 the consideration may also be in money's worth, i.e. such as suitable exchange land: see section 3.

Where no notice to treat has been served by the authority, and an agreement is made, the agreement will only be enforceable if it complies with the provisions of section 2 of the Law of Property (Miscellaneous Provisions) Act 1989. Section 2 of the 1989 Act was enacted to replace section 40 of the Law of Property Act 1925, which provided that no agreement for the sale or other disposition of land could be enforced unless there was some memorandum or note in writing evidencing the agreement. It has been held that compliance with section 40 was not necessary where the parties have agreed a price, and where a notice to treat has been served on the owner by the authority. The notice to treat and the agreement as to price constitute a 'statutory' contract which is enforceable as such: see *Pollard* v *Middlesex County Council* [1906] and *Williams* v *Secretary of State for Environment* [1976]. However, it is not entirely clear that the principle of the 'statutory' contract has survived section 2 of the 1989 Act, although the Lands Tribunal considered it had in *Llanelec Precision Engineering Co* v *Neath Talbot CBC* [2000]. But even this 'statutory' contract will be unenforceable if one party makes his offer or acceptance of the other's terms, 'subject to contract': *Munton* v *Greater London Council* [1976] and *Duttons Breweries Ltd* v *Leeds City Council* [1982].

Where no notice to treat has been served, it would appear that the parties are free to agree the terms and price without regard to the statutory rules of compensation, although a local authority would have to justify the payment of compensation above the statutory code, to avoid the members being surcharged. Where a notice to treat has been served, any agreement reached must be within the statutory code. However, a mere offer in writing to purchase will bring into effect the statutory planning assumption, including a right to apply for a certificate of appropriate alternative development: see section 22 of the Land Compensation Act 1961.

As an agreement might be made at any stage following the confirmation of a compulsory purchase order, not all the necessary steps, such as the service of a notice to treat, may have been taken. These steps in the exercise of compulsory powers are described in the next part of this book. It is by no means clear that the provisions of the Compulsory Purchase Act 1965 and the statutory rules of compensation will apply in every such purchase by agreement, and therefore, as discussed earlier, any such agreement should include sufficient terms to protect the vendor's interest. Thus the date of valuation for the purpose of assessing compensation ought to be defined if the compensation is stated as that which would have been payable had the acquisition been compulsory. In *Bamlings (Washington) Ltd* v *Washington District Council* [1985] CA, the contract stated that the price for the land was to be settled by the Lands Tribunal 'as if the necessary steps for acquiring such interest compulsorily had been taken ... and a notice to treat had been served on date hereof'. The Court of Appeal, upholding the earlier decision of the Lands Tribunal, said it was the duty of the Tribunal, under this contract, to ask itself: 'What would have been the proper date for ascertaining the price payable ... if the necessary steps for acquiring the claimant's interest in the land compulsorily had been taken ... and a notice to treat had been served'. The proper date for ascertaining this price, in the contingency postulated by the words of the contract, was the date that values were agreed, (or the date that possession was taken if earlier) applying the normal compulsory purchase rule on valuation dates: see Chapter 11. (In private contract law the date of the contract is the date where the equity in the property passes to the purchaser, and would be the valuation date.)

A vendor who concludes an agreement with an acquiring authority possessing powers of compulsory purchase should be careful not to bind himself to a contract that takes away rights he would ordinarily enjoy under the Land Compensation Act 1961. In *Crabb* v *Surrey County Council* [1982] LT the claimant agreed to substitute for the statutory procedure for determining some potential development value (application for a certificate of appropriate alternative development) the use of an application for planning permission. The latter procedure is quite inappropriate where the land has been taken for a public purpose – hypothetical planning permission cannot be given, but the claimant was held bound by the procedure he agreed to use in his contract.

An acquiring authority that agrees to purchase a freehold, or other reversionary interest, will be bound by the interests of any tenant or tenants. If the reversionary interest is purchased by agreement, and therefore no notice to treat has been served, it will not be possible to serve a notice of entry on tenants with interests of less than a year, or from year to year, under section 11(1) of the Compulsory Purchase Act 1965. If tenants are not willing to agree terms for possession it will be necessary to serve a notice to treat in respect of their interests.

Where land is tenanted at the moment of entry, and landlord and tenant have agreed terms with the acquiring authority for the surrender of the lease, compensation under the agreement is assessed in accordance with the terms of the agreement and the factual matrix; compensation therefore reflects the lease: see *Tozer Kemsley & Millbourne Estates plc* v *Secretary of State for Transport* [1996].

6.5 Disposal of land

Public authorities that have exercised powers of compulsory purchase may need to sell surplus land, or land that is no longer required for the purpose for which it was acquired. Provisions in Part X of the Local Government, Planning and Land Act 1980 and in Schedule 5 to the Local Government Act 1988 require registers of unused land held by public authorities; there are powers for the Secretary of State to issue directions to sell.

1. Crichel Down rules

Following a major political scandal in the 1950s, what became known as the 'Crichel Down' principles were instituted in the case of the disposal of land owned by central government and these principles were recommended to other bodies. Under these principles land should first be offered back to the original owners, at market value, where the land remained in substantially the same state. In the case of local government, those principles are subject to the requirements of the Local Government Act 1972, section 123 (and there are similar provisions in the New Towns Act 1981). The present and revised 'Crichel Down Rules' were published in 1992: see Circular 6/93 and [1993] JPL 325. They were considered in *R* v *Trent Regional Health Authority, ex parte Westerman Ltd* [1995] where it was held that an acquiring authority was obliged to offer land back to a consortium of previous owners and could not rely on an exception to the rules designed to avoid fragmented sales. The DETR published a research report called *The Operation of the Crichel Down Rules* in 2000. The Rules were also considered in *R* v *Secretary of State for Defence, ex parte Wilkins* [2000] and *R* v *Secretary of State for the Environment, ex parte Wheeler* [2001].

2. Sale at best consideration reasonably obtainable

Section 123 of the Local Government Act 1972 provides that although councils may dispose of land in any manner they wish, they must not, without the consent of the Secretary of State, dispose of land 'for a consideration less than the best that can reasonably be obtained'. There are similar, but specific, powers to dispose in section 233 of the Town and Country Planning Act 1990. The obligation to get the best price reasonably obtainable means that where there are factors suggesting a higher price may be obtained than a bid which has been received, those factors must be pursued: see *R* v *Essex County Council, ex parte Clearbrook Contractors Ltd* [1981] applying the principle relating to the duty of trustee in *Buttle* v *Saunders* [1950]. In the *Buttle* case it was accepted that although trustees have an overriding duty to obtain the best price, that does not mean that they must necessarily accept an increased offer at any stage.

In the case of land with development value, where it is difficult to place an accurate value on the land, the only method of disposal that would comply with the duty to get the best consideration would be by auction or tender. In such a circumstance a previous owner cannot insist on being able to repurchase if the authority believes it must sell by these methods to comply with its duty: see *Tomkins* v *Commission for the New Towns* [1989]. Where a local authority is exercising its power under section 123 to dispose land, its duty to sell at a consideration of not less than the best that can reasonably be obtained means that it must consider all factors, including the possibility of an auction: see *R* v *Lancashire County Council, ex parte Telegraph Service Stations* [1988].

Employment-creation benefits are not relevant in deciding whether the best consideration reasonably obtainable test under section 123 has been satisfied: see *R (Leman Land Ltd)* v *Hackney London Borough Council* [2002].

The release of restrictions affecting land owned by a local authority is not a disposal for the purposes of section 123.

In *R* v *Hackney London Borough Council, ex parte Structadene* Ltd [2001] a local authority sold property to its tenants at an undervalue prior to an auction. It was held that as the transaction had reached contract stage, but not completion, and as the authority was in breach of law, the provisions of section 128(2) of the Local Government Act 1972, that protect third parties such as purchasers, did not apply.

Purchasers of land from public authorities should not necessarily assume that third-party rights, such as easements and restrictive covenants, have been extinguished; they may revive: see *Marten* v *Flight Refuelling Ltd* [1961]. Where land is acquired or appropriated under the wide powers of the Town and Country Planning Act 1990, section 226, and passed on to developers or others, section 237 of the 1990 Act gives immunity to building operations carried out with planning permission against the rights of third parties owning the benefit of easements or restrictive covenants over the land. Appropriation is more than a mere formal resolution. There must be proposals for the land for which it could be acquired under section 226 of the 1990 Act: see *Sutton London Borough Council* v *Bolton* [1993]. However, those rights are not extinguished and may affect the title in respect of matters and activities not specified as immune in section 237. However there are important restrictions on the effect of section 237, which are considered in Chapter 8 below.

3. *Pre-emption rights*

Sometimes rights of pre-emption may still affect land surplus to the needs of a scheme. However, this depends on the construction of the pre-emption rights and the relevant legislation: see *Freedman* v *British Railways Board* [1992] CA. Pre-emption rights are found in section 128 of the Lands Clauses Consolidation Act 1845, section 5(3) of the Defence of the Realm (Acquisition of Land) Act 1916 and section 156 of the Water Industry Act 1991 (the latter is subject to ministerial directions). If a contractual right of pre-emption is based on the statutory wording, it will be construed according to the intention shown by the wording: see *Naylor* v *British Railways Board* [1983].

4. *Liability for additional development compensation*

In certain circumstances compensation is payable to an owner where planning permission is granted within a 10-year period for additional development after the acquisition. This is fully considered in Chapter 13 below. Where an acquiring authority is disposing of land within that 10-year period, it may well require any purchaser to indemnify it against any claim for additional compensation payable to the original owner as a result of planning permission granted within that period.

PART II

EXERCISING THE POWERS OF COMPULSORY PURCHASE

The effective powers of compulsory purchase are as follows: the acquiring authority serves what is called a notice to treat and may then lawfully take possession of the land without the owner's consent upon giving a notice of entry. If the owner will not submit a claim for, or negotiate compensation, the authority may refer the matter to the Lands Tribunal. The assessment of the Lands Tribunal and the notice to treat together constitute a statutory contract, and the authority can obtain an order of court to compel the owner to convey, and, if he has not already done so, give up possession. In any event, if the owner refuses to convey after agreed compensation has been tendered, or a sum is awarded by the Tribunal, the authority may pay the sum into court and convey the land to itself by deed poll. Finally, if an owner or occupier refuses to give up possession, the authority may request the sheriff to obtain possession for them. Alternatively, a general vesting declaration is made and entry taken following the vesting date.

The Lands Clauses Consolidation Act 1845 contained the standard provisions governing the exercise of powers of compulsory purchase; its main provisions have been re-enacted in the Compulsory Purchase Act 1965. Today, the 1965 Act is applicable to most compulsory purchase orders made by a local authority, statutory undertaker or minister.

Chapter 7

Commencing a Compulsory Purchase

Introduction
Notice to treat
Deemed notice to treat
General vesting declaration

7.1 Introduction

A notice to treat is the first step in the exercise of compulsory powers following the confirmation of a compulsory purchase order. There are occasions where a notice to treat is not served as such, but is deemed to have been served (blight and purchase notices): the consequences that follow a deemed notice to treat are the same as if an actual notice to treat had been served. A relatively new procedure, the general vesting declaration, expedites the purchase of land; although a notice to treat is not served if this procedure is used, the effect of a general vesting declaration is, for certain purposes, as if a notice to treat had been served.

Section 4 of the Compulsory Purchase Act 1965 stipulates that the powers of compulsory purchase must not be exercised after the expiration of three years from the date the compulsory purchase order becomes operative. An order becomes operative when proper notice of the minister's confirmation is given the required publicity: see Chapter 4. In *Co-operative Insurance Society Ltd* v *Hastings Borough Council* [1993], and not following, *Westminster City Council* v *Quereshi* [1991], Vinelott J held that the service of a notice under section 3 of the Compulsory Purchase (Vesting Declaration) Act 1981 was not an exercise of compulsory powers, and that therefore the making of a general vesting declaration after the three-year time-limit would be of no legal effect.

It is sufficient if the notice to treat is served within the time-limit, and, provided the completion of the purchase takes place within a reasonable time thereafter, it does not matter if the acquiring authority completes and takes possession after the time-limit: *Marquis of Salisbury* v *Great Northern Railway* [1852]. However, where a compulsory purchase order is made, or in the case of one made by a minister, notices are published, after September 25 1991, a notice to treat shall cease to have effect at the expiration of three years from its service unless compensation is agreed, awarded, paid or paid into court: see section 67 of the Planning and Compensation Act 1991.

If, following the service of the notice to treat, the authority does not proceed to negotiate the purchase in good faith, the notice to treat can be set aside by the court and damages awarded to the owner for any loss: *Bremer* v *Haringey London Borough Council* [1983].

7.2 Notice to treat

When an acquiring authority wishes to exercise its powers under a compulsory purchase order, it must first serve a notice to treat as provided in section 5 of the 1965 Act.

1. Contents and service of a notice to treat

The notice must describe the land to which it relates, demand particulars of the interest in the land and the claim of the recipient, and state that the acquiring authority is willing to treat for the purchase of the land, and as to the compensation for any other damage that may be sustained as a consequence of the execution of the works: section 5, Compulsory Purchase Act 1965. There is no prescribed form of notice to treat and a letter that clearly contains the matters just outlined can be regarded as a notice to treat: see *Hull & Humber Investment Co* v *Hull Corporation* [1963] (letter from the district valuer of the Inland Revenue was accepted without any dispute). The notice must give particulars of the land to which it relates: see *Lewis* v *Hackney London Borough Council* [1990]. In *Bostock, Chater & Sons Ltd* v *Chelmsford Corp* [1973] the Lands Tribunal held that a letter from a minister that he had decided to confirm a compulsory purchase order was not a notice to treat.

A notice to treat must be served on an owner personally, or where he cannot be traced, affixed to the land: section 30. A notice cannot be validly served on an agent: *Fagan* v *Knowsley Metropolitan Borough Council* [1985].

2. *Persons entitled to a notice to treat*

All persons, with exceptions mentioned below, who have an interest in the land and have power to sell and convey or release the land are entitled to a notice to treat. If any owner cannot be traced after diligent inquiry by the acquiring authority, the special provisions mentioned in Chapter 9 will apply before they take possession. Diligent inquiry means reasonable diligence, but no very great inquiry is required: see *R* v *Secretary of State for Transport, ex parte Blackett* [1992].

A mortgagee is entitled to a notice to treat (see *Advance Ground Rents Ltd* v *Middlesborough Borough Council* [1986]), as is an owner with a possessory title (*Perry* v *Clissold* [1907]) and a person with an equitable interest in the land by reason of a contract to purchase or an option: see *Oppenheimer* v *Minister of Transport* [1942]. In *DHN Food Distributors Ltd* v *Tower Hamlets London Borough Council* [1976] CA, a company was held to have an irrevocable contractual licence to carry on business on premises owned by one of its subsidiaries; as that licence gave rise to a constructive trust, DHN had an equitable interest in the land which entitled them to compensation: it followed that DHN had an interest which entitled them to a notice to treat. In the case of groups of companies it will always be a question of fact whether a company is in a position to receive a notice to treat; this can be important as compensation usually depends on this: see *Marzell* v *Greater London Council* [1975].

The owner of each separate interest in the land, freehold, leases, subleases, etc. will be entitled to a notice, although, where the land is subject to a strict settlement trust or a trust for sale, only the tenant for life or the trustees, respectively, need be served and not any other beneficiaries: this is because the tenant for life or the trustees, as the case may be, have full power to sell the land free of interests of the beneficiaries.

Certain parties are not entitled to a notice to treat. A licensee is not, although the interest of a contractual licensee may be protected by a constructive trust by reason of the licence having an equity which the courts will protect (as in the *DHN* case above). Persons owning the benefit of an easement or restrictive covenant which affects the land concerned are not entitled as an acquiring authority is not obliged to acquire their interests: *Clark* v *School Board for London* [1874]. The rights over the land taken will subsist in the hands of the dominant tenant owners, although to the extent that the rights cannot be exercised by reason of the statutory powers of the authority and the dominant tenement is injured in value, there is usually a compensation claim: section 10 of the 1965 Act. A few statutes provide that such rights are extinguished upon acquisition of the land, but even in these cases there may be no obligation to serve a notice to treat on the owners of the rights: *London Regional Transport* v *Imperial Group Pension Trust Ltd* [1987].

Although a notice to treat may be served on any lessee or tenant, whatever the length of his term, it need not be served on any tenant who has an interest no greater than a year or from year to year as special compensation provisions apply in such a case: see further Chapter 19. It was pointed out in *Newham London Borough Council* v *Benjamin* [1968] CA, that one of the purposes of a notice to treat is to obtain details of the recipient's interest. In practice a notice to treat need not be served if the acquiring authority first acquire the reversionary interest of the landlord and then either serve notice to quit under the terms of the tenancy or allow the lease or tenancy to expire. In other cases, where a lease with an unexpired term exceeding one year is to be acquired, a notice to treat will have to be served on the lessee.

A person in occupation under an agreement for a tenancy for life is entitled to a notice to treat: see *Blamires* v *Bradford Corporation* [1964].

3. The consequences of a notice to treat

There are a number of consequences that follow the service of a notice to treat:

(a) Notice of claim

A notice to treat demands that the recipient states his interest and his claim in respect of the land. There is usually a time-limit for this, generally 21 days. Failure to respond to a notice to treat with a notice of claim will not prevent the acquiring authority from proceeding; but the Lands Tribunal, in any reference to it for compensation to be assessed, may penalise the owner in costs if he has failed to state the exact nature of his interest and failed to give details of the compensation he claims, 'distinguishing the amounts under separate heads and showing how the amount claimed under each head is calculated': section 4 of the Land Compensation Act 1961. The Tribunal may require such an owner to bear his own costs and to pay the costs of the acquiring authority from the time the notice of claim could have been made.

If a notice of claim is not submitted containing 'the amounts under separate heads and showing how the amount claimed under each head is calculated', the acquiring authority may withdraw its notice to treat and abandon its intention to purchase. In *Trustees for Methodist Church Purposes v North Tyneside Metropolitan Borough Council* [1979] ChD, the claimants completed the notice of claim as follows: for the value of the claimant's interest in the land, they wrote: 'compensation under rule (5) basis to represent the cost of acquiring a simple site and erecting an alternative place of worship'; for disturbance they wrote: 'A claim is reserved under the head'. The court decided that because the actual figures of cost and expense had not been inserted, it was an invalid claim and the authority was entitled to withdraw the notice to treat: section 31, Land Compensation Act 1961. The right to claim compensation is assignable and can therefore pass with the title: see *Dawson v Great Northern Rly* [1905].

(b) The interests in the land are fixed

The owner of the land affected by a notice to treat remains free to sell his interest to anyone. A contract to sell is not frustrated by a proposal to acquire the land: see *E Johnson & Co (Barbados) Ltd v NSR Ltd* [1996]. Where land that is subject to a notice to treat is sold, the purchaser is entitled to claim compensation and it is no argument that the claimant may have paid a price that reflects the impending acquisition: *Landlink Two Ltd v Sevenoaks District Council* [1985]. A contract of sale, made before the notice to treat, is binding on the purchaser: *Hillingdon Estates Ltd v Stonefield Estates Ltd* [1952]. However, if the purchaser does not complete, he will probably not be entitled to claim compensation: see the *Hillingdon* case.

The owner may also grant leases, but a tenant under a lease granted after the notice to treat cannot be compensated: see *Mercer v Liverpool, St Helen's & South Lancashire Rly* [1904] and *Re Marylebone Improvement Act, ex parte Edwards* [1871]. If an existing lease is assigned after the notice to treat, and the assignee submits an amended claim for a higher amount of compensation, it will be paid as no new interest has been created: *Cardiff Corpn v Cook* [1923] and *Carnochan v Norwich & Spalding Railway Co* [1858].

Most acquisitions are within the Acquisition of Land Act 1981, and section 4 provides that an owner must not unnecessarily create new interests or carry out building or other works 'with a view to obtaining compensation or increased compensation'. In *Hefferon* v *City of Liverpool* [1989] the compensation was reduced to reflect improvements carried out immediately before the vesting date. Otherwise, where property is merely subject to a compulsory purchase order, an owner would be inhibited from dealing with his property in circumstances where a notice to treat might never be served. An analogy is found in *Ravenseft Properties* v *Hillingdon London Borough Council* [1968] where the Lands Tribunal considered that a claimant who had acquired land with prior knowledge of an acquisition proposal was not deprived of a right to serve a counternotice under section 8 of the Compulsory Purchase Act 1965.

Thus, in *Neeson* v *Department of Environment for Northern Ireland* [1985] a claimant who had carried out works of improvement to premises after the date of the notice of an intention to vest property was entitled to be compensated for the improvements as his intention had not been to increase the compensation.

In *Penny* v *Penny* [1868], it was said that the valuation of land taken ought to be made as at the time when the land was about to be taken, 'and should be of the exact interest which the (claimant) would have had...'. Therefore until 1969 it was generally accepted that not only did the notice to treat fix the interest in the land to be valued but it also fixed the date for making the valuations. This is no longer so in respect of the date of valuation as a result of *Birmingham City Corpn* v *West Midlands Baptist Trust* [1969] HL: see Chapter 11. If an interest in land is altered prior to the notice to treat, the case of *Penny* v *Penny* can be distinguished. In *Rugby Joint Water Board* v *Foottit* [1972], the reversionary freehold interest had originally been to an agricultural tenancy protected by the agricultural holdings legislation; as a result of the scheme, but prior to the notice to treat, the tenancy lost its protection and it was held that the reversionary interest could be valued accordingly. In that case it was said that the nature of a claimant's interest is to be ascertained at the date of the notice to treat. (Land Compensation Act 1973, section 48 abrogates the effect of this decision in the case of agricultural tenancies, but does not alter the general principle.) Because a notice to treat may fix the interests to be acquired, and to be valued at the later valuation date, claimants should heed the case of *Pyrah (Doddington) Ltd* v *Northampton County Council* [1982] LT. Agricultural land was owned by P Ltd and tenanted under an agricultural tenancy by P & B Ltd, both companies effectively controlled by Mr P. It was held that despite the voting power of Mr P, the principal shareholder in the tenant company, that latter company would have served a counternotice to any notice to quit, and it therefore enjoyed security of tenure under the agricultural holdings legislation. The value of the freehold interest subject to this tenancy was therefore £68,500, and not £90,000 claimed on the basis of vacant possession. Although the tenant company had surrendered its interest before the date of entry, the surrender was after the dates of the notice to treat and notice of entry.

Young and Rowan-Robinson [1986] JPL 727 point out what they see as a confusion since the *West Midland Baptist* case as to whether the rule that the notice to treat fixes the interests to be valued still holds good. There is confusion, but only because a clear distinction has not been made between the purpose of the notice to treat as a step in identifying the interests which are to be the subject of a conveyance, by way of compulsory purchase, and the valuation of whatever interests are in fact taken on the date entry is effected. The *West Midlands Baptist* case decided that the date of valuation of an interest is either the date that possession is taken, or the date values are agreed (or awarded by the Lands Tribunal), whichever is the earlier, and that it is not the date of the notice to treat. Thus, it may happen that a lease, which subsisted at the date of the notice to treat, determines or is surrendered before the valuation date. This raises two questions: first, will the tenant have any claim to compensation: and, second, is the reversionary interest to be valued as subject to the lease or with vacant possession? In *Bradford Property Trust Ltd* v *Hertfordshire County Council* [1973] the Lands Tribunal decided that only interests subsisting at the date of the notice to treat will qualify for compensation.

If a tenant is served with a notice to treat and submits a claim for compensation, the notice to treat establishes that the lease is one that must be acquired by conveyance. Where the lease is acquired and possession is taken by the authority, the lease must be valued as at the date determined in accordance with the *West Midlands Baptist* case. If the lease ceases before the date possession is taken by the acquiring authority, there is no tenant upon whom a notice of entry can be served, and no lease to acquire; consequently there can be no claim to compensation: *per* Lord Morris in *West Midlands Baptist* and see *JV Cleaners* v *Luton County Borough Council* [1968]. That was also the position in *Holloway* v *Dover Corporation* [1960]. Similarly, where a lease is created after the notice to treat, it will not have been identified by the notice as required for compulsory purchase and is not compensatable: see the *ex parte Edwards* case above.

Turning to the position of the owner of the reversionary interest, which is subject to a lease at the date of the notice to treat, the practical problem is whether the ending of the lease after the notice to treat and before entry permits the owner of the reversionary interest to claim compensation on the basis of being able to offer vacant possession; of some importance if vacant possession value is higher. It must not be forgotten that the main effect of the notice to treat is to establish the interest to be acquired; if that interest still subsists at the date of entry, its value on that later date will have to be determined. Accordingly, where a lease determines, the reversionary interest may be more valuable, but it is not altered in kind and remains the same interest as identified by the notice to treat. It should be valued on the basis of vacant possession value if that is its true value on the date of entry: *Banham* v *Hackney London Borough Council* [1970]. However, the Land Compensation Act 1973 (sections 48 and 50) may deny vacant possession values in specific situations involving agricultural and residential tenancies: see *Paul* v *Newham London Borough Council* [1991].

(c) Acquiring authority has a right to take possession

Once a notice to treat has been served, an acquiring authority has the right to take possession upon giving a notice of entry under section 11 of the Compulsory Purchase Act 1965: see Chapter 9. If an acquiring authority has unlawfully taken possession because the notice to treat and notice of entry have been served on the wrong person, it may regularise its position by serving a further notice to treat, and of entry on the correct person, and backdating the effect of such notices: *Cohen* v *Haringey London Borough Council* [1981] CA (the owner in this case had negotiated compensation for about a year before raising the unlawfulness of the authority's entry; quite apart from the court's decision that a notice to treat can be backdated, it was considered that he was estopped by reason of his conduct from relying on any unlawfulness).

(d) Amount of compensation may be referred to Lands Tribunal

Section 6 of the 1965 Act provides that if a person fails to respond to a notice to treat with a notice of claim within 21 days, or, the owner and the acquiring authority cannot reach agreement as to the amount of compensation, the matter can be referred to the Lands Tribunal.

(e) Right to compensation assignable

It is possible that the owner may assign his right to claim compensation: see *Dawson* v *Great Northern & City Railway* [1905].

4. The legal relationships of the parties after notice to treat

There is no contract between an acquiring authority and an owner of land who has been served with a notice to treat. Indeed we have seen that the owner is free to sell or otherwise deal with his property: the *Hillingdon* case. The notice to treat is not registerable as a land charge under the Land Charges Act 1972 as it is not an estate contract: *Capital Investments Ltd* v *Wednesfield Urban District Council* [1965]. However, the notice to treat creates an equitable interest binding the land (whether or not compensation has been assessed), and the owner may not create any interest in the affected land to the prejudice of the person taking under the notice to treat: see *Mercer* v *Liverpool, St Helens and South Lancashire Railway Co* [1904]. But it is frequently registered as a local land charge, and a purchaser will learn of the intended compulsory purchase in a response to the enquiries he makes of the local authority.

A contract to sell land is not frustrated by the service of a notice of intention to acquire the land compulsorily: see *E Johnson & Co (Barbados) Ltd* v *NSR Ltd* [1996] and *Korogluyan* v *Matheou* [1976].

If compensation is agreed between the parties, or determined by the Lands Tribunal, the relationship between the parties changes. In *Harding* v *Metropolitan Ry* [1872] it was held that the notice to treat and the agreement as to compensation amounted to a quasi-contract, and the court could order specific performance of that contract so as to compel the acquiring authority to take the title and interest of, in that case, the lessee-claimant. See also *Grice* v *Dudley*

Corporation [1957], *Watts* v *Watts* [1874] and *Re Cary-Elwes Contract* [1906]. No section 40 memorandum was required in *Williams* v *Secretary of State for the Environment* [1976]. Although the quasi-contract did not have to satisfy section 40 of the Law of Property Act 1925 (see Chapter 6 *Pollard* v *Middlesex CC* [1906]); the requirements of section 2 of the Law of Property (Miscellaneous Provisions) Act 1989 probably do not have to be satisfied: see *Llanelec Precision Engineering Co Ltd* v *Neath Port Talbot CBC* [2000].

However, although regarded as a quasi-contract, it will have to satisfy the requirements of a binding agreement in other respects:

> *Munton* v *Greater London Council* [1976] CA
> Notice to treat had been served on M, and the district valuer made an offer of £3,400 for his house. M's surveyor accepted 'subject to contract'. Meanwhile property values increased and at the date that M gave up possession his house was worth £5,100. It was held that as he accepted the earlier figure 'subject to contract' there was no contract between the parties and M was entitled to the higher value.

> *Duttons Breweries Ltd* v *Leeds City Council* [1982] CA
> In May 1968 the figure for compensation to be paid for the acquisition of a public house was approved by the city council, whose town clerk wrote: 'at the price of £15,000 subject to a Contract to be approved by me'. Possession of the premises was not taken until June 1976 by which date the brewers were claiming £78,000. The Court of Appeal decided that there was no implied term that completion was to be within a reasonable time, rather, there never was a binding agreement as to price because of the town clerk's letter. The brewers were therefore entitled to reopen negotiations for compensations based on 1976 values.

5. Time-limit

Where a compulsory purchase order is made, or notice of one made by a minister is published, after September 25 1991, a notice to treat ceases to have effect after three years of the date when the CPO becomes operative. This is the date of publication: see section 4 of the Compulsory Purchase Act 1965 and section 26 of the Acquisiton of Land Act 1981. This applies unless compensation is agreed, awarded, paid or paid into court, the acquiring authority has taken possession, or the question of compensation has been referred to the Lands Tribunal: see section 67 of the Planning and Compensation Act 1991. The period of three years can be extended by agreement: section 5(2B) of the Compulsory Purchase Act 1965. Where a notice ceases to have effect, compensation for any loss is payable: section 5(2C) of the 1965 Act.

6. *Validity of a notice to treat*

A notice to treat may lose its validity in certain circumstances; it may also be withdrawn.

In *Simpsons Motor Sales (London) Ltd* v *Hendon Corpn* [1964] HL a notice to treat was served in 1952, but because of certain changes in the acquiring authority's proposals they took little further action and eventually Simpsons issued a writ in 1959 to challenge the validity of the notice. The House of Lords held that a notice to treat could be invalid if: (1) the authority unreasonably delays its acquisition – in this case there was no unreasonable delay as the authority had difficult public duties to perform (but applied in *Collector of Land Revenue* v *Kam Gin Paik* [1986] PC); (2) the authority has shown an intention to abandon its rights under the notice to treat; or, (3) that the authority is purporting to use the notice to treat for a purpose not within the original compulsory purchase order. With regard to the second point delay may be good evidence that the authority has abandoned its original proposals; a resolution of the authority would also make this clear. See also *Chocolat Express* v *London Passenger Transport Board* [1935]. The cases that follow illustrate the points made in the *Simpson* case:

> *Grice* v *Dudley Corpn* [1957] ChD
> Notice to treat was served on the owner of premises in 1939. Owing to the war the acquisition did not proceed and by 1955 the corporation had adopted a very different scheme, but still intended to purchase under the original notice to treat. It was held by Upjohn J that as the original compulsory purchase order was for a very specific scheme of development – road widening and market hall – and as these specific proposals were no longer part of the new proposals, the corporation had clearly shown an intention to abandon the original order and, accordingly, the notice to treat was not valid for the new proposal.

Bremer v *Haringey London Borough Council* [1983] ChD
A purchase notice was accepted in 1975 by the authority
(deemed notice to treat). There was a considerable period of
inactivity on the part of the authority and no serious intention
to negotiate. In 1980 Bremer obtained a declaration that the
notice to treat was of no effect and then claimed damages.
Damages amounting to £25,735 for lost rent and rates paid on
empty property were awarded to him because of a
reprehensible degree of bad faith on the part of the authority
which was under a duty to negotiate in good faith.

If a notice to treat is declared invalid, a new notice may only be
served within three years of the confirmation of the CPO. If this
time-limit has expired, another CPO will have to be made. The
wide powers of authorities to appropriate land or sell to other
authorities for a purpose different from the original proposals can
make the challenge of a notice to treat difficult:

Capital Investments Ltd v *Wednesfield Urban District Council*
[1965]
The compulsory purchase order was made under the housing
Acts, and, in the original proposal, the land owned by Capital
Investments was to be for housing. After serving the notice to
treat, the council resolved to use part of Capital's land for a
school; Capital challenged the notice to treat. It was decided
that although the acquisition was under housing Acts, that
did not necessarily mean that only houses would be built;
educational use was ancillary to housing and the council had
power to sell the land to the educational authority: the notice
to treat was valid.

7. *Withdrawing a notice to treat*

Where an owner has served a notice of claim, the acquiring
authority may, within six weeks of that notice, withdraw the notice
to treat served on that owner or a notice to treat served on any other
person with an interest in the land: section 31(1) of the Land
Compensation Act 1961. In *R* v *Northumberland Water Ltd, ex parte
Able UK Ltd* [1996] it was held that a notice to treat may be
withdrawn even where possession has been taken. If no notice of
claim is served, or a notice does not contain the details specified by
section 4(1)(b) of the 1961 Act, the acquiring authority may

withdraw the notice to treat: *Trustees for Methodist Church Purposes v North Tyneside Metropolitan Borough Council* [1979] ChD (see p89 above). It is therefore important to serve a proper notice of claim setting out the full details.

Where an owner has failed to serve a notice of claim containing the details required by section 4(1)(b) of the 1961 Act, in time to enable the acquiring authority to make a proper offer, the authority may withdraw any notice to treat concerning the land within six weeks of a decision of the Lands Tribunal, or, if later, final determination of the case in the courts, provided possession has not been taken: section 31(2) of the 1961 Act. Where an acquiring authority withdraws a notice to treat, the authority is liable to pay compensation for any loss or expense incurred by the claimant: section 31(3) of the 1961 Act. This will not apply to loss and expense incurred after the proper time for making a notice of claim and the notice to treat is withdrawn under section 31(2) following the Lands Tribunal decision.

If a notice to treat is withdrawn, any advance payment of compensation paid under section 52 of the Land Compensation Act 1973 is recoverable by the authority: see *R* v *Northumberland Water Ltd, ex parte Able UK Ltd* [1996].

In *Williams* v *Blaenau Gwent Borough Council* [1994] the Lands Tribunal decided that although a notice to treat had not been withdrawn in accordance with section 31 of the 1961 Act, it could be withdrawn by agreement with the owner on payment of compensation.

8. Events that follow a notice to treat

After a notice to treat has been served, and the owner concerned has put in his notice of claim, the compensation will have to be agreed. If the parties cannot agree, the matter is referred to the Lands Tribunal: see Chapter 10. The acquiring authority may, if they need the land urgently, serve a notice of entry and take possession: see Chapter 9. When compensation has been settled or determined, the owner will convey his interest in the land to the authority.

7.3 Deemed notice to treat

There are circumstances where a notice to treat is not served by an acquiring authority, but some other process is deemed to be equivalent to the service of a notice to treat. In Chapter 5 we saw that a purchase or blight notice could, in certain circumstances, be served by a landowner on a local authority. If such a notice is accepted or confirmed by the minister, a notice to treat is deemed to have been served. The various points made in the preceding part of this chapter will therefore apply, with the qualification that the 'deemed notice to treat' cannot be withdrawn by the authority as the initiative for the purchase is with the owner: see Chapter 5 for the time-limit of three years which may apply to the validity of the deemed notice to treat.

7.4 General vesting declaration

The provisions concerning the expedited procedure are contained in the Compulsory Purchase (Vesting Declarations) Act 1981. Where the traditional notice to treat is used, the title to the land or the interest in the land will have to be conveyed to the acquiring authority by its owner. The use of a general vesting declaration ('GVD') simplifies this process as it replaces the notice to treat and the conveyance with one procedure which, on a certain date, automatically vests title in the land with the authority.

The use of a notice to treat may reveal ownership problems, i.e. it may not be possible to identify the owners of some land. In these circumstances the GVD procedure is more convenient. The decision to use the procedure can be the subject of judicial review: see *R v Carmarthen District Council, ex parte Blewin Trust* [1990].

1. The procedure

(a) Notice of intention

The acquiring authority must first publish in a local newspaper, and serve a notice of intention to make or 'execute' a general vesting declaration on any owner, lessee or occupier (except tenants for a month or any period less than a month – minor tenancies). Such a notice may be served with the notice given to those persons of the making or the confirmation of the compulsory purchase order, or it may be served at some later stage, but before any notice to treat is served in respect of the land concerned. In *Westminster City Council v Quereshi* [1991] it was held that the publication of a notice of intention is sufficient exercise of powers of compulsory purchase for the purposes of the three-year time-limit under section 4 of the Compulsory Purchase Act 1965.

This case was not followed in *Co-operative Insurance Society Ltd* v *Hastings Borough Council* [1993] on the same facts on the ground that a section 3 notice of intention did not give rise to the same reciprocity of rights as a notice to treat: it was merely a warning of the possible use of a GVD.

It is possible to use the GVD procedure for only some of the land in a compulsory purchase order, and a notice to treat for the rest; it cannot be used in respect of an interest in the land that has already been subject to a notice to treat.

The notice of intention must state the effect of the GVD procedure and demand the recipient's name, address and interest: section 3.

If no ownership problems are revealed by the notice of intention the authority may choose to proceed by the way of notice to treat if it prefers.

Unlike a notice to treat, the aforegoing notice is registrable as a local land charge.

(b) Execution of declaration

The general vesting declaration is then executed by the acquiring authority on a date at least two months after the notice of intention was first published. That period of time can be less than two months if every occupier of the land concerned consents in writing: section 5(1). The general vesting declaration must be in a prescribed form: see Compulsory Purchase of Land Regulations 1994.

(c) Notice of making vesting declaration

The acquiring authority must then serve a notice, as soon as reasonably possible, stating the effect of the declaration and specifying the affected land, on the following persons (section 6):

(i) on every occupier (other than a person with a minor tenancy or a long tenancy about to expire); and

(ii) on any other person who responded to the notice of intention (see (a) above).

The special position of tenants is considered below.

(d) Vesting date

The general vesting declaration takes effect on a date specified in the notice referred to in (c) above which is at least 28 days after the execution of the declaration: section 4. The title to the interest in the land will then vest with the authority together with the right to enter and take possession.

2. The effect of a general vesting declaration: Part III of the 1981 Act

Once a general vesting declaration has been executed, then, at the end of the 28-day period (or such longer period as may be specified), the acquiring authority is regarded as if it had served a notice to treat on the date of the declaration. This will then bring into play the compensation provisions of the Compulsory Purchase Act 1965 and the Land Compensation Act 1961, thus enabling a claim and, if necessary, a reference to have a disputed claim to compensation dealt with by the Lands Tribunal: section 7(1). The 'notice to treat', which the authority is deemed to have served, will not apply if an actual notice to treat has been served, nor will it apply to a minor tenancy or a long tenancy about to expire. The power to withdraw a notice to treat does not apply where a general vesting declaration has been used: section 7(3). Presumably the three-year time-limit on the validity of a notice to treat does not apply if legal title has vested with the authority. On the vesting date the land specified in the general vesting declaration, together with the right to enter upon and take possession of it rest with the acquiring authority: section 8(1). The position is as if the authority had conveyed the title to themselves by deed poll.

3. Tenancies: section 9

Section 9 makes special provision for tenancies. The right of entry, and thus the obligation to pay compensation, does not apply to a minor tenancy or a long tenancy which is about to expire. A minor tenancy is tenancy for a year or from year to year or any lesser interest, e.g. weekly, monthly. A long tenancy which is about to expire is a tenancy granted for a period greater than a year but which has, at the date of the GVD, a period still to run which is less than some period specified for the purpose in the GVD. The effect of this is that the authority can exclude from the GVD all long tenancies which have, for example, five years or less to run (or such other period they choose which is convenient to their requirements).

The reason for excluding these tenancies is to save the authority having to deal with and compensate tenants who can remain in occupation for the time being. The vesting of any superior title in the land with the authority will be subject to these tenancies until they expire or are determined by notice to quit. However, if the authority needs to take early possession it may do so after serving a notice to treat and a notice of entry (of at least 14 days).

4. Compensation: section 10

Where land has become vested in an acquiring authority under a GVD, the authority is liable to pay compensation, and interest thereon, as they would have had to pay had they obtained possession under a notice of entry: section 10(1). This really means that the vesting date is the proper date for assessing compensation:

> *Hussain* v *Oldham Metropolitan Borough Council* [1981] LT
> The vesting date was December 26 1974, but the acquiring authority allowed owners and occupiers to remain in occupation provided they repaired and insured the properties. The property was vacated in December 1979, and the claim based on values at this date was for £48,124. The Tribunal rejected this claim as the proper valuation date was in December 1974; it awarded £14,678.

There is a time-limit of six years from the deemed notice to treat, or such time as a person first knew, or could reasonably have known, for referring a question as to compensation to the Lands Tribunal: section 10(3). In *Royal Bank of Scotland* v *Clydebank District Council* [1995] it was held that where the time-limit had expired, the Scottish Lands Tribunal did not have any jurisdiction to determine a claim, and the claim could not be pursued. In *Co-operative Wholesale Society* v *Chester le Street District Council* [1996] the Lands Tribunal decided that the limitation period in section 10(3) is capable of being waived, and was waived because both parties had proceeded on the basis of a common assumption that they were negotiating settlement of a valid claim for compensation without regard to the limitation period.

5. Severance: Schedule 1

This Schedule makes special provision for an owner to object to the severance of his property by a GVD. Because the procedure is similar to that where a notice to treat is used, it is considered in detail in the next chapter.

Chapter 8

The Land: What is Acquired

Introduction
The definition of land
Interests in land that can be acquired
Severed land
Power to override third party rights
Omitted land

8.1 Introduction

In the usual case of a compulsory purchase of land, the enabling Act will authorise the taking of land by a compulsory purchase order made under the Acquisition of Land Act 1981. It is important to know what is the meaning and definition of land and what interests the acquiring authority can compel an owner to grant. If an authority has powers to acquire land, but only wants an easement, it must have statutory powers to compel the owner to grant an easement.

An acquiring authority must therefore ask itself, these questions:

1. What rights are required for the purposes of their scheme? and
2. What statutory powers are available to compel an owner to grant the rights required?

Another matter dealt with in this chapter concerns severed land. The authority will have specified the land it requires for its purposes, say, a road, on a plan attached to the CPO, but the land may not coincide with ownership or occupational units; the owner who is to lose his front sitting-room to a road widening scheme might feel aggrieved if he could not sell the whole house to the authority.

8.2 The definition of land

One tends to think of land as the physical surface of the earth, but, in English law, the word land can have a wider meaning so as to include interests in land such as easements, as well as buildings and other fixtures on the land. The definition of land, and therefore what can be compulsorily acquired, must first be sought from the enabling Act authorising the acquisition. Some of these Acts provide a definition, others do not.

In the absence of a definition of land in an Act of Parliament, the Interpretation Act 1978, Schedule 1, defines land as including 'buildings and other structures, land covered with water, and any estate, interest, easement, servitude or right in or over land'. The Town and Country Planning Act 1990 defines land that may be acquired as 'any corporeal hereditament, including a building ... and ... any interest in or right over land' (a corporeal hereditament is property which has physical existence in the form of land); there is no definition in the New Towns Act 1981. The Housing Act 1985, section 17 authorises an authority to acquire 'land ... houses, or buildings'.

In *Sovmots Investment Ltd* v *Secretary of State for the Environment* [1977] the House of Lords had to consider whether the power in the Housing Act 1957 to acquire 'any rights over land' could include the power to compel an owner to grant 'rights' that did not exist. It was decided that existing rights, such as easements, could be acquired, but not those that did not exist at the time. In any event the compulsory purchase order must clearly specify the rights the authority is seeking to acquire. This case must now be considered in the light of the Local Government (Miscellaneous Provisions) Act 1976, which is discussed below.

Neither the Acquisition of Land Act 1981 nor the Compulsory Purchase Act 1965 define land; one is referred to the enabling Act. Although the Land Compensation Act 1961 contains a definition, it is useful only for the purposes of that Act, namely the assessment of compensation, and does not deal with the problem of what can be acquired.

Subject to any limitations in the enabling Act, the power to acquire land will be a power to compel the owner to convey his interest or estate in the land. In relation to a conveyance of land, land for this purpose will have the meaning given to it in connection with the Law of Property Act 1925 and includes mines, and minerals, buildings or parts of buildings (however divided), fixtures, trees and plants (but not annual crops called *fructus industriales*), easements, rights and privileges.

Mines and minerals can be excluded from a compulsory purchase by applying the 'mining code'. This refers to Schedule 2 to the Acquisition of Land Act 1981 which re-enacts sections 77 to 85 of the Railway Clauses (Consolidation) Act 1845; the provisions can be incorporated by reference in a compulsory purchase order: the minerals will not be acquired, and subject to the provisions of the code, the original owner can work them: see further on this in Chapter 21. Although *fructus industriales* will not be acquired by the conveyance of land, any loss in respect of them will be compensated as part of the claim for disturbance: see Chapters 17 and 20.

The expropriated owner, therefore, is called upon to convey whatever interests in the land he has, freehold or leasehold; and, in the case of a general vesting declaration, the acquiring authority will be regarded as being vested absolutely with whatever estates and interests are necessary to give them immediate possession of the land with the exception of certain tenancies – see Chapter 7. But if the estate or interest conveyed to the acquiring authority is subject to an option to purchase in favour of a third party, the title conveyed is subject to this and the authority must compensate the owner of the option: *Oppenheimer v Minister of Transport* [1942].

Where only a stratum of land is required, such as for a tunnel, it is usual for the enabling Act to specifically authorise such a taking: the London Transport Act 1969 is an example and is one of several Acts authorising London Transport Executive to acquire land below ground for an underground railway; the required land is specified by reference numbers in a Schedule to the Act and books of reference detailing the land are deposited in the library at the Houses of Parliament. Another example is the Public Health Act 1936, which contained powers to lay a sewer (section 15): the freehold of the sewer is held by the water authority together with the necessary rights of support and access (see *Thurrock, Grays and Tilbury Joint Sewerage Board v Thames Land Company Ltd* [1925]); see now section 159 of the Water Industry Act 1991 which replaced the 1936 Act.

If the enabling Act does not expressly authorise the taking of a stratum of land the authority will probably have to acquire the land as a whole (see *Ramsden v Manchester etc Ry Co* [1848], or specify rights only in the CPO (under the 1976 Act).

8.3 Interests in land that can be acquired

1. Freehold

Clearly the freehold can be acquired and usually this is the interest
of most use to the acquiring authority. But in the *Sovmots* case,
considered above, the freehold of the building concerned, Centre
Point in London, was owned by the Greater London Council, and
as the acquiring authority, Camden London Borough Council, was
interested in acquiring certain flats in the building, it would
probably have been satisfied to have acquired only the interests of
the lessees of those flats: a 150-year lease owned by Sovmots and
sublease of 45 years owned by another company.

2. Leasehold

The power to take land compulsorily includes the power to compel
the owner of any leasehold interest to convey or assign his interest,
and, if the authority acquire the freehold or other reversionary
interest, the lease will merge with that superior interest.

Where a lease is to be acquired, and a notice to treat has been
served, the tenant remains liable under the covenants until the
formal assignment: see *Mills* v *East London Union* [1872]. However
where a lease prohibits any assignment without the landlord's
consent, such consent is not required: see *Slipper* v *Tottenham and
Hampstead Junction Railway Co* [1867].

In the case of a tenant having no greater interest in the land than
as a tenant for a year, or from year to year, his interest may be
terminated by notice of entry, and he is then entitled to
compensation: Compulsory Purchase Act 1965, section 20.

Security of tenure under the Agricultural Holdings Act 1986,
Landlord and Tenant Act 1954 (business tenancies) or the Rent Act
1977 or Housing Act 1988 (residential tenancies) does not prevail
against a compulsory purchase.

The acquiring authority is entitled to acquire the reversionary
interest, and, as landlord, it can then determine rather than acquire
a lease: see Chapter 19 for a full treatment of this in terms of the
compensation.

3. Land subject to rights and interests

A private purchaser of a freehold or leasehold interest in land will
be subject to any legal interests, such as mortgages and easements,

and to any equitable interests, such as restrictive covenants and interests under a trust, of which he has notice and which are not overreached by the conveyance. Easements and restrictive covenants are considered below at 4. Interests under a trust will usually be overreached by the purchaser treating with the trustees, and the same will apply to an acquiring authority, but the *DHN* case (see Chapter 7) illustrates a situation where a beneficial interest under a (constructive) trust did bind the authority who had to pay compensation to the owner of the beneficial interest.

Special provision is made for mortgages and this is dealt with in Chapter 21. A licence to occupy land is not an interest in land and will not, usually, bind a purchaser. But if the licensee has an 'equity', the courts may protect that licence by a constructive trust, as in the *DHN* case; an equity arises if some promise or undertaking has been given to the licensee and it would be unjust and inequitable if it could be broken and the licensee turned off the land.

4. *Easements and restrictive covenants*

Easements and restrictive covenants do not prevail against an acquiring authority where the land compulsorily purchased or acquired by agreement is being used for purposes authorised by statute: see *Kirby* v *School Board for Harrogate* [1896], approved in *Long Eaton Recreation Grounds Co* v *Midland Ry* [1902]. The interests are not, with some exceptions, acquired and a notice to treat need not be served on the owners of the benefit of such interests: see *Clark* v *School Board for London* [1874]. The interests are not extinguished by the compulsory acquisition and will remain enforceable against successors in title: see *Ellis* v *Rogers* [1885]. There is an exception to this rule where land is acquired or appropriated for planning purposes: see below.

If interests are interfered with by the acquiring authority, the person with the benefit of such interests may claim compensation: section 10 of the Compulsory Purchase Act 1965 (see Chapter 23). The same point now applies in respect of restrictive covenants that affect land purchased by agreement; the authority may breach the covenants but must pay compensation: section 120 of the Local Government Act 1972 and section 14 of the Local Government (Miscellaneous Provisions) Act 1976.

If compensation is claimed for the interference with an interest, it is usual to insist that the owner of the interest agrees to its extinguishment, or partial extinguishment, in consideration for the payment of compensation. Apart from those circumstances, some of which are set out below, where interests are specifically extinguished with the exercise of compulsory purchase of the servient land, if the owner of a third party interest is not paid compensation, his interest will remain binding against the title. This means that although an interest is unenforceable against an acquiring authority exercising its statutory powers, if the land is sold the interest will revive and bind subsequent purchasers: see *Marten* v *Flight Refuelling Ltd* [1961].

Where a housing authority acquires land under the clearance area provisions of the Housing Act 1985, on completion of the purchase of such land, all private rights and easements are extinguished: Housing Act 1985, section 295. The Town and Country Planning Act 1990, section 237, contains a limited immunity to carry out building operations (with the benefit of planning permission) on land acquired for planning purposes. This immunity does not extend to a use contrary to a covenant restrictive against a particular use: see *Thames Water Utilities* v *Oxford City Council* [1999]. This provision does not extinguish private third-party rights, such as easements and restrictive covenants, and these may revive where the land is passed on to private purchasers who put the land to a use not given immunity by section 237.

5. Acquisition of rights

The question here is whether an owner of land can be compelled to grant a right, such as an easement, to an authority with statutory powers. It was decided in the *Sovmots* case that an owner could not be compelled if the easement did not already exist. However, section 13 of the Local Government (Miscellaneous Provisions) Act 1976 provides that in all cases where an authority is authorised to acquire land, it may be authorised to acquire specified rights over land. The rights, primarily, though not necessarily, easements, must be specified in the compulsory purchase order. The acquisition of such rights will then be regarded as an acquisition of land so that the compulsory purchase procedures and compensation rules will apply.

Of course, many enabling Acts specifically authorise an authority to acquire an easement: section 250 of the Highways Act 1980 provides a good example. This Act enables a highway authority to acquire a right, perhaps to erect a traffic sign, if full ownership of the land is unnecessary, although the owner can serve a notice requiring the authority to take his full interest if he so desires:

section 252 of the 1980 Act. The electricity, gas and water authorities all have enabling Acts which authorise the compulsory acquisition of easements for their installations.

A water undertaker has the right to lay a public sewer through private land upon giving reasonable notice (section 159 of the Water Industry Act 1991); in this case none of the procedures so far discussed in this book applies: there is no compulsory purchase order and no right to object. The earlier, and analogous power in section 15 of the Public Health Act 1936 was held to give the power to lay sewers through any building on the land:

> *Hutton* v *Esher Urban District Council* [1973] CA
> The council served notice to lay a sewer through Hutton's bungalow, the demolition of which was inescapable. It was held that as land included buildings, then, by definition, the sewer could be laid through the bungalow.

Perhaps it should be added that compensation was payable under section 278 of the 1936 Act. Strictly this right to lay a sewer did not involve the acquisition of an easement; the public sewer was owned, in freehold by the authority so long as it remains a sewer, but the authority had rights to have the sewer supported and to enter land for the purposes of inspection and maintenance.

The Pipe-lines Act 1962 enables private enterprises to compulsorily acquire easements and construct pipe-lines without the need of a private Act. The Secretary of State for Energy may authorise a compulsory purchase order, or a compulsory rights order for ancillary rights such as inspection and maintenance, for what is called a cross-country pipe-line – the oil companies have made use of this Act. For further rights see Chapter 21 below.

8.4 Severed land

There will be many cases where the boundary or outer line of an acquiring authority's proposal severs units of occupation; the map attached to the compulsory purchase order will indicate the land needed for that proposal and this will not necessarily coincide with the ownership boundaries concerned. This can give rise to problems for the affected owners; the loss of a front or back garden can seriously affect the amenities of a house; the severance of a farm can leave small and inconvenient areas of land; and the taking of only part of a building may be very inconvenient.

A landowner faced with this problem may do one of two things. He may sell only that land the authority requires and claim compensation, not only for the value of the land lost, but also for the depreciation in the value of the land retained: see Chapter 15. In this way he will obtain the financial equivalent of the taking and severing of his land, but he is left with land or buildings so inconvenienced by the severance that he would probably wish to sell and use the proceeds, plus his compensation, to reinstate himself elsewhere.

The second solution to this problem is to see if the acquiring authority can be made to acquire all his land so that the owner has compensation money, sufficient to enable him to purchase new property immediately, and to leave the problem of reselling the severed land to the acquiring authority. The Compulsory Purchase Act 1965 sets out the circumstances for compelling an authority to acquire the whole of an owner's land, or just small areas of divided land (Schedule 1 to the Compulsory Purchase (Vesting Declarations) Act 1981 has similar effect where a GVD is used); and the Land Compensation Act 1973 makes further provision for severed agricultural land. Similar problems can arise where a compulsory purchase order authorises the taking of 'rights' over land under section 13 of the Local Government (Miscellaneous Provisions) Act 1976 or section 252 of the Highways Act 1980; the affected owner can claim compensation for the depreciation in value, or compel the acquiring authority to purchase his whole interest. The procedures now described apply to the taking of part of land, but they also apply with the appropriate modifications to the taking of rights: Schedule 1 to the 1976 Act.

The procedure to be used when a general vesting declaration vests only part of an owner's property in the acquiring authority is slightly different, and is described below at 4.

1. Circumstances under which an owner can require an authority to acquire the whole of his land: section 8(1) of the 1965 Act

This subsection states: 'No person shall be required to sell part only of any house, building or manufactory, or of a part or garden belonging to a house if he is willing or able to sell the whole of the house, building, manufactory, park or garden'. The owner's counternotice must be served before entry by the authority: see *Glasshouse*

Properties Ltd v *Department of Transport* [1994]. This is subject to a qualification that the authority need not take the whole if:

(a) in the case of a house, building or manufactory the part proposed to be acquired can be taken without material detriment to the house, building or manufactory: or

(b) in the case of a park or garden, the part proposed to be acquired can be taken without seriously affecting the amenity or convenience of the house.

There are similar provisions in relation to blight notices: see section 166 of the Town and Country Planning Act 1990. In *Halliday* v *Secretary of State for Transport* [1991] a blight notice in respect of a flat and garden was upheld in relation to a proposal to acquire only the garden. See also *Smith* v *Kent County Council* [1995].

If the authority refuses to take the whole of the land under this provision, it will be for the Lands Tribunal to determine whether or not there will be material detriment or a serious effect on the amenity or convenience of the house, as the case may be. In deciding this, section 58 of the Land Compensation Act 1973 additionally requires the Tribunal to take into account the proposed use of the part to be acquired, and, where other land is involved, the effect of the whole of the proposed works or use.

A very wide meaning has been given to a 'house' or a 'building' and a shop or an office will be included in these terms. Land may be included as part of the definition of a building: see *Caledonian Railway* v *Turcan* [1898]. The garden attached to a house is regarded as part of the house. In *Richards* v *Swansea Improvement and Tramways Co* [1878] a cottage abutted on to the back of a house, the house was used for residential purposes, the cottage as a store, and there was an internal communication; it was held that the cottage and house were one house for the purposes of what is now section 8. A church is a 'house or other buildings' and a hall and adjoining car park are part of it; the church can therefore require the acquiring authority to take the whole property and not just the hall and car park: *London Transport Executive* v *Congregational Union of England & Wales* [1979].

In *Ravenseft Properties Ltd* v *Hillingdon London Borough Council* [1968] LT, a case involving business premises, the Tribunal put forward a test for deciding what amounted to material detriment: the remaining part must be 'less useful or less valuable in some significant degree'. The fact that compensation for the severance would be available is irrelevant: see also *Genders* v *London County*

Council [1915]. But see *McMillan* v *Strathclyde Regional Council* [1983] where, applying the *Ravenseft* test, there was no material difference before and after.

One difficulty may arise where an acquiring authority accepts or is required to accept a section 8 notice to acquire the whole of the owner's land. Where the acquiring authority has already served a notice to treat and of entry in respect of the land it originally required, but after the section 8 notice enters that land, is it deemed to have entered all the land for valuation purposes? In *Christos* v *Secretary of State for the Environment, Transport and Regions* [2002], the Lands Tribunal thought so.

2. Small intersected land: section 8(2) and (3) of the 1965 Act

If the works of the acquiring authority intersect land not situated in a town or built upon, and leave an owner with an area which is less than half an acre, and which cannot be conveniently occupied with other adjoining land, if any, of that owner, then the authority can be compelled to purchase such land. Where the intersected land could be conveniently occupied with other adjoining land of the owner, the authority can be required, at their expense, to remove fences and carry out levelling and soiling to achieve this.

Sometimes the enabling Act (called the special Act) permits an owner to require the authority to provide communication between intersected land by a bridge or culvert. If the cost of providing that communication exceeds the value of the isolated land, or the isolated land is less than half an acre, and it cannot be added to other adjoining land of the same owner, the acquiring authority may compel the owner to sell it to them instead of providing the communication. Disputes as to value or costs of communication are settled by the Lands Tribunal.

In practice it may be possible to reach an agreement with the acquiring authority over unique problems caused by severance. In *Wilson* v *Minister of Transport* [1980] LT, the Department agreed to purchase replacement land for sheep pens that needed to be suitably located to suit sheep handling practices.

3. Procedure

If section 8 of the 1965 Act is thought to apply, the owner need merely write to the authority requiring it to purchase the whole of his land, or the intersected piece, and must do so before entry is effected by the acquiring authority: see *Glasshouse Properties* v *Department of Transport* [1994]. In the circumstances where the owner requires the authority to purchase the whole of his land, the authority must either comply or it will not be able to purchase any of his land. As mentioned above, certain questions can be put to the Lands Tribunal. If a notice is served, and if disputed, upheld, the acquiring authority can be compelled to take the whole of the claimant's land: see *Marson* v *London, Chatham & Dover Railway* [1868]. Further, if a notice to treat is served, and a counternotice which has been assented to by the acquiring authority, the authority is then authorised to acquire all the land even the time-limit for the exercise of compulsory purchase powers has expired: see *Schwinge* v *London & Blackwall Railway Co* [1855].

4. *Severed land and general vesting declarations*

Section 8(1), which covers the circumstances considered at 1 above, only applies where the acquiring authority has used a notice to treat and has no application where a general vesting declaration has been used. In the latter case, Schedule 1 to the Compulsory Purchase (Vesting Declarations) Act 1981 provides a complicated procedure:

   (a) following the execution of the general vesting declaration and receipt of the notice thereof, an owner who believes the circumstances set out at 1 above are satisfied, must serve a notice of objection to severance within 28 days of the notification of the execution of the declaration (para 2);

   (b) where a notice of objection to severance has been served, the vesting declaration will not take effect and the authority will not be entitled to take possession (para 3);

   (c) within three months of the notice of objection to severance, the acquiring authority must either notify the owner that it is no longer proceeding with the acquisition of his property; or notify the owner that the whole of his land is now included in the general vesting declaration; or refer the notice of objection to severance to the Lands Tribunal, notifying the owner at the same time (para 4);

   (d) a failure by the acquiring authority to take any of the steps at (c) above within the time-limit will be regarded as a withdrawal from any acquisition of the land concerned (para 5);

   (e) the Lands Tribunal may consider not only the question of material detriment and amenity or convenience of the house, as described above at 1, but also the extent of the owner's land that the authority ought to acquire.

This last point is rather wider than the equivalent provision under the 1965 Act, as the Tribunal can substitute for the whole of an owner's land, a smaller area (including the part proposed to be severed). The Tribunal is required to consider not only the effect of the severance, but also the proposed use of the land required by the authority and the effect of the whole of the authority's works (para 8). The Schedule also makes provision for a situation where an owner fails to receive a notice and thereby fails to serve a notice of objection to severance in time: the vesting declaration will still take effect, but the authority may agree to take all the owner's land or the questions at (e) above can be referred to the Lands Tribunal (para 10).

5. *Severance of Agricultural Land: sections 53–57 of the Land Compensation Act 1973*

In addition to section 8(2) of the 1965 Act, discussed at 2 above, the 1973 Act contains provisions enabling owners and lessees of agricultural property to compel the acquiring authority to take more than just the land it needs for its purposes. The idea behind these further provisions is to empower a person, who is left with an area of land that is not economically viable, to require the authority to buy the whole.

Notice to treat in respect of part of a farm

Section 53 of the 1973 Act provides that where an acquiring authority serves a notice to treat, in respect of any agricultural land which is part of an agricultural unit (a farm), on a person who has a greater interest in the land than as tenant for a year or from year to year (whether he is in occupation or not), that person may serve a counternotice:

(a) claiming that the part of the unit not required is not reasonably capable of being farmed, either by itself or in conjunction with other relevant land, as a separate unit; and
(b) requiring the acquiring authority to purchase his interest in the whole unit.

In relation to (a) and the meaning of 'other relevant land', the claimant must first consider whether the land not required can be farmed with any other land in the same unit in respect of which he has a yearly tenancy, or with any other land in another unit he occupies as a freeholder or as a tenant for a term longer than a year or from year to year: see *Johnson v North Yorks County Council* [1992].

This provision also applies to a notice to treat deemed to have been served following a blight notice under the Town and Country Planning Act 1990, and to a general vesting declaration made under the Compulsory Purchase (Vesting Declarations) Act 1981: see Chapter 7. The counternotice must be served within two months of the notice to treat and, if the claimant serving the counternotice is a landlord or a tenant, he must serve a copy on the other party. The procedure after the counternotice is as follows (section 54):

(a) within two months of the counternotice the acquiring authority may accept it in writing; if it does not do so in that period, either the claimant or the authority may refer the question to the Lands Tribunal;

(b) the Tribunal will then determine whether the claim in the counternotice is justified and will declare that counternotice valid or invalid as they think appropriate. In *Johnson v North Yorkshire County Council* [1992] the claimant failed to show that upon the compulsory purchase of three acres of land for a gypsy site, the remaining holding of 137 acres could not be farmed;

(c) if the counternotice is accepted, or declared valid by the Land Tribunal, the authority shall be deemed to have served a notice to treat, on the date of the original notice to treat, in respect of the claimant's interest in the land covered by the counternotice, as well as the claimant's interest in the land covered by the original notice to treat.

The assessment of compensation for the land specified in the counternotice cannot, unlike the land specified in the original notice to treat, include development value: see further on this in Chapter 20. A claimant may, therefore, withdraw a counternotice at any time up until the end of six weeks after the Lands Tribunal determine the compensation: section 54(3) and (5).

If a lessee has served a counternotice and this is accepted or declared valid, and the lessor has not served such a notice, the authority shall offer to surrender the lessee's interest, after it has acquired it, to the lessor. The surrender is to be on terms that the authority consider reasonable, although the matter may be referred by either party to the Lands Tribunal: section 54(6).

Notice of entry in respect of part of an agricultural holding

If a notice of entry is served on a yearly tenant of an agricultural holding under section 11 of the Compulsory Purchase Act 1965, and that notice relates to part only of that holding, the tenant in occupation may, within two months, serve a counternotice on the acquiring authority (section 55):

(a) claiming that the remainder of the holding is not reasonably capable of being farmed, either by itself or in conjunction with other relevant land, as a separate agricultural unit; and
(b) electing to treat the notice of entry as a notice relating to the entire holding.

The tenant must also serve a copy of the counternotice on his landlord within the two-month period.

In relation to (a) and the meaning of 'other relevant land', the tenant must first consider whether the land in the holding he rents, which is not required by the authority, can be farmed with other land in the same agricultural unit as the holding, or can be farmed with land in any other unit occupied by the tenant but as a freeholder or lessee with an interest greater than a year or from year to year.

The procedure that follows and the effect of a counternotice, served under section 55, is similar to that considered above in relation to counternotices under section 53. However, if the acquiring authority has not been authorised to acquire the landlord's interest in the land specified in the counternotice, say because the landlord has not served a counternotice, it shall give up possession of this land to the landlord. In these circumstances, the acquiring authority is liable to the tenant in respect of tenant-right, though any increase in the value of the land returned to the landlord shall be deducted from the compensation payable in respect of the acquisition of his interest in the remainder of the holding: section 56.

A tenant may have to give up possession of part of his holding under a notice of entry before the validity of his counternotice in respect of the rest of the holding can be determined. Section 56(2) provides that if, in the event of the counternotice being accepted or declared valid, the tenant gives up possession of every part of the holding within 12 months of the counternotice, he will be regarded as having given up possession of the whole holding under a notice of entry on the day before the expiration of the current year of the tenancy. The purpose of this provision is to establish the most favourable basis for compensating the tenant: see Chapter 20.

8.5 Power to override third party rights

Where land has been acquired by a body with powers of compulsory purchase, and the land is burdened by third-party rights, such as easements or restrictive covenants, those rights are normally unenforceable against a purchaser exercising statutory powers: see *Ayr Harbour Trustees* v *Oswald* [1883] and *Dowty Boulton Paul Ltd* v *Wolverhampton Corporation (No 2)* [1973]. Such rights are not necessarily extinguished and may remain binding against the title and survive the compulsory purchase conveyance: see *Marten* v *Flight Refuelling Ltd* [1962]. In the *Marten* case, Wilberforce J (as he then was) held that a restrictive covenant, affecting certain land that had been acquired by the Crown under statutory powers, was enforceable against a party having rights in the nature of a tenancy held from the Crown where that party was using the acquired land for a purpose that did not enjoy the immunity given by the statutory powers. He said that the covenant survives the exercise of compulsory purchase and is only extinguished if the covenant is taken over or extinguished by statutory procedure under the Land Clauses (Consolidation) Act 1845: see *Bird* v *Eggleton* [1885]. He gave as his authority *Clark* v *School Board for London* [1874]. It is not clear that the *Clark* case is authority for the proposition that the payment of compensation, say under section 10 of the Compulsory Purchase Act 1965 (see Chapter 23), extinguishes a third-party right. The position is probably as follows.

The payment of compensation is in lieu of an action for an injunction or damages: see Chapter 23. If the owner of the third-party right had been awarded damages at common law for an interference with his right, he would not be entitled to make a further claim in respect of the same interference. Neither would he be likely to obtain an injunction after the expiration of a reasonable period of time from the initial interference. There seems no reason why the payment of compensation under statutory provisions should have any different effect. Accordingly, if compensation is paid, no further payment can be made in respect of the same interference. But if the original cause of interference is removed or the scheme terminated, there seems no reason in principle why the third-party right cannot then be potentially enforceable, subject of course to the statutory powers of the acquiring authority. Accordingly, if the acquiring authority were to dispose of land subject to third-party rights, and the cause of the original interference of those rights ceases or is removed, it may be possible to argue that the third-party right continues to bind the affected land in the hands of successors to the acquiring authority, even in cases where compensation has been paid: in the latter respect it is arguable that the *Marten* case is wrong.

On account of the doubt as to whether a third-party right is extinguished by the mere payment of compensation, acquiring authorities will normally stipulate that upon payment of compensation the owner of the third-party right releases any interest in that right.

Third-party rights under the Town and Country Planning Act 1990

Section 226 of the 1990 Act contains wide powers for local planning authorities to acquire land which is suitable for and required in order to secure the carrying out of development, redevelopment or improvement, or is required for a purpose which it is necessary to achieve in the interests of the proper planning of an area in which the land is situated. Land may also be acquired by agreement for the same purposes: see section 227 of the 1990 Act. These powers are likely to be amended in 2003.

Section 237 of the 1990 Act contains a power to override easements and other rights where land has been acquired or appropriated by a local authority for planning purposes. The erection, construction or carrying out, or maintenance of any building or work on land which has been so acquired (whether done by the local authority or by a person deriving title under it) is authorised if it is done in accordance with planning permission, notwithstanding that it involves an interference with an interest or right or is a breach of a restriction as to the user of the land arising by virtue of a contract. The interests and rights to which the section applies are any easement, liberty, privilege, right or advantage annexed to land and adversely affecting other land, including any natural right to support: see section 237(2). Normally this section will be concerned with overriding easements and restrictive covenants. The owner of any such third-party right has a claim for compensation: see section 237(4).

The land subject to the third-party rights must either have been acquired, compulsorily or by agreement, for planning purposes under the 1990 Act, or must have been appropriated to planning purposes. A local authority has wide powers of appropriation in section 122 of the Local Government Act 1972. However, appropriation is not a mere formality of passing the appropriate council resolutions from one committee to another: the appropriation must be for planning purposes and not as a mere exercise to override third-party rights prior to the sale of surplus land: see *Sutton London Borough Council* v *Bolton* [1993].

Section 237 authorises the buildings and works specified, so long as there is planning permission for such matters. It seems strongly arguable that if planning permission was obtained for a material change of use of land, section 237 would not override a restrictive covenant against the proposed user. In *Thames Water Utilities Ltd* v *Oxford City Council* [1999] a restriction against the use of land otherwise than for certain specified purposes was in issue. It was held that section 237 did not authorise a use in contravention of the restrictive covenant; the erection of a building may be authorised by section 237, but its subsequent use would not be. The unavailability of compensation for the interference with the benefit of a restriction against a use was a material factor in the decision.

It has been held that the reference to 'the restriction as to use of land arising by virtue of a contract' includes a restrictive covenant: see *Edmunds* v *Stockport Metropolitan Borough Council* [1990]. It was held in the *Edmunds* case that the restriction as to the type of building that might be erected on land was on analysis inevitably in some degree a restriction as to the user of land, and accordingly came within what is now section 237(1).

There is therefore a possible conflict between *Thames Water* and *Edmunds*, with the former nullifying the principal purpose of section 237. One serious consequence of the *Thames Water* decision is that it appears to have cut down what the law would have been if the section had not been enacted; a body exercising statutory powers has immunity from proceedings if it does something that would otherwise have been a breach of a restrictive covenant. The only safe advice to an acquiring authority is that it should now acquire the land with the benefit of the covenant, if it has the necessary powers.

In *R* v *City of London Corporation, ex parte Mystery of Barbers* [1996], it was held that section 237(1) did not cease to apply once the original purpose for which an authority has acquired the land has been achieved. Where land has been acquired, and the authority continues to hold it for planning purposes and proposes to redevelop the land for a second time, section 237(1) will authorise that second development in accordance with the planning permission. Accordingly, the provision authorised the interference with a covenant not to interfere with light or air to an adjoining building.

Where a local authority decides to dispose of land affected by a restrictive covenant, it may consider appropriating the land to planning purposes under section 122 of the Local Government Act 1972. If it then disposes of land so appropriated, it may rely on section 237(1). Provided there are proper motives and reasons for such steps, they will be lawful, even though the effect on the owner of the benefit of the restrictive covenant is that he will forego a ransom sum for a deed of release for the much lower compensation sum under section 237(4): see *R v Leeds City Council, ex parte Leeds Industrial Co-operative Society Ltd* [1996].

8.6 Omitted land

It sometimes happens that an acquiring body enters land that is outside any notice to treat. Subject to the affected land being within the area of the CPO, section 22 of the Compulsory Act 1965 will protect the acquiring body. This is more fully dealt with in Chapter 21.

Chapter 9

Taking Possession and Conveyance

Introduction
Survey and preliminary works
Entry under the Compulsory Purchase Act 1965
Entry under a general vesting declaration
Consequences of entry
Advance payment of compensation
Unlawful entry
Enforcing entry
Absent or untraced owners
Compelling an authority to take possession
Conveyance

9.1 Introduction

The ultimate and most significant power, in relation to a compulsory purchase, is the right of the acquiring authority to enter and take possession of land without the consent of the owner: indeed that entry can be enforced, if necessary. There are also powers to enter land to carry out surveys, etc.

9.2 Survey and preliminary works

The Local Government (Miscellaneous Provisions) Act 1976, section 15, contains wide powers for local authorities to survey land. A person authorised in writing by a local authority may at any reasonable time:

(a) survey any land in connection with a proposal by the authority to acquire compulsorily an interest in the land or a right over the land which is not an interest (for an acquisition of a 'right': see Chapter 8); and

(b) accordingly, for the purpose of surveying any such land, enter on the land and other land.

This power includes a 'power to search and bore on and in the land for the purpose of ascertaining the nature of the subsoil or whether minerals are present in the subsoil'. Any necessary apparatus for use in connection with the survey may be left on or in the land and may be removed when finished with.

The authorised person must produce evidence of his authorisation, if requested, and may be accompanied by others if necessary for the survey. If the land is occupied, he must give not less than 14 days' notice; and, if unoccupied, he must leave the land as effectively secured against trespassers as he found it.

If the authorised person wishes to leave apparatus on or in the land he must first give notice to the owner, or if the land is occupied, at least 14 days' notice to the occupier. There are certain limitations if the land is owned by a statutory undertaker.

Compensation is payable to any person with any interest in the land if damage occurs. Any dispute as to a person's entitlement to compensation is to be determined by the Lands Tribunal: section 15(5) and (6).

It is a criminal offence to obstruct a person authorised to enter land or to enter with his apparatus. It is also an offence for the authorised person, who enters the land, to wrongfully disclose information he obtains of a manufacturing process or trade secret: section 15(7) and (8).

Similar, though not so wide powers to enter and survey, are found in the Highways Act 1980, in connection with highway functions; the Town and Country Planning Act 1990, in connection with the acquisition of land for planning purposes and the necessary survey and valuation thereof; and in the Compulsory Purchase Act 1965. The power in the 1965 Act is found in section 11(3) and permits the acquiring authority, after giving between three and 14 days' notice to the owners and occupiers, to enter land for the purpose of surveying and levelling any land subject to a compulsory purchase order, and to probe or bore to ascertain the nature of the soil or to set out the line of the works. Compensation is payable for any damage, and any dispute as to compensation is referred to the Lands Tribunal.

9.3 Entry under the Compulsory Purchase Act 1965

The acquiring authority may not, without the consent of the owners and occupiers, enter on any land until the amount of compensation has been agreed by the parties, or determined by the

Lands Tribunal, and has been paid to the persons concerned or, where an owner cannot be found or refuses to convey, has been paid into court: section 11(4).

If the authority seeks possession of certain land before compensation has been agreed or determined, then provided a notice to treat has been served in respect of any of the land, it may use one of the two procedures described below to effect an entry without the owner's consent.

Where an acquiring authority has taken possession of any land, the owner of any affected interest may claim an advance payment of compensation: Land Compensation Act 1973, section 52. The amount is 90% of the agreed compensation, or, where there is no agreement, 90% of the acquiring authority's estimate. The advance must be paid within three months of the request, to effect an entry without the owner's consent.

For the effect of handing over keys to the acquiring authority, see *Simmonds* v *Kent County Council* [1991] and *Pandit* v *Leicester City Council* [1989].

1. Powers of entry: section 11(1) of the 1965 Act

Provided a notice to treat has been served in respect of any of the land and notice of entry is served on the owner, lessee and occupier of that land at least 14 days before possession is required, the authority may then enter and take possession of that land, or of such part of that land as is specified in the notice.

Where one notice of entry is served on an owner, and the acquiring authority takes physical possession in stages over a period of time, the authority is deemed to have taken legal possession of the whole of the land covered by that notice on the date of the first entry: *Chilton* v *Telford Development Corpn* [1987]. This means that to the extent that an owner remains on some of his land covered by a notice of entry, he is a trespasser, or at best a licensee of the authority. Where a notice to treat and of entry has been served in respect of part of a claimant's land, and the acquiring authority is required, and accepts that it has to acquire the remainder of the land on the grounds of material detriment under section 8 of the Compulsory Purchase Act 1965, the authority will probably be deemed to have entered the whole of the land on the date it entered the part that was subject to the original notice of entry: see also Chapter 8 above and **Severed Land**.

Section 11(1) is not well expressed, but it is presumed that the word 'land' includes an interest in land so that separate interests, freehold and leasehold, must be dealt with separately. Thus, a notice to treat and notice of entry must be served on the owner of each interest the authority desires to take possession of.

When compensation is ultimately agreed or determined, it will bear interest at a rate prescribed from time to time from the date of entry. That date will usually be appropriate for making the valuations: see Chapter 11. See the *Chilton* case, above, for the date of entry, where entry is taken in stages under one notice of entry.

An acquiring authority is not deemed to have entered the land at the expiration of the notice of entry: see *Burson* v *Wantage Rural District Council* [1974].

2. Alternative procedure for obtaining Right of Entry: Schedule 3 to the 1965 Act

This procedure is rather involved, and in practice is rarely resorted to because of the convenience of the notice of entry procedure above. The authority must first pay into court the amount of compensation claimed by the owner, or a sum equal to the value of the owner's interest determined by an able and practical surveyor appointed by two justices; it must then give a bond (that is contract by deed) to pay the amount to the owner, or any other sum awarded, plus interest. When the authority has paid the owner, the sum in court is repaid to them.

3. Entry under the Housing Act 1985

Where a housing authority is authorised to purchase compulsorily a house, and has served a notice under section 11(1) of the 1965 Act, it may, instead of taking actual possession of the house, serve a notice on the occupier authorising him to continue in occupation upon terms specified in the notice: Housing Act 1985 section 583.

Where a housing authority has agreed to purchase land for housing, for area improvement or in relation to clearance areas, it may, after giving not less that 14 days' notice enter and take possession against any tenant with an interest of less than a year or from year to year: Housing Act 1985, section 584.

4. What amounts to entry

In *Pandit* v *Leicester City Council* [1989] it has held that entry was effected when the keys to the property were handed to the authority and accepted. However, the handing over of the keys on the expected completion date in *Simmonds* v *Kent County Council* [1990] did not amount to entry.

9.4 Entry under a general vesting declaration

The general vesting declaration is an alternative procedure to the notice to treat: see Chapter 7.

Section 8 of the Compulsory Purchase (Vesting Declarations) Act 1981 provides that on the date specified in a general vesting declaration, the land and the right to enter upon and take possession of it vests in the acquiring authority; no further special procedure is required. There is excepted from this right of entry any minor tenancy or a long tenancy about to expire; it will be recalled that for reasons of convenience such tenancies will still bind an authority, even though the reversionary interest may vest in the authority. If entry is required against these tenancies, a notice to treat and notice of entry under the 1965 Act (see above) must be served on the tenants concerned.

9.5 Consequences of entry

Where an authority has lawfully entered land the subject of a notice of entry, it becomes liable to pay interest on unpaid compensation under section 11 of the 1965 Act. An advance payment of compensation may be claimed under section 52 of the Land Compensation Act 1973 (see below). The date of entry is the date the dispossessed owner will have been disturbed and is relevant for the recovery of compensation for that disturbance. It is also the valuation date in valuing the land, if that has not already been agreed.

9.6 Advance payment of compensation

If the acquiring authority takes possession before compensation has been agreed, it is obliged, if requested, to make an advance payment on account of any compensation which is due for the acquisition of any interest in land: section 52, Land Compensation Act 1973. The claimant must make his request in writing and give particulars of his interest in the land and such other details as the acquiring authority may reasonably require to enable it to estimate the amount of compensation. The amount of any advance payment shall be equal to 90% of the acquiring authority's estimate of compensation or, if the amount of the compensation has been agreed, 90% of this figure. The advance payment must then be made within three months of the written request; if the three months expires before possession is taken, then it must be paid at the date of possession. If an advance payment is made, that fact together with details of the interest in the land to which it relates is entered as a local land charge. This ensures that if the owner disposes of his interest, a purchaser will have notice that an advance of compensation has already been made in respect of that interest and any further compensation to be paid will take into account the advance payment. If the advance payment is found, eventually, to have exceeded the proper amount of compensation due to the claimant, the excess must he repaid. Finally, if the interest in the land is mortgaged, the acquiring authority will not make any advance payment if the outstanding loan exceeds the 90% figure, and if it is less, the advance payment will be reduced to ensure that sufficient sums are retained by the acquiring authority to enable it to pay off the mortgagee.

If it appears that the acquiring authority's estimate of value was too low, the authority shall pay the balance of the advance payment following a request: section 52(4A).

Section 52A of the 1973 Act provides for the payment of accrued interest on the estimate of compensation from the date of entry until payment. If an additional sum is payable under section 52(4A) because the initial estimate was too low, interest becomes payable in respect of the difference between the original estimated value and the revised estimate.

9.7 Unlawful entry

There is a penalty of £10 and an obligation to compensate for any damage done should the acquiring authority, or any of their contractors, wilfully enter land without serving the notice of entry, or following the alternative procedure, as required under the Compulsory Purchase Act 1965 (see **9.3** above); the words 'wilfully enter' connote an absence of honest belief that the procedural requirements have been satisfied: section 12.

The acquiring authority may remain in possession of land it has entered upon, where it appears that through mistake or inadvertence the authority has failed or omitted to purchase or to pay compensation for any interest in that land. Section 22 of the 1965 Act, which provides for this, requires the authority to purchase or pay compensation for the omitted interest and to pay the profits the land could have made for the owner from entry to payment of compensation, within six months of the authority becoming aware of that interest. In these circumstances it would seem that an owner may be entitled to interest on the unpaid compensation from date of entry, under section 11(1), and lost profits, under section 22. If the interest is disputed, the time-limit is six months from the date of a decision of a court establishing the claimant's right to that interest. Compensation is assessed as at the date of entry and without regard to any improvements carried out by the authority meanwhile.

In *Advance Ground Rents Ltd* v *Middlesbrough Borough Council* [1986], notices to treat and of entry were served on the reputed owner, and entry was taken. However, there was a mortgagee, and a notice to treat was not served on the mortgagee until more than three years after the date of the CPO, and more than six months after the mortgagee proved his title. The Tribunal decided that the time-limit for the service of the notice to treat had expired, and so too had the time-limit in section 22 of six months for correcting an error. Accordingly, the Tribunal had no jurisdiction to determine the compensation.

Where the acquiring authority, or any of its contractors, unlawfully and without consent, enter any land which is not subject to compulsory purchase, the provisions of sections 12 or 22 of the 1965 Act will not apply. The affected owner is left with his remedies under the common law; he must sue for trespass or, if he has lost possession of the land, he must bring an action for the recovery of the land: see *National Provident Institution* v *Avon County Council* [1992] for an award of damages against an authority for a trespass based on a nominal licence fee. In *Cohen* v *Haringey London Borough Council* [1981] CA, it was held that an acquiring authority could regularise an unlawful possession, where it had served notices on the wrong person, by serving fresh notices to treat and entry and backdating their effect. It was also held that an owner who negotiated with an authority which had unlawfully taken possession might be estopped if he sought to recover possession against that authority.

9.8 Enforcing entry

If the acquiring authority has served the requisite notice of entry, or has paid compensation, it is entitled to enter and take possession of the land. If the owner refuses consent to enter, the authority may take possession without the use of force (if the land is unoccupied or the occupier offers no resistance): *Loosemore v Tiverton and North Devon Railway Co* [1884]. Otherwise the authority may issue a warrant to the sheriff who is then authorised to take possession of the land using sufficient force to enable this to be achieved: section 13 of the 1965 Act. The sheriff is the chief officer of the Crown in each county, and his duties include carrying into effect certain court orders; the less glamorous tasks are delegated to an authorised deputy!

The costs of enforcement by the sheriff are not deductable from the compensation: see *Matthews v Lewisham London Borough Council* [1982].

9.9 Absent or untraced owners

There is a procedure in Schedule 2 to the Compulsory Purchase Act 1965 for dealing with absent or untraced owners who cannot be found after diligent inquiry. A valuer member of the Lands Tribunal makes a valuation, and the acquiring authority pays into court the appropriate compensation and conveys the land to itself by deed poll. If the owner turns up and proves his title, he is entitled to the compensation. He may refer the amount to the Lands Tribunal if he is dissatisfied. The Tribunal members handle some 250 such valuations a year. Any money paid into court and not claimed can be recovered by the acquiring authority after 12 years: Local Government (Miscellaneous Provisions) Act 1976, section 29.

See further *Doe d, Hutchinson v Manchester* [1845] and *Douglas v London NW Rly Co* [1857] for the possible liability of an authority which has not wilfully entered land without following the prior procedure.

9.10 Compelling an authority to take possession

Frequently, authorities delay taking possession in order to avoid paying interest on unpaid compensation, or to avoid relieving a tenant of an obligation to pay rent. The remedies available to an owner where he has received a notice of entry and the authority will not take possession are not clear. It may be possible to argue that where, as a result of receiving a notice of entry, the owner has incurred expenditure in seeking alternative accommodation, or has otherwise acted to his detriment, the authority is estopped from denying that it has not taken constructive entry. Alternatively, it may be possible to seek a mandatory order in the High Court, under Part 54.2 of the Civil Procedure Rules, where it can be shown that there is a duty to enter without delay: see *Morgan* v *Metropolitan Railway Co* [1868]. Otherwise all an owner can do is to make an expedited application to the Lands Tribunal for a determination of compensation, and then enforce 'statutory' contract compelling the authority to complete the conveyance and pay the compensation as was suggested in *Simpson* v *Stoke-on-Trent City Council* [1982].

9.11 Conveyance

1. *Conveyance follows agreement on compensation*

Where acquisition proceeds by way of notice to treat, conveyance follows agreement as to compensation or its determination by the Lands Tribunal. This is the case even where entry has already been taken.

2. *Owners without power to sell or disabilities*

Some owners may hold land inalienably, such as the National Trust; others have legal disabilities. The power to purchase land compulsorily is exercisable notwithstanding some enactment providing that the land shall be inalienable: see section 9 of the Acquisition of Land Act 1981. Some land held by the National Trust is inalienable under section 21 of the National Trust Act 1907 or section 8 of the National Trust Act 1939.

Where National Trust land is held inalienably, special Parliamentary procedure may arise in relation to the making of a compulsory purchase order in certain circumstances: see p38 above.

Land may be held inalienably, such as some National Trust land, or owned by persons without power to sell their interests. In these circumstances an acquiring authority will be concerned with two matters: whether they will acquire a good title to such land, and whether it is safe to pay compensation directly to the trustees or their owners concerned. Section 2 of and Schedule 1 to the Compulsory Purchase Act 1965 contains provisions addressing these matters.

Para 2 of Schedule 1 makes it lawful for all persons who are possessed of or entitled to any of the land subject to compulsory purchase, or any estate or interest in any of that land, to sell and convey or release to the acquiring authority, and to enter into all necessary agreements for the purpose. Thus, such persons are entitled to enter into a contract to sell land to an acquiring authority, and can lawfully convey such land.

Para 4 of Schedule 1 provides that where land is being acquired from a person with a legal disability, the compensation must be determined by the valuation of two surveyors, one of whom shall be nominated by the acquiring authority, and the other by the other party, alternatively by the Lands Tribunal. Para 6 provides that the compensation in respect of any land or interest 'shall be paid into Court'. Once paid into Court it may only be paid out in certain circumstances such as in payment to any party becoming absolutely entitled to the compensation.

However, it would appear that an acquiring authority will obtain a good title to land held by persons without power to sell for the following reasons. Schedule 1 to the 1965 Act is subject to section 42(7) of the Law of Property Act 1925. Under this provision an express contract can be made by which the acquiring authority agreed to pay compensation directly to the owners of the land who otherwise have no power to sell. A good title is then made. Section 42(7) is arguably a statutory enactment of the decision in *Re Milnes* [1875] where it was held that in the absence of what is now section 42(7) an acquiring authority would still get a good title even if compensation were not paid into Court. This would probably cover the position where a contract arises merely under the notice to treat and agreement of compensation. The only concern for an acquiring authority would be whether some third party might claim that the compensation has been paid to the wrong persons. However, if the compensation is paid to trustees they would be bound to hold it for the benefit of the beneficiaries.

Chapter 10

The Lands Tribunal

Introduction
Reference to the Lands Tribunal
Valuation methods and evidence
Small claims
Appealing an award

10.1 Introduction

Mention has been made of the Lands Tribunal on several occasions so far and further reference will be made in subsequent chapters. It seems appropriate to consider its purpose at this stage, as the Tribunal is concerned with the assessment of compensation in accordance with rules and principles, many of its own creation, that are the subject of the rest of this book.

The Lands Tribunal was established by the Lands Tribunal Act 1949; it replaced the system of official arbitrators set up in 1919. The Tribunal consists of a President, a person who has held judicial office or is a barrister, and other members who are either barristers, solicitors or valuers. Each member is a person of some standing and experience in the legal or valuation professions.

Any one or more members of the Tribunal may exercise its jurisdiction. The President may select a member or members to deal with a case. The nature of the case will suggest whether a legal or a valuation member should be selected, and in certain cases involving both legal and valuation problems, two appropriate members may be selected. In connection with the assessment of compensation, the dispute between the parties may not be one of different opinions as to the land values, or the quantification of other claims, but of the interpretation of legal rules which govern compensation assessment, hence the legal members of the Tribunal.

1. Jurisdiction

The Tribunal does not have any inherent jurisdiction and can only exercise such jurisdiction as is conferred by legislation: see *Re Richard and Great Western Railway* [1905]; *Re London & Winchester Properties Ltd's Application* [1983] and *Simmonds* v *Kent County Council* [1990]. In *Donovan* v *Welsh Water* [1993] the Tribunal decided that it had jurisdiction to hear a claim for compensation under the Water Act 1989 (now the Water Industry Act 1991) for damage caused by the water company's contractor on land which was not within the line of a sewer depicted on the plan attached to the notice of entry. There was also jurisdiction in *Williams* v *Blaenau Gwent Borough Council* [1994] where a notice to treat was withdrawn by consent and not in accordance with the requirements of section 31 of the Land Compensation Act 1961. In *Royal Bank of Scotland* v *Clydebank District Council* [1995] it was held that the Scottish Lands Tribunal had no jurisdiction to determine compensation where a reference was not made within the period stipulated by the equivalent of section 10 of the Compulsory Purchase (Vesting Declarations) Act 1981.

However, the Tribunal did not have jurisdiction in *Harford* v *Birmingham City Council* [1993] where the claimant's advisers accepted an offer of compensation without qualification; there was a binding agreement which settled the amount of compensation. The Tribunal does not have jurisdiction to determine compensation disputes under the telecommunications code under the Telecommunications Act 1984: see *Mercury Communications Ltd* v *London & India Dock Investments Ltd* [1994] and *Finsbury Business Centre* v *Mercury Communications* [1994] for county court cases. However, jurisdiction can be conferred by consent: see section 1(3) of the Lands Tribunal Act 1949. Nevertheless, the Tribunal has a wide jurisdiction to determine matters related to land. These may include hearing rating appeals from local valuation courts and the removal or modification of restrictive covenants. We are concerned here with the role of the Tribunal to determine disputes as to compensation in connection with the acquisition of land (section 1 of the Land Compensation Act 1961); or, in connection with a claim under Part I of the Land Compensation Act 1973 where a depreciation in value has been caused by public works. The Tribunal also declares the validity or otherwise of blight notices, and, under section 8 of the Compulsory Purchase Act 1965, counternotices, to an acquiring authority to take the whole or none of an owner's property: see Chapter 5. A special problem arose in *Shraff Tip Ltd* v *Highways Agency* [1999], where the Tribunal made its decision on all the substantive issues other than costs. It decided it was not *functus officio* and the reference could be reopened to hear additional evidence on pre-acquisition costs.

2. *Referring claims*

The parties to a dispute may agree to refer the matter to the Tribunal, known as a reference by consent; the Tribunal then has jurisdiction to act as an arbitrator and make a decision which will bind the parties: see section 1(3) of the Lands Tribunal Act 1949. For this purpose it sits in private. If agreement to refer cannot be reached, a dispute can only be referred to the Tribunal unilaterally where expressly provided by statute.

Section 6 of the Compulsory Purchase Act 1965 provides that if a person does not respond to a notice to treat with a claim for compensation within 21 days, or if he and the acquiring authority cannot agree the amount of compensation, the question of compensation shall be referred to the Lands Tribunal. Section 1 of the Lands Compensation Act 1961 further provides that whenever land is authorised to be acquired compulsorily, any question of disputed compensation shall be referred to the Tribunal and the amount determined in accordance with the provisions of the 1961 Act: see Part III of this book.

3. *Limitation period for references*

Where a general vesting declaration has been made, section 10(3) of the Compulsory Purchase (Vesting Declarations) Act 1981 provides that a reference must be made within six years from the date at which the claimant, or a person under whom he derives title, first knew, or could reasonably expected to have known, of the vesting of the subject land. Once this limitation period has expired, there is no longer any enforceable right to compensation: see *Royal Bank of Scotland plc* v *Clydebank District Council* [1995]. However the time-limit is procedural, and is capable of being waived by estoppel by and on behalf of the acquiring authority, as in *Co-operative Wholesale Society Ltd* v *Chester-le-Street District Council* [1998].

There would appear to be no express limitation period for compensation claims for land taken and injurious affection under sections 7 and 10 of the Compulsory Purchase Act 1965. However, in *Vincent* v *Thames Conservancy* [1953] the Tribunal decided that a reference to it under section 34(3) of the Land Drainage Act 1930 was an arbitration within the meaning of section 27(6) of the

Limitation Act 1939 (now section 34 of the Limitation Act 1980) and the period of limitation prescribed by that Act applied. The arbitral character of the Tribunal is supported by the incorporation of certain provisions of the Arbitration Act 1950 in the Lands Tribunal Rules 1996 (rule 32). The six-year limitation period prescribed by section 9 of the Limitation Act 1980 in respect of actions to recover any sum recoverable by statute applies to the statutory right to compensation in sections 7 and 10 of the 1965 Act: see *Hillingdon London Borough Council* v *ARC Ltd* [1998]. A reference should therefore be made within that period to the Tribunal: see *Williams* v *Blaenau Gwent County Borough Council (No 2)* [1999] for claims following the withdrawal of a notice to treat.

In respect of claims under Part I of the Land Compensation Act 1973 (see Chapter 23), section 19(2A) of that Act provides that for the purposes of the Limitation Act 1980 a person's right of action to recover compensation shall be deemed to have accrued on the first claim day (which is the first anniversary of the opening of the public works in question). In *Bateman* v *Lancashire County Council* [1999] the Tribunal decided that the principle in *Hillingdon London Borough Council* v *ARC Ltd* [1998] applied and a claim would be time-barred six years after the first claim day. A first claim day is the first anniversary of the opening of the works.

The Tribunal will hear a reference after the expiration of a limitation period where waiver or estoppel applies: see *Co-operative Wholesale Society* v *Chester-le-Street District Council* [1996] where waiver was found. However, for estoppel to arise, there must be a common assumption of a valid claim and an agreement that the acquiring authority will not take the point of the expiration of the limitation period: see *Hillingdon London Borough Council* v *ARC Ltd (No 2)* [2000]. The making of an advance payment, under section 52 of the Lands Compensation Act 1973, after the expiration of the limitation period was not sufficient to waive the authority's right to rely on the expiration of the limitation period in the absence of an agreement: see *Wiberg* v *Swansea City Council* [2002].

Section 3(6)(a)(ii) of the Lands Tribunal Act 1949 provides that the Tribunal may make rules as to the time within which any proceedings before it are to be instituted; no rules have been.

4. *Precedent and decision of the Tribunal*

The doctrine of precedent does not bind the Tribunal to the extent that it must follow its previous decisions. Even on a question of law, there are plenty of conflicting decisions. There are two reasons for this. In the past, decisions of the Tribunal have not been comprehensively reported or properly indexed. And, perhaps more importantly, the Tribunal is primarily one of fact.

In *W Clibbett Ltd* v *Avon County Council* [1976], the President of the Tribunal said:

> I was asked to look at certain previous decisions of the tribunal, but, as I have said and emphasised before, decisions are relevant only to argument on law or procedure. The assessment of compensation must be decided on, and only on, the evidence.

10.2 Reference to the Lands Tribunal

Where any question of disputed compensation is referred to the Tribunal under section 1 of the 1961 Act, the Tribunal will normally sit in public; the parties are allowed not more than one expert witness, unless the Tribunal directs otherwise, or the claim involves minerals, or disturbance of business, as well as the land. The member of the Tribunal is authorised to enter and inspect any of the land which is the subject of the reference. Although the Tribunal normally sits in London, it frequently holds sittings throughout the country.

Since a claim for compensation is regarded as one claim, although it may contain several elements, such as the value of land taken, severance and disturbance, only one reference can be made to determine all losses: see *Thameside* v *Greater London Council* [1979].

The procedure of the Tribunal is governed by rules: see the Lands Tribunal Rules 1996. Reference should also be made to the Practice Directions issued in April 2001.

1. Procedure

(a) Preliminary matters

A reference to the Tribunal is commenced by the completion of a notice of reference containing certain information specified by rule 10. It may be made at any time after a period of 28 days from the notice to treat. There is provision for what are called interlocutory matters, such as how many expert witnesses, or for a hearing of a preliminary issue: see rules 38 and 43. A pre-trial review can be held: see rule 39 and Lands Tribunal Practice Directions para 3. The Tribunal can order documents to be produced (known as discovery): see rule 34.

For the listing and hearing of references, see Lands Tribunal Practice Directions para 8.

(b) Case management

Para 2 of the Lands Tribunal Practice Directions states that the Tribunal will follow its procedures on the basis of the overriding objective that applies in the Civil Courts. That overriding objective requires that in dealing with a case, so far as is practicable, the parties should be on an equal footing, there should be a saving of expense, the case should be dealt with in ways which are proportionate to the amount of money involved, to the importance of the case, to the complexity of the issues, and to the financial position of each party, the Tribunal will ensure that the case is dealt with expeditiously and fairly and that it is allotted an appropriate share of the Tribunal's resources.

Under para 3 of the Lands Tribunal Practice Directions, every case will be assigned to one of four procedures, as soon as that can be done. The four procedures are:

(a) the standard procedure;
(b) the special procedure;
(c) the simplified procedure;
(d) the written representations procedure.

A case will be assigned to the special procedure if it requires case management by a Member in view of its complexity, the amount in issue or its wider importance. There will be a pre-trial review to be held under rule 39 in order that all appropriate directions are given for the fair, expeditious and economical conduct of the proceedings. The simplified procedure is considered further below; a case will be assigned to it where no substantial issue of law or valuation practice, or a substantial conflict of fact, is likely to arise. The written representation procedure, which is also considered further below, will be used only if the Tribunal is of the view that oral evidence and argument can properly be dispensed with. All other cases will be assigned to the standard procedure.

(c) Evidence

Rule 42 deals with expert evidence, the number of expert witnesses and their proofs of evidence: see also Lands Tribunal Practice Directions para 13.

Evidence of an expert nature is usually given orally, but

evidence may be given in writing (an affidavit) if the parties agree or the Tribunal orders: rule 33(1). The ordinary rules of evidence apply. Under the Civil Evidence Act 1995 hearsay evidence can be given, subject to appropriate weight being given. So a valuer who is called to give evidence ought to ensure that he does not give what is called hearsay evidence because little weight may be given to it; he must only give evidence of transactions and comparables within his personal knowledge, though he is entitled to give his expert opinion of the significance of these and of other generalised factors affecting land values: *English Exporters (London) Ltd* v *Eldonwall Ltd* [1973] ChD approved by the Tribunal in *Nuttal* v *Leeds City Council* [1982]. The parties may agree certain facts or the use of evidence that would otherwise be inadmissible as hearsay.

For valuation methods and other evidence, see below.

(d) Preliminary issue

Under rule 43, the Tribunal may determine a preliminary issue. However, in *Harrison & Hetherington* v *Cumbria County Council* [1985] the House of Lords said that the Tribunal should not hear as a preliminary issue an application for the determination of compensation under rule 5 of section 5 of the Land Compensation Act 1961 because evidence is necessary to exercise discretion under the rule. That case is, however, unlikely to apply to the wording of the new rule. For guidance see Lands Tribunal Practice Directions, at para 6.

(e) Simplified procedure

Rule 28 permits the Tribunal to direct that the new simplified procedure should apply to a claim hearing. Where this procedure is to apply, directions are given for the filing and contents of a statement of claim. Not less than 14 days before the appointed hearing date, each party shall send to all other parties copies of all documents which are to be relied on; not less than seven days before the hearing experts' reports must be sent together with a list of witnesses. If one party objects to this procedure, it is likely that the Tribunal will order a directions hearing to determine whether to accept the objection or not.

The hearing is to be informal and the strict rules of evidence will not apply. Unless otherwise ordered, evidence will not be on oath: rule 28(10). No award of costs is to be made, save in certain circumstances:

(i) where section 4 of the Land Compensation Act 1961 applies – section 4 applies where an acquiring authority has made a written offer to settle and the sum awarded does not exceed that offer: see *Nicholls* v *Highway Agency* [2000], and it also applies where a claimant has failed to make a properly particularised claim;

(ii) where an offer of settlement has been made by a party, and the Tribunal considers it appropriate to have regard to the fact that an offer has been made; or

(iii) in cases in which the Tribunal regards the circumstances as exceptional.

If, exceptionally, an award of costs is made, the costs will be on the county court scales: rule 28(11).

(f) Right of audience

A party may appear in person or be represented by counsel, solicitor or by any other person by leave of the Tribunal: see rule 37. There is a guidance note on direct professional access where a party wishes to access a barrister through a surveyor or valuer in Lands Tribunal Practice Directions para 14.

(g) Decision

The decision of the Tribunal is given in writing, though it may be given orally if there would be no inconvenience or injustice to the parties; it must include reasons: rule 50. If the amount of compensation depends on a point of law that is likely to be taken to the Court of Appeal, the Tribunal will usually give alternative awards depending on which way the point of law is decided.

(h) Written representations

Rule 27 provides that the parties may agree to the Tribunal determining the dispute by way of written representations and without an oral hearing. The Registrar must be satisfied that the parties can present their cases in this manner. Very few cases are conducted by way of written representation.

(i) Arbitration Acts and interest

Rule 32 applies the following sections of the Arbitration Act 1996 to the Tribunal's proceedings: sections 47 (awards on different issues), 49 (power to award interest), and 57(3) to (7) (power to correct awards).

2. Costs

The costs of bringing a case before the Tribunal include the costs of legal representation and the expert witnesses. They do not include surveyor's fees incurred in negotiating claims; these are usually allowed as a matter of course: see Chapter 18.

Subject to section 4 of the Land Compensation Act 1961 and rule 28(11) of the Lands Tribunal Rules 1996 (the latter deals with the simplified procedure), the Tribunal has a discretion to order that the costs of the proceedings before it incurred by one party shall be paid by the other party. The Lands Tribunal Practice Directions, para 19, recognises that the Tribunal will normally exercise its discretion and award costs to the claimant. In practice if the Tribunal's award is higher than the acquiring authority's offer of compensation, the claimant will have his costs paid. But in *Pepys* v *London Transport Executive* [1975], the Court of Appeal decided that where a claimant failed to establish before the Tribunal a claim for compensation, the Tribunal should normally treat the claimant as an unsuccessful litigant in a court action, and order that the claimant pay the authority's costs. In *Purfleet Farms Ltd* v *Secretary of State for Transport* [2003], the Court of Appeal said that the proper approach of the Tribunal is that a successful claimant, who is awarded more than the amount of an unconditional offer by the acquiring authority, should be entitled to his costs in the absence of some 'special reasons' to the contrary. A 'special reason' should only be regarded as established where an item of costs or an issue raised was such that it could not on any sensible basis be regarded as part of the reasonable and necessary expense of determining the amount of the compensation.

The Tribunal may have regard to any offers to settle, including a 'without prejudice offer save as to costs': see Lands Tribunal Practice Directions, para 19. See also *Phipps* v *Wiltshire County Council* [1983]. Subject to the claimant acting reasonably, his costs are recoverable as part of his claim for losses: see *Lesquende Ltd* v *Planning and Environment Committee of State of Jersey* [1998].

Section 4(1) of the Land Compensation Act 1961 provides for circumstances where either: (a) the acquiring authority has made an unconditional offer in writing, and the sum awarded by the Tribunal does not exceed that sum; or (b) the Tribunal is satisfied that the claimant has failed to deliver, in time for the acquiring authority to make a proper offer, a claim stating the interest of the claimant and details of the claim, distinguishing the amounts claimed under each head, and how calculated; then the Tribunal shall order that the claimant shall bear his own costs and pay the costs of the acquiring authority so far as incurred after the date of the offer, or the time when the Tribunal is of the opinion the notice should have been delivered. Where an advance payment is made under section 52 of the Land Compensation Act 1973, and the Tribunal awards a sum less than the advance payment, the acquiring authority is still likely to have to pay all the claimant's costs according to the Scottish decision in *Emslie & Simpson Ltd* v *Aberdeen District Council (No 2)* [1995].

Where a claimant has delivered a notice of claim, as described above, and has made an unconditional offer to accept any sum as compensation, then if the sum awarded by the Tribunal exceeds that sum, the Tribunal shall normally order the acquiring authority to pay the claimant's costs: see section 4(3) of the 1961 Act. The Tribunal might depart from this normal rule where a sealed offer is made only shortly before the hearing, as in *Shevlin* v *Trafford Park Development Corporation* [1998] where offer was made two days beforehand. However, there is a risk in a claimant making an offer; he may find that the award beats the acquiring authority's offer but not his own. The Tribunal might then not award him his costs; see *Toye* v *Kensington and Chelsea Royal London Borough Council* [1994] where the award was above the sealed offers of both parties and the claimant was awarded costs only from the date of his sealed offer.

A sealed offer must offer compensation and compromise the reference. An offer that omits counsel's fees and surveyors' fees other than Rydes Scale is inadequate: see *Shevlin* v *Trafford Park Development Corporation* [1998] and *Taque* v *Lancester City Council* [1999], where an offer was made two days before the hearing and omitted the claimant's costs.

To encourage the settlement of a compensation dispute and to reduce the costs that would be incurred, if a reference was heard by the Tribunal, either party may make an unconditional offer in respect of the amount of compensation. Usually such an offer is only made by the acquiring authority; the claimant may refuse the offer, and the reference will proceed, or he may accept the offer and such acceptance is binding on him. In the latter case, the reference before the Tribunal is withdrawn. The unconditional offer has an important bearing on the award of costs. The offer is put in a sealed cover and sent to the Registrar; it is opened after the Tribunal has made its decision and determined the amount of compensation: rule 50. Section 4 of the Land Compensation Act 1961 makes provision for the award of costs where a sealed offer has been made by the acquiring authority. If the sum awarded by the Tribunal does not exceed the offer, the claimant, unless there are special reasons, is ordered to bear his own costs and to pay the costs of the acquiring authority incurred after the date of the offer. See the *Toye* case above for the danger to the claimant in making a sealed offer.

Where a sealed offer is made which the claimant accepts, the Tribunal retains its jurisdiction to order that the authority pays the claimant's costs up to the date of the offer: see *Marshall* v *Basildon Development Corporation* [1970]. Where a sealed offer is accepted on the day of the hearing, section 4 of the 1961 Act does not apply because the reference does not proceed to a determination; the Tribunal retains its discretion to determine the date by which the claimant ought to have accepted the offer: see *Stanford Marsh Ltd* v *Secretary of State for the Environment* [1997].

There is a very high chance that acquiring authorities' sealed offers will be close to the Tribunal's award, but the Tribunal has severely criticised an authority for putting in a sealed offer higher than the valuation being spoken to: *Fawcett* v *Newcastle-upon-Tyne* [1980]. That criticism is probably misplaced; the whole purpose of a sealed offer is to make an offer with a sufficient margin above the likely award in order to avoid the costs of a reference: see *R* v *High Bailiff for Westminster, ex parte London County Council* [1903].

There are circumstances, particularly where part of a claimant's land is acquired, and the claimant suffers injurious affection and severance, where the acquiring authority would like to consider making an offer consisting partly of money and partly of some practicable measure to minimise or reduce the effect of the injurious affection or severance. It would appear that an offer not of money may not amount to a sealed offer: see *Fisher* v *Great Western Railway* [1911].

The Tribunal may also award costs to the authority where the claimant has failed to deliver a notice of claim, with the necessary particulars, in sufficient time to enable the authority to make a proper offer: the costs of the authority from a date when the notice should have been delivered will have to be paid by the claimant unless there are special reasons: section 4(1) of the 1961 Act.

For a case where a successful party was deprived of an award of costs where a purchase notice was not upheld, see *Cook* v *Winchester City Council* [1995].

Where there is doubt as to whether a limited liability company to a reference will be able to meet an award of costs, an application can be made for security for costs. This is done by an application to a Master in the High Court. For the necessary balancing exercise, see *Keary Developments Ltd* v *Tarmac* [1995].

In *Durnsford* v *South Gloucestershire District Council* [1999], the surveyors agreed to act for a number of claimants without the claimants being liable to the surveyors. It was held that the claimants could not recover any costs from the authority as they had not incurred any costs; further that the surveyors were only entitled to Ryde's Scale fees, not their litigation costs. Costs of a reference may be recoverable under rule (6).

3. Interest on awards and on costs

According to *Barclays Bank plc* v *Kent County Council* [1998], section 29 of the Arbitration Act 1950 applied to proceedings in the Lands Tribunal (now section 49 of the Arbitration Act 1996). Accordingly interest was payable on an award of costs. For interest on compensation see Chapter 18.

10.3 Valuation methods and evidence

Collected here are references to a number of tribunal decisions where valuations methods have been considered or other matters relating to evidence.

1. Residual valuations

It is not the purpose of this book to describe the valuation methods that will find acceptability in compensation negotiation or before the Lands Tribunal. But it seems appropriate to draw attention to the few cases where the Tribunal has criticised a particular valuation method, or drawn attention to its unreliability. In *Essex Incorporated Congregational Union* v *Colchester Borough Council* [1982], the Tribunal drew attention to the inherent defects in the use of residual valuations. Under this method, the final value of a proposed development is first computed, the costs of carrying out the development are then deducted and the balance or 'residual' is the value that can be attributed to the property and the potential development at a stage before any work is started. It was said that a small change in one of the factors can cause a very large change in the residue. The case concerned the valuation of a church and its potential for office use. An estimated rental value of something over £21,000 had been made to which was applied a year's purchase of six. It was said that if there was an alteration of one in this multiplier, it would cause a change of 43% to the land value.

However, the method was accepted as a helpful test to apply as a check to the primary valuation based on comparable transactions in *Co-operative Retail Services Ltd* v *Wycombe District Council* [1989]. A residual method was adopted as the primary method in *Tudor Properties Ltd* v *Bolton Metropolitan Borough Council* [2000].

In *Richmond Gateway* v *Richmond London Borough Council* [1989] it was accepted that one of the common deductions, for developer's profit, need not be made. However that may have been because the case concerned a claim for compensation for refusal of planning permission, and the Tribunal and the Court of Appeal probably could not otherwise accept that there would have been any loss of value.

2. Comparable transactions

Valuation methods that rely upon direct comparable transactions are generally preferred by the Tribunal. In the Essex Incorporated case itself, the building was actually resold by the acquiring authority for £5,000 and this was the best evidence of its value and found acceptance with the Tribunal. See also *Windward Properties Ltd* v *Government of Saint Vincent and the Grenadines* [1996].

3. Tone of settlements

Another difficulty is that in many circumstances valuers, and particularly those acting for acquiring authorities, may place some reliance upon the settlements that are made with other claimants. In the case of *Lewars* v *Greater London Council* [1981], the Tribunal remarked that it had on more than one occasion preferred evidence of transactions in the open market to evidence of settlements. It was said that claimants were reluctant to come to the Tribunal because of the trouble involved and the potential liability for costs of the reference: generally they preferred to settle and avoid uncertainty. This is known as the 'Delaforce' effect from *Delaforce* v *Evans* [1970]. In *Ken Newbridge Ltd* v *Ipswich Borough Council* [1983], evidence was given on the basis of settlements but the claimant pointed out the reluctance of parties to come to the Tribunal because of delay and possible costs. The Member in that case came to the conclusion on the evidence that he had heard that the acquiring authority had made the first settlement at a figure advantageous to it, and at a level which was below that which was indicated by settlements at a later date. See also *Farr* v *Millersons Investments Ltd* [1970].

In *Dhenin* v *Department of Transport* [1990] the Tribunal did not accept evidence of settlements of compensation claims under Part I of the Land Compensation Act 1973 because these had been achieved against the background of severe underestimates of traffic predictions.

In *Hallows* v *Welsh Office* [1995] the Lands Tribunal said that the witness most likely to assist will be a surveyor practising in the locality, experienced in selling and valuing property, the evidence of the claimant's valuer concerning Tribunal decisions and settlements in other parts of the country was irrelevant and little weight was attached to them.

4. *Analysis or experience*

In *Marson* v *Hasley* [1975] LT, criticism was made by one of the parties of the 'academic' approach of the valuer for the other party: it was said reliance on analysis could be described as a mere juggling with figures. The valuer who made that criticism said that he did not belong to the 'Analytical School' of surveyors, but regarded himself as belonging to the 'Forty-years-man-and-boy School'. In that case the Tribunal said:

> It had every respect for able and practical surveyors who belong to the latter 'School', but the fact should be recognised that when a member of this 'School' finds himself unable to agree values with an equally able and practical member of the 'Analytical School' then on a reference to the Lands Tribunal, the latter surveyor is apt to have the easier passage. The reason for this is quite simple, the Tribunal reaches its decisions on the evidence presented and although it does of course draw on its own skill, that skill is applied not to the valuation of the subject property but to weighing the evidence given – a process conven-iently described as 'valuing the valuations' (and which may involve also 'valuing the valuers'). Opinion evidence, if it is to be certain of carrying weight, needs not only to be based on factual evidence but also to be demonstrably so based. Factual evidence bearing on the value of any land commonly takes the form of comparables: and the purpose of analysing the comparables is to enable unlike features to be identified and distinguished and to enable like features to be compared.

Similar views were expressed in *Mears* v *St Pancras Metropolitan Borough Council* [1963] where the Tribunal indicated that it was prepared to accept spot valuations direct to capital values of houses with vacant possession provided the valuer had been concerned with the transaction on which he relied and was therefore aware of any special circumstances. But in the case the 'Academic' approach of taking a rental value and capitalising this, then comparing it with settlements, was relied on.

In *Re Hayes Will Trusts* [1971] Ungoed-Thomas J said, in connection with the valuation of property for taxation purposes under section 7(5) of the Finance Act 1894 that:

> it has been established time and again in these Courts, as it was in this case, that there is a range of price, in some circumstances wide, which competent valuers would recognise as the price at which 'property would fetch if sold in the open market' ... the section ... [does not] require that the proper price of that range should be the price fixed for estate duty. That price together with the lowest price in the range may be expected to be the least likely price within the range, to be obtained from the open market. The most likely price, in the absence of consultation between the valuers representing conflicting interests, would presumably be the mean price. The habitual well recognised process of arriving at that price is for executors to put in the lowest price within the range and then to confer with the district valuer who acts to safeguard the Revenue. Such has been the accepted process of arriving at the price which the 'property would fetch if sold in the open market' and it seems to me to be as likely as any to arrive at that price within the margin which is the price most likely to be the market price.

It may be said that exactly the same process is used, as a matter of practice, in seeking to agree compulsory purchase compensation. The difference is that the price first submitted on behalf of a claimant would be a price at the top of the range, on the basis that the claimant's advisers would envisage a settlement within the range and at the mean price.

5. *Post valuation date evidence*

Where such evidence is of values, the evidence is admissible and goes to weight: see *Melwood Units Pty Ltd* v *Commissioners of Main Roads* [1979] and *Segama* v *Penny Le Roy Ltd* [1984]. In relation to other post valuation events, the decision in *Bwllfa & Merthyr Dare Steam Collieries Ltd* v *Pontypridd Waterworks Co* [1903] allows evidence of post valuation date events to replace speculation in certain circumstances, as described below. See also *Dingleside Development Co Ltd* v *Powys County Council* [1995].

6 *The* Bwllfa *principle*

In *Dhenin* v *Department of Transport* [1990] the Lands Tribunal decided that the *Bwllfa* principle did not apply to the assessment of compensation under Part I of the Land Compensation Act 1973: see *Bwllfa & Merthyr Dare Steam Colleries (1981) Ltd* v *Pontypridd Waterworks Co* [1903] AC 426. In that case the claimant sought to rely on actual traffic counts after the date of valuation, rather than projected figures estimated before that date. The principle had no application because the 1973 Act provides for the assessment of compensation as at a specific date, on the facts at that date, on prices then current at that date and on any intensification of the depreciation which could be anticipated at that date: see *Wickham Growers Ltd* v *Southern Water plc* [1997].

However the *Bwllfa* principle will apply to the assessment of compensation for disturbance as that is not concerned with establishing the open market value of land on a particular date: see *Wickham Growers* and *London County Council* v *Tobin* [1959].

In *ADP & E Farmers* v *Department of Transport* [1988] the application of the *Bwllfa* principle became an issue in relation to whether certain post-valuation date events could be taken into account that indicated that there was no longer any hope value in relation to certain retained land. The Tribunal decided that, as a matter of principle, the *Bwllfa* principle was capable of being applied to the case, but considered that, as a matter of fact, it should not be. What had to be ascertained in the case was the compensation payable under section 7 of the Compulsory Purchase Act 1965 sustained by the owner of the land by reason of a severance. The damage was said to be the measure of the owner's loss as at a certain date, and that this could be distinguished from damage that results from an occurrence at a certain date but where the loss is experienced or can be better calculated, subsequently. The Member said:

> Thus the damage in this case is the measure of the owner's loss as at a certain date. This can be distinguished from damage which results from an occurrence at a certain date but where the loss is experienced, or can be better calculated, subsequently. It is easy to imagine cases of injurious affectation under section 7 of the 1965 Act coming within the second category. It seems to me that damages in *Bwllfa* and *Carslogi Steamship Co Ltd* v *Royal Norwegian Government* [1952] AC 292 also come within the second category.
>
> The damage due to severance in this case is not ongoing; both valuers approach the problem on a 'before and after' basis of valuation

as at the date of severance. The events which occurred after that date ... are all factors which subsequently affected the hope value of the retained land, but it is not suggested that they had any bearing on the hope value estimated as at the date of severance.

In my view it would be wrong in valuing damages due to severance to take account of subsequent events which had no bearing on the valuation as at the date of severance. I would distinguish this case from cases where subsequent transactions in land might be called in aid to establish a valuation at a previous date or where damages for injurious affection can be better identified or valued some time after the date of severance.

In *Gaze* v *Holden* [1983], a decision in the Chancery Division of the High Court, the judge had to consider the proper valuation of a farm for the purposes of an option to purchase. In issue was whether the fact that a lease had been surrendered after the valuation date could be taken into account under the *Bwllfa* principle. It was held that the valuation had to be carried out at a particular date and should not take into account subsequent events which showed how certain possibilities and prospects in fact turned out: the *Bwllfa* was not applicable.

It follows that the *Bwllfa* principle should be restricted to those claims concerning compensation for disturbance or other losses under rule 6 where the measure is the loss to the claimant and the exercise is not that of determining a particular value on a particular date. That is precisely what the decision of the House of Lords in *Bwllfa* was dealing with.

7. Proof of evidence

An expert, instructed to appear as a witness before the Lands Tribunal, will have to prepare a proof of evidence. This document first sets out the expert's qualifications and experience, without which he would not be entitled to give his opinion. In a simple case where the value of the land acquired is in dispute, the document will then set out the expert's opinion of value, supported by any necessary valuation calculations. Normally an opinion of value will need to be supported by the evidence of comparable transactions.

Under the Civil Evidence Act 1995, hearsay evidence will be admissible. Accordingly, it will then be possible for a valuer to rely on transactions not within his first hand knowledge. However, the less detail he knows of a particular transaction, the less weight that transaction is likely to be given.

An expert owes a duty to the Tribunal to give his true opinion; he is likely to be under oath. He is not a negotiator advancing his client's particular interest. In the *Ikarian Reefer* [1993] Cresswell J said: The duties and responsibilities of expert witnesses in civil cases include the following:

1. Expert evidence presented to the court should be, and should be seen to be, the independent product of the expert uninfluenced as to form or content by the exigencies of litigation: see *Whitehouse v Jordan* [1981] 1 WLR 246 at p256, *per* Lord Wilberforce.
2. An expert witness should provide independent assistance to the court by way of objective unbiased opinion in relation to matters within his expertise: see *Polivitte Ltd* v *Commercial Union Assurance Co plc* [1987] 1 Lloyd's Rep 379 at p386; *Garland J and Re J* [1990] FCR 193 *per* Cazalet J. An expert witness in the High Court should never assume the role of an advocate.
3. An expert witness should state the facts or assumptions upon which his opinion is based. He should not omit to consider material facts which could detract from his concluded opinion: see *Re J supra*.
4. An expert witness should make clear when a particular question or issue falls outside his expertise.
5. If an expert's opinion is not properly researched because he considers that insufficient data is available, then this must be stated with an indication that the opinion is no more than a provisional one: see *Re J supra*. In cases where an expert witness, who has prepared a report, could not assert that the report contained the truth, the whole truth and nothing but the truth without some qualification, that qualification should be stated in the report: see *Derby & Co Ltd* v *Weldon (No 9) The Times*, November 9 1990, *per* Staughton LJ.
6. If, after exchange of reports, an expert witness changes his view on a material matter having read the other side's expert's report or for any other reason, such change of view should be communicated (through legal representatives) to the other side without delay and when appropriate to the court.
7. Where expert evidence refers to photographs, plans, calculations, analyses, measurements, survey reports or other similar documents, these must be provided to the opposite party at the same time as the exchange of reports: see Guide to Commercial Court Practice 15.5.

10.4 Small claims

The expense and uncertainty of a reference to the Tribunal does deter the use of that form for the settlement of small claims. In theory a claimant may conduct his own case before the Tribunal, or, with the Tribunal's consent, he may be represented by a person who is not a solicitor or a barrister. In practice the problems of preparing a case, determining the type of evidence that needs to be produced, considering whether to accept a sealed offer to avoid paying costs, and cross-examining expert witnesses, are formidable. The uncertainty as to the award of costs must be one of the biggest deterrents to a small claim, although to the credit of the Tribunal and acquiring authorities, costs may not always be awarded against an unsuccessful claimant if his claim was not frivolous. In *Streak & Streak* v *Berkshire County Council* [1976] LT, Mr Streak appeared in person and failed in his claim for compensation under Part I of the Land Compensation Act 1973; he was ordered to pay only £100 of the authority's substantial costs. The claimant in the *Pepys* case (see above) failed in a claim for compensation arising out of the construction of an underground railway (Victoria Line) that caused noise and vibration to her house; she, however, was ordered (although the order was not subsequently enforced) to pay all the costs of the authority.

The costs of referring small claims can be reduced if use is made of the new simplified procedure in rule 28 of the Lands Tribunal Rules 1996. Costs will not usually be awarded where this procedure applies, and therefore a claimant will usually avoid the risk of having costs awarded against him. These costs are considerable; a day's hearing with counsel, solicitor and one expert witness on either side can cost up to £15,000 per day (2003).

There are upwards of 60,000 compensation claims a year, and only about 200 are ever referred to the Tribunal of which about 55 are actually heard. It is said that more use is not made of the Tribunal because of the formalities and uncertainties as to costs. It is the view of this author that some new procedure is required to handle small claims and it is suggested that the practice of the Lands Tribunal in holding sittings outside London should be extended. The uncertainty as to costs can be removed if the Tribunal had no power to order costs where the sum claimed is below a prescribed amount. During the period 1979–83, some 30% of claimants who succeeded in obtaining an improvement in the offer made by the acquiring authority, were still unsuccessful in persuading the Tribunal to order the acquiring authority to pay their costs.

10.5 Appealing an award

A decision of the Lands Tribunal is final, there is no further appeal
on questions of fact or valuation. However, if one of the parties
considers the decision is erroneous in point of law, he may appeal
to the Court of Appeal: see section 3(4) of the Lands Tribunal Act
1949. An appeal is made by filing an appellant's notice of appeal at
the Court of Appeal within 28 days of the Tribunal's decision: see
CPR Practice Directions para 21.9. Permission to appeal is required
from the Court of Appeal: see Lands Tribunal Practice Directions,
para 20.

Prior to 2000, the procedure of appealing by case stated required
the questions of law which arose from the Tribunal's decision to be
stated specifically: see *RA Vine (Engineering) Ltd* v *Havant Borough
Council* [1989]. That meant that, to the extent that the Tribunal's
decision involved questions of valuation, there could be no further
appeal, but where the reasons in a decision disclosed an error of
law, this could be referred to the Court of Appeal. It is considered
the same position arises under the new form of appeal. The Court
of Appeal will not reconsider the valuations, but it may remit the
case back to the Tribunal to determine the amount of compensation
within stated legal criteria: the case of *Myers* v *Milton Keynes
Development Corporation* [1974] CA is a good illustration of the roles
of the Court of Appeal and the Lands Tribunal in this regard (how
the effect of the authority's scheme should be disregarded).

An award of the Tribunal may be successfully challenged if 'on
its face it is wrong in law' or there was no evidence upon which a
conclusion was reached: *Baker Britt & Co Ltd* v *Hampsher (VO)*
[1976] and *Edwards* v *Bairstow* [1956]. A decision of the Tribunal on
an interlocutory matter cannot be the subject of an appeal: *R* v
Lands Tribunal, ex parte City of London Corporation [1982].

Where the Tribunal did not accept any of the valuations
submitted, but made its award on its own valuation, the award
must be remitted to give the parties an opportunity of dealing
with the new valuation: see *Aquilina* v *Havering London Borough
Council* [1993].

However, the fact that the Tribunal does not support every step
in a valuation in an award with evidence does not necessarily mean
there has been an error of law. It is a specialist tribunal charged
with problems of compensation and entitled to come to its own
judgment on certain matters: see Glidewell LJ at p22L in *Abbey
Homesteads* v *Northampton County Council* [1992].

Although the Tribunal's award is final, and it cannot hear further evidence or argument to make good omissions or errors in the evidence, it could correct clerical errors or errors arising from accidental steps or omissions under the slip rule: see *Craske* v *Norfolk County Council* [1991].

PART III

COMPENSATION FOR THE COMPULSORY PURCHASE OF LAND

Chapter 11

Introduction to the Assessment of Compensation for Land Acquired

Introduction

The purpose of compensation

Legal presumptions in favour of compensation

Meaning of compensation

The development of the market value rule

The present statutory entitlement to compensation and the basic rules of valuation

Persons entitled to compensation

Date of valuation or assessment of compensation

11.1 Introduction

Before considering certain preliminary matters, such as the entitlement to compensation, this chapter first raises questions about the purpose of compensation, considers legal presumptions in favour of full compensation for the taking of private property and then describes the development of the basic rule for the assessment of the price to be paid for the taking of land: the market value. It also deals with certain problems inherent in the use of a market value basis.

11.2 The purpose of compensation

The assumption that because it is land that is expropriated, and as every piece of land has a price in the market-place, the expropriated owner should be adequately compensated with that price is too easily made. Much attention has been paid in the past to the problems of determining market value, and too little in determining and then fulfilling the true purpose of compensation. What is the true purpose of compensation and what are the expectations of expropriated owners? Clearly there are no certain answers and the purpose of compensation may vary according to

155

whether the expropriated owner is losing a home, a business or a form of investment; so also will the expectations vary. The home owner and businessman may suffer considerable inconvenience and demoralisation which the investor in land does not share.

Compulsory purchase at a market value basis can give rise to opposition to the proposals and scheme of the acquiring authority as owners may be unwilling sellers at that price. It can be argued that one purpose of compensation should be to overcome this opposition by the payment of a price which turns an unwilling seller into a willing seller. A great deal of compulsory purchase in the past has been in urban areas where housing and other premises are old and in bad condition, if the purpose of the compulsory purchase is to improve those areas, possibly the compensation to the affected owners should be at a level to enable reinstatement in homes and businesses of a better standard to be achieved.

When Parliament was considering what is now the Channel Tunnel Act 1987, there was evidence of considerable disquiet about the level of compensation for the 'commercial' aspects of the project. Landowners might grudgingly have parted with their land for the main parts of the project on a compensation basis that ignored the scheme, but were incensed at parting with land for warehousing, service areas and offices at a level of compensation that did not reflect those intended uses.

These points are deliberately left open; the reader should bear them in mind in considering the adequacy of the rules in the succeeding chapters. What seems clear is that landowners have expectations about compensation which are related, not only to their personal problems of relocation, but also to the intended use of the land taken. If market value is used as the basis of compensation, an important question is going to be whether that market value is to reflect the intended scheme.

Parliament has now provided that compensation may be paid in money or money's worth, thus opening up the possibility of land exchange as another means of compensating owners: see section 3 of the Compulsory Purchase Act 1965.

11.3 Legal presumptions in favour of compensation

There are two separate aspects to the development of legal presumptions in favour of compensation in the English courts. The first is the principle *restitutio in integrum* used in the English common law for the assessment of damages in actions in contract or tort. The second is a presumption of interpretation of statutes that Parliament does not intend to authorise the taking of private property without compensation except where it clearly so expressly directs. For the effect of the Human Rights Act 1998, see Chapter 27.

1. The principle of equivalence

Considering the first principle, this was stated by Lord Blackburn in *Livingstone* v *Rawyards Coal Company* [1880] as follows:

> In settling a sum of money to be given for reparation of damages, you should as nearly as possible get at that sum of money which will put the party who has been injured, in the same position as he would have been in if he had not sustained the wrong for which he is now gaining his compensation or reparation.

In relation to the assessment of compensation for land taken, section 63 of the Lands Clauses (Consolidation) Act 1845 provided:

> In estimating the purchase money or compensation to be paid ... regard shall be had ... to the value of the land to be purchased or taken.

(Now re-enacted as section 7 of the Compulsory Purchase Act 1965.) The Act did not contain a precise definition, but the court applied the same financial equivalency principle as used in common law actions. In *Ricket* v *Metropolitan Railway Company* [1865] Erle CJ had this comment to make:

> The Company claiming to take land by compulsory process, expel the owner from his property, and are bound to compensate him for all the loss caused by the expulsion; and the principle of compensation, then, is the same as in trespass for expulsion ...

Scott LJ in *Horn* v *Sunderland Corporation* [1941] said:

> The principle of equivalence ... is at the root of statutory compensation, which lays it down that the owner shall be paid neither less nor more than his loss.

More recently the Privy Council in *Director of Buildings and Lands* v *Shun Fung Ironworks* [1995] gave approval to this principle when Lord Nicholls said:

> The purpose of these provisions, in Hong Kong and England, is to provide fair compensation for a claimant whose land has been compulsorily taken from him. This is sometimes described as the

principle of equivalence. No allowance is to be made because the resumption or acquisition was compulsory; and land is to be valued at the price it might be expected to realise if sold by a willing seller, not an unwilling seller. But subject to these qualifications, a claimant is entitled to be compensated fairly and fully for his loss. Conversely, and built into the concept of fair compensation, is the corollary that a claimant is not entitled to receive more than fair compensation: a person is entitled to compensation for losses fairly attributable to the taking of his land, but not to any greater amount. It is ultimately by this touchstone, with its two facets, that all claims for compensation succeed or fail.

2. *Parliament does not authorise a taking without compensation*

The second aspect, namely the presumption in aid of interpretation of legislation, that Parliament is not intended to authorise the taking of private property without compensation, is found in a number of cases. Thus in *Central Control Board* v *Cannon Brewery* [1919] the House of Lords decided that where property was taken by statutory authority without any compensation procedure, compensation was to be assessed under the Lands Clauses (Consolidation) Act 1845.

11.4 Meaning of compensation

In *Blundell* v *R* [1905] Ridley J was concerned with the meaning of 'compensation' in the Defence Act 1842. He held that where land had been acquired under that Act, that expression included not only the price for the land, but also any injurious affection to retained land. He took into account submissions that compensation must mean an indemnity – full satisfaction for the land taken and any injurious affection to other land must be included in the term.

In *Nelungaloo Proprietary Ltd* v *The Commonwealth* [1948] 75 CLR 495 at p 571, Dixon J in the High Court of Australia said:

> Now 'compensation' is a very well understood expression. It is true that its meaning has been developed in relation to the compulsory acquisition of land. But the purpose of compensation is the same, whether the property taken is real or personal. It is to place in the hands of the owner expropriated the full money equivalent of the thing of which he has been deprived.
>
> Compensation prima facie means recompense for loss and when an owner is to receive compensation for being deprived of real or personal property his pecuniary loss must be ascertained by determining the value to him of the property taken from him. As the object is to find the

money equivalent for the loss or, in other words, the pecuniary value to the owner contained in the asset, it cannot be less than the money value into which he might have converted his property had the law not deprived him of it.

11.5 The development of the market value rule

1. *Value to the owner*

The Lands Clauses Act 1845 was passed to provide standard provisions with regard to acquisition procedures and the assessment of compensation. The standard clauses in this Act would usually be incorporated by reference in subsequent Acts authorising compulsory acquisition. Section 63 provided for the assessment of compensation as follows:

> In estimating the purchase money or compensation to be paid by the promoters of the undertaking... regard shall be had by the justices, arbitrators, or surveyors, as the case may be, not only to the value of the land to be purchased or taken by the promoters of the undertaking, but also to the damage, if any, to be sustained by the owner of the land by reason of the severance of the lands taken from the other lands of such owner, or otherwise injuriously affecting such other lands by the exercise of the powers of this or the Special Act, or any Act incorporated therewith.

But the 1845 Act did not lay down any definition of valuation, a fact acknowledged in the Report of the Acquisition and Valuation of Land Committee on Valuation for the Purposes of Compulsory Acquisition (the Scott Report – Cmnd 8998) published in 1918. Until the First World War, the generally accepted legal proposition was that compensation was to be the value of the land to the expropriated owner; it was his loss that was to be compensated, ascertained by determining what price the owner would have obtained for his land had he put it on the market, but ignoring any value the land had to the acquiring authority. In one of the first cases on the 1845 Act, *Penny v Penny* [1868], Page Wood, V-C said:

> I think the valuation ought to be made as at the time when the house was about to be taken, and ... assuming that the house had not been taken.

He continued:

> It is not the interest which has been acquired by the (acquiring

authority) that has to be estimated, but the value of the interest taken from the person with whom the [acquiring authority] deals.

The next case was *Stebbing* v *Metropolitan Board of Works* [1870], where the board was acquiring land in three graveyards owned by Stebbing, the rector of the parishes concerned. Stebbing contended that as land was being taken for secular purposes (new street and building sites) and would be divested of its ecclesiastical character, he was entitled to the value of the land for secular purposes. It was accepted that as ecclesiastical land it was virtually valueless to the rector. Cockburn CJ said:

> It is argued for the plaintiff, that although in his hands the churchyards are valueless, yet when they pass to the defendants, under compulsory powers of the Act of Parliament, they acquire a value from the fact that they may be applied to secular purposes ... When Parliament gives compulsory powers, and provides that compensation shall be made to the person from whom property is taken, for the loss that he sustains, it is intended that he shall be compensated to the extent of his loss; and that his loss shall be tested by what was the value of the thing to him, not by what will be its value to the persons acquiring it.

These two cases established the principle, underlying the assessment of compensation under the 1845 Act, that the measure of compensation was the value of the expropriated land to the owner: the value the land would have had, had it not been acquired. In practice, this was usually represented by market value.

The value to owner basis applied to all elements of the single claim to compensation provided by section 63: value of the land itself, and for all other losses suffered by the claimant: see *Ricket* v *Metropolitan Railway Co* [1865]. Although the land element of a claim is now valued by reference to its market value, the House of Lords in *Hughes* v *Doncaster Metropolitan Borough Council* [1991] has recently approved these earlier cases in recognising that a compensation claim is one claim for all losses suffered by a claimant.

2. Potential value

It was decided in *R* v *Brown* [1867] that where land had a prospective value, say for building purposes, this could be taken into consideration, for otherwise the expropriated owner would not be compensated for his full loss – the value of the land to him.

But a new problem of valuation was to come before the courts – the incorporation of private and often rival water companies, with statutory powers of expropriation, acquiring land which had some special suitability or adaptability for the purposes of reservoirs or water supply. It did not seem unreasonable to assume that where land was specially suited for such purposes, it might fairly become in private hands the subject of competition between rival public authorities desiring to take advantage of that special suitability.

In the unreported case of *Countess Ossalinsky* v *Manchester Corporation* [1883] (Browne & Allan, *Law of Compensation*, 2nd ed p659) certain land belonging to the plaintiff, bounding Lake Thirlmere, was acquired in connection with a scheme for converting the lake into a reservoir. The arbitrator had assessed the compensation payable with reference to the enhanced value of the land for its adaptability for forming a reservoir. The court approved this basis on the ground that if the land had an adventitious value, beyond its mere agricultural or existing use value, and this value was marketable in the sense that a higher priced could be obtained, the arbitrator could take this into account. But both judges had to reconcile this with the fundamental principle, already well established, that the compensation must not be assessed with reference to the particular purpose for which the land is being acquired. It was the owner's loss that had to be ascertained. On this point Stephen J said:

> When a railway company, or any other person who takes land under compulsory power, is to pay for that land, you are not to make them, as it were, buy it from themselves; you are not to take the value which, in their hands, it would acquire, and make them pay for it as if they had no compulsory power. That seems to rest upon a basis of perfect good sense, because if you were, there would be really no value in those compulsory powers at all...

The court was satisfied that the arbitrator had not, in his award, taken into consideration the fact that the corporation had compulsory powers, and the value of the land to them in carrying out the objects of the authorising Act.

In a later case, *Re Lucas and Chesterfield Gas and Water Board* [1909], Fletcher Moulton LJ explained special adaptability, he said:

> ...the phrase is not a happy one, for special adaptability for some purpose or other is the very basis of the market value of all land ... in agricultural land extra fertility, in town lands advantages of site, are true cases of special adaptability for farming or building purposes. These tend so directly to increase both the value and the market price of lands in the hands of a private owner that it has never been doubted that he

could urge them in augmentation of the compensation which he was entitled to receive.

His lordship considered this was a proper application of the principles upon which compensation is assessed under the Lands Clauses Acts; he continued:

> The owner receives for the lands he gives up their equivalent ie that which they were worth to him in money. His property is therefore not diminished in amount, but to that extent it is compulsorily changed in form. But the equivalent is estimated as the value to him, and not the value to the purchaser ...

Fletcher Moulton LJ also restated the principle that where land had a special value to a particular purchaser who has obtained powers of compulsory purchase it cannot be taken into consideration in finding the price:

> ... because to do otherwise would be to allow the existence of the scheme to enhance the value of the land to be purchased under it ... you are to look at the value to the seller and not at the value to the purchaser. The scheme which authorises the new reservoir only entitles the owner of the land to receive as compensation the value of the land unenhanced by the scheme ... I do not think that the single possible purchaser that has obtained parliamentary powers can be made to pay a price based on special suitability merely by reason of the fact that it was easy to foresee that the situation of the land would lead to compulsory powers being some day obtained to purchase it.

In this case land was again being acquired for a reservoir and the Court of Appeal followed the earlier cases in permitting account to be taken of special adaptability for storage of water and leaving the question of possible demand and competition for that purpose to the arbitrator. Although in 1908 the possibility of rival public authorities desirous of competing for such land was more unreal than 30 years earlier, the court refused to interfere with the arbitrator's award to the extent that he did consider there existed a possibility of more than one undertaking desiring to supply water in the district.

The *Lucas* case was approved by the Privy Council in *Cedar Rapids Manufacturing and Power Company* v *Lacoste* [1914]. In this case the respondent owned two islands in the rapids, the great value of which was their character and position to any person desiring to develop water power. In allowing an appeal against an award of compensation based on the value of the islands as proportional parts of the whole undertaking, a member of the Board, Lord Dunedin, confirmed, yet again, the principle that the value to be paid for was the value to the owner as it existed at the date of the taking, not the value to the taker, and, therefore, the value was not a proportionate part of the assumed value of the whole undertaking to develop water power as intended by the appellants. It was merely the price, enhanced above the bare value because of the land's special suitability, and tested by an imaginary market which would have ruled had the land been exposed for sale before any undertakers had secured the powers, or acquired the other subjects which made the undertaking as a whole a realised possibility.

3. Betterment

Betterment can be defined as 'the enhancement in the value of land resulting from the actions or decisions of central or local government or by a statutory body, or from the expectations of such actions or decisions': *The Land Problem – A Fresh Approach –* RICS 1975. The fact that schemes of promoters and undertakers may increase the value of land in the neighbourhood by virtue of their advantages and benefits has long been appreciated and the recoupment of that increased value, or betterment, occasionally legislated for. The Act for the Rebuilding of London 1667 (after the Great Fire) provided that where streets were widened or new streets laid out, the owners of sites that benefited were required to pay that benefit to the City Corporation. But the Lands Clauses Act made no provision for recoupment and the problem for arbitrators, in applying the principle of assessing a price which was compensation for an expropriated owner's loss, was whether to deduct any gain which an owner might realise because a scheme caused some of his land, which was not being acquired, to increase in value.

In *South Eastern Railway* v *London County Council* [1915] part of the railway company's land was being acquired to widen the Strand, and the remaining land was substantially increased in value as a consequence. The judgment of Eve J was upheld in the Court of Appeal. He clearly saw that if a deduction was made:

> ... it would be calculated to work injustice in that a vendor compelled to sell, and who the Legislature intended should be compensated for being compelled to sell, might have to accept from the undertakers a price far less than he would have obtained from any other purchaser, and out of all proportion to the true value of the land had it been ascertained

without reference to the fortuitous circumstances of his being also interested in the contiguous land.

Lord Cozens-Hardy MR and Warrington LJ in the Court of Appeal both agreed that there was no provision in the enabling Act for taking betterment into consideration. No cases were referred to in either of their judgments, but Eve J in the court below stated certain propositions which he regarded as established by authorities binding on him. These included:

(1) The value to be ascertained is the value to the vendor, not its value to the purchaser; (2) in fixing the value to the vendor all restrictions imposed on the user and enjoyment of the land in his lands are to be taken into account, but the possibility of such restrictions being modified or removed for his benefit is not to be overlooked; (3) market price is not a conclusive test of real value; (4) increase in value consequent on the execution of the undertaking for or in connection with which the purchase is made must be disregarded; (5) the value to be ascertained is the price to be paid for the land with all its potentialities and with all the use made of it by the vendor.

These propositions substantiate the principles of compensation so far discussed. In the event, none of these propositions had any relevance to the case before Eve J; he found no authority which established the principle of deducting any enhanced value due to betterment and declined to establish such a proposition himself. (What is of interest at this stage is that although the restatement of these propositions must properly be regarded as *obiter*, it was to be particularly relied upon by the Privy Council in the notorious *Pointe Gourde* case: see p223.)

Eve J's propositions reflect the principles of compensation established by valuers and the courts by the First World War. They can be summarised as follows:

(a) the expropriated owner should be compensated for the loss that resulted from the expropriation;
(b) the owner's loss was the value of the expropriated land to him, not the value to the purchaser with compulsory powers;
(c) if the land had an increased value for some potential use or development, this could have been included, but if the potential was due to special suitability or adaptability for the very purpose the acquiring authority required the land, this had to be disregarded, unless there was some rival demand for that purpose; this was because the value to be ascertained

was the value to the owner, not the value to the acquiring authority;

(d) betterment to any retained land could not be set off against the compensation;

(e) the market value would usually, but not invariably, be the value of the land to the owner.

If there was one principle underlying these, it was that the compensation to be ascertained for the land was the value to the owner.

4. *The change to market value*

A mass of evidence was given to the Scott Committee that reported in 1918; this convinced its members that in practice there was excessive valuation for compensation purposes and the owner was too often given the benefit of the doubt. The committee recommended that the price to be paid should be defined as the 'market value as between a willing seller and a willing buyer'. In predicating market value, rather than value to the owner, as the proper basis for compensation, the committee did not, and probably could not, foresee the consequences in the decades of local authority acquisitions that were to follow and the introduction of planning controls; an owner's loss may well have been the market value of the land at the time, but the market value was not necessarily his loss in all circumstances. This paradox is central to the contemporary difficulty in dealing with the effect on market values of acquiring authorities' schemes and the application of what is known as the *Pointe Gourde* principle. The committee made no recommendation as to how market value was to be established when affected by betterment (an increase in values) or by its counterpart, worsenment (a decrease in values); up to 1918 these value influences had not become as significant as they are today. The following example will indicate the problem in using market value as a basis for compensation instead of value to the owner.

Blackacre is agricultural land and has potential for residential development by reason of its proximity to roads, other development and services; planning permission is not forthcoming only because Blackacre is to be acquired for a highway improvement scheme. If planning permission could have been expected, the value of Blackacre is assumed to be £5,000. The present market value is assumed to be £1,000; knowledge of the proposed highway improvement deters potential purchasers who may be prepared to pay no more than its value for agricultural purposes, if that.

At the moment of acquisition the market value is only £1,000, but the owner's loss is a further £4,000, to give him the value he could have expected to obtain but for the highway scheme. We shall see later that, today, statutory rules and some judicial principles may avoid these influences on market values.

The market value basis has presented further problems in the era since regulatory development control commenced following the Town and Country Planning Act 1947. In recommending market value, the Committee accepted as logical that market value would reflect any value the land had for some potential use or development. But since July 1948 the development of land or buildings requires planning permission and this raises the question as to whether the right to develop land is part of the proprietary rights of ownership of land that should be compensated upon the land's compulsory acquisition. Between 1948 and 1953, the right to develop was, in effect, nationalised; if planning permission was obtained, the value of it was payable by way of a development charge, and if land was compulsorily acquired, then the compensation did not include anything for the potential the land might have had for development. This last point was quite logical; if no right to develop existed, it had already been taken away from owners by the 1947 Act, and it need not be compensated when the land was acquired. The development charge was abolished in 1953. The effect of this was that market value of land would thereafter reflect any potential land might have; the existence or expectation of planning permission and the right to develop were then factors that possible purchasers might pay extra for. However, the right to develop land without permission was not restored to land owners, and so compensation for the compulsory acquisition of land still did not include the value of any such rights.

This basis of compensation was, in principle, correct; the right to develop land without planning permission was no longer part of the rights of landownership; it need not be paid for under the compulsory acquisition of the land. The case of *Belfast Corpn v OD Cars Ltd* [1960] HL concerned the legality of legislation in Northern Ireland that took away development rights without compensation. The House of Lords said that the right to develop land was not property. But the principle was inequitable once the development charge, the payment for the value of a planning permission, was abolished as market value then reflected the existence or possibility of planning permission but the compensation did not. The Town and Country Planning Act 1959 sought to remove this inequity by providing that market value could thereafter reflect the value of any existing planning permission. In addition, it provided a number of assumptions as to planning permission that could be made. The purpose of these assumptions was to establish what planning permission the owner of land might have obtained were his land not being compulsorily acquired.

With the restoration of the right to include potential or development value in 1959, betterment caused by decisions and activities of public authorities began to have a more profound influence on market values than ever before. This was anticipated in 1959 and certain rules were enacted to ensure that in assessing market value certain increases or decreases in value caused by development or the prospect of development were to be disregarded if they were due to the scheme under which the acquiring authority was purchasing and, but for that scheme, such development would have been unlikely. The new rules defined with particularity the scheme. Before 1959 there were no statutory rules for excluding the effects of betterment on market value (these were, of course, not needed between 1948–1959 as potential or development value could not be compensated for anyway), nor were there any judicial principles as the *South Eastern Railway* v *London County Council* case confirmed: see p163. It is true that following the *Ossalinsky* case, any potential value the land has because of some special suitability or adaptability for the purpose the acquiring authority require the land must be ignored. This is because any increased value due to the acquiring authority's need for the land is excluded. But this rule did not exclude any increased value caused by the acquiring authority's scheme: the latter is strictly betterment. If a scheme of an acquiring authority causes betterment to land values, the market value of land both within and outside the scheme area may be increased; thus, even if a particular plot of land within a scheme is not compulsorily acquired, its market value will still be affected by betterment. It is important to see the distinction between increased value of a particular plot of land *to* a scheme (which of course disappears if the plot is not acquired) and increased value caused *by* a scheme, because the latter increase is a real increase in market value that will be payable unless precluded by rules to exclude such betterment. We shall see later that the courts failed to make this distinction when the *Pointe Gourde* case was decided and in that case developed a new principle to disregard certain betterment not otherwise disregarded by the statutory rules.

5. Claimant entitled to market value for land, but value to owner for other losses

The recommendation of the Scott Committee, that market value should be the basis of compensation for the acquisition of 'land', was enacted by the Acquisition of Land (Assessment of Compensation) Act 1919: see now rule 2 of section 5, Land Compensation Act 1961. The statutory definition of market value for land does not apply to other items of compensation such as for disturbance. If a claimant is claiming loss of goodwill, the proper basis is the value of the claimant, not its market value: *Afzal* v *Rochdale Metropolitan Borough Council* [1980] LT.

In *Horn* v *Sunderland Corpn* [1941] CA Scott LJ said that an owner compelled to sell is entitled to compensation:

> ... the right to be put, so far as money can do it, in the same position as if his land had not been taken from him. In other words, he gains the right to receive a money payment not less than the loss imposed on him in the public interest, but, on the other, no greater.

These words refer to the position of the law before compensation for 'land' was defined as market value in 1919. While they correctly state the entitlement to disturbance compensation – they are quite inappropriate in the case of compensation for 'land' – an owner is entitled to the market value for land, and if he suffers a greater or lesser loss than this in respect of his 'land', that is irrelevant. However, other losses remain recoverable as disturbance compensation as part of the single claim for compensation: see *Hughes* v *Doncaster Metropolitan Borough Council* HL [1991] and *Director of Buildings and Lands* v *Shun Fung Ironworks Ltd* [1995].

6. Case against market value

As compensation for the taking of land, market value has many advantages. It satisfies criteria of fairness and efficiency: the claimant obtains a sum of money that he can use to purchase comparable substitute property, and compensation assessment is carried out by an existing profession of valuers using market data. But market value will not always equal a claimant's loss.

Hobbs (Quarries) Ltd v *Somerset County Council* [1975] illustrates the difference between loss to the owner and market value, in the context of a compensation claim following the revocation of a planning permission for the working and winning of limestone from the claimant's quarry. The depreciation of the market value of the quarry was agreed at £72,000; the loss of profits the claimant was expected to earn was £250,000 (allowing for deferment). The members of the Lands Tribunal said:

> We see some force in the argument that the loss to the claimants cannot be more than the depreciation in the market value. That argument, however, presupposes that there was another quarry available to be bought at market value which could serve the claimant's purposes and provide them with an equal profit: but there was no evidence to that effect. Thus it is clear that the claimants have been deprived of the profits they would have earned ...

Another illustration can be given. A veterinary surgeon buys a large house for £40,000, which he adapts and extends for his professional requirements at a cost of £10,000: the premises are then compulsorily purchased. The owner's loss is £50,000, but the adaptations and extension may add very little to the market value of £40,000 because they are only suitable if the premises are used for a veterinary surgery. The market value may reflect the inclinations of a wider class of buyers for whom the special adaptations are of no use: market value does not necessarily reflect the seller's expenditure on the property being sold – what may be called non-marketable improvements.

The limitations of market value were considered by Forbes J in *Reynolds* v *Phoenix Assurance Co Ltd* [1978]. After referring to the classic statement of Scott LJ in *Horn* v *Sunderland Corporation* [1941], that an owner compelled to sell is entitled to compensation – the right to be put as far as money can do it in the same position as if his land had not been taken from him, Forbes J said:

> But these are all broad principles – you are not to enrich or impoverish: the difficulty lies in deciding whether the award of a particular sum amounts to enrichment or impoverishment. This question cannot depend in my view on an automatic or inevitable assumption that market value is the appropriate measure of the loss. Indeed in many, perhaps most cases, market value seems singularly inept, as its choice subsumes the proposition that the assured can be forced to go into the market (if there is one) and buy a replacement. But buildings are not like tons of coffee or bales of cloth or other commodities unless perhaps

the owner is one who deals in real property. To force an owner who is not a property dealer to accept market value if he has no desire to go to market seems to me a conclusion to which one should not easily arrive.

11.6 The present statutory entitlement to compensation and the basic rules of valuation

This chapter has so far considered the development of the principles of compensation. An understanding of these principles is sometimes helpful as many of the older cases are still referred to by the courts today. The rest of this chapter is concerned with the present statutory entitlement to compensation, the basic rules and certain other preliminary matters.

1. The entitlement to compensation

Certain provisions of the Lands Clauses Act 1845 have now been enacted in the Compulsory Purchase Act 1965. The 1965 Act applies whenever the acquisition procedure is under the Acquisition of Land Act 1981 and this is usually the case with acquisitions by local authorities, central government and other public authorities.

Section 63 of the 1845 Act appears with slight textual changes as section 7 of the Compulsory Purchase Act 1965 as follows:

> in assessing the compensation to be paid by the acquiring authority under this Act regard shall be had not only to the value of the land to be purchased by the acquiring authority, but also to the damage, if any, to be sustained by the owner of the land by reason of the severing of the land purchased from the other land of the owner, or otherwise injuriously affecting that other land by the exercise of the powers conferred ...

The owner of an interest in land being compulsorily purchased is therefore entitled to the value of his land and, where he retains some land held with the land to be acquired and this retained land is depreciated in value, he is entitled to be compensated for this depreciation whether it be caused by the severance of the two parts of his land or the injurious affection to the retained land. Although this section does not mention it, an owner will be entitled to be compensated for his losses, above the value of the land being compulsorily purchased, that are a consequence of being compelled to vacate the land: this compensation is called disturbance. These rights to compensation and certain other payments are dealt with in succeeding chapters as follows:

(a) Compensation for land acquired:
   Market value: Chapter 12
   Reinstatement and special cases: Chapter 16
(b) Compensation for severance and or injurious affection where part of a claimant's land acquired: Chapter 15
(c) Compensation for disturbance: Chapter 17
(d) Other payments:
   Legal costs and other fees
   Home loss payment   } Chapter 18
   Disturbance payments

In *Landlink Two Ltd* v *Sevenoaks District Council* [1985] LT, a submission was made on the part of the authority that the claimant had acquired the subject property after possession had been taken of part required for a road scheme, and that as they must have paid a price to reflect the compulsory acquisition, they had received 'money's worth' and no compensation was due. This was rejected by the Tribunal: see also *Ravenseft Properties* v *Hillingdon London Borough Council* [1968].

These statutory rights to compensation for the acquisition of land can be lost if no reference is made to the Lands Tribunal within a six-year limitation period: see Chapter 10.

2. The basic rules of valuation

The recommendations of the 1918 committee were enacted in the Acquisition of Land (Assessment of Compensation) Act 1919 as six basic rules of valuation. These rules, and rules for making assumptions as to planning permission and for dealing with betterment are now found in the Land Compensation Act 1961.

In addition to these statutory rules for valuation, there are many judicial decisions which have interpreted these rules. The cases considered at the beginning of this chapter remain important as they are cases on the interpretation of the word 'value' used in the Lands Clauses Act 1845 and now enacted in the Compulsory Purchase Act 1965. These rules will be considered in detail in the succeeding chapters.

11.7 Persons entitled to compensation

It will be recalled that a notice to treat must be served on all persons interested in, or having power to sell and convey the land to be compulsorily acquired. In practice this will include the freeholder, an owner of a possessory title (*Perry* v *Clissold* [1907]), and the owners of any leasehold interests in the land. Such persons have proprietary interests in the land, they are bound to convey those interests to the acquiring authority, and they are therefore entitled to compensation by virtue of section 7 of the 1965 Act. However, certain tenants and the owners of other interests present special problems.

1. Tenants

We have seen that although all tenants may be served with a notice to treat, where a tenant has no greater interest in the land than as tenant for a year or from year to year (e.g. weekly, monthly, yearly or an unexpired term of less than a year), and is required to give up possession by notice of entry before the expiration of his term, he is entitled to compensation under section 20 and not section 7 of the 1965 Act.

Even if a tenant has been served with a notice to treat, and his term expires before the authority requires possession, he will have no interest to give up and will not be entitled to any compensation: *Holloway* v *Dover Corporation* [1960]. Similarly, a tenant under a lease containing a proviso for determination upon a compulsory acquisition will not have a compensatable interest: *Murray Bookmakers Ltd* v *Glasgow District Council* [1979]. A tenant who takes a tenancy after notice to treat has been served in respect of the lessor's interest may also go without compensation: Lord Romilly MR in *Re Marylebone Improvement Act, ex parte Edwards* [1871] said:

> I am of opinion that the owner's power of dealing with his property is concluded when the notice to treat is served, and that a lease granted subsequently to that period to a tenant cannot properly be compensated for.

However, to provide some compensation to a person displaced from land of which he had lawful possession (as a tenant at will, or a tenant holding over) but no compensatable interest, section 37 of the Land Compensation Act 1973 requires the authority to make a 'disturbance payment': see generally Chapter 18.

Where a lessee was served with a notice to treat some two and half years before the expiration of a 14-year lease, and then served with a notice of entry that took effect some six months before the expiration, it was held by the Lands Tribunal in *Runcorn Association Football Club* v *Warrington and Runcorn Dev Corpn* [1982] that the basis of compensation was as a lessee under section 7 rather than as a short tenancy under section 20 of the Compulsory Purchase Act

1965. It was the date of the notice to treat that determined the compensation basis. The lessee football club were therefore entitled to compensation on the basis of equivalent reinstatement under rule 5 of section 5, 1961 Act: see Chapter 16.

2. Mortgagees

A mortgagee has an interest in land and he is entitled to a notice to treat and to compensation: the special procedures are explained in Chapter 21. But, in practice, the compensation for the value of the land may be paid to the mortgagor, leaving him to redeem the mortgage before conveyance to the authority. In *Provincial Building Society* v *Hammersmith and Fulham* [1982], the freeholders let the mortgaged house in breach of a covenant in the mortgage and had then disappeared. The building society obtained a court order for possession against the tenants, but the house was then first made subject to a housing control order (under which the local authority takes over the owner's powers) and later compulsorily purchased. At the date of entry, the control order ceased, and the Lands Tribunal decided that the mortgagee claimant could at that time, but for the compulsory purchase, have obtained possession: compensation to the mortgagee was therefore on vacant possession basis.

3. Easements and restrictive covenants

The acquiring authority may serve notice to treat on the owner of Blackacre but the owners of adjoining land, not being acquired, may have the benefit of easements or restrictive covenants over Blackacre. If these rights are interfered with by the acquiring authority using its powers, for example by the construction of a road authorised by statutory powers, the owners of these interests and rights have a right to claim compensation under section 10 of the Compulsory Purchase Act 1965 to the extent that their lands are injuriously affected: see Chapter 23. For the effect of these rights, see also Chapter 8.

4. Licences

An owner of land may give permission to another person to use or occupy his land for some purpose. This will not usually confer any interest in the land to the licensee and no compensation is payable under the Compulsory Purchase Act 1965.

To this general rule there would appear to be two exceptions. Section 37 of the Land Compensation Act 1973 permits a 'disturbance payment' to persons displaced from land. No person is entitled to this payment unless he is in lawful possession of the land from which he is displaced, and he has no interest in the land which entitles him to compensation under any other provision: section 37(2). The use of the term lawful possession is probably not intended to mean possession of an estate or interest in the land (which would be compensatable) but lawful occupation. The claim is limited to the costs of being disturbed: see Chapter 18.

The second exception concerns the licensee whose licence is irrevocable and which the courts will protect against revocation. This arises where an owner has permitted another to use or occupy his land, and it would be unjust and inequitable to allow him to revoke the licence and remove the licensee. A court may thus exercise its equitable jurisdiction and protect the licensee by imposing a constructive trust; the licensee has an equitable interest under that trust, and is entitled to compensation: consider the case of *DHN Food Distributors Ltd* v *Tower Hamlets London Borough Council* [1976] CA, where there were special facts as the occupier controlled the owner.

A common problem in practice is where business property is owned by an individual who trades through a limited liability company; the company having no formal legal interest in the property. The company may recover compensation as a licensee under an irrevocable licence: see the *DHN* case above. See also *Wrexham Maelor Borough Council* v *MacDougall* [1993] for the general approach to this problem: see p270.

11.8 Date of valuation or assessment of compensation

Although an acquiring authority may serve a notice to treat, it may be some months or even years before they require possession of the land. During periods of rising land values it is important to know the correct date for making a valuation or calculating items for the compensation assessment. As the statutes do not stipulate these dates as such, most of the law is found in decisions of the courts. What follows is an explanation of the law in relation to a compulsory purchase; the position where there is an agreement is explained in Chapter 6.

1. The old rule

Penny v *Penny* [1868]

The unexpired portion of a lease held by an executor was compulsorily acquired and both the executor and beneficiaries under the will submitted claims for their respective interests. The beneficiaries were also the tenants and were paying a very low rent for the lease to the executor in accordance with the terms of the will. The executor's interest in the reversion was therefore of little value but the value of the unexpired term to the acquiring authority was much greater as it, after acquisition, could obtain a full improved rent. In the course of his judgment Page-Wood V-C said:

> It is not the interest which has been acquired by the Board that has to be estimated, but the value of the interest taken from the person with whom the Board deals...The scheme of the Act I take to be this: that every man's interest shall be valued, *rebus sic stantibus*, just as it occurs at the very moment when the notice to treat was given. Any difference in the result which is due to the accident of the property being acquired by a public body is not to be thrown into the compensation fund.

For a century these words were regarded as authority for making the valuation of the interest to be acquired at the date of notice to treat. Although this has now been changed, the case is still good authority for considering the date of the notice to treat as the date for ascertaining the interests which will later be valued; although the reader is referred to the discussion on p88 as to the effect of a notice to treat. The interest of the executor being acquired was, at the date of the notice to treat, a reversionary interest to a lease at a low rent; the fact that the interest in the hands of the acquiring authority was not subject to the lease at a low rent was irrelevant.

2. The new rule

Birmingham Corporation v *West Midlands Baptist (Trust) Association* [1970] HL

Notice to treat was deemed to have been served on the Association, the owners of 'The People's Chapel', on August 14 1947. It was agreed that the claimants should have the cost of reinstating the chapel, instead of market value of the premises, under rule (5) of the six basic rules of valuation (see Chapter 16), and that the cost of reinstating at the date of notice to treat was accepted as £50,025. But reinstatement did not become possible until April 30 1961 at which date the cost of reinstatement was £89,575.

In this case the House of Lords considered the case of *Penny* v *Penny* and the practice of assessing compensation at the date of notice to treat that had followed. Lord Morris explained the authority the case had when he said:

> the whole point of the decision in that case was that in valuing the leasehold interest of the executor full regard had to be paid to the fact that the [beneficiaries'] rights undoubtedly existed and that because they existed the value of the interest of the executor was depreciated. In my view, the case is no sort of authority for the proposition that a notice to treat is so far binding that it always determines the time by reference to which an interest being acquired is to be valued.

He then gives an example to confirm his view:

> A case may be supposed where land subject to a lease is being acquired. Suppose that notices to treat are served on the owner and on a lessee whose lease has two years to run, and suppose that nothing is done for a period of three years but that compensation is then to be assessed by the Lands Tribunal. In my view, the lessee would have no claim then to receive compensation.

Lord Morris then said that he considered the date by reference to which the value of land should be assessed under rule (2) is the date when the value is being agreed or is being assessed by the Lands Tribunal or, if it is earlier, the date when possession was taken. A majority of the House of Lords agreed with this and decided that in the case before them the appropriate date under rule (5) for assessing the cost of reinstatement is the date when in all the circumstances the claimant can reasonably begin replacement. The West Midlands Baptist Association were therefore entitled to £89,575.

(a) Date of agreement

If compensation is agreed, that agreement and the notice to treat are regarded as a binding contract which can be enforced by the courts (*Harding* v *Metropolitan Railway Co* [1872]). The date of the agreement as to compensation will therefore be ascertained in accordance with the ordinary rules of contract; if one party makes an unconditional offer to pay or to accept a certain sum of compensation, an agreement will arise when the other party communicates his acceptance of that sum to the first party.

In *Munton* v *Greater London Council* [1976] CA it was held that an offer of a compensation figure 'subject to contract' was not a binding agreement, and similarly in *Duttons Breweries Ltd* v *Leeds City Council* [1982] where the town clerk accepted a figure for compensation 'subject to a contract to be approved by me'. The claimants could therefore obtain the value of their respective properties at a later date of entry.

(b) Date of possession

In *Buckingham Street Investments Ltd* v *Greater London Council* [1975] the acquiring authority was considered to have taken possession when it sent officers to padlock the doors. This was an act amounting to entry upon and taking possession of the premises and, as it occurred some days after the tenants had vacated, the landlord successfully claimed that at the date of possession the premises were vacant and had to be valued on that basis.

However, if an acquiring authority rehouses a tenant of residential accommodation under its statutory obligation in section 39 of the Land Compensation Act 1973, and the premises at the date of the notice to treat were subject to a tenancy, then by virtue of section 50(2) of the same Act, for the purpose of determining the date by reference to which compensation is to be assessed, the acquiring authority is deemed to have taken possession on the date on which the tenant gives up possession to be rehoused. On that date the premises will still be tenanted and must be valued on that basis. Though presumably if the tenant leaves before entry by the acquiring authority for any other reason, the premises must be regarded as vacant at the date of entry.

In *Chilton* v *Telford Development Corpn* [1987] the Court of Appeal decided that where a notice of entry is served, and physical entry of the land covered by that notice is effected in stages, there is lawful entry of all of the land covered by the notice of entry on the date when physical entry is taken of the first part of the land. Although that was a decision in relation to the running of interest, there is no reason why it should not also be applied in determining the date of entry for valuation purposes.

If the general vesting declaration procedure is used in place of the conventional notice to treat, the title to the land and a right to enter upon and take possession passes to the acquiring authority on the date of vesting: section 8, Compulsory Purchase (Vesting Declarations) Act 1981. The acquiring authority is then liable to pay compensation as if it had entered following a notice to enter. The date of vesting is therefore the date of valuation: *Hussain* v *Oldham Metropolitan Borough Council* [1981] LT. Interest on unpaid compensation will therefore run from this date: *Birrell Ltd* v *City of Edinburgh District Council* [1982].

One effect of the rule that the date of valuation is the earlier of the date of agreement, or date of possession, rather than the date of the notice to treat, is that any factors that influence land values after the notice to treat will have to be taken into account. Although the claimant will be happy if land values rise, he may be less so if the value of his property falls because it is vandalised before compensation can be agreed. In *Lewars* v *Greater London Council* [1974] the Tribunal said that a vandalised house (which would cost £4,665 to repair) must be valued in the actual state in which it was at the valuation date. (It may be possible to argue that vandalism is due to the scheme of the authority – see the *Pointe Gourde* principle on p223).

(c) *Date when reference to the Lands Tribunal*
In *W & S (Long Eaton) Ltd* v *Derbyshire County Council* [1975] the Court of Appeal considered they were bound by the *Birmingham Corporation* case and that the date of valuation, when the compensation is to be assessed by the Lands Tribunal, is the date of the award, this being the last day of the hearing before the Tribunal.

Where there is an appeal to the Court of Appeal, and the case is then remitted to the Tribunal, the date of the original hearing before the Tribunal is the date of valuation: *Hoveringham Gravels Ltd* v *Chiltern District Council* [1979] LT.

3. *The relevant date for considering surrounding circumstances*

Although the *West Midland Baptist* case decided the date by reference to which land values fall to be assessed, there has remained some doubt as to whether the date of the notice to treat is still the relevant date for identifying the interest to be valued and the other relevant circumstances to be considered. The question is not free from doubt. Thus, the House of Lords decided in *Rugby*

Joint Water Board v *Foottit* [1973] that if the scheme of the acquiring authority changes the nature of the interest of a claimant, for example from a reversion to a protected tenancy, to a reversion to an unprotected tenancy, the change in the interest does not have to be disregarded under the *Pointe Gourde* principle: see Chapter 14 below. This then begs the question as to whether the nature of the interest to be valued is fixed at the date of the notice to treat.

There are three matters that may affect the value of property: the nature of the interest of the claimant (e.g. whether an interest in possession or subject to a tenancy); the planning background; and the condition of the property to be valued. The relevant date for identifying the planning background is considered in Chapter 13 below in connection with the statutory planning assumptions. It would appear that any change in the condition of the property will be taken into account at the valuation date: see *Gately* v *Central Lancashire New Town Development Corporation* [1984] and *Blackadder* v *Grampian Regional Council* [1992].

Section 4 of the Acquisition of Land Act 1981 provides that the Lands Tribunal shall not take into account any interest in land, or any enhancement of the value of any interest in land, by reason of any building erected, work done or improvement or alteration made, whether on the land purchased or any other land with which the claimant is (or was) directly or indirectly concerned, if the Lands Tribunal is satisfied that the creation of the interest, the erection of the building, the doing of the work, the making of the improvement or the alteration, as the case may be, was not reasonably necessary and was undertaken with a view to obtaining compensation or increased compensation. This particular provision does prevent a claimant from unnecessarily creating a new interest or carrying out works 'with a view to obtaining compensation or increased compensation'. It probably does not apply until a compensation right has arisen, such as following the service of a notice to treat. For otherwise an owner might be inhibited from doing work etc. in circumstances where his land might never be acquired.

The remaining matter is whether the notice to treat fixes the date for identifying the nature of the interest to be valued. This was fully considered in Chapter 7 above.

Chapter 12

Compensation for Land Acquired: Market Value

Introduction
The market value rules
Development and hope value
Marriage and ransom value
The *Stokes* principle
Lotting
Special types of properties

12.1 Introduction

This chapter is concerned with the rules for the assessment of compensation for land acquired where the market value is used: this is the normal basis unless it has been agreed that an owner shall be paid the costs of his reinstatement or he comes within one of the special cases dealt with in Chapter 16.

The use of market value in preference to some other basis for assessing compensation presents special problems. If Blackacre is being purchased under compulsory purchase powers, it may no longer have any market value: the existence of the compulsory purchase order or the special Act may destroy demand, and once a valid notice to treat has been served and cannot be withdrawn, realistically the owner has only one purchaser, the acquiring authority, to whom he is bound to sell.

The statutory and judicial rules concerning market value seek to establish a price that the owner of Blackacre would have obtained had there been no compulsory purchase. This is done in a number of ways that disregard the fact that the land is being compulsorily purchased. First, the principal rule directs that the price to be paid is the value of the land if sold in the open market by a willing seller: rule (2). Second, if the land could have been developed, one or more planning permission assumptions can be made to determine what development might have been permitted: see Chapter 13.

Third, the effect on land values of the scheme or proposals underlying the compulsory purchase is disregarded by either a statutory rule (section 6 of the Land Compensation Act 1961) or a judicial rule (the *Pointe Gourde* principle). Finally, any depreciation in the value of land due to the prospect of compulsory purchase is to be disregarded: section 9 of the Land Compensation Act 1961. The effect of the scheme is considered in Chapter 14.

12.2 The market value rules

The first four of the six basic rules of valuation in section 5 of the Land Compensation Act 1961 concern market value, and of these, rule (2) is the principal rule.

1. Rule (1)

'No allowance shall be made on account of the acquisition being compulsory'
Before this rule was originally enacted in 1919, it was common for valuers to add additional sums to the value of the land as a solatium to the owner who was being compulsorily acquired. However, rule (1) does not forbid the home loss payment that is payable under section 29 of the Land Compensation Act 1973: see Chapter 18.

2. Rule (2)

'The value of land shall, subject as hereinafter provided, be taken to be the amount which the land if sold in the open market by a willing seller might be expected to realise'
This rule replaces the original principle of 'value to owner' with a more objective definition of market value which applies to that element of a compensation claim which relates to land as such. A number of issues arise for discussion.

(a) Open market
Where land is being compulsorily acquired, there will be no sale 'in the open market'; the valuer must determine what price the land would fetch if put on the open market. In *Inland Revenue Commissioners* v *Clay & Buchanan* [1914], a case concerned with similar wording in the Finance Act 1910, it was said that 'open market includes a sale by auction, but is not

confined to that'. The point was made in that case that if land is to be assumed to be sold in the open market, it would be 'offered under conditions enabling every person desirous of purchasing to come in and make an offer'; full publicity to all facts likely to enhance the price would be given by the vendor.

The open market hypothesis must be applied to the property as it actually existed and not to some other property, even if in real life a vendor would have been likely to make some changes or improvements before putting it on the market: see *Buccleuch* v *Inland Revenue* [1967]. In *Lady Fox's Executors* v *Commissioners for Inland Revenue* [1994], Hoffmann LJ added to this as follows:

> In all other respects, the theme which runs through the authorities is that one assumes that the hypothetical vendor and purchaser did whatever reasonable people buying and selling such property would be likely to have done in real life. The hypothetical vendor is an anonymous but reasonable vendor, who goes about the sale as a prudent man of business, negotiating seriously without giving the impression of being either over-anxious or unduly reluctant. The hypothetical buyer is slightly less anonymous. He too is assumed to have behaved reasonably, making proper inquiries about the property and not appearing too eager to buy. But he also reflects reality in that he embodies whatever was actually the demand for that property at the relevant time. It cannot be too strongly emphasised that, although the sale is hypothetical, there is nothing hypothetical about the open market in which it is supposed to have taken place. The concept of the open market involves assuming that the whole world was free to bid, and then forming a view about what in those circumstances would in real life have been the best price reasonably obtainable.
>
> The practical nature of this exercise will usually mean that although in principle no one is excluded from consideration, most of the world will usually play no part in the calculation. The inquiry will often focus upon what a relatively small number of people would be likely to have paid. It may have to arrive at a figure within a range of prices which the evidence shows that various people would have been likely to pay, reflecting, for example, the fact that one person had a particular reason for paying a higher price than others, but taking into account, if appropriate, the possibility that through accident or whim he might not actually have bought. The valuation is thus a retrospective exercise in probabilities, wholly derived from the real world, but rarely committed to the proposition that a sale to a particular purchaser would definitely have happened.

(b) Willing seller

The meaning of a 'willing seller' was also considered in the *Clay & Buchanan* case: 'it does not mean a sale by a person willing to sell his property without reserve for any price he can obtain'. In *Raja Vyricherla Narayana Gajapatiraju v Revenue Divisional Officer, Vizagapatam (The Indian case)* [1939] Lord Romer said:

> The compensation must be determined, therefore, by reference to the price which a willing vendor might reasonably expect to obtain from a willing purchaser. The disinclination of the vendor to part with his land and the urgent necessity of the purchaser to buy must alike be disregarded. Neither must be considered as acting under compulsion. This is implied in the common saying that the value of the land is not to be estimated at its value to the purchaser. But this does not mean that the fact that some particular purchaser might desire the land more than others is to be disregarded. The wish of a particular purchaser, though not his compulsion, may always be taken into consideration for what it is worth.

A willing seller is not an anxious seller. In non-compulsory purchase transactions, a vendor is sometimes advised to wait for an improvement in market prices; in compulsory purchase the vendor is to be regarded as a 'willing seller' at the time of assessing compensation, and the price is assessed according to the state of the market at that time. It should be noted that the rule does not mention the requirement of a 'willing buyer'. This is entirely logical as, by definition, any buyer in the market is 'willing', and if there are no buyers, then this is merely evidence of no demand: should this be the case then there is the discretionary alternative basis of compensation (see Chapter 16 – Equivalent reinstatement).

In *FR Evans (Leeds) Ltd v English Electric Co Ltd* [1977] and *First Leisure Trading Ltd v Dorita Properties Ltd* [1991] the meaning of 'willing lessee' was considered in relation to the determination of the open market rental value of premises in circumstances where it was arguable that the subject premises would only be of interest to the sitting tenants – a monopoly position. A party to a hypothetical transaction who is to be regarded as 'willing' is neither reluctant nor importunate.

One assumes that the hypothetical vendor and purchaser would otherwise do whatever reasonable people buying and selling the subject property would be likely to do in real life:

see *Lady Fox's Executors* v *Commissioners of Inland Revenue* [1994].

In *Trocette Property Co* v *Greater London Council* [1974] the Court of Appeal said the willing seller is:

> a hypothetical character. There is no justification for attaching to him, so as to increase or reduce the assessment of compensation, any special characteristics. He is to be assumed to be willing to sell at the best price which he can reasonably get in the open market.

This echoes the *FR Evans* case (see above) where it was said that the actual attributes of an actual occupier must be disregarded in determining the open market rental value of premises in a rent review dispute, although it must be assumed that an actual transaction would take place.

In *Abbey Homesteads Group Ltd* v *Secretary of State for Transport* [1982], the member said that there was no justification for assuming that the hypothetical seller owns adjoining land that might be held with the land taken. This view can present problems where an authority is taking only part of a claimant's land. Where there is a marriage value in owning the two parts as one, a seller in the real world would be most reluctant to sell part of his land if this destroys some of the marriage value of the land he retains. By assuming that the willing seller may not necessarily own the retained land, it must follow that the price he would receive will only reflect some, and not all, of the marriage value (see further below).

(c) Willing buyer

The statutory definition of 'open market value', in rule (2), does not refer to a willing buyer. There are several obvious reasons for this. The first is that if the open market value concept is adopted, there must be a hypothetical seller willing to sell. But whether there would be a willing buyer and, if so, how many or how interested such buyers would be, are matters that are the characteristics of the open market at the relevant time. This was recognised in *The Indian* case [1939] (see above).

Hoare v *National Trust* [1999] illustrates an analogous situation that arises where an unusual property has to be valued for rating purposes. The case involved two historic houses owned by the National Trust. Because of the costs involved the only realistic 'willing tenant' would have been

the National Trust itself. But the rent that the Trust would
have been prepared to pay would have been nil.

(d) Land subject to restrictions and tenancies

It is important that when valuing land, any restrictions,
covenants or adverse rights are taken into account. In *Abbey
Homesteads (Developments) Ltd* v *Northamptonshire County
Council* [1992] CA, the subject land was the subject of a
reservation for school purposes in a planning agreement. The
court decided that the land must be valued, as subject to a
restrictive covenant, but the Lands Tribunal was entitled to
conclude on the evidence that in the no-scheme world there
was a high chance of discharging the restrictions under
section 84 of the Law of Property Act 1925. Where the
freehold is subject to leases and tenancies the freehold interest
must be valued having regard to the terms of any tenancy
agreement, and whether the tenancy is protected by social
legislation. In *Harris* v *Commissioners for Inland Revenue* [1961],
a case involving the valuation of land for taxation purposes,
it was held that in making any assumption about obtaining
vacant possession the valuer was to assume the maximum
difficulty in obtaining possession.

Where the freehold has a possible marriage value to any
leasehold interest, that must be taken into account: see **12.4
Marriage and ransom value**, below.

For the effect of the scheme on a leasehold interest, see
Chapter 14 below, and for the valuation of leasehold interests
see Chapter 19 below.

(e) Development value

We have already seen in Chapter 11 that potential value can
be taken into account; the assumptions as to planning
permission are considered in detail in Chapter 13. However,
it is arguable that where part of a claimant's land is being
taken, and that part has some development value, the *Horn*
principle (see p239) may preclude all or some part of a claim
for injurious affection to the claimant's retained: see *BP
Petroleum Developments Ltd* v *Ryder* [1987]. This is because the
valuations of the land acquired and for injurious affection to
the retained land must be consistent. If the valuation of the
land acquired assumes its development, either there may be
no injury to the retained land in that hypothesis, or there

would be injury which the claimant must be assumed to accept in order to obtain the higher development value.

3. Rule (3)

'The special suitability or adaptability of the land for any purpose shall not be taken into account if that purpose is a purpose to which it could be applied only in pursuance of statutory powers, or for which there is no market apart from [the special needs of a particular purchaser] the requirements of any authority possessing compulsory purchase powers'

When land has special suitability for any purpose, this rule will apply to disregard increases in the market value in the following circumstances; when that purpose needs statutory powers or where there is no market for that purpose except to meet the requirements of an authority possessing compulsory purchase powers: see (b) below. However, the words in rule (3) above in square brackets, which referred to the special needs of a particular purchaser were repealed by section 70 of the Planning and Compensation Act 1991 from September 25 1991: the rule therefore no longer applies to the second situation, however see (c) below.

(a) 'Special suitability or adaptability any purpose'

The meaning of this part of the rule was considered in Chapter 11 in connection with the problem of potential value of land.

In the case of *Pointe Gourde Quarrying Co Ltd* v *Sub-Intendent of Crown Lands* [1947] PC, the products of a quarry, namely limestone, had a special suitability to the acquiring authority (for building a naval base) which gave the quarry an enhanced value in their hands. Rule (3) could not be applied to exclude any enhanced value of land due to the 'purpose' to which its products (limestone) could be applied: the rule only applied to a 'purpose' to which the land could be applied: see p223 for a different point decided in this case.

Similarly in *Lambe* v *Secretary of State for War* [1955] (see above), the special suitability of the freehold interest to merge with the leasehold interest (and which enhanced the value of the freehold interest due to the marriage value) was not within rule (3): the rule only applies to the special suitability of the land for any purpose.

In *Batchelor* v *Kent County Council* [1990] the Court of Appeal decided that 'special suitability' did not mean the 'most suitable'.

In *Blandrent Investment Developments Ltd* v *British Gas Corporation* [1979] HL, it was accepted that the land being acquired had 'special suitability or adaptability' for the purpose of joint development with some adjoining land. In the event rule (3) did not apply for reasons given at (c) below.

In *Edmonstone* v *Central Regional Council* [1984], where planning permission was assumed for the purpose of the acquisition, a road depot, the Lands Tribunal for Scotland decided that the existence of a planning permission was not a physical quality of the land for the purpose of rule (3); the additional value it brought to the land therefore did not have to be disregarded.

In *Waters* v *Welsh Development Agency* [2001] the Lands Tribunal decided that an area of agricultural land did not have 'special suitability or adaptability' for the purpose of creating a wetland nature reserve; rule (3) therefore did not apply.

(b) *'a purpose to which it could be applied only in pursuance of statutory powers, or for which there is no market apart from ... the requirements of any authority possessing compulsory purchase powers'*

If the land is shown to have special suitability or adaptability for any purpose, that fact shall be disregarded if the purpose needs statutory powers or the only market for that special suitability or adaptability is created by the requirements of authorities with compulsory purchase powers. In Chapter 11, in the *Ossalinsky*, *Re Lucas* and *Cedar Rapids* cases, special suitability of the land was found to exist in each case, in two cases to build reservoirs and in the third to develop water power. It was held in these cases that the owner was entitled to any enhanced value if the valuer had evidence of a market for the special suitability. In the 19th century, water companies might compete for sites of special suitability for their purposes. Today rule (3) now clearly precludes any enhanced value in these circumstances. The rule was applied in *Livesey* v *CEGB* [1965], and the Tribunal excluded a substantial part of the claim based on the proposed use of the land as a power station.

In *Ozanne* v *Hertfordshire County Council* [1991], where land was taken to improve and provide a public highway access for a large development site, the acquiring authority argued that the replacement of an existing highway could only be achieved with statutory powers, namely, the powers to stop up a public highway. This fell within this part of rule (3) and any ransom value had to be ignored. The Lands Tribunal decided that statutory powers were not necessary for this purpose; accordingly the ransom value was not precluded by this part of rule (3). In finally dismissing the acquiring authority's appeal, the House of Lords decided that rule (3) had no application; the stopping up powers did not affect the land acquired and the reference to statutory powers in rule (3) is a reference to powers affecting the land to be acquired, not other land. It also said that the rule did not preclude any enhanced value due to a planning permission.

(c) *'a purpose ... for which there is no market apart from the special needs of a particular purchaser'*
It is generally accepted that these words were added to meet the circumstances that arose in the case of *Inland Revenue Commissioners* v *Clay & Buchanan* [1914]. This part of rule (3) was repealed by section 70 of the Planning and Compensation Act 1991. However, it remains applicable if any of the following events occurred before September 25 1991: (i) a non-ministerial compulsory purchase was made; (ii) in relation to a compulsory purchase order made by a minister, the notice of its making was published; (iii) in relation to a purchase notice, the planning decision; and (iv) in relation to a blight notice, the land becomes blighted within the meaning of Schedule 13 to the 1990 Act. In *Clay & Buchanan*, a house worth £750 as a private residence was bought by the owners of an adjoining nursing home for £1,000 to enable their premises to be extended. At the time of enacting the statutory rules in 1919 it was considered that a special price that could be obtained because of the necessities of the adjoining owner should be excluded in establishing market value.

It is this part of the rule which may exclude marriage or ransom value where the land being valued has a special suitability for any purpose. 'Any purpose' can include the 'marriage' to adjoining land and the joint development of both. Such circumstances arose in the *Blandrent* case (see above) and in *Barstow* v *Rothwell Urban District Council* [1970], but in both cases the rule was held not to apply as there was evidence of a market for the purpose for which the land had special suitability apart from the needs of the adjoining owner.

Front land may have special suitability for the purpose of providing access to back land which can then be developed. The land having this special suitability will have enhanced value to the owner of the back land, but whether there is a market for this purpose apart from his special needs will depend on the facts. In *Dicconson Holdings Ltd* v *St Helens Metropolitan Borough* [1979], the Lands Tribunal, by way of *obiter*, held that rule (3) will only preclude such enhanced value if there is an actual purchaser or an actual identifiable living person who has made an actual inflated bid forcing up the market value of the land.

The member in the *Dicconson* case referred to the earlier Tribunal decision of *Rathgar Property Co Ltd* v *Haringey London Borough Council* [1978]; there it was said that if other bidders can be found for land with special suitability for an access, a speculator as well as the owner of any back land, there would be more than one potential purchaser, and a normal market: rule (3) would not apply.

Lord Scarman in the House of Lords in *Blandrent* (see above) said that the application of rule (3) was really a question of evidence: if there was evidence of a market, the rule would not apply. In *Chapman, Lowry & Puttick Ltd* v *Chichester District Council* [1984] the authority was acquiring an access to housing land it already owned. It was agreed between the parties that if rule (3) applied to exclude the value of the access land for that purpose, its value was £200; if rule (3) did not apply, the land had a value of £25,000 because of its special suitability for the purpose of providing the access to the housing land. The member of the Tribunal decided that the needs of the acquiring authority to provide access to its site were not needs peculiar to itself. He thought it reasonable to take into account the needs of some hypothetical owner or developer of the rear land who would also have obtained planning permission to build houses: he would also need access. For that reason, that in the hypothetical market, others besides the acquiring authority had a need for this access the rule had no application.

4. Rule (4)

'Where the value of the land is increased by reason of the use thereof or of any premises thereon in a manner which could be restrained by any Court, or is contrary to law, or is detrimental to the health of the occupants of the premises or to the public health, the amount of that increase shall not be taken into account'

If development has been carried out in breach of planning consent, it may be said that the use of the land 'is contrary to law'. After 10 years, a use of land commenced without planning permission is immune from enforcement: see section 171B of the Town and Country Planning Act 1990. Until the expiration of this time-limit, a use will be unlawful. For a Tribunal case, see *British Electricity Authority* v *Cardiff Corpn* [1951].

Where, because of the scheme of the acquiring authority, a claimant abandoned use of his property for two years prior to the valuation date and was unable to obtain an established use certificate, rule (4) did not exclude compensation assessed on the basis that he had continued such use: see *Ullah* v *Leicester City Council* [1996].

In *Hughes* v *Doncaster Metropolitan Borough Council* [1991], the House of Lords decided that as rule (4) referred to the value of land, and 'value' referred to the total claim for compensation, land and other losses, rule (4) therefore applied to a claim for disturbance compensation. In the *Hughes* case, it was accepted that development which had become immune from enforcement proceedings under the town and country planning legislation cannot be said to be 'contrary to law', though it may not be 'lawful' within the planning legislation. Accordingly, in relation to compensation law, rule (4) only applies to disregard any enhanced value that is due to development that can be the subject of enforcement action.

Premises being used contrary to the overcrowding provisions of the Housing Acts, places of entertainment or hotels which do not satisfy rules regarding fire precautions and escape, places of work which do not satisfy the requirements of the Health and Safety at Work Act 1974, and property used for a purpose which causes a nuisance which could be restrained by an injunction are all examples where the rule may apply.

However, in *Bolton* v *North Dorset District Council* [1997] rule (4) did not apply to negate the value of land for motocross purposes because such purposes might constitute a statutory nuisance.

12.3 Development and hope value

Whenever market value reflects development value, this may be taken into account: see *R* v *Brown* [1867] considered in Chapter 11. The fact that there is no planning permission for any development is irrelevant if value in the open market reflects any 'hope value' that may exist in respect of the land being valued: it is market value that is payable. Evidence of sales of comparable land, or of the planning background, time-tabling of development and provision of roads and services which support the probability of planning permission being granted for development will be necessary to prove 'hope value'. In *Corrin and others (Trustees of Northampton Church Charities)* v *Northampton Borough Council* [1980], the Lands Tribunal accepted agreed evidence that the subject land had hope value for residential development and that a vendor would be unwilling to sell the land at a price which did not reflect this. Hope value was awarded notwithstanding that no planning permission existed for residential development, that the subject land was just outside the designated area of the new town of Northampton and that the local planning authority had issued a certificate that planning permission could not reasonably have been expected to be granted for residential development: see Chapter 13. However, following amendments made by the Planning and Compensation Act 1991 if a certificate is now issued stating that but for the compulsory acquisition planning permission would not have been granted, that must be taken into account: see section 14(3A) of the 1961 Act.

The question of development value raises two problems, both of which are explained in detail in Chapters 13 and 14. In many cases of compulsory purchase, the fact of impending acquisition will mean that no planning permission for development will be forthcoming; this problem is avoided by being able to make what are called statutory planning assumptions (see Chapter 13). Second, any development value attributable only to the scheme underlying the acquisition must be ignored (see Chapter 14).

12.4 Marriage and ransom value

If there is any evidence to suggest that the plot of land might fetch a higher price because of the possibility of combining it with an adjoining plot, or that a reversionary interest may be more valuable to the lessee than to other buyers, the higher value or 'marriage value' will be accepted as a factor in the market value:

1. Merging two interests

Lambe v *Secretary of State for War* [1955] CA

The Territorial Association were lessees of a house for a term expiring in 1990. The Secretary of State compulsorily acquired the freehold reversion expectant on the lease. (The lease would then merge with the freehold and certain restrictive covenants on the lessee would cease.) If the marriage value to the sitting tenant was ignored, the value of the reversion was agreed to be only £600, but the Court of Appeal accepted a valuation of £1,400 which took into account the marriage value to the tenant: 'the statutory basis of compensation laid down in Rule (2) is the value in the open market', that is 'the amount which the acquiring authority in a friendly negotiation would be willing to pay in acquiring a freehold interest for its purposes and as though no compulsory powers of acquisition had been obtained'.

The reference to a 'friendly negotiation' is derived from what is called the *Indian case*: *Vyricherla Narayana Gajapatiraju* v Revenue District Officer, Vizagapatam [1939].

In the *Lambe* case the acquiring authority so happened to be the sitting tenant and had to pay a price which it was considered a sitting tenant would have had to pay for the freehold: but if the acquiring authority had not been the sitting tenant and were merely acquiring the freehold reversion, the possibility of the sitting tenant paying more than other investors for the freehold can still be taken into account.

The *Lambe* case was applied in *Hearts of Oak Benefit Society* v *Lewisham Borough Council* [1979] LT where a number of freehold interests subject to long leases were acquired. Evidence was accepted that if the freehold interests were put on the market, the lessees might not be interested in purchasing.

The value of the property was agreed at £20,100 if the freehold and leasehold interests were merged, the value of the leasehold interest alone was said to be £8,750 and the freehold interests (excluding marriage value) to be £3,850. Without giving reasons, the Tribunal awarded £5,500 for the freehold interest to include an element for the large marriage value to the lessees had they been purchasers.

In the discussion on the marriage value of merging two interests, it has been assumed so far that the merging of the interests is a possibility which the market-place will recognise. In other words there are no known facts to show that a merger would not be likely. Obviously if there are facts known to bidders in the market to show that a merger of the interests will not take place, there will be little chance of the sale of one of the interests showing a marriage value. Thus, in *Trocette Property Co Ltd* v *Greater London Council* [1974] CA, where a lease with an unexpired term of 11 years was being acquired, it was held that the known fact that the GLC as freeholders would not have been interested in participating in any marriage value had to be accepted. The site was ripe for development, and a hypothetical freeholder would have been expected either to buy in the lease to bring forward the development, or to grant a new and longer lease to the lessees at a premium or higher rent to share in the development. However, the GLC would not have taken either course as they wanted the site for a road scheme.

This case must be contrasted with *Chapman, Lowry Puttick* v *Chichester District Council* [1984] where the Tribunal was dealing with the marriage of an access to an area of landlocked development land already owned by the authority. The member said that one should consider the needs of a hypothetical owner or developer rather than simply the needs of the actual owner in the real world. On that basis, the *Trocette* case presents difficulties. (In fact, in the *Trocette* case, the claimant lessees were able to recover the marriage value under a further rule – see p223.)

2. Merging two sites: ransom land

Marriage value may exist where two pieces of land are more valuable held in one ownership than the sum of the values of the two pieces held in different ownerships. This may arise because both parcels are necessary to enable development to take place, either as such, or because one piece is the 'key' to unlocking the development of the other. Potential purchasers in the open market for one of the parcels will pay a 'ransom value' to acquire such land subject to a discount for the risk in not achieving the 'marriage' of the two sites. An owner of one of the sites, who does not face that risk, can afford to dispense with that discount. In *Dicconson Holdings Ltd* v *St Helens Metropolitan Borough Council* [1979] LT 0.488 acres of land was being acquired following a purchase notice; it was accepted that this land would provide satisfactory access to residential development on 14 acres of rear land. This potential access land had a value in the open market above its intrinsic value; not only would the owner of the rear land be prepared to pay more than its intrinsic value, so would speculators with a view to reselling to the owner of the rear land.

Land may also have ransom value in the sense that land cannot be developed unless roads or infrastructure are provided, and further land is the most suitable and appropriate for the purpose. In the real world, anyone owning this further land has property with a ransom value in the market-place.

Where land has a marriage or ransom value, by reason of its geographical position, and that value would exist in the absence of the scheme of acquiring authority, it is a genuine market value for compensation purposes; see *Ozanne v Hertfordshire County Council* [1992] where the reference land was held in the 'no-scheme world' to have had a ransom value as soon as the prospect of development of land nearby became known, and the development of that development required highway improvements affecting the reference land.

It will be a question of fact in each case whether the land in question really is the 'key' that 'unlocks' the development value of some adjoining land. In *Laing Homes Ltd v Eastleigh Borough Council* [1979] LT, a claim for a marriage value of £1m was rejected because it was said that the potential development value of the adjoining land had already been released; planning permission for that other land had already been granted and it was not absolutely essential that the 'Laing's' land be acquired to provide access. It was also accepted by the Tribunal that rule (3) prevented any ransom value being paid because, on the facts, only 'particular purchasers' were interested. Later cases have not followed this decision and rule (3), in this particular application, has been repealed.

The taking of part of an area of land belonging to a single owner may of course destroy marriage value already in his hands. In *Salop County Council v Craddock* [1970] CA, where the claimant had received an offer to purchase his property at a price that reflected marriage value, Lord Denning said that the effect of the scheme of acquisition must be ignored, and the claimant should be entitled to that marriage value if there was adequate evidence that it represented the market value of the land. Although there is a separate claim for the depreciation in value of any retained land (see Chapter 13), the marriage value in the land taken has often been forgotten by claimants: see *Bolton Metropolitan Borough Council v Waterworth* [1981] CA and *Hoveringham Gravels Ltd v Chiltern District Council* [1977] CA. This is because the effect of severance may be to damage the value of the land taken rather than the land retained: a point long recognised in the United States, and belatedly in this country: see *Sams* [1982].

For a case involving cross-claims to ransom value where two potential developers are involved, see *Dingleside Development Co Ltd* v *Powys County Council* [1995].

12.5 The *Stokes* principle

If the land being acquired has development potential if a satisfactory access could be provided, market value will be the full development value less the estimated cost of acquiring additional land:

> *Stokes* v *Cambridge Corporation* [1961]
>
> Certain land owned by Stokes was compulsorily acquired for industrial development. For the purposes of valuing the land, it was assumed that Stokes had planning permission for industrial development (see Chapter 13 for statutory planning assumptions), but subject to a condition that satisfactory access be provided. There was no satisfactory access to this land; the only suitable access land was already owned by the acquiring authority. The fact that the acquiring authority was the owner of the access land had to be ignored; but it could be assumed that the owner of the access land might well be induced to sell as it would also enable development of further land of their own; the cost of acquiring the access land was considered to be one-third of the profit that would be realised by the development of Stokes' land.

In *BP Petroleum Developments Ltd* v *Ryder* [1987] Peter Gibson J considered the *Stokes* principle and thought that the Lands Tribunal must have treated the market as comprising more than one would-be developer and that bidders would be prepared to bid substantially more than the existing use value of the strip. It must be remembered that *Stokes* is merely a valuation approach; it is not a rule of law and therefore its application and any appropriate percentage depends on expert evidence. Thus, in *Batchelor* v *Kent County Council* [1992] the Tribunal decided that 15% was the appropriate proportion attributable to the land acquired under *Stokes*. The Court of Appeal decided that although the resulting figure was high, the *Stokes* principle is a principle of valuation and the Tribunal was entitled to decide that it was a useful starting point for valuation.

12.6 Lotting

The application of estate duty on scattered rural estates threw up a problem in the use of the market value concept as defined by section 7(5) of the Finance Act 1894: whether the price the property would fetch on the market was the aggregate of the prices which the several parts would have fetched if an estate was broken up and sold in suitable lots. In *Earl of Ellesmere* v *Commissioners of Inland Revenue* [1918] the High Court accepted as correct a determination of the open market value of a rural estate based upon the sale of its aggregate parts. This decision was applied in the *Buccleuch (Duke)* v *Inland Revenue Commissioners* [1967] where the Inland Revenue had valued the estates of the 10th Duke of Devonshire on the assumption that each estate would be lotted and each lot sold on the open market at the best price. In the House of Lords it was held that what had to be valued was the 'property' and the 'property' was not the whole estate but a unit for valuation purposes which would consist of easily identifiable natural units. The House of Lords accepted that the estates could be divided into 532 units, a natural division which would not have involved undue expenditure of time and effort, but it did not accept the revenue's more extreme proposition that the hypothetical vendor must be assumed to have divided up the estate into whatever units would have produced the best possible price. A further division of the 'natural units', requiring substantial further work, would not have been a valuation of the property as it actually was. The *Buccleuch* case was applied by the Lands Tribunal in *First Garden City Ltd* v *Letchworth Garden City Corporation* [1966] in relation to the very diverse assets of the Garden City. The Tribunal made a deduction in the market values for bulk and diversity.

In *Maori Trustee* v *Ministry of Works* [1959] some 91 acres of land were acquired, in respect of which, on the valuation date, there was no more than a paper plan of a proposal subdivision into lots. If ministerial approval had been obtained for a subdivision, and the subdivision carried out, the land would have been more valuable. The open market value on the valuation date could not reflect a subdivision that had not taken place, it could only reflect the potential for subdivision.

12.7 Special types of properties

It is not always possible to find comparable sales transactions for special types of property. Thus, in the case of petrol filling stations, valuers normally value such properties by reference to the throughput in gallons of petrol sold, as in *Telegraph Service Stations Ltd* v *Trafford Borough Council* [2000]. In the case of hotels and pubs, values are by reference to beds and barrels respectively.

Chapter 13

Statutory Planning Assumptions

Introduction
Planning assumptions: general
Assumptions not directly derived from development plans
Special assumptions derived from development plans
Certificate of appropriate alternative development
Compensation for additional development permitted after
    acquisition

13.1 Introduction

We have seen that market value may include any potential or development value. If land is being sold in the open market purchasers will take into account the value of existing planning permission, or the possibility of obtaining planning permission if permission is not immediately forthcoming. When land is compulsorily acquired, certain assumptions as to planning permission may be made in order to establish the planning background had there been no proposal to acquire the land: section 14 of the Land Compensation Act 1961. These assumptions generally apply to the land being acquired, and not to any retained land of the claimant.

The true purpose of these planning permission assumptions is to determine the market value of the land had no compulsory acquisition taken place. But these planning assumptions are not exclusive. They permit an assumption to be made that planning permission would be granted for certain development, but this does not mean that planning permission would be refused for any other form of development: section 14(3) of the 1961 Act.

13.2 Planning assumptions: general

In determining whether planning permission could reasonably have been expected to be granted in respect of any land, and whether any of the statutory planning assumptions are applicable, regard must be had to any contrary opinion expressed in a certificate of appropriate alternative development (see section **13.5** below): section 14(3A) of the 1961 Act.

1. Land acquired for highway purposes

Where land is acquired for highway purposes and a determination has to be made whether planning permission might reasonably expect to be granted, or, under section 17 of the 1961 Act (certificate of appropriate alternative development), whether planning would or would not have granted but for the compulsory acquisition, section 14(6) of the 1961 Act provides for an assumption to be made. The assumption is that if the relevant land were not used for highway purposes, no highway would be constructed to meet the same or substantially the same need as the highway the subject of the scheme. This assumption prevents alternative highway schemes from being taken into account, for example, in order to unlock the development value of land being acquired in the no-scheme world.

2. Existing planning permission: section 14(2) of the 1961 Act

This is not really an assumption, but any planning permission which is in force at the date of notice to treat and relates to the land or part of the land may be taken into account in assessing market value, regard being had to any restrictions or conditions, whether the permission is outline, whether it is a personal permission and so on. Existing planning permission will include any permission contained in a development order (such as the General Permitted Development Order 1995) and any deemed planning permission. The assumptions as to planning permission that follow are in addition to any existing planning permission.

Akin to an existing planning permission is a right to continue a use by reason of having an established use certificate (under the pre-1991 planning legislation) or a certificate of lawful use under section 191 of the Town and Country Planning Act 1990. In *Ullah* v *Leicester City Council* [1996] a claimant was refused an established use certificate because he had abandoned a light industry use. However, the Lands Tribunal decided that his abandonment was because of the scheme of the acquiring authority and that therefore he was entitled to be compensated on the assumption that the land could be lawfully used for light industry.

13.3 Assumptions not directly derived from development plans

1. Planning permission for the acquiring authority proposals: section 15(1) of the 1961 Act

An acquiring authority usually has planning permission for any purposes involving development by the time it exercises its powers of acquisition. If this is so, the owner concerned may rely on that planning permission: see above.

Where an acquiring authority is acquiring land for carrying out certain proposals, and those proposals involve the development of land for which there is no planning permission by the date of the service of a notice to treat, 'it shall be assumed that planning permission would be granted in respect of the ... land (or part of it) such as would permit development thereof in accordance with the proposals of the acquiring authority'. In this case 'land' means the land being acquired from a particular landowner. This assumption is of little value if the proposal is a highway scheme or similar public works; but it could be more valuable if the proposal is for commercial, residential or industrial development. Thus in *Roberts v South Gloucestershire District Council* [2003], where planning permission was for a road, it could not be assumed that there was a permission for the extraction of minerals necessary to construct the road, and which had additional value.

Although it is therefore possible to assume planning permission for the development to be carried out by the acquiring authority, the demand for land with that planning permission may be attributed to the scheme underlying the compulsory acquisition:

> *Myers v Milton Keynes Development Corpn* [1974] CA
> Some 300 acres of agricultural land were acquired in 1970 for residential development in about 1980, and as part of the new town. Lord Denning MR said that the claimant was entitled to assume planning permission by virtue of section 15(1) of the 1961 Act for such development at the end of the 10-year period. But, in determining the value of the land with this assumed planning permission, one must disregard the scheme of the acquiring authority – the new town. The valuer must disregard the existence of the new town development corporation, and the development – infrastructure, roads, factories, shops – the corporation is responsible for. The valuer must value the benefit of the assumed planning

permission taking into account the development that might have taken place in the locality had there been no scheme.

The problem of ignoring the effect of the scheme underlying the acquisition is dealt with in Chapter 14. For the payment of compensation where additional development is permitted after acquisition, see section **13.6** below.

2. *Planning permission for Third Schedule Development: section 15(3) of the 1961 Act*

'It shall be assumed that, in respect of the relevant land or any part of it, planning permission would be granted:

(a) subject to the condition set out in Schedule 10 to the Town and Country Planning Act 1990, for any development of a class specified in paragraph 1 of Schedule 3 to that Act; and

(b) for any development of a class specified in paragraph 2 of Schedule 3 to that Act.'

The development in Schedule 3, originally referred to as the 'existing use development of land', is a hangover from the Town and Country Planning Act 1947 and the 'nationalisation' of the right to develop land. Although planning permission is required for the classes of development set out in Schedule 3, permission may be granted in some cases by the General Permitted Development Order 1995.

The purpose of this planning permission assumption is to ensure that the compensation for the compulsory purchase of land includes compensation for any value attributable to the right to rebuild and alter buildings within certain limitations. Until its amendment by the Planning and Compensation Act 1991, Schedule 3 included other classes of existing use development in what was Part II of the Schedule. If planning permission was refused for any development in Part II, compensation was payable. That right has now gone: see Chapter 25.

The classes of development in Schedule 3 are briefly summarised at this point:

Para 1: The carrying out of:

(a) the rebuilding, as often as occasion may require, of any building which was in existence on July 1 1948, or of any

building which was in existence before that date but was destroyed or demolished after January 7 1937, including the making good of war damage sustained by any such building;
(b) the rebuilding, as often as occasion may require, of any building erected after July 1 1948, which was in existence at a material date;
(c) the carrying out for the maintenance, improvement or other alteration of any building, or works which:

(i) affect only the interior of the building, or do not materially affect the external appearance of the building, and
(ii) are works for making good war damage, so long as the cubic content of the original building is not substantially exceeded.

Ivens & Sons v *Daventry District Council* [1976] LT
Until 1964 a house stood on the subject land; it was demolished and in 1966 the local highway authority and the claimant used the site to dump soil until the level of the land was raised by 20 ft. There was a deemed compulsory purchase on the land and the claimant contended that planning permission could be assumed to rebuild the house as this was development within what is now Part I of the Third Schedule: the land would then have had a value of £9,000. The Lands Tribunal held that planning permission could not be assumed as it was no longer possible to rebuild the house as the level of the land was so much higher than the site of the original house: the proper amount of compensation was £300.

Old England Properties Ltd v *Telford & Wrekin Council* [2001] LT
The rebuilding must constitute the original building and not the erection of a different building. The rebuilding must be on the foundations of the original building, subject to such deviations as allow for permitted increases in size, and for the original purposes. There is no scope for any hope value under this planning assumption.

Para 2: The use of two or more separate dwellinghouses of any building which at a material date was used as a single dwellinghouse.

The planning assumption for the development in para 1 of the third Schedule is subject to the conditions in the 10th Schedule of the 1990 Act. These limit the additional floorspace which may be assumed in relation to a building to be rebuilt or altered to no more that 10% of the original building, and to nil if the building is the result of rebuilding or alteration: see *Walton-on-Thames Charities* v *Walton and Weybridge Urban District Council* [1968] for the nature of this assumed planning permission.

13.4 Special assumptions derived from development plans

The development plan means the plan in force on the date of the notice to treat: see section 39(1) of the 1961 Act.

1. Planning permission for development of a specific description as defined in the current development plan: section 16(1) of the 1961 Act

Apart, possibly, from roads, it is now uncommon to find a site of proposed development of a specific description defined on a development plan. When a plan does define such a site, and it will usually be of a public works nature, it may be assumed that planning permission would be granted for development of the description specified. Such an assumption is unlikely, if the development is of a public works nature, to add anything to the market value. It cannot be made if the land is part of an action area or a comprehensive development area.

2. Planning permission for development where the land is allocated primarily for a use specified in the current development plan: section 16(2) of the 1961 Act

If, for example, land is within an area allocated on the development plan for housing purposes, planning permission may be assumed for any development for the purposes of housing: see *Margate Corporation* v *Devotwill* [1970] for assumptions relating to highways. However, this assumption can only be made if planning permission might reasonably have been expected to be granted for the land, or that part of the land, so allocated, if no part of the land were proposed to be compulsorily purchased:

> *Provincial Properties Ltd* v *Caterham and Warlingham Urban District Council* [1972] CA
> The land being acquired was part of an area allocated for residential use but because this land lay on top of the North

Downs, planning permission had been consistently refused as development on top of the Downs would spoil the scenic amenities of the area. It was held by the Court of Appeal that planning permission could not, therefore, have been reasonably expected to be granted and this planning assumption could not be made.

Under the older development plans, this assumption cannot be made if the land is part of an action area or a comprehensive development area.

3. *Planning permission for development where the land is allocated primarily for a range of two or more uses specified in the current development plan: section 16(3) of the 1961 Act*

This assumption is similar to the preceding assumption and subject to the same important proviso: planning permission for development for the purposes of a use falling within a range of uses can be assumed if planning permission might reasonably have been expected to be granted if no part of the land were proposed to be compulsorily acquired: see section 16(7) of the 1961 Act and *Margate Corporation* v *Devotwill Investment Ltd* [1970].

This assumption is also only applicable to that part of the land allocated for the specified uses on the plan. It cannot be made if the land is part of an action area or a comprehensive development area.

4. *Planning permission for development where the land is within a comprehensive development area or an action area: section 16(4) of the 1961 Act*

Planning permission may be assumed for any development for the purposes of a use falling within the planned range of uses as indicated in the current development plan for the area. This assumption can only be made if planning permission might reasonably have been expected to be granted if no part of the land were proposed to be compulsorily acquired: see section 16(7) of the 1961 Act and *Margate Corporation* v *Devotwill Investment Ltd* [1970].

However, in making this assumption, the fact that the area has been defined as a comprehensive development area, or an action area, must be ignored; any particulars or proposals for those areas must also be ignored; and, if at the date of notice to treat some of the land in the comprehensive development area or action area has already been developed in accordance with the plan, it must be assumed that no such development has taken place before that date.

Example

Blackacre is a small private car park lying behind the High Street to which it has poor access. It is to be acquired for development as a large shopping unit: shopping is one of the planned uses. Although the owner may make the planning assumption for a shopping use, he cannot do so if the planning permission would have been unlikely had there been no CDA or action area; the fact that Blackacre is to be used for a large shopping unit must be ignored.

13.5 Certificate of appropriate alternative development

1. Procedure

It shall be assumed that planning permission would be granted for any development specified in a certificate of appropriate alternative development provided that the certificate states that the specified development would have been permitted if the land concerned were not proposed to be acquired compulsorily: section 15(5).

The circumstances when an application for a certificate may be made, and the procedure to be followed, are set out in section 17 of the 1961 Act (as amended by section 65 of the Planning and Compensation Act 1991). As planning permission for development other than that to be carried out by the acquiring authority will not be granted, the certificate is the only way of establishing what development might have been permitted: *Crabb* v *Surrey County Council* [1982]. In *Williamson* v *Cambridgeshire County Council* [1977] the Lands Tribunal stated that this procedure should be used to determine the planning basis for the assessment of compensation rather than the tribunal; there is a tendency for the tribunal to take on the nature of a planning inquiry at times. However, there are circumstances where this is inevitable. A certificate cannot be sought to determine the planning basis of any retained land where this is relevant to a claim for injurious affection or set-off arises.

An application can only to made where 'an interest in land is proposed to be acquired by an authority possessing compulsory powers': see section 17(1). An interest is so proposed to be acquired where (see section 22(2)):

(a) a notice required to be published or served in connection with compulsory acquisition has been so published or served;

(b) where a notice has been served which is a deemed notice to treat; or

(c) where an offer in writing has been made by or on behalf of the authority to negotiate for the purchase of that interest.

An application is made for a certificate to the local planning authority. Either the landowner or the acquiring authority may apply: see section 17(1). Prior to the amendments made by the Planning and Compensation Act 1991, a certificate could not be applied for if the land to be compulsorily acquired was, or was part of, a comprehensive development area, an action area, or 'an area shown in the development plan as an area allocated primarily for a use which is of a residential, commercial or industrial character, or for a range of two or more uses any of which is of such a character'. There is now no such limitation.

An application for a certificate cannot be made, subject to specified exceptions, where a notice to treat has been served, or there is an agreement for sale of the land, and there is a reference to the Lands Tribunal for the determination of compensation. The exceptions are that both parties consent or the tribunal gives leave: see section 17(3).

It must be remembered that the planning assumptions permitted by the 1961 Act do not preclude the possibility of making an assumption that planning permission would be granted for some development outside those assumptions. However, if a certificate (perhaps in this situation obtained by the acquiring authority) states that planning permission would not have been granted for any development had there been no compulsory purchase, regard shall be had to that fact: section 14(3A) of the 1961 Act. A nil certificate was issued in the *Corrin* case (see above at p192) but this did not prevent the assumption of 'hope value' on the basis that development might be permitted in the future.

When an application is made for such a certificate, the applicant must state:

(a) Whether there are any classes of development which in the applicant's opinion would be appropriate for the land in question, either immediately or at a future time, if the land were not being compulsorily acquired; and

(b) the grounds for the opinion of the applicant.

The application for a certificate should be treated by the local planning authority in the same way as a planning application. The applicant does not have to prove his case; if he submits that planning permission would have been granted for some development, it is for the local planning authority (or the minister on appeal) to show a good reason why the development would not have been permitted: *JD White Ltd* v *Secretary of State for the Environment* [1982] QBD (minister dismissed the appeal, but as the inspector had said he might have recommended a positive certificate had a more detailed scheme been presented the minister's decision was quashed as it was unfair to the applicant).

The party applying for a certificate must enclose a map. A copy of his application is sent to the other party, and 21 days is allowed for any representations.

Not earlier than 21 days after the application the local planning authority shall issue a certificate within two months stating either (section 17(4)):

(a) that planning permission would have been granted for development of one or more classes specified in the certificate (whether specified in the application or not) and for any development for which the land is to be acquired, but would not have been granted for any other development; or

(b) that planning permission would have been granted for any development of which the land is to be acquired, but would not have been granted for any other development.

In a positive certificate, conditions and timing may be added: see section 17(5) and (6). The form of certificate is invalid unless it contains a statement of the rights of appeal: *London & Clydeside Estates Ltd* v *Aberdeen District Council* [1979] HL.

2. Relying on certificates in the Lands Tribunal

In *Porter* v *Secretary of State for Transport* [1996] the Court of Appeal decided that a certificate is not conclusive on the planning issues in relation to the assessment of compensation for severance or injurious affection of retained land. It is therefore open for either party before the Lands Tribunal to lead evidence to show that the conclusions by which a certificate was issued should not be followed in relation to retained land. This is not the case for land taken. Accordingly, issue estoppel only arises in relation to land taken and does not apply to retained land.

Where a certificate is issued with conditions, the land must be valued with the benefit of the planning permission deemed by the certificate but taking into account the practical difficulties under it: see *Pearce* v *Augton* [1973].

3. Right of appeal

The claimant, any successor in title and any acquiring authority proposing to acquire the land may appeal to the Secretary of State against a certificate within one month of its issue: section 18. There is no right of appeal against a certificate successfully obtained: see *R* v *Secretary of State for the Environment, ex parte Ward* [1995]. Until amendment by the Planning and Compensation Act 1991, the costs of such appeal could not be recovered as part of the compensation: *Hull & Humber Investment Co* v *Hull Corporation* [1965]. Now in assessing compensation, there shall be taken into account any expenses reasonably incurred in connection with an application for a certificate, or of appealing where the appeal is successful: see section 17(9A).

4. Relevant date

The certificate procedure does not provide for the question as to what is the date at which the planning authority is to consider whether planning permission would or would not have been granted. This is important if there has been a change of planning policy after the date of the notice to treat; a change of planning policy could mean that planning permission would be granted after the change but not before, or vice-versa. In *Hitchins Builders Ltd* v *Secretary of State for the Environment* [1979] QBD, Sir Douglas Frank QC decided that the purpose of the certificate procedure was to establish the market value of the land in question. It followed that the local planning authority, or the Secretary of State, on an appeal, should have regard to planning policies as near as possible to the date of assessment. This appeared also to be the view of the House of Lords in *Grampian Regional Council* v *Secretary of State for Scotland* [1983].

However, in *Fox* v *Secretary of State for the Environment* [1991] Roch J decided that the date at which relevant factors were to be considered was the date of the acquiring authority's offer to purchase and not the date when the Secretary of State makes his decision. The problem was resolved in the House of Lords in *Fletcher Estates* v *Secretary of State* [2000]. It was accepted by the parties that the Court of Appeal had been correct in deciding that the relevant date for the determination of certificates was the date for the purposes of section 22(2)(a) of the 1961 Act, namely the date of the notice of the making of the compulsory purchase order.

5. Ignoring the scheme

There might be a temptation on the part of the local planning authority, particularly if it were also the acquiring authority, to issue a 'nil' certificate on the ground that no development would have been permitted but for that for which the land in question is being compulsorily acquired. This was first answered in *Grampian Regional Council* v *Secretary of State for Scotland* [1983] where the land in question was being acquired for the erection of two schools and a certificate had been issued stating that planning permission would not have been granted for any development other than that proposed by the education authority. Lord Bridge said that the whole purpose of the certificate procedure was to secure fair compensation to claimants using planning assumptions that ignored the scheme of the acquiring authority. In *Fletcher Estates* v *Secretary of State* [2000] the House of Lords decided that, under section 17(4) of the 1961 Act, the local planning authority must assume that the scheme for which the land is proposed to be acquired, together with the underlying proposal, which may appear in any of the underlying documents, has been cancelled. No assumption has to be made as to what may or may not have happened in the past. The decision in the *Grampian* case was distinguished as it concerned different facts and different arguments. The effect of *Fletcher* must be that the need for a similar scheme and the likelihood of such a similar scheme does not necessarily have to be disregarded.

Where the acquiring authority is only taking part of a claimant's land, and the balance is to be retained by the claimant, it may be important to establish the planning assumptions in respect of both the land taken and the land retained. This is because the compensation is payable not only for the land taken, but may also be payable for the depreciation in the value of the retained land by virtue of its severance. In *Abbey Homesteads Group Ltd* v *Secretary of*

State for Transport [1982], the Tribunal said that in assessing the compensation for the land taken, regard must be had to the certificate and any density development that it might prescribe. However, regard could not be had to the certificate in the case of the land retained by the claimant. This is because section 17 of the 1961 Act clearly states that a certificate may only be obtained in respect of the land proposed to be acquired. While this is a correct view of the law, it does mean that a claimant has no fair procedure to determine the planning basis for valuing the land that he retains: see also *Portsmouth Roman Catholic Diocesan Trustees* v *Hampshire County Council* [1980]. However, in *ADP & E Farmers* v *Department of Transport* [1988], the Tribunal decided that matters of fact or judgment leading to the grant of a certificate may well be strong or decisive evidence in relation to adjoining land.

If a certificate is issued for an area of land, and then only part of that land is compulsorily acquired, the certificate is not divisible. That means that it cannot be relied on as a matter of course without taking into account the fresh circumstances that have arisen because only part of the land is being taken: see *Hoveringham Gravels Ltd* v *Chiltern District Council* [1977].

Another difficulty in issuing a certificate is that whereas development might have been permitted on a large area of land of which the claimant's is only part, permission might be refused merely for the claimant's own land. In *Sutton* v *Secretary of State for the Environment* [1984] QBD, it was decided that the local planning authority should issue a certificate for the claimant's land alone provided there were circumstances to justify that, but for the compulsory purchase, development of the claimant's and other surrounding land might have been permitted. It was also said in the same case that the likelihood or unlikelihood of particular development taking place was not relevant in deciding whether a positive certificate for an exceptional project of development (a large car factory) would have been permitted. The likelihood of development actually taking place was a matter of valuation judgment.

In *Maidstone Borough Council* v *Secretary of State for the Environment* [1996] the Court of Appeal held, in the case of the acquisition of allotment land, that the Secretary of State, on an appeal, was entitled to consider the loss of public open space. It was also held that rule (2) of section 5 of the 1961 Act (the market value rule) has nothing to do with assumptions as to planning permission.

13.6 Compensation for additional development permitted after acquisition

The Planning and Compensation Act 1991 made amendments to the Land Compensation Act 1961 to provide for compensation where permission for additional development is granted after the acquisition of land. These amendments apply to an acquisition where the date of completion is on or after September 25 1991: see section 66(2) of the 1991 Act.

1. Compensation where planning decision made after acquisition

Where an interest in land is compulsorily acquired, or is sold to an authority possessing compulsory purchase powers, the person to whom the compensation or purchase price was payable is entitled to claim additional compensation where a planning decision is made granting permission for the carrying out of additional development on any of the land before the end of a period of 10 years beginning with the date of completion of the purchase: section 23.

The additional compensation is an amount equal to the difference between the principal amount of compensation which was payable, or the amount of the purchase price, and the amount which would have been payable in respect of a compulsory acquisition of the interest by the acquiring authority, in pursuance of a notice to treat served on the relevant date if:

(a) the planning decision which is made after acquisition had been made before the relevant date; and
(b) the permission granted by it had been in force on that date.

The relevant date is the date of the notice to treat or the date of any contract: see section 29. What is not provided for is what happens where the planning permission is granted after the relevant date but before the completion date. It follows from the above that a fresh valuation is made using the original valuation date, and taking into account facts known on that date, and not later, on the assumption that the new planning permission was in force.

Compensation is not payable in respect of a planning decision in so far as it relates to land acquired by an acquiring authority under section 142 or 143 of the Local Government, Planning and Land Act 1980 (acquisitions by urban development corporations and by highway authorities in connection with urban development areas); under the New Towns Act 1981; or where the compulsory purchase order included a direction under section 50 of the Planning (Listed Buildings and Conservation Areas) Act 1990 (minimum compensation where building deliberately allowed to fall into disrepair): see section 23(3) of the 1961 Act.

Further, compensation is not payable in respect of development permitted for purposes of local authority functions or for development for the purposes of the project underlying the acquisition: see section 29(1).

Where the person who would otherwise have been entitled to claim the additional compensation has died, the right to the compensation devolves to his estate: see section 23(4) of the 1961 Act.

Compensation under section 23 carries interest from the date of the planning decision in question until payment: see section 23(5).

2. *Procedure*

Section 24 of the 1961 Act makes provision for the registering of a claimant's address for the service by the acquiring authority of notice of any planning decision giving rise to additional compensation. By section 24(4) a claim for compensation in respect of a planning decision shall not have effect if more than six months after the following dates:

(a) the claim is made by a person who has not given the acquiring authority an address for service under the section, the date of the decision;

(b) the claim is made by a person who has given the acquiring authority such an address, the date on which notice of the decision is given to him by the acquiring authority.

3. *Extension to planning permission where no planning decision made*

The provisions of sections 23 and 24 of the 1961 Act have effect in relation to any planning permission falling within column one of the following table for any development as if a planning decision granting that permission had been made on the date shown in column 2.

Planning permission	Date of decision
Permission granted by a development order	When development is initiated
Permission granted by the adoption or approval of a simplified planning zone scheme	When the scheme is approved or adopted
Permission granted by an order designating an enterprise zone	When the designation takes effect
Permission deemed to be granted by a direction under section 90 of the Town and Country Planning Act 1990	When the direction is given
Permission deemed to be granted by a local planning authority	The occurrence of the event in consequence of which the permission is deemed to be granted

Again there are provisions for the giving of notice by the acquiring authority to persons who have provided the authority with an address for service: see section 25(2) and (3). Again there is a time-limit of six months within which to make a claim for compensation: see section 25(4).

4. Extension to Crown development

Where development is initiated by or on behalf of the Crown, or the Crown or the Duchy of Cornwall have an interest in the land and the development is initiated in right of that interest, planning permission may not be required under the Town and Country Planning Act 1990. Section 26 of the 1961 Act provides that the provisions of sections 23 and 24 of the 1961 Act shall apply as if the planning decision granting permission for that development had been made at the time when the additional development is so initiated: see section 26 of the 1961 Act.

5. Assessment of compensation

The provisions of Part I of the 1961 Act apply to the determination of the additional compensation under these sections.

In assessing the principal amount of the compensation paid to a claimant, or which ought to have been paid had the planning decision permitting additional development been made before acquisition, the principal amount of any compensation shall be construed as including any sum attributable to disturbance, severance or injurious affection: see para 1 of the Third Schedule to the 1961 Act.

Where a person becomes entitled to compensation under section 23 of the 1961 Act, but at the time of the planning decision in question no longer owns an interest in other land which he owned contiguous or adjacent to the land acquired or purchased, the principal amount of compensation, or the amount of the purchase price, paid to him originally, will be construed as excluding so much of the compensation or purchase price as was or would have been attributable to severance or injurious affection of that land: see para 2 of the Third Schedule to the 1961 Act.

6. *Retained land*

Where a claimant retains contiguous or adjacent land, the assessment of compensation may be reduced (whether by virtue of section 7 of the 1961 Act or otherwise) by reason of an increase in value of the interest in the contiguous or adjacent land. Where, because the owner has an interest in contiguous or adjacent land at the time of acquisition, the compensation or the purchase price was or would have been reduced by reason of an increase in value of his interest in contiguous or adjacent land, but at the time of the planning decision giving rise to additional compensation the person so entitled is not entitled to an interest in contiguous or adjacent land (or only has an interest in part of the contiguous or adjacent land), it shall be assumed in calculating the principal amount of compensation which was payable, and which should have been payable, that the circumstances giving rise to a reduction in compensation for an increase in value of the contiguous or adjacent land had not existed: see para 3 of the Third Schedule to the 1961 Act.

7. *Land sold by acquiring authority*

Where an acquiring authority purchases land, perhaps in consequence of a blight notice, and then later re-sells it, the authority will remain potentially liable to pay compensation if planning permission is subsequently obtained by any successor in title to the authority within the 10-year period. To protect itself, an authority in such a position may seek to impose an obligation on any purchaser to reimburse such liability if the purchaser obtains planning permission.

Chapter 14

The Effect of the Scheme

Introduction
Statutory rules for disregarding the 'scheme'
Section 9 of the Land Compensation Act 1961
The *Pointe Gourde* principle
Summary

14.1 Introduction

It is a general principle of the law of damages that, at common law, a person who has suffered harm to his property for which he can recover, should be put in a position where he is neither better nor worse off. This principle is frequently echoed in relation to compulsory purchase compensation: see *Horn* v *Sunderland Corpn* [1941]. However, by virtue of the Land Compensation Act 1961, section 5, rule (2), compensation is defined, not as loss, but as market value. Generally market value will give to a claimant financial equivalence; sometimes the scheme of the acquiring authority will increase or decrease market values. There are special rules to disregard the effect of the scheme, and to ensure that the claimant is neither better nor worse off.

The natural market value must first be determined in accordance with the rules so far considered in this chapter. But that value may have been increased or decreased by factors known as betterment or worsenment: the cause of which are decisions or activities of central or local authorities. Where such value increases or decreases are attributable to the scheme underlying the compulsory acquisition of land, there are three rules for disregarding those influences to land values. The first is a statutory rule to disregard increases and decreases in value in certain cases of defined 'schemes' of acquisition; the second, a statutory rule to disregard decreases in value due to the prospect of the use of compulsory powers; and, the third is a judicial rule to disregard increases and decreases in value due to the scheme underlying the acquisition.

14.2 The statutory rules for disregarding the 'scheme'

Section 6 and Schedule 1 to the Land Compensation Act 1961
contain the rules. These complicated provisions are best described
by reference to a diagram:

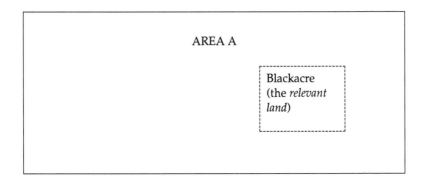

Let us assume that a claimant has an interest, freehold or leasehold,
in Blackacre, in respect of which he has received a notice to treat.
He is then regarded as having a relevant interest in the relevant
land. Blackacre is part of the scheme of the acquiring authority, the
area of which we can call area A.

Section 6 provides that no account shall be taken of any increase
or diminution in the value of the relevant interest (in Blackacre)
which is attributable to the carrying out, or the prospect of, certain
specified development in the rest of Area A. The development
disregarded in this way is not only development by the acquiring
authority. Section 6 refers to four cases involving the compulsory
purchase of land, and, in each case the specified development that
must be disregarded if that development causes an increase or
diminution in the value of this relevant interest (in Blackacre). In
each case, the increase or diminution in value is only disregarded if
the specific development would have been unlikely to be carried
out if the land was not being compulsorily acquired; and, in cases
2 and 4, if the areas had not been so defined or designated (see
below).

The four cases and the specified development to be disregarded
in each case, are found in the First Schedule. The effect of section 6
and the First Schedule is as follows:

The circumstances of compulsory purchase (a description of Area A)	No account shall be taken of any increase or diminution in the value of the *relevant interest* (in Blackacre) attributable to the development in this column:
Case 1: the land (Area A) is the land authorised to be acquired and is either the aggregate of the land in a compulsory purchase order or the aggregate of land authorised to be acquired by a Special Act.	Development of any of the land (Area A), other than the *relevant land* (Blackacre), being development for any of the purposes for which the land is being acquired.
Case 2. The land (Area A) is defined in the current development plan as a comprehensive development area.	Development of any of the land (Area A), other than the *relevant land* (Blackacre), in the course of the development or redevelopment of the area in accordance with the current development plan.
Case 3 and 3A: The land (Area A) is designated as the site of a new town, or is an area designated as an extension of the site of a new town.	Development of any land in the area (Area A), other than the relevant land (Blackacre), in the course of the development of that area as a new town.
Case 4: The land (Area A) forms part of an area defined in the current development plan as an area of town development	Development of any land in the area (Area A), other than the *relevant land* (Blackacre), in the course of town development within the meaning of the Town Development Act 1952.
Case 4A: The land (Area A) forms part of an urban development area, e.g. Liverpool docks or London Docklands	Development of any land in the area (Area A), other than the *relevant land* (Blackacre), in the course of the development or redevelopment of the urban development area.
Case 4B: Land forms part of a housing action trust area under Housing Act 1985.	Development of any land other than the relevant land in course of development or redevelopment of housing action trust area.

Case 1 includes the usual circumstances of a compulsory purchase order. An increase or decrease in the value of Blackacre attributable to development for any of the purposes for which the land is being acquired must be disregarded. However, if there are two compulsory purchase orders, one for Area A, and another for some adjoining land, say Area B, development carried out or proposed to be carried out in Area B may increase or decrease the value of Blackacre in Area A. Section 6 and the First Schedule does not provide for this problem under this or any of the other cases. The increase or decrease in value cannot therefore be disregarded under the statute: see *Sprinz* v *Kingston-upon-Hull Corpn* [1975] LT where a similar problem arose involving two adjoining schemes and where it was held that section 6 could not apply as between the two areas (but the two areas may constitute one scheme for the purposes of the *Pointe Gourde* principle – see below).

The direction to disregard 'development' that would not have taken place but for the scheme includes clearance of buildings: section 6(3) of the 1961 Act. In *Davy* v *Leeds Corpn* [1965] the House of Lords decided that the clearance of buildings around the claimant's properties had to be ignored; they could not assume that the surrounding land was cleared of buildings and available for development.

It was also said in the *Davy* case that what is now section 6 was a statutory enactment of the *Pointe Gourde* principle, a common law principle of like effect (and discussed below). While the statutory rule and the common law principle are indeed similar, Parliament, in enacting the statutory rule (originally in 1959), was at the same time restoring full market value as the basis of compensation; the concern at the time was to ensure that an acquiring authority should not pay for the benefit it created by its scheme, and the claimant should not lose if a scheme caused depreciation. The relationship between the statutory rule and the *Pointe Gourde* principle was also explained in *Camrose* v *Basingstoke Corporation* [1966], where it said that the Tribunal was to ignore any increase in value due to development both on the relevant and other land.

If Area A is to be designated as the site of a new town (or the extension of a new town) and the main purpose of the new town (or extension to a new town) is housing or other facilities for any public development, the Secretary of State may make a direction under section 51 of the Land Compensation Act 1973 before making his new town order. The effect of such a direction is to provide that any increase or diminution in value due to the housing or other facilities for public development shall be disregarded whether or not the public development is in the designated area (Area A). This provision can therefore widen the effect of case 3 above.

Rank Leisure v *Castle Vale Housing Action Trust* [2001] concerned Case 4B. The claimants were the last remaining tenants in a shopping centre owned by a housing trust; they were awarded existing use value only as any development value was unlikely in the absence of a designation and ownership by the trust within the meaning of Case 4B.

It is the task of the valuers to determine the value of the subject land in the 'no-scheme' world. They must imagine what would have happened, and what development might have been permitted, had the scheme of acquisition not taken place:

> *Myers* v *Milton Keynes Development Corpn* [1974] CA
> For the details, see p201 above. Lord Denning MR said:
>
> In assessing the value, it is important to consider what would have happened if there had been no scheme ... The valuer must cast aside his knowledge of what has in fact happened ... due to the scheme. He must ignore the developments which will in all probability take place in the future...owing to the scheme. Instead, he must let his imagination take flight to the clouds. He must conjure up a land of make-believe, where there has not been, nor will be, a brave new town, but where there is to be supposed the old order of things continuing ...

The idea is simple to state, but there are great practical difficulties in determining the value a particular property might have had had there been no scheme.

14.3 Section 9 of the Land Compensation Act 1961

Any suggestion that a piece of land may be compulsorily acquired will affect its market value; indeed once an intention to compulsorily acquire becomes definite, the land may have little or no value in the open market. Section 9 provides that 'no account shall be taken of any depreciation of the value of the relevant interest (which has the same meaning as under section 6 above) which is attributable to the fact that (whether by way of designation, allocation or other particulars contained in the current development plan, or by any other means) an indication has been given that the relevant land is, or is likely, to be acquired by an authority possessing compulsory purchase powers'.

What must be disregarded is the effect on values of an indication of compulsory purchase: an indication of the use of the compulsory purchase powers may depreciate market values. This section is intended to provide that market value is to be assessed on the basis of what the land would have fetched had there been no possibility of the land being compulsorily acquired.

In *Leek* v *Birmingham City Council* [1982] LT, it was agreed that the value of the lessor's interest in certain properties on the date of vesting was £8,000; if the lessor's interest had not been compulsorily acquired, and she enforced her repairing covenants, it was agreed the properties would have been worth £15,000. The lessor argued unsuccessfully that section 9 should apply to disregard this difference as the loss of the full value was due to the indication of compulsory purchase. The loss of the right to enforce the repairing covenant was not due to an indication of compulsory purchase, but to the actual act of compulsory purchase; the Tribunal awarded £12,629 to reflect a speculative 'overbid' to purchase the right to enforce the covenants, but not the full loss under section 9.

> *Trocette Property Co Ltd* v *Greater London Council* [1974] CA
> The GLC held a freehold reversion to a lease to Trocette of a disused cinema; the lease had 11 years to run. Because the GLC had plans for a new road through the site, they indicated that a new lease could not be granted. Trocette applied for planning permission to develop the site and upon having the application refused served a purchase notice. The evidence indicated that had a new lease been granted and development of the site taken place, Trocette could have participated in the development value that would have resulted. Section 9 was applied to disregard the loss of this development value to Trocette by reason of the indication that the land was likely to be compulsorily acquired for the road.

> *Jelson Ltd* v *Blaby District Council* [1978] CA
> Planning permission was refused to develop a strip of land which had originally been reserved through a housing development for a new road. The proposal for a new road having been abandoned, it was accepted that had this road proposal never existed the strip of land could have been

developed along with the adjoining housing development. The Court of Appeal held that the strip of land was depreciated in value because of the original intention to compulsorily acquire it for a new road, and the development value which had been lost must be compensated for now that strip was being acquired following a purchase notice: see also below under the *Pointe Gourde* principle.

Where restrictive covenants affected land, and these were imposed by a planning agreement which was part of the acquiring authority's scheme, section 9 was held not apply to disregard the restrictive covenants: see *Abbey Homesteads* v *Northampton County Council* [1992]. In *Thornton* v *Wakefield Metropolitan District Council* [1991] it was decided that although section 9 applied to disregard notification in a planning permission of a likelihood of acquisition, in the circumstances the property had to be valued in its actual state at valuation date.

14.4 The *Pointe Gourde* principle

1. The principle stated

The *Pointe Gourde* principle may be stated in the following terms:

> compensation for the compulsory acquisition of land cannot include an increase in value which is entirely due to the scheme underlying the acquisition.

Whenever there is a scheme underlying a compulsory purchase, the 'principle' will apply. If the scheme of the acquiring authority comes within any of the four cases considered at p219, the statutory rule will also apply. Whenever both 'principle' and statutory rule are applicable, the statutory rule should first be applied (*Sprinz* v *Kingston-upon-Hull Corpn* [1975] LT); the 'principle' is applied second to disregard any increase or decrease in the value of the land due to the scheme which is not disregarded by the statutory rule. The 'principle' is therefore wider in effect than the statutory rule.

The *Pointe Gourde* principle is derived from the following case:

> *Pointe Gourde Quarrying and Transport Company Ltd* v *Sub-Intendent of Crown Lands* [1947] PC
> The Crown compulsorily acquired lands in Trinidad which were required in connection with the establishment of a naval base nearby. On part of the land was a quarry containing

stone which could be used in building the base. The original award of compensation included £15,000 which was identified as the value of the increased profits the quarry could make supplying stone to the proposed naval base. The quarry land was not needed for the naval base but the purpose of its acquisition seems to have been to requisition a suitable and convenient source of stone. The proximity of the naval base, and the probability of increased profits from supplying stone to the base, would have given the quarry land an enhanced value had it not been compulsorily acquired. This enhanced value, or betterment, was said to be due to the scheme of the acquiring authority (construction of a naval base) and was excluded by following previously decided cases that had excluded increased value to the acquiring authority: see previous chapter. Clearly the quarry did have an increased value to the Crown but it also had an enhanced market value due to the scheme. This latter value increase was betterment and for the first time it was excluded from the compensation. Hence the significance of this case to present-day acquisitions where market value may well be enhanced by acquiring authority schemes.

The *Pointe Gourde* principle is a legal idea not a valuation step. The legal idea is that a claimant should neither gain nor lose out of a compulsory purchase. The principle is therefore concerned with establishing fair compensation using market values; market values that would have prevailed had there been no 'scheme'. In *Batchelor v Kent County Council* [1990] the Court of Appeal held that any pre-existent value to the scheme need not be ignored. Because the scheme for the purpose of the *Pointe Gourde* principle is not defined with the precision of the statutory rule in section 6, it may not always be clear how, or whether to apply the principle. Valuers should look for evidence that the market value of the land in question has been increased or decreased due to causes entirely attributable to the scheme underlying the acquisition, and those increases or decreases cannot be disregarded under any of the statutory rules so far discussed.

2. Disregard value not interest

In *Rugby Joint Water Board v Shaw Fox* [1973] the House of Lords held that the principle did not apply to the ascertainment of the interest in the land to be valued. In that case, and by virtue of the scheme, an owner of agricultural land was entitled to serve an incontestable notice to quit under the agricultural holdings legislation, and his interest became a reversionary interest to an unprotected tenancy; that interest did not have to be disregarded under the scheme. That was the interest existing at the date of the notice to treat and that was the interest to be valued.

Similarly, in *Abbey Homesteads* v *Northampton County Council* [1992] where the reference land was subject to a planning agreement containing restrictive covenants, as the interest to be valued was subject to the restrictive covenants, it had to be valued subject to them. The *Pointe Gourde* principle did not apply to disregard the restrictive covenants, notwithstanding the fact that the planning agreement imposing them was part of the scheme.

3. Identifying the scheme

In *JA Pye (Oxford) Ltd* v *Kingswood Borough Council* [1998], the Court of Appeal decided that the compulsory acquisition itself could not be the scheme; there must always be an underlying scheme, in consequence of which the compulsory purchase order was made.

The *Pointe Gourde* principle has been held to apply where the scheme of the acquiring authority is wider in effect than the scheme as defined in the statutory rule. This may arise if the acquiring authority make a compulsory purchase order covering only part of a scheme area, or where they make two or more compulsory purchase orders in respect of the same scheme:

> *Wilson* v *Liverpool City Council* [1971] CA
> The acquiring authority had a scheme of housing development covering 391 acres, and most of this land had been acquired by agreement, but some 86 acres was the subject of a compulsory purchase order of which 73 acres was owned by Wilson. It was agreed that the market value of Wilson's land had been enhanced by the scheme, and the installation of sewerage works, from £5,350 per acre to £6,700, its deadripe value. The statutory rule (see Case 1 above) only excludes an increase in value due to development in the rest of the area of the compulsory purchase order (i.e. the rest of Area A in the diagram on p218), but the increase in value in this case was not due to development in the rest of the compulsory purchase order (scattered pockets of land amounting to 13

acres) but due to activities and development in the wider scheme and outside the compulsory purchase order. The increase in value not being excluded by the statutory rule, it was disregarded by applying the *Pointe Gourde* principle.

If the scheme underlying the acquisition is a scheme of an authority other than the actual acquiring authority, the 'principle' may still apply even where the acquisition area is only a small part of the scheme:

> *Bird* v *Wakefield Metropolitan District Council* [1978] CA
> The county council had a scheme for the reclamation and redevelopment of 770 acres for industrial purposes. Their scheme did not provide for the compulsory acquisition of any land. The district council had a scheme for the compulsory purchase of about 30 acres, within the 770 acres, for industrial development. The Lands Tribunal had held that the county council's scheme was the scheme underlying the acquisition by the district council, the district council's scheme having 'merged', or become part of the wider scheme. This was upheld by the Court of Appeal. Any increase in value due to this wider scheme was to be disregarded.

The *Pointe Gourde* principle will therefore apply whenever there is a scheme. And the scheme for the purposes of the 'principle' can be wider in scope and effect than a scheme within the four cases under the statutory rule. As the purpose of the 'principle' is to disregard an increase in market value due to the scheme, it is important to know, in each circumstance, what is the scheme. Unlike the statutory rule, the scheme for the purpose of the 'principle' is not defined with any particularity. It is a question of fact, in each case of acquisition, to be determined, where there is disagreement, by the Lands Tribunal. In the *Wilson* case Lord Denning MR said:

> A scheme is a progressive thing. It starts vague and known to few. It becomes more precise and better known as time goes on. Eventually it becomes precise and definite, and known to all.

Widgery LJ, as he then was, in the same case said:

> Whenever land is to be compulsorily acquired, this must be in consequence of some scheme or undertaking or project ... it is for the tribunal ... to consider just what activities – past, present or future – are properly to be regarded as the scheme.

The greatest difficulty in identifying a scheme is identifying the commencement of a scheme, and the components of a scheme as distinct from other improvements and developments in the area: *Bolton Metropolitan Borough Council* v *Tudor Properties Ltd* [2000].

Where land has acquired naturally a value in excess of its existing use value by reason of its geographical position, and that enhanced value would exist in the absence of the scheme of the acquiring authority, the *Pointe Gourde* principle has no application: see *Chapman, Lowry & Puttick Ltd* v *Chichester DC* [1984].

Where a landowner serves a purchase notice (see Chapter 5) there is a deemed compulsory purchase. In this circumstance it may be difficult to identify any scheme underlying the acquisition, as the acquiring authority would not have initiated the purchase in pursuance of a particular project or scheme. This problem arose in the following case where the court accepted an abandoned scheme as the 'Scheme' underlying the acquisition:

> *Jelson Ltd* v *Blaby District Council* [1978] CA
> Jelson obtained planning permission for residential development of an area of land with the exception of a strip of land running through the centre reserved for a highway scheme. After the development was completed, the highway scheme was abandoned and Jelson sought planning permission for the strip of land. This was refused because of the difficulty of developing along this strip. It was accepted that had there been no highway scheme in the first place, planning permission could have been obtained and the strip developed with the adjoining land. Jelson served a purchase notice on the ground that the strip of land was incapable of reasonable beneficial use. The dispute concerned the proper value of the strip of land. Without the planning permission, its market value was only £6,700. If the strip of land could have been developed with the adjoining land, it was worth £60,000. The court accepted that the abandoned highway scheme was the scheme for the purpose of applying the *Pointe Gourde* principle, and this scheme had caused the depreciation in value which should be disregarded. The higher value was payable. (The court accepted that section 9 of the 1961 Act – see p221 – also disregarded the depreciation.)

In *Ozanne* v *Hertfordshire County Council* [1992] it was said that releasing a large area for development and highway access was not one broad scheme.

However, there will not always be a scheme or project underlying the acquisition in purchase notice cases. In *Birmingham City District Council* v *Morris & Jacombs Ltd* [1976] CA, where land was rendered incapable of reasonable beneficial use by the imposition of a planning condition, it was held that the imposition of planning conditions could not be a scheme. The depreciated value of the land due to the planning condition could therefore not be disregarded.

The imposition of restrictive covenants under a planning agreement can be part of a scheme, although in so far as it affects the interest to be valued the principle does not apply: see *Abbey Homesteads* v *Northamptonshire County Council* [1992].

In *Vyricherla Narayana Gajapatiraju* v *Vizagapatam* [1939] the Privy Council considered that the obtaining of compulsory powers of acquisition could be part of the 'scheme': 'the valuation must always be made as though no such powers had been acquired'. That follows from *Re Lucas and Chesterfield Gas and Water Board* [1909] where Fletcher Moulton LJ said that any additional value that land has because of compulsory powers must be disregarded. It is not a requirement that a project can only be a scheme if it is a project of the acquiring authority.

> *Waters* v *Welsh Development Agency* [2002] CA
> In early 1998 the Land Authority for Wales (LAW) acquired some 1,000 acres of land for a bird reserve. The reserve was required in order to meet serious environmental objections arising from the loss of wetlands in connection with the construction of the Cardiff Bay Barrage by the Cardiff Bay Development Corporation. Some 225 acres of the land was low-lying farmland adjacent to the Severn Estuary and owned by the appellant owners. The barrage project was already underway in 1995 when the subject land was identified for the nature reserve. The owners claimed compensation on four alternative bases: £28,000 pa for 'barrage inhibition value', £13,000 pa for 'nature reserve value', £9,000 pa for 'development hope value' and £4,500 pa for agricultural value. The 'barrage inhibition value' was advanced on the basis that the land commanded an additional or ransom value consequent upon its indispensable status to the Cardiff Bay barrage scheme. The Court of Appeal decided that the nature reserve was part of the scheme. Identifying the purpose of the acquisition may be relevant to the definition of the 'scheme',

but it is not a substitute for it. It was not a requirement that a project could only be a scheme if it was a project of the acquiring authority. There was no temporal limitation on the matters that can be regarded as included in the scheme; the mere fact that the owners' land was not identified until 1995, when the barrage project was already underway, did not prevent it being treated as part of the same project. The project for the nature reserve was directly linked to the purposes of the urban development area, which included the barrage project. The owners were entitled to 'nature reserve value', but not to 'barrage inhibition value'.

4. Decrease in value due to scheme

In the *Jelson* case, the 'principle' was applied to disregard a decrease in value due to a scheme. This also arose in *Melwood Units Pty Ltd* v *Commissioner of Main Roads* [1979] PC where the Privy Council decided that an expressway project (in Australia) destroyed the potential of the affected land for development as a drive-in shopping centre, notwithstanding the fact that planning permission had not been given because of that project. The claimant was entitled to have the diminution in potential value disregarded by applying the 'principle'. In this country, the statutory planning assumptions may have applied in the circumstances of the *Melwood* case to disregard the acquiring authority's project.

So far we have been considering the application of the *Pointe Gourde* principle to schemes wider in scope than a scheme under the four cases of the statutory rule; we have also been considering whether there is always a scheme in purchase notice cases. The next case deals with a special problem. Here the scheme under one of the cases of the statutory rule is the same as the scheme area of the *Pointe Gourde* principle. But the claimant owns so much of the area of the scheme that the statutory rule cannot apply. The point is that it is the actual or prospective development in the rest of the scheme (see Area A on the diagram above) that must be disregarded under the statutory rule, but no provision is made if the claimant owns most of the scheme area (Area A) and it is actual or prospective development on some of his land (Blackacre on the diagram) that is causing an increase in value of other parts of Blackacre:

Camrose v *Basingstoke Corporation* [1966] CA
Under the Town Development Act 1952 the corporation

compulsorily purchased an area of land for development of which a goodly portion belonged to the Earl of Camrose. His land was enhanced in value, not by the development or prospect of development in the rest of the town development area (which the statutory rule could have excluded) but by the prospect of development on and within the relevant land owned by the Earl himself (and which would not be excluded by the statutory rule). The Court of Appeal held that the enhanced value could be disregarded by the application of the *Pointe Gourde* principle which would apply whenever betterment was not excluded by the statutory rule.

5. *Vandalism*

Any diminution in market value of property that is attributable to vandalism will be the claimant's loss unless he can prove that the vandalism was due to the scheme of the acquiring authority:

> *Gately* v *Central Lancashire New Town Development Corpn* [1984] LT
> Under a scheme for urban renewal, the corporation demolished a large number of properties surrounding the house of the claimant. This encouraged vandalism, and the claimant's house was badly damaged before possession was taken by the corporation. It was held that the manner in which the corporation implemented the scheme encouraged vandals: the method of implementation was itself part of the scheme. The Corporation was held 50% liable for the diminution in its value which was entirely attributable to the scheme underlying the acquisition: the *Pointe Gourde* principle was satisfied.

In *Blackadder* v *Grampian Regional Council* [1992] it was decided that although the scheme caused vandalism to the subject property, the real reason for the vandalism was the claimant giving up possession too early.

14.6 Summary

To assess compensation when market value is the statutory basis:

(a) establish natural market value on the date for assessment on the assumption the land was not being compulsorily acquired and no proposal has ever been made for its acquisition: rule (1) and section 9 of the 1961 Act;

(b) in establishing the natural market value in (a) above, regard may be had to such one or more planning permission assumptions as give the highest natural market value: sections 14–17 of the 1961 Act;

(c) apply the special suitability rule to disregard value due to purposes actual or potential covered by the rule: rule (3) of the 1961 Act;

(d) apply the statutory rule to disregard betterment or worsenment to the natural market value: section 6 of, and First Schedule to the 1961 Act; and

(e) apply the *Pointe Gourde* principle to disregard any betterment or worsenment not disregarded by the statutory rule and attributable to a scheme underlying the acquisition.

Any valuer who finds difficulty in establishing the market value of land having regard to one or more of the planning assumptions and yet having to disregard the scheme should take comfort in the following words of advice from Lord Denning MR in the *Myers* case:

> ... he must let his imagination take flight to the clouds. He must conjure up a land of make believe.

That is exactly what the interaction of the rules considered in this chapter amount to!

Chapter 15

Depreciation or Enhancement of Retained Land: Compensation or Set-off

Introduction
Severance and injurious affection
Set-off
Subsequent acquisition of retained land: section 8 of the Land
  Compensation Act 1961

15.1 Introduction

We have seen in the previous chapters that the expropriated owner is compensated for the land acquired from him; but there will be occasions when the authority only takes part of his land for its scheme. His retained land may be less valuable, either because the part taken was important to the value of the whole, or because the proposals or scheme of the acquiring authority are such as to cause values to drop by reason of the noise, visual intrusion, or other deleterious effect that is likely to occur. On the other hand, the authority's decisions and activities may increase the value of an expropriated owner's retained land.

This chapter deals with the depreciation or enhancement in the value of land retained, and the compensation that can be claimed (injurious affection and severance), or the deductions that are made (set-off), where an owner has some land compulsorily acquired. If no land is acquired from an owner, and his land is depreciated in value by the activities of an authority with statutory powers, the much more limited rights to compensation are considered in Chapter 23.

15.2 Severance and injurious affection

1. General

The right to claim compensation for severance and injurious

affection is found in section 7 of the Compulsory Purchase Act 1965 which provides that in addition to the value of the land to be purchased the owner is entitled:

> to the damage, if any, to be sustained ... by reason of the severing of the land purchased from the other land of the owner, or otherwise injuriously affecting that other land by the exercise of the powers ...

Severance occurs where the land acquired from the claimant contributes to the value of the retained land, so that when severed from it the retained land loses value. Injurious affection is the depreciation in value of retained land as a result of the compulsory acquisition and the proposed use of all the land acquired by the acquiring authority. Severance can be said to be one cause of injurious affection to the retained land. The rules on the problem of the effect of severance are deficient. They assume that damage due to severance only harms the retained land. It has long been recognised in the United States (*Sackman* [1972]) and more recently in this country (*Sams* [1982]) that severance may cause damage to the value of the land taken.

The classic test for establishing a claim for compensation for severance or injurious affection is found in *Cowper Essex* v *Acton Local Board* [1889] HL. Cowper owned land laid out for a building estate and part was taken for a sewage farm. The remaining part, which was depreciated in value by the sewage farm, was separated from the part acquired by a railway line. It was decided that a claim could be made, even if the two parts were not contiguous, provided that where a claimant has separate pieces of land, they are so near to each other, and so situated, that possession and control of each gives an enhanced value to all of them. Lord Watson said:

> ... where several pieces of land, owned by the same person, are so near to each other, and so situated that the possession and control of each gives an enhanced value to all of them, they are lands held together within the meaning of the Act: so that if one piece is compulsorily taken, and converted to uses which depreciate the value of the rest, the owner has a right to compensation.

In *Holditch* v *Canadian Northern Ontario Railway* [1916] Lord Sumner in the Privy Council said:

> The basis of a claim for lands injuriously affected by severance must be that the lands taken are so connected with or related to the lands left

that the owner of the latter is prejudiced in his ability to use or dispose of them to advantage by reason of the severance. The bare fact that before the exercise of the compulsory power to take land he was the common owner of both parcels is insufficient, for in such a case taking some of his land does no more harm to the rest than would have been done if the land taken had belonged to his neighbour. Compensation for severance therefore turns ultimately on the circumstances of the case.

The claim in the *Holditch* case failed because, prior to any notice to take the land, the owner had parcelled out the entirety and stereotyped a scheme, parting with numerous plots in all parts of it. There was therefore one owner of many holdings, with no common connections and the unity of ownership did not 'conduce to the advantage or protection' of them all as one holding.

The land retained and the land taken need not be held by the same interest or title:

> *Oppenheimer* v *Minister of Transport* [1942]
> The claimant had a freehold interest in a house and an option to purchase some adjoining fields. Part of these fields were acquired for a road and the claimant successfully obtained compensation for the depreciation in the value of the house which would result from the new road. The option to purchase the fields compulsorily acquired was regarded as land held with the land he retained.

In *Holt* v *Gas, Light and Coke Company* [1872] certain land was held under two leases for the purposes of a rifle range. Further parcels of land beyond the target butts were held under a separate lease (granted by a Mr Raphael) and under a verbal agreement. Part of this further land was compulsorily acquired. The court held that the owners of the rifle range were entitled to severance and injurious affection compensation under what is now, in effect, section 7 of the Compulsory Purchase Act 1965. In the course of his judgment Blackburn J said:

> Raphael's land was occupied not by the same title, but occupied by the same occupier, or the same parties, for the same common object. I think therefore, in every sense of the word, it was held 'therewith'. ... I cannot see, however, when the two [lands] are occupied together for a common purpose, and the possession of both is essential for that purpose, why any person who has lost the benefit of the parts taken away should not be compensated ...

That case, together with the decision in *Oppenheimer*, appears to be authority for an entitlement to compensation for the effects of severance and/or injurious affection even where the claimant holds land under different interests. Further, it would not seem necessary that a claimant must be both an owner and occupier of the land taken and land retained; common occupation is not a requirement. Provided the proximity test can be satisfied, and that can be shown where there is an enhanced value to the owner of interests (legal or equitable) (or mixed legal and equitable) in two parcels of land by reason of having possession and control of both, then that person is *prima facie* entitled to make a claim for compensation and injurious affection under section 7. The reference to the expression 'possession and control' in the *Cowper Essex* case is unlikely to mean just physical possession, but must also include legal possession of the particular interest in land in issue.

The question of related trusts of adjoining land was considered in *Rothera* v *Nottingham City Council* [1980].

There are circumstances, particularly where part of a claimant's land is acquired, and the claimant suffers injurious affection and severance, where the acquiring authority would like to consider making an offer consisting of some practicable measure to minimise or reduce the effect of the injurious affection or severance. If such an offer is made, or remedial measures are undertaken, these should be disregarded if they occur after the date of severance (normally the date of valuation). A claimant is entitled to be compensated in monetary terms for the severance and injurious affection: see *Fisher* v *Great Western Railway* [1911].

2. Severance

Severance may injuriously affect retained land because the loss of the part acquired depreciates the value of that retained, or because the claimant's land is severed into two or more parts, such as a farm by a motorway, and the severed parts are depreciated in value because of the increased cost of working:

> *Holt* v *Gas, Light and Coke Co* [1872]
> The claimant had a leasehold interest in a rifle range and a 'safe area' beyond the butts. The company acquired a small area of land in the 'safe area' to build a road for which amounted to £300. But because the road would go through the 'safe area', the rifle range could no longer be used for rifle

practice and the claimant was held to be entitled to £2,500 as compensation for the depreciation in the value of the rest of the land retained because of the severance of the small area.

The compulsory acquisition may take some of the claimant's land, and leave the retained land with no access so that planning permission for that retained land is delayed: *Bolton Metropolitan Borough Council* v *Waterworth* [1981]. Alternatively, if land with potential development value is severed, the density or timing of development on the retained land can be seriously affected: *Hoveringham Gravels Ltd* v *Chiltern District Council* [1979] and *Abbey Homesteads Group Ltd* v *Secretary of State for Transport* [1982]. The effect of taking part of a claimant's land is to destroy the marriage value that existed in the claimant's total ownership: in this chapter we are concerned, not simply with the value of the land taken, but the effect on the value of what is retained. It has already been noted that damage due to severance may harm the value of the land taken, rather than, or as well as, the retained land.

It must be appreciated that in certain circumstances, where an owner's land is severed, he may be able to compel the acquiring authority to acquire the whole of his land by the service of a counternotice: see Chapter 8.

3. *Injurious affection*

If the execution of the works by the acquiring authority, or the intended use of those works, depreciates the value of land retained by a claimant who has some land compulsorily acquired, he will have a claim for compensation for that injurious affection to the full extent of his loss:

> *Duke of Buccleuch* v *Metropolitan Board of Works* [1872]
> The Duke was the lessee of Montagu House, the garden of which ran down to the Thames; from his garden he had direct access to the river along a causeway which was regarded as part of his land. The Board constructed an embankment between the end of the garden and the river across the site of the causeway. The Duke successfully claimed compensation not only for the loss of the causeway but for the depreciation in the value of the house.

This depreciation was caused by the construction of the embankment and a public highway thereon which resulted in loss of privacy and traffic, dust, dirt and noise which altered the character of the house. It must be noted that the claim is for a depreciation in value caused either by the execution of the authorised works or the subsequent use of those works. Loss of privacy and a deterioration in the character of an area which tend to affect market value will therefore be compensated if due to the exercise of the statutory powers: see *Turris Investments Ltd* v *CEGB* [1981] LT for the injurious affect of electricity lines and pylons. This must be contrasted with the position of an owner who loses no land but yet suffers depreciation in the value of his land; his claim, if any, is more limited: see Chapter 23.

4. *Measure of compensation*

The case of *Horn* v *Sunderland Corporation* [1941] CA is often cited as authority for the principle that a claimant should receive compensation that is neither no greater, nor no less than his loss. It is then argued that in the case of the severance of land, where the claimant loses some land and retains other land, then the most appropriate way of determining his loss is to value his whole property before severance and then deduct from this the value of his retained land after severance. There is also a question whether the reference in section 7 of the 1965 Act, that an owner is entitled not only to the value of the land purchased from him but also to the damage sustained by reason of the severance, suggests that compensation for 'damage' is a reference to a claim not solely related to the depreciation in the market value of the interest in the remaining land, as suggested by the Tribunal in *Rathgar Property Company Ltd* v *Haringay London Borough Council* [1978].

There are two possible methods for determining the loss to an expropriated owner in a case of severance. The first is to value the land that is taken and add to this the decrease in value, if any, of the retained land. The second method is the 'before and after' method in which the expropriated owner's entire interest is valued before severance and from this is deducted the value of the land he retains. There are advantages and disadvantages with each method. Under the first method the expropriated owner will always receive the value of the land that is taken from him. On the other hand, the act of severance may destroy the marriage value in having the land in its entirety. This first method also presents problems of valuation, especially where there is marriage value in the land in its entirety, as it may be difficult to determine the market value of the part taken and the depreciation in the value of that retained, if both valuations are to be carried out as separate exercises.

The 'before and after' method has the advantage of being the easier valuation exercise, but it was said by the Tribunal in *Abbey Homesteads Group Ltd* v *Secretary of State for Transport* [1982] that compensation for the land taken must be assessed separately from compensation for severance and injurious affection: a 'before and after' valuation was said to be based on a wrong legal premise. The Tribunal in the *Abbey Homesteads* case found support for the view that compensation for land taken must be assessed as a separate exercise from compensation for severance and injurious affection in both earlier case authority and in the statutory scheme set out in the Land Compensation Act 1961. For judicial authority, there is the judgment of Eve J in *South Eastern Railway* v *London County Council* [1915], and approved by the Court of Appeal, and the judgments of the Court of Appeal in *Hoveringham Gravels Ltd* v *Chiltern District Council* [1977], in particular that of Roskill LJ who said: 'It seems to us clear that the section [7] in its true construction is envisaging an additional head of compensation for the owner of the land being taken by reason of other retained land of his being less valuable to him through that retained land being severed from or otherwise injuriously affected by the compulsory acquisition of the land taken'. The *Abbey Homesteads* case and the method of valuing the land taken and the land retained as two separate interests, was followed in *ADP&E Farmers* v *Department of Transport* [1988], where it was said that this accords with rule (2) of section 5 of the 1961 Act and section 7 of the Compulsory Purchase Act 1965; it also allows the *Stokes* payment to be allowed for in determining any ransom payment.

Despite these strictures, the 'before and after' method of valuation will no doubt still be used on behalf of claimants and acquiring authorities alike because of its advantages in most cases of severance. It probably best achieves the true loss of a claimant for which he is entitled to compensation: see *Hughes* v *Doncaster Metropolitan Borough Council* [1991].

The valuation of the land taken and the effect of severance and injurious affection must be on a consistent basis: see *Horn* v *Sunderland Corporation* [1941] as applied in *RA Vine (Engineering) Ltd* v *Havant Borough Council* [1989] and *BP Petroleum Developments Ltd* v *Ryder* [1987]; see also *St John's College, Oxford* v *Thames Water Authority* [1990]. Thus, if the land being acquired is valued on a development value basis, or valued on some basis which assumes it is being severed from any retained land of the claimant, the claimant should not be entitled to compensation for injurious affection or severance if the depreciation in value to the retained land would have come about in the valuation hypothesis used for the land acquired.

The illustration that now follows shows the difference between the use of the two methods of determining compensation in the case of a severance:

Example

Assume that Blackacre is owned in its entirety by one freehold owner and that it has planning permission for the erection of one house. Its value for this purpose is £30,000. The acquiring authority takes a strip of front land for the widening of a road and the effect of this is that the land retained is now too small for building purposes. Assume that the back land on its own now has a value of £5,000, possibly as an addition to someone's garden, and the front land on its own, and without considering marriage value with a view to development, has a value of £1,000

Land taken	**Front land**
Land retained	**Back land**

Valuation of land taken and damage to retained land assessed separately

	£	£
Value of land taken:		
Front land has an existing value on its own of £1,000 but assume a marriage value of 30% of the unlocked development value in the whole plot.		8,200

Depreciation in value of retained land:	£	£
The back land has a value of £5,000 but assume again it has a marriage value of 30% of the unlocked development value.	12,200	
Less the value of the retained land without any prospect of marriage.	5,000	7,200
Total compensation equals value of land taken and depreciation in value of retained land.		£15,400

(Marriage value = £30,000 – (£1,000 + £5,000) = £24,000)

'Before and after' valuation	£
Value of Blackacre as a building plot with the benefit of planning permission.	30,000
Value of the retained land as a possible addition to someone's garden:	5,000
Difference in values equals loss to the expropriated owner:	25,000

The first valuation method would seem to be the correct method following the *Abbey Homesteads* case, but it denies to the expropriated owner the depreciation in the value of the land taken that is attributable to the loss of the marriage value. In this sort of circumstance, it may be possible to argue that the *Pointe Gourde* principle is applicable and that any depreciation in value is attributable to the scheme of acquisition that has destroyed the chance of realising a building plot with the value of planning permission. This argument was accepted by the Court of Appeal in *Jelson Ltd* v *Blaby District Council* [1978] in the case of a strip of land that had been sterilised by a proposed highway scheme. The severance effect on the value of the land taken was disregarded by applying the *Pointe Gourde* principle (see p223 above). It was also accepted in *Salop County Council* v *Craddock* [1970] and in *Melwood Units Property Ltd* v *Commissioner of Main Roads* [1979]: see also *South Eastern Rly* v *London County Council* [1915]; *Hoveringham Gravels* v *Chiltern District Council* [1977] and *Turris Investments* v *CEGB* [1981] for related difficulties.

The various statutory planning assumptions set out in the Land Compensation Act 1961 are not relevant in the case of retained land. This is because sections 14–17 refer to the 'relevant land', a reference which means the land which is being acquired. Thus, in the *Abbey Homesteads* case where a certificate of appropriate alternative development had been issued, the Tribunal said that it was wrong to have regard to the certificate in the case of the retained land in a severance situation. But, as the member said: 'Of course, although the certificate has no relevance or usefulness save in respect of the land acquired, the material which gave rise to its being issued or its contents being agreed can be referred to on the wider issue'. This means that although the precise development which might have been permitted and as specified in the certificate cannot be relied on in determining values for the retained land, none the less, the fact that a certificate has been issued means that the planning background, and the sort of development that may or may not have been permitted, will be relevant. This was followed in *ADP&E Farmers* v *Department of Transport* [1988]. But see *Porter* v *Secretary of State for Transport* CA[1996].

In assessing the compensation, damage that may result from an anticipated use of the authorised works must be taken into account:

> *Rockingham Sisters of Charity* v *R* [1922] PC
> Two small parcels of land were acquired from a school, but at the time of assessing compensation were then little used. It was held that the school could claim compensation for depreciation in the value of the land it retained by virtue of an anticipated legal user of the acquired land as a railway shunting yard.

The amount of compensation for severance and injurious affection is the depreciation in the value of the retained land not the extra costs to the owner:

> *Cooke* v *Secretary of State for Environment* [1973] LT
> Cooke owned a farm of 141 acres which was severed by a road improvement scheme into two parts. The consequences of the scheme were as follows. A small area of land was acquired, including the site of the farming buildings; the farmhouse was left without direct access to the farm land and about a half mile from the new site of the buildings; and, cattle could no longer be driven across the new road from one side of the farm to the other. Cooke claimed the costs of providing new buildings, access road, capitalised cost of car travel from the old farmhouse and the capitalised cost of transporting the

cattle by lorry across the road, all amounting to £19,000. The Lands Tribunal decided that proper basis of a claim for damage due to severance is the difference between the value of the land before the severance, but less the land actually acquired, and its value afterwards. The amount awarded was:

Value of land taken	£3,376
Compensation for severance and injurious affection	£3,048

It can be seen from this case that the depreciation in market value may be less than the full cost to the claimant of the severance. It is not necessarily true that the loss of essential buildings or adequate access between severed portions of land will reduce the value of the remainder of the land by the costs of replacement or increased working costs as the case may be. In *Frederick Powell & Son Ltd* v *Devon County Council* [1979] LT the acquisition of part of a development site meant the development costs had to be averaged over the smaller area of retained land. These extra costs could not be compensated as there was no evidence that there had been any depreciation in value of the retained land.

The valuation must be made at the date of severance to find the depreciation in the market value of the severed land; but section 7 directs that it is the damage due to severance that must be ascertained and the question that might arise is whether events following that date of severance can be considered where these enable a more precise calculation of the severed owner's loss to be made:

Bolton Metropolitan Borough Council v *Waterworth* [1981] CA
Thirty acres of agricultural land were purchased by agreement from the claimants in 1972. It was a term of the agreement that the claimants could submit a claim for compensation for severance in respect of 8.5 acres that was retained. Several planning applications for the development of the retained land were refused on the grounds of inadequate access. Although the 8.5 acres could have been developed along with the 30 acres already acquired, the effect of severance was to land-lock the 8.5 acres and the claimants submitted a claim for compensation for the effect of severance of £97,750. In March 1976 the claimants sold the 8.5 acres for £50,000, the purchasers were able to obtain planning permission for its development, together with some more land they already

owned. The acquiring authority submitted that the claim for severance should be limited to the deferment of the entitlement to the development value from the date of severance to the date when this successful planning permission was issued: a sum of £39,372 was offered. The Lands Tribunal accepted that the act of severance caused the delay in obtaining planning permission because of the lack of access, but considered that a deferment of seven years was a reasonable estimate to the date of severance and awarded damages due to severance of £63,648. One issue was whether the Tribunal was entitled to take into account events occurring after the date of severance under what is known as the *'Bwllfa* principle' *(Bwllfa and Merthyr Dare Steam Collieries (1891) Ltd v Pontypridd Water Works Company* [1903]). The Tribunal's decision that the *Bwllfa* principle should be followed was accepted by the Court of Appeal and its decision that the evidence of the subsequent sale and the connection between the price and the planning permission was unsatisfactory and could not be relied on was also supported. The Court of Appeal found a further reason for upholding the decision of the Tribunal, namely that when the planning permission for the severed land was eventually given, it was not for that land alone, but for that and other land together.

In making the 'before' valuation, the valuer must apply the *Pointe Gourde* principle and disregard any increase or decrease in value due to the scheme underlying the acquisition:

> *Clarke v Wareham and Purbeck Rural District Council* [1972] LT
> Clark owned a farm adjoining an outmoded, overloaded and malodorous sewage works. About three acres of land were acquired from Clark to enable the existing sewage works to be enlarged and modernised ('with-scheme world'). Had this scheme not been proceeded with, the original works would have been modernised within the limitation of the existing site ('no-scheme world'). The Lands Tribunal decided that the damage to Clark's retained land due to injurious affection was the difference between the value of the retained land in the 'no-scheme world' and its value in the 'with-scheme world'; but as the Tribunal found the value of the retained land in the 'with-scheme world' no less than its value would have been in the 'no-scheme world', no injurious affection existed.

In the following case the *Pointe Gourde* principle was applied in determining the value of the land acquired and the depreciation due to severance of the retained land of the claimant:

> *Melwood Units Property Ltd* v *Commissioner of Main Roads* [1979] PC
> The claimant purchased 37 acres of land on the outskirts of Brisbane (Australia); it was intended to develop the land as a drive-in shopping centre, although at the time of purchase it was known that an expressway was to be built through the centre of the land. But for the proposed expressway, the claimant would have been granted planning permission for the whole 37 acres; in the event they obtained planning permission for a shopping centre on 25 acres north of the proposed expressway. The Privy Council decided that the value of the land acquired for the expressway (5 acres), and the value of the land to the south of the expressway (7 acres) retained by the claimant but no longer capable of shopping centre development, should first be determined as if part of a drive-in shopping centre that could have been developed on the 37 acres had there been no expressway. In respect of the severed 7 acres, there is deducted from this 'before' value its value after severance; the difference represents compensation for severance.

It was decided in the case of *Edwards* v *Minister of Transport* [1964] CA that where a claimant seeks compensation for injurious affection to his retained land, he could only succeed in respect of the injurious affection attributable to the use of the land acquired from him. So, if a noisy road is built by an acquiring authority which depreciates the value of a person's property, and the land taken from that person is used as a grass verge or hard shoulder, a use which is not noisy, he will have no claim to compensation for what could be substantial depreciation. This unsatisfactory position was reversed by section 44 of the Land Compensation Act 1973. Now, in determining compensation for injurious affection, the compensation is assessed by reference to the effect of the whole of the works of the acquiring authority and not only the part of the works situated on land acquired from a claimant.

In *Garrett* v *Department of the Environment for Northern Ireland* [1985] where a garage lost petrol sales due to road works and a stopping-up order, it was held that the whole of the loss was attributable to the road works, and no deduction need be made for the stopping-up order. It was agreed that a stopping-up order is not, alone, compensatable.

In *Countess of Malmesbury* v *Secretary of State for Transport* [1982] it was decided that the construction of a motorway affected the water table which caused subsidence damage. This was compensatable as injurious affection.

The acquiring authority may carry out accommodation works (see Chapter 21) or other works of mitigation such as tree planting, erection of sound baffles or noise insulation (see Chapter 24); the value of such work is taken into account in assessing compensation for severance and injurious affection.

A final point needs to be appreciated in a case of severance. If the expropriated owner claims compensation for the land taken on a basis that assumes a different purpose to the land retained (e.g. some form of development), so that severance is inevitable, he may reduce or destroy his claim for severance compensation. An example will illustrate this:

Example

Blackberry Farm is 50 acres in area and the highway authority require five acres for a new road; this will sever the farm into two parts, two acres to the north of the proposed road containing the buildings, and 43 acres of land to the south. The depreciation in value of the retained 45 acres as farming land due to severance is considerable and amounts to, say £10,000. But if the owner succeeds in claiming some development value for the five acres acquired, which value could only be realised by the separate sale of the five acres and the severance of the farm, the depreciation due to severance will be disallowed as it is inconsistent with the basis of the claim for the land taken. To avoid this, the claimant should claim existing use value for the land taken and then he can claim depreciation in the existing use value of the land retained as his severance claim.

5. *Acquisition of rights: section 13 of the Local Government (Miscellaneous Provisions) Act 1976*

Where a right, such as an easement, is acquired over land under the 1976 Act, the acquisition of the right is to be considered as part of the owner's land. Accordingly, the owner of the land over which the new right is acquired is entitled to compensation for severance and injurious affection to that retained land. For this purpose, section 7 of the 1965 Act is adapted to read as follows:

> In assessing compensation ... regard shall be had not only to the extent, if any, to which the value of the land over which the right is purchased is depreciated by the purchase but also to the damage, if any, to be sustained by the owner of the land by reason of injurious affection of other land of the owner by the exercise of the right.

All the principles so far discussed in relation to severance and injurious affection will apply in respect of the taking of a right as they apply in respect of the taking of a part of land of an owner. *Turris Investments Ltd* v *CEGB* [1981] LT was concerned with the acquisition of rights, not under the 1976 Act, but under equivalent powers available to the electricity authorities. The member accepted taking separately the value of the land taken and the injurious affection due to pylons and cables. Visual intrusion was acknowledged and depreciation in value of land immediately affected by the pylons and cables was awarded at 12.5% of land value, with a further sum of 3% of land values for land further away and not immediately under the cable.

15.3 Set-off

The Land Compensation Act 1961 (sections 7 and 8), certain other public general Acts, such as the Highways Act 1980 (section 261), and many local Acts, provide that where an owner, who has had some land compulsorily acquired, retains land which increases in value because of the acquiring authority's scheme, that increase in value shall be deducted or set off against the compensation to be paid for land taken. This is a form of betterment recoupment. But if the betterment to retained land exceeds the compensation for the land taken, the excess cannot be recovered, nor can any betterment be recovered from an owner who has no land taken from him.

Legislation authorising the recovery of betterment has a long pedigree. The Act for the Rebuilding of London 1667 after the Great Fire authorised the common council to recover betterment following the improvement and widening of streets. The House of Lords, in a report in 1895, recommended that betterment clauses should be inserted in statutory powers: e.g. London County Council (Improvements) Act 1897. Although the idea that individual landowners should not keep the benefit created by schemes funded by tax or ratepayers finds a measure of approval, in practice there seems both reluctance and difficulty in recovering betterment.

It should also be pointed out that where a landowner expects betterment to accrue to his retained land by virtue of a scheme, he would be well advised to transfer his interest in the retained land to some other party before the date of the notice to treat.

1. Non-statutory betterment

A distinction must be made between the statutory rules for the deduction of betterment and other benefits which may arise directly or indirectly from the scheme which may be called 'non-statutory betterment'. For example, in connection with the construction of a motorway through an agricultural holding, the contractors might make arrangements with the owner for the use of land to extract gravel for road construction use, or to deposit surplus material: large sums of money may be payable for such benefits. The acquiring authority will normally try to set off against compensation the benefits obtained by these contracts. The question in issue is whether at the valuation date the value of the land retained by the claimant in the open market is higher by reason of these benefits than it would otherwise have been in the absence of the scheme. This will depend upon whether or not the contract has been entered into prior to the valuation date, and whether the benefit and burdens of any such contract bind a successor in title. If no contract has been entered into by the valuation date, the value of the retained land might, possibly, reflect the possibility of entering into such contracts. However, it must be borne in mind that there may be other possible 'sellers' of such benefits along the route of the motorway. If the contract is entered into prior to the valuation date, then the question will arise as to whether the benefits and burdens of the contract bind any successor in title, and will therefore be a factor in the open market. In any event it cannot be the consideration payable under such a contract which must be deducted, but only the increased value attributable to the benefit of any such contract. In determining the effect of severance and injurious affection, it must be remembered that it is the 'after value' which is to be determined in identifying the loss attributable to such matters.

Another example of non-statutory betterment might arise where part of a claimant's property is taken for a road, and by reason of the underlying scheme of the acquiring authority planning permission to develop the claimant's retained land becomes more certain. In the absence of statutory rules to deduct betterment to retained land from the compensation otherwise payable for the land taken, there is an argument for the deduction on basic principles in the absence of specific rules. *Horn* v *Sunderland Corporation* [1941], as approved in *Director of Buildings and Lands* v *Shun Fung Ironworks Ltd* [1995], is authority that a claimant is entitled to his loss and no more or less. Accordingly, where some land is taken by a scheme, but some is retained and is enhanced, the total net effect on the claimant should be considered.

However, there is strong authority in the Court of Appeal's decision in *South Eastern Railway* v *London County Council* [1915] that betterment should not be deducted from compensation for land taken unless it is done under statutory authority. Such statutory provisions are now considered.

2. *The general set-off provision: section 7 of the Land Compensation Act 1961*

Where an owner has some land compulsorily acquired and owns in the same capacity an interest in other land which is contiguous or adjacent to the land taken, there is deducted from the compensation payable the amount of any increase in value of the retained land which is due to development or the prospect of development in the following circumstances:

(a) development or the prospect of development in the compulsory purchase order or the area authorised to be acquired and which would have been unlikely had there been no proposal to acquire any of the land; and

(b) development or the prospect of development in the comprehensive development area, action area, site of a new town (or extension thereto) and an area for town development under the Town Development Act 1952, being in each case development for those purposes and development which would have been unlikely had there been no such designation or definition of the areas concerned.

This requirement to deduct increases in value due to development or the prospect of development in the defined scheme, and which would have been unlikely but for that scheme, makes reference to section 6 of and the First Schedule to the 1961 Act for the purpose of defining the circumstances of the scheme (see previous chapter).

> *Laing Homes Ltd* v *Eastleigh Borough Council* [1979] LT
> 0.68 acres of land were acquired for a spine road, and Laing Homes were left with 2.7 acres. All the land had some development potential with a suitable spine road access. Laing Homes claimed £1m. The authority offered a nominal £1 on the basis that its construction of a spine road saved Laing Homes the construction costs resulting in betterment to the retained 2.7 acres: section 7 of the 1961 Act and the *Pointe Gourde* principle were said to apply. The Tribunal found as an issue of fact that there was no evidence that Laing's land could not be developed in the absence of the spine road (there were other access alternatives – although less satisfactory), betterment could not be recovered under section 7. The Tribunal awarded £12,750 after making a 25% deduction to allow for the cost of acquiring an access with no-scheme world.

3. *Other provisions for set-off*

The general set-off provision described above applies to every compulsory acquisition unless the Act authorising acquisition itself contains a set-off provision: see section 8(5). Probably the most common example is section 261 of Highways Act 1980 which provides that where land is compulsorily acquired under that Act for the construction or improvement of a highway, then, in assessing compensation for the land taken, regard shall be had to the extent to which the remaining contiguous lands belonging to the same person may be benefited by the purpose for which the land is authorised to be acquired:

> *Cooke* v *Secretary of State for Environment* [1973] LT (for full facts see p242)
> Cooke had permitted the contractors building the road to dump soil on his land: he was paid £6,000. This was said to have increased the value of his contiguous land and ought to have been deducted from any compensation for land taken. The Lands Tribunal decided that the set-off provision did not apply to the circumstances as there must be some increase in value of the contiguous land, attributable to the new road itself, 'by reason of having a new or improved access' which

would enhance the possibility of, say, development; in any event, the contiguous land was not benefited by the construction of the road, but by the dumping of soil which was purely incidental to the construction of the road.

In *Cooke*, therefore, the purpose of section 261 was said 'to set-off any value the land would have, particularly for development purposes, by reason of having a new or improved access to it'. In *Leicester City Council* v *Leicester County Council* [1995], where the retained land had the benefit of planning permission and an enhanced value of £4m, the Lands Tribunal added to those words 'or an enhanced capacity in the local highway network to facilitate development of the retained land'. The Tribunal went further and decided in the *Leicester* case that there was no ground for exercising any discretion it might have to determine the compensation for the land taken at the agricultural existing use value. Accordingly no compensation was payable.

> *Portsmouth Roman Catholic Diocesan Trustees* v *Hampshire County Council* [1980] LT
> Certain land was acquired to form a distributor road; the claimants retained 6.64 acres. The authority argued that planning permission to develop this land could not have been expected without the construction of the road, and that its benefit should be set off against compensation for the land taken. The increment in value was £182,600. The Tribunal accepted that planning permission for the retained land would not have been granted until the road was constructed, but did not accept that this was the kind of benefit to be taken into account. The grant of planning permission is an indirect effect of the road; it is too remote especially if the permission results from a policy which itself was referable to the purpose for which the land taken was acquired. The kind of benefit to be set-off must be 'directly referable to the purpose for which the land is authorised to be acquired, such as where the coming of the road will provide access to the retained land of a new or improved kind (including the creation of a frontage to a widened highway), which benefit increases the value of the land.'

The member of the Tribunal added that the expression 'shall have regard' gave him a discretion not to deduct betterment from existing value.

In *Lorbright Ltd* v *Staffordshire County Council* [1980] LT the widening and improvement of a road junction which benefited land retained by the claimant did accord with the requirements of benefit which the Tribunal should have regard, but no betterment could be deducted in that case, as the value of the land taken was determined as £1 after deducting the cost of the access.

The Act additionally specifically directs that in the case of land acquired for widening a highway, there shall be set off against the value of the land acquired any increase in the value of other land belonging to the same person which will accrue to him by reason of the creation of a frontage to the highway as widened (section 261(1)):

> *Grosvenor Motor Co* v *Chester Corpn* [1963] LT
> Land was acquired from the claimant company to widen a street; the widening so improving the utility of that street that the value of all frontages increased most noticeably. As the value of the land taken came to £6,800 and the increase in value of the retained land was £8,745, no compensation was payable for the land taken.

15.4 Subsequent acquisition of retained land: section 8 of the Land Compensation Act 1961

If the acquiring authority subsequently acquires land retained by an owner, and that land has already been the subject of a payment for compensation for injurious affection, then that depreciated value shall not be disregarded by virtue of section 6 (see Chapter 12), for to do otherwise would mean that a depreciated value would be compensated twice over, once on the first acquisition by injurious affection compensation and again on a subsequent acquisition by disregarding the depreciated value and paying its non-depreciated value: this would be wrong.

If the acquiring authority subsequently acquires land retained by an owner and that land was increased in value by an earlier acquisition and that increase in value has already been taken into account and set off against the compensation paid on the first acquisition under section 7 (see section **15.3.1** above), then that increased value shall not be disregarded, as would otherwise be the case, under section 6.

Finally, if an area of retained land has, upon an earlier acquisition of other land of a claimant, increased in value so that the set-off provisions in section 7 have been applied in the first acquisition, then the same increase in value need not be set off against compensation for land taken from the claimant in any subsequent acquisition.

The provisions described in the three foregoing paragraphs refer to first and subsequent acquisitions for the same scheme (as defined in Part I of the First Schedule, 1961 Act) and the reference to owner or claimant will include any successor in title.

Chapter 16

Compensation for Land Acquired: Special Cases

Introduction
Equivalent reinstatement
Houses unfit for human habitation
Listed buildings

16.1 Introduction

Chapter 12 was concerned with the compensation payable for land compulsorily purchased and where the market value is the appropriate basis. This chapter deals with certain special cases where the market value is either not used or is significantly modified. Market value may be inappropriate if a claimant's property is used for a purpose for which there is no market; he may be able to claim the cost of purchasing, building or adapting other property for his particular purpose under the rule permitting 'equivalent reinstatement'. In other cases, where a building does not comply with the law, or a listed building has not been repaired after a direction requiring repair, it is considered that as a matter of policy owners of such buildings should not benefit from their omissions: less than market value may be payable.

16.2 Equivalent reinstatement

Rule (5) of Section 5 of the Land Compensation Act 1961 provides:

> Where land is, and but for the compulsory acquisition would continue to be, devoted to a purpose of such a nature that there is no general demand or market for land for that purpose, the compensation may, if the Lands Tribunal is satisfied that reinstatement in some other place is bona fide intended, be assessed on the basis of the reasonable cost of equivalent reinstatement

This rule will apply in the case of the acquisition of a freehold interest. In *Runcorn Association Football Club* v *Warrington and Runcorn Development Corpn* [1982] the Tribunal held that the rule will also apply in the case of a leasehold interest that had more than a year's unexpired term at the date of the notice to treat. Even if the interest acquired had had less than a year to run, and the basis of compensation was under section 20 of the Compulsory Purchase Act 1965 (see Chapter 19), the rule might still apply because the tenant's right to a new lease under the Landlord and Tenant Act 1954 has to be taken into account: section 47, Land Compensation Act 1973. In *Conservative and Unionist Club* v *Manchester City Council* [1975] the Lands Tribunal accepted that a rule (5) claim could be pursued where property owned by a company formed by a local political association was let on a yearly tenancy to a political club. However, no decision was made as to whether the landlord company or the tenant club was the correct claimant under rule (5).

1. *The conditions for the application of rule (5)*

This rule was analysed in *Sparks* v *Leeds City Council* [1977] LT, a case involving the compulsory purchase of the premises of a members' social club; the member of the Lands Tribunal put forward four essentials of rule (5) to be satisfied by the claimants, on whom is the burden of proof:

> (a) 'That the subject land is devoted to a purpose, and but for the compulsory acquisition would continue to be so devoted.'
> It was said in *Aston Charities Trust* v *Stepney Borough Council* [1952] CA that 'devoted to a purpose' is a question of intention rather than the *de facto* use at the date of the notice to treat, so that where bombing of property caused a temporary interruption of the purposes, the actual or de facto use for a storage could be ignored as the intention to use the premises for the charitable purpose had not been abandoned. The date of the notice to treat is the proper date for determining whether land is devoted to a purpose within rule (5). This was confirmed in *Zoar Independent Church Trustees* v *Rochester Corpn* [1974]; in this case the land consisted of a chapel which, at the date of the notice to treat, was used by a very small congregation; later, the roof fell in and the congregation, having considered that repairs would be rendered otiose by the impending acquisition, abandoned

regular use of the chapel and met elsewhere. The Court of Appeal decided that it was 'devoted to a purpose' and, but for the acquisition, would have continued to be devoted to public worship; 'continuity of devotion', it was held, is not directed to perpetuity; it is sufficient if the intention to continue that purpose existed at the time of the notice to treat.

(b) *'That the purpose is one for which there is no general demand or market for the land for that purpose'*

The example of a 'purpose ... for which there is no general demand or market for the land' include religious purposes (the *Zoar* case), charitable purposes (the *Aston* case), clubs (*St John's Wood Working Men's Club* v *LCC* [1947]), and hospitals or clinics (*Trustees of the Manchester Homeopathic Clinic* v *Manchester Corpn* [1970]).

The test, however, is the absence of any general demand or market for land devoted to the purpose. This is a question of fact; in the Sparks case the absence of a general demand or market for a club was accepted, whereas in *Wilkinson* v *Middlesborough Borough Council* [1979] the claimants failed to satisfy the Lands Tribunal that there would be no market for premises for a multi-principal veterinary surgeon's practice. The member accepted that it was customary to accept a new partner who would buy out a retiring partner, and that although this was the normal method of disposal, he had no reason to doubt that for premises occupied by a multi-principal firm there would be a market. The decision of the Tribunal was upheld by the Court of Appeal with one dissentient. Waller LJ thought that just because there was a market in the disposal of a partnership share in multi-principal firms did not entitle the Tribunal to conclude that there would be a market in land for such firms.

A more definitive meaning of 'no general demand or market' was given by the House of Lords in *Harrison & Hetherington Ltd* v *Cumbria County Council* [1985], a case involving the acquisition of a livestock market. It was accepted that livestock markets rarely came into the market for sale, and that a small number of transactions meant there was hardly a market in such premises. But intermittent demand is not general demand. The fact that a particular property would sell if put up for sale is not, of itself, evidence of a general demand or market; latent demand is not general demand.

(c) *'The bona fide intention to reinstate on another site'*

In *Edge Hill Light Railway Co* v *Secretary of State for War* [1956] LT, in respect of the acquisition of part of a railway, the claimants failed to satisfy the Tribunal that they intended to reinstate the railway undertaking elsewhere.

The bona fide intention to reinstate was accepted in the *Sparks* case, although the member of the Tribunal considered that intention must connote also financial ability, and he looked at the claimant's accounts and a rebuilding fund: he was satisfied that reinstatement was, and remained, a bona fide intention by reason of negotiations for the new site and a commitment to a feasibility study. In the *Zoar* case, the Court of Appeal was satisfied that an intention to reinstate was present; the question was not whether the former congregation or any part of it was to be reinstated, or a chapel with a particular name, but whether the purposes of the former chapel were to be reinstated. The fact that some members of the original congregation joined with others to form a chapel with a new name, but which continued the purposes of the original chapel, did not negate a bona fide intention to reinstate.

If reinstatement is intended some way from the original premises, it will only be within rule (5) if the original purpose of the premises can be reinstated at that distance. Thus, in the *Aston* case, the Court of Appeal decided it would be a question of degree whether a purpose was so local as to be incapable of being reinstated very far away; although the reinstatement of a church hall four miles away was held to be within the rule.

It was said in the *Zoar* case that the bona fide intention of the claimant is not in question if the realisation of the intention to reinstate depends on receiving compensation under rule (5) on the basis of the reasonable cost of equivalent reinstatement.

(d) *'these conditions being satisfied, that the Tribunal's reasonable discretion should be exercised in [the claimant's] favour'*

The Tribunal has discretion as to whether compensation is to be assessed in accordance with this rule (in practice the discretion may first be exercised by the district valuer):

Festiniog Railway Co v *Central Electricity Generating Board* [1962] CA:
The acquiring authority compulsorily purchased part of a railway line and tunnel. Although the railway had not been

used for a time it was reopened and run for pleasure trips and the new owners intended to replace that part of the line taken. The Court of Appeal upheld the decision of the Lands Tribunal that rule (5) should not apply as the costs of reinstatement (£180,000) were so disproportionate to the value of the railway undertaking (about £3,000).

(Despite the decision, the CEGB did make a contribution to the costs of rebuilding the line as railway enthusiasts will know.)

Although the discretion as to whether to allow the application of rule (5) is the Land Tribunal's, it must not unreasonably exercise its discretion against a claimant. With a commercial undertaking, the question of the relation between the cost of reinstatement and the value of the undertaking was considered by Ormerod LJ, in the *Festiniog* case, to be a relevant or even a paramount question for the Tribunal in considering the exercise of its discretion, but it was not a conclusive factor.

In practice, an acquiring authority may agree to rule (5) compensation without any need for the claimant to first apply to the Lands Tribunal. However, an authority which attempts to withdraw from such an agreement may be estopped: see *Trustees of the Manchester Homeopathic Clinic* v *Manchester Corpn* [1970].

Lands Tribunal decisions

In *Kolbe House Society* v *Department of Transport* [1995] the Lands Tribunal accepted that a building used as a home for Polish and Central European refugees was devoted to a purpose of a non profit-making charity; there was no general demand and compensation could be awarded under rule (5).

2. Cost of reinstatement

The date for ascertaining the cost of reinstatement is the date when in all the circumstances the claimant can reasonably begin replacement: *Birmingham Corpn* v *West Midlands Baptist (Trust) Association* [1970]: see Chapter 11.

The claimant is entitled to the cost of acquiring an alternative site, constructing replacement buildings together with architects' fees and other consequential costs. If the premises to be reinstated require repair, a deduction to reflect this will be made:

Cunningham v *Sunderland CBC* [1963] LT
Upon the acquisition of premises used for parochial church purposes, the Lands Tribunal, having decided that rule (5) applied, adopted the following figures for the equivalent reinstatement basis: (1) cost of site, with fees, £1,554; (2) cost of new equivalent building, £17,000; (3) site works, £1,330; (4) architect's and quantity surveyor's fees, £1,650; deduction for cost of essential repairs to existing buildings at date of notice to treat, £3,000.

The deduction for repairs is made in accordance with the principle that the compensation should not put a claimant in a better position because of the compulsory acquisition: he is only entitled to equivalent reinstatement: *Runcorn Association Football Club* v *Warrington and Runcorn Development Corpn* [1982].

3. Disturbance

Disturbance compensation, in addition to reinstatement costs, is payable for those matters attributable to disturbance in Chapter 17, such as loss of profits: see *Eronpark Ltd* v *Secretary of State for Transport* [2000] LT.

4. Interest

Statutory interest on unpaid compensation is payable from the date of entry until the date when compensation is received as during this period the claimant has neither the land nor its value: see *Halstead* v *Manchester City Council* [1998] CA.

5. Disabled person's home

Section 45 of the Land Compensation Act 1973 provides that where a dwelling has been constructed or substantially modified to meet the special needs of a disabled person and is occupied by such a person as his residence, then, if the claimant so elects, the compensation can be assessed in accordance with the provisions of rule (5).

16.3 Houses unfit for human habitation

It will be recalled that rule (4) precludes the payment of compensation for any increase in value by reason of premises being used in a manner which is contrary to law, or is detrimental to the health of the occupants or to the public health.

Housing authorities may deal with areas of bad housing by making clearance areas or redevelopment areas under Part IX of the Housing Act 1985, and then compulsorily acquire the land. Individual unfit houses may be acquired compulsorily under Part VI of the Act. Until its repeal, section 585 of the 1985 Act provided that compensation was the value of the site of the house, cleared and available for development in accordance with the requirements of building regulations. The original purpose of this basis was to discourage the provision of unhealthy houses by landlords and to ensure that acquiring authorities did not pay for buildings that were contrary to public health standards. However, the value of a bare site on this basis may be very low if the site is too small to permit rebuilding in accordance with building regulations. The Local Government and Housing Act 1989 repealed the provisions relating to site value compensation in respect of any unfitness orders made after March 31 1990. Accordingly, claimants are now entitled to compensation assessed by reference to market values.

Injustice may be caused to an owner, especially an owner-occupier or a person who has maintained the house in a reasonable condition, if only the bare site value is paid. Accordingly, a number of additional payments were made to mitigate such injustice, in addition to the bare site value. Reference should be made to the 4th edition of this book for details of the determination of site value and the additional payments.

16.4 Listed buildings

The usual compensation rules for the compulsory acquisition of a listed building will normally apply.

However, if a listed building is being compulsorily acquired under the Planning (Listed Buildings and Conservation Areas) Act 1990, section 51, because reasonable steps are not being taken for properly preserving it, the Secretary of State may direct that minimum compensation shall be paid if he is satisfied the building has been deliberately allowed to fall into disrepair for the purpose of justifying its demolition and the development or redevelopment of the site.

Before such compulsory acquisition commences, the owner must be served, at least two months previously, with a repairs notice specifying the works considered reasonably necessary for the proper preservation of the building and explaining the consequences of compulsory acquisition and a direction for minimum compensation: section 48.

When a direction for minimum compensation has been made, compensation is assessed as the market value but on the assumption that, contrary to the statutory planning assumptions in the Land Compensation Act 1961, planning permission would not be granted for development or redevelopment of the site and listed building consent would not be granted for any works for the demolition, alteration or extension of the building other than development or works necessary for preserving it. Such a direction can be challenged in the magistrates court: section 50; see also *Cook v Southend Borough Council* [1990].

Chapter 17

Compensation for Disturbance

Introduction
The principle of equivalence
Persons entitled to disturbance compensation
The general principles of the disturbance claim
Disturbance: particular compensatable losses
Other matters under rule (6)

17.1 Introduction

If the purpose of compensation is to put a person, who has some
interest in land acquired from him, in the same position, financially,
had his interest not been compulsorily acquired, then in many cases
compensation for the market value of the land will not achieve this.
For not only must the expropriated owner buy another house, land
or premises, but he will have to remove himself, and if he is in the
same business, he may lose customers, temporarily or permanently.
Rule (6) of section 5 of the Land Compensation Act 1961 provides:

> The provisions of rule (2) shall not affect the assessment of
> compensation for disturbance or any other matter not directly based on
> the value of land.

Rule (6) has two limbs, disturbance, and other matters not directly
based on the value of land. This Chapter is primarily concerned
with the first of these two limbs: the claim for disturbance.
Underlying the claim for disturbance is the principle of equivalence
or fair compensation. Losses that are compensable under the
second limb of rule (6) are considered at the end of this chapter and
also in Chapter 18.

17.2 The principle of equivalence

This principle, of fair compensation, was first considered in

Chapter 11. In *Director of Buildings and Lands* v *Shun Fung Ironworks Ltd* [1995] Lord Nicholls in the Privy Council said:

> The purpose of [the legislation] in ... England, is to provide fair compensation for a claimant whose land has been compulsorily taken from him. This is sometimes described as the principle of equivalence. No allowance is to be made because the resumption or acquisition was compulsory; and land is to be valued at the price it might be expected to realise if sold by a willing seller, not an unwilling seller. But subject to these qualifications, a claimant is entitled to be compensated fairly and fully for his loss. Conversely, and built into the concept of fair compensation, is the corollary that a claimant is not entitled to receive more than fair compensation: a person is entitled to compensation for losses fairly attributable to the taking of his land, but not to any greater amount. It is ultimately by this touchstone, with its two facets, that all claims for compensation succeed or fail.
>
> Land may, of course, have a special value to a claimant over and above the price it would fetch if sold in the open market. Fair compensation requires that he should be paid for the value of the land to him, not its value generally or its value to the acquiring authority. As already noted, this is well established. If he is using the land to carry on a business, the value of the land to him will include the value of his being able to conduct his business there without disturbance. Compensation should cover this disturbance loss as well as the market value of the land itself. The authority which takes the land on resumption or compulsory acquisition does not acquire the business, but the resumption or acquisition prevents the claimant from continuing his business on the land. So the claimant loses the land and, with it, the special value it had for him as the site of his business. The expenses and any losses he incurs in moving his business to a new site will ordinarily be the measure of the special loss he sustains by being deprived of the land and disturbed in his enjoyment of it. If, exceptionally, the business cannot be moved elsewhere, so it simply has to close down, prima facie his loss will be measured by the value of the business as a going concern. In practice it is customary and convenient to assess the value of the land and the disturbance loss separately, but strictly in law these are no more than two inseparable elements of a single whole in that together they make up the value of the land to the owner: see *Hughes* v *Doncaster Metropolitan Borough Council* [1991] 1 AC 382, *per* Lord Bridge of Harwich at p392.

1. *Disturbance as one element of compensation for land*

In Chapter 11, in examining the background to the present rules for the assessment of compensation, it was said that the underlying principle, until 1919, was that compensation should represent the 'value to owner'. Although this is said to be a principle established by judicial decisions, it originated as an interpretation of the appropriate sections of the Lands Clauses Consolidation Act 1845 which provided that an owner who had land acquired was entitled to 'purchase money or compensation' and in estimating this, the Act directed that 'regard shall be had ... to the value of the land.'

The compensation money was regarded as one sum for the compulsory purchase of the owner's land. This was restated by the House of Lords in *Hughes* v *Doncaster Metropolitan Borough Council* [1991] and by the Privy Council in the *Director of Buildings* case considered above. Apart from compensation for injurious severance, if any, the sum contained two different elements of the expropriated owners loss, value of the land acquired, and other losses occasioned by the owner being turned out or 'disturbed' from his land or premises. Each of these two elements was part of one sum which was supposed to represent the value to the owner of his land. The statute said the expropriated owner was entitled to compensation, having regard to the value of his land, and value was interpreted as value to the owner: the owner's entitlement was therefore to compensation for his loss. The authority for regarding other losses as but one element of the price to be paid for the land acquired is generally said to be *Jubb* v *Hull Dock Co* [1846], where a brewer was held to be entitled to temporary loss of profits as well as the value of his land.

Following the Acquisition of Land (Assessment of Compensation) Act 1919, the basis for assessing compensation for the land was changed from 'value to owner' to open market value (see now Land Compensation Act 1961, section 5, rule (2)), but the second element in the total compensation sum, compensation for disturbance, was left on the original basis of 'value of owner'. Indeed rule (6), in the 1961 Act, clearly says:

> The provisions of Rule (2) shall not affect the assessment of compensation for disturbance or any other matter not directly based on the value of the value of the land.

The provisions of the Lands Clauses Act 1845 as to entitlement to compensation have been substantially re-enacted in the Compulsory Purchase Act 1965, section 7 (see p170) and the totality of the compensation sum, though composed of the two elements, value of land and other losses, is therefore preserved. It is frequently argued that it is the totality of the compensation which is to compensate the owner for his loss: the total sum, including, where applicable, compensation for injurious affection or severance, shall be no more nor less than his loss due to the compulsory acquisition: see *Horn* v *Sunderland Corpn* [1941] confirmed in *Hughes* v *Doncaster Metropolitan Borough Council* [1991].

The position can be stated in this form:

Entitlement to compensation	Basis of assessment
1. Compensation for land acquired (a) Value of land ... ... + (b) Disturbance ... ... + 2. Compensation for damage due to injurious affection or severance (if any)	... ... open market value (rule (2)) ... ... "value to owner" (preserved by rule (6)) ... depreciation in market value (rule (2))
Total compensation sum	Must be neither greater nor less than owner's loss

2. Disturbance only compensatable if consistent with land value

Before the change to open market value as the basis for valuing land, the underlying principle of determining the 'value to owner' meant that the total compensation sum would usually represent the owner's loss. But in the following case, the court considered that where the market value of the land was on a basis that presupposed the owner being 'disturbed' anyway, he could not have, as total compensation, more than his loss:

Mizen v *Mitcham Urban District Council* [1929] Div C
The land being acquired was used as a market garden which had erected upon it greenhouses and other trade fixtures. The value of the land as a market garden was £12,000. But the land was ripe for immediate development for building and on that basis was valued at £17,280, this sum being obtained if vacant possession was given. The cost of being 'disturbed' and removing from the land (removal of greenhouses and

other trade fixtures, forced sale or removal of crops and plants, and compensation for disturbance and loss of business) was put at £4,640. The Divisional Court held that the claimant could not have the disturbance sum of £4,640 and the development value of £17,280 because in order to realise the development value he would be disturbed in any event.

The doubtful reasoning behind this case must be that had there been no compulsory acquisition and Mizen had sold the market garden on the open market for building purposes, he would only have got £17,280. (Upon the sale of market garden land to a purchaser who wishes to use the land for that purpose, it is customary for the purchaser to pay over and above the value of the land for many of the items of claim in Mizen's claim for disturbance.)

The case was approved in *Horn v Sunderland Corpn* [1941] by a majority of the Court of Appeal. The facts were similar: farmland was being acquired which had development value for building purposes. The point at issue was similar: whether the claimant was entitled to compensation for disturbance and development value; or whether he was only entitled to disturbance when claiming agricultural value for the land acquired. Green MR said that where the claim for the land is to be treated, for the purposes of valuation, as building land, the claimant must be regarded as willing to abandon his farming business in order to realise that higher development value; he could not claim in addition a sum for disturbance of his farming business. He said that the two claims were inconsistent; the claimant can only obtain compensation for disturbance to his farming business where he is saying he is not willing to abandon that business and, but for the compulsory acquisition, would have continued to farm the land. In the same case Scott LJ after saying 'the [1845] Act, ... gives to the owner compelled to sell ... compensation – the right to be put, so far as money can do it, in the same position as if his land had not been taken from him', added, 'the statutory compensation cannot and must not exceed the owner's total loss.'

The effect of *Mizen's* case and *Horn's* case is as follows. The claimant is entitled to:

(a) the value of the land for its existing use plus disturbance to that use (business, farming or personal use); or

(b) the value of the land for development or other potential use

(which presupposes that the existing use will cease and the
owner removing himself at his own expense);

whichever is the greater sum.

There is a significant flaw in the majority decision of the Court of
Appeal in the *Horn* case, a flaw which the dissenting judge
(Goddard LJ) saw, and writers have also pointed out: RE Megarry
– *Law Quarterly Review*, vol CCXXIX, p29. Since 1919, a claimant,
who is disturbed from possession, is entitled to the market value of
his land (rule (2)) and the costs of being disturbed (rule (6)). It was
said by the majority in the *Horn* case that if development value was
claimed, this supposed the abandonment of farming and so
disturbance costs could not be recovered. But if the owner sells his
land for agricultural values, he will also abandon his farming.
There is nothing in the present Land Compensation Act 1961 to
suggest that entitlement to disturbance depends on the basis of
valuation of the land taken. Megarry points out the absurdity of the
Horn decision; where land has something less than dead ripe
development value – hope value – is the claimant entitled to
disturbance compensation, or some proportion of it? It is submitted
that the majority decision in *Horn* is both unworkable and contrary
to the statutory provisions.

3. *Other matters*

As explained below, only a claimant disturbed from occupation of
land may claim compensation under the first limb of rule (6). However non-occupiers may suffer losses in addition to the value of land
taken (and severance and injurious affection). They may be entitled
to compensation under the second limb of rule (6) (see below).

17.3 Persons entitled to disturbance compensation

Compensation is payable to the person who is expelled from the
land: see *Jubb* v *Hull Dock Co* [1846]. To claim compensation for
disturbance, the claimant must have been the occupier of the land
or premises acquired, be displaced from occupation, and be a
person entitled to have received a notice to treat, ie the freeholder
or lessee with an expired term exceeding a year. The compensation
for short tenancies is dealt with in Chapter 19.

In certain circumstances a claimant not in occupation, and who
suffers loss in consequence of the acquisition, may recover

compensation for that loss under section 5, rule (6), of the 1961 Act: see *Wrexham Maelor Borough Council* v *MacDougall* [1993].

1. Investment owner

The rule that disturbance compensation is only payable to disturbed occupiers has meant that an investment owner cannot recover the costs of reinvestment. However, following amendments made by the Planning and Compensation Act 1991, section 10A of the Land Compensation Act 1961 provides compensation for an owner of an interest in land not in occupation. Compensation is payable for charges or expenses incurred in acquiring, within a period of one year of date of entry, an interest in other land in the United Kingdom.

There are arguments against the rule that an investment owner is not entitled to disturbance compensation. In *Tull's Personal Representatives* v *Secretary of State for Air* [1957] a claimant landlord recovered compensation for the value of an on-licence in respect of a public house as disturbance compensation, rather than as part of the value of the land acquired. Further, in *Ryde International plc* v *London Regional Transport* [2001], an investment owner/developer, compelled to hold flats that he was developing for sale because of the compulsory acquisition, was awarded compensation in respect of the holding costs. In both of these cases the claimants, who had not been disturbed from possession, obtained compensation for non-land value items. It might also be possible to argue that, following the enactment of the Human Rights Act 1998, the English rules relating to compensation must now be read and given effect in a way that is compatible with the requirements with the European Convention on Human Rights: see section 3. This matter is considered further at Chapter 27 below.

2. Disturbance to occupation

Save where a claim can be made under section 10A of the Land Compensation Act 1961, disturbance to occupation is fundamental to a claim for compensation:

> *Roberts* v *Coventry Corpn* [1947] DC
> Mrs Roberts owned premises which were let to a family company in which she had shares. Upon the acquisition of the premises, the value of her shares depreciated. It was held

that as she was not the occupier of the premises, she had no claim for compensation for the depreciation of her shares. It was irrelevant that she owned the freehold and had a shareholding in the tenant-company.

However, in *Wrexham Maelor Borough Council* v *MacDougall* [1993] the Court of Appeal decided that a claimant, who had no rights of occupation, and who had a service contract with a company which was disturbed from occupation, was entitled to compensation by reason of the second limb to rule (6) of section 5 of the 1961 Act. The claimant did, however, own a lease of the subject property and his losses were regarded as consequential to the loss of the lease (see further below).

The rule that it is only the disturbed occupier who can claim disturbance compensation can have serious consequences where ownership and occupation are split between two separate legal personalities (such as companies) that are none the less related in some way. If the occupier has no interest in the land, he has no claim for disturbance compensation: see *Woolfson* v *Strathclyde Regional Council* [1978] HL (however the claimant may have a claim under section 37 of the Land Compensation Act 1973).

Where the occupier and owner are related companies, it is, in certain circumstances, possible for the court to lift 'the corporate veil' and to look at the realities of the situation. In this way two companies might be regarded as one. Alternatively, it might be possible to argue that the occupier has a licence or other interest in the land which would be regarded as an equitable interest, and thus a compensatable interest:

> *DHN Food Distributors Ltd* v *Tower Hamlets London Borough Council* [1976] CA
> DHN were the occupiers of premises owned by Bronze Ltd, they had no formal lease. Four years before the acquisition, DHN contracted to purchase the premises, the contract was never completed as DHN purchased the share capital in Bronze, instead, to save the stamp duty on a conveyance. The premises were compulsorily acquired and Bronze were paid for the value of the land. DHN, who ran a grocery provision business, claimed disturbance compensation. The court allowed the claim for the following reasons:
>
> (i) The two companies could be regarded as one because Bronze was a subsidiary of DHN with common directors,

the 'firm' was effectively DHN (piercing the corporate veil); or

(ii) DHN had an equitable interest in the premises by reason of having an irrevocable contractual licence to carry on business on the premises. The licence giving rise to a constructive trust under which Bronze could not turn out DHN. The equitable interest under the trust was a sufficient interest in the land for DHN to claim compensation.

The Lands Tribunal will usually adopt a strict approach to the problem of whether the occupier has a compensatable interest, although in *Wharvesto Ltd* v *Cheshire County Council* [1984] the Tribunal did apply the *DHN* principle, and treated two companies (one owned the freehold, and the other a lease) as one company able to offer a freehold with vacant possession; a disturbance claim was also allowed. It could be that the problems that arose in the *Woolfson* and *DHN* cases are unlikely to arise again. This is because section 37 of the Lands Compensation Act 1973 provides a disturbance payment to claimants disturbed from lawful possession but who do not otherwise have compensatable interests in land: see next chapter. See also *Wrexham Maelor Borough Council* v *MacDougall* [1993].

3. Disturbance following a blight or purchase notice

Despite the abolition in 1968 of a statutory rule preventing the payment of disturbance compensation following a blight notice, it might be argued that where the acquisition follows the service of a blight or purchase notice, the owner should not be entitled to disturbance compensation as he is not being 'disturbed' but has brought the acquisition and disturbance upon himself through his own initiative.

But, in each case, once the notice has been accepted or confirmed, a notice to treat is deemed to have been served and the authority concerned is regarded as compulsorily acquiring the land. Disturbance compensation must then be payable in the ordinary way. For a case on a deemed compulsory purchase under the New Towns Act 1965, section 11, which is analogous to that following a blight notice under the Town and Country Planning Act 1990, see *Elmer-Smith* v *Stevenage Development Corpn* [1972].

In a case from the Scottish Lands Tribunal, *Campbell Douglas & Co Ltd* v *Hamilton District Council* [1983], a light engineering firm claimed £35,000 removal expenses following the acceptance of a blight notice. It was said that proposals for the redevelopment of the town centre prevented the firm expanding and caused the blight; the loss and expense of moving was imposed on the claimants and they were entitled to be compensated.

In *Budgen* v *Secretary of State for Wales* [1985] LT, it was held that the costs incurred in making reasonable endeavours to sell to establish the right to serve a valid blight were not recoverable following a deemed or actual notice to treat.

4. *Disturbance when part of the claimant's land is acquired*

If a claimant has part of his land or premises acquired, he will be entitled to claim disturbance compensation in respect of being 'disturbed' from the land taken. The validity of each item in such a claim must be considered in relation to the general principles affecting a claim for disturbance compensation considered throughout this chapter: see *Budgen* v *Secretary of State for Wales* [1985].

It is questionable whether a claimant is entitled to disturbance compensation in respect of the land not taken from him; that was the position in the *Budgen* case. If there is a depreciation in value of this retained land caused by severance or injurious affection, he will be entitled to compensation for this (see Chapter 13), but he is not 'disturbed' from this retained land by being expelled or dispossessed in the sense usually associated with a disturbance claim. In *Brickell* v *Shaftesbury Rural District Council* [1955] LT, the Tribunal awarded, as compensation, the reduction of profits of a retail business when the owner had some two acres of market garden some distance away compulsorily purchased and was thereby deprived of some of his produce for retailing.

However, in *Bisset* v *Secretary of State for Scotland* [1992] the acquiring authority appeared to have accepted that a claim could be made for temporary loss of profits in circumstances where the claimant was not disturbed from that part of his land which was acquired. The case is unsatisfactory in its reasoning. In *TG O'Fee* v *Highways Agency* [1999] the Lands Tribunal saw no reason why disturbance compensation should not be claimed in respect of land not taken if not otherwise compensation by the claim for severance and injurious affection.

17.4 The general principles of the disturbance claim

There are some general principles that apply to the entitlement to, and assessment of, a claim for disturbance compensation. All losses are recoverable which are (1) not too remote and are a natural and reasonable consequence of the dispossession of the owner: see *Venables* v *Department of Agriculture* [1932], *Harvey* v *Crawley Development Corp* [1957]; (2) there is a causal connection between dispossession and the loss: *Prasad* v *Wolverhampton Borough Council* [1983]; and (3) the duty to mitigate has been discharged.

These principles were slightly restated as conditions in *Director of Buildings and Lands* v *Shun Fung Ironworks Ltd* [1995]:

(1) there must be a causal connection between the resumption or acquisition and the loss in question;
(2) the loss must not be too remote; and
(3) losses or expenditure incurred unreasonably cannot sensibly be said to be caused by, or be in consequence of, or be due to the acquisition.

A further principle can be added. A claimant cannot recover compensation where he receives value for a head of expenditure; value for money: see *Service Welding Ltd* v *Tyne & Wear County Council* [1979].

1. Losses must not be too remote

In *Harvey* v *Crawley Development Corpn* [1957] CA, Romer LJ said that 'any loss sustained by a dispossessed owner which flows from a compulsory acquisition may properly be regarded as the subject of compensation for disturbance, provided first that it is not too remote and, second, that it is the natural and reasonable consequence of the dispossession of the owner'. In that case the claimant's expenditure on surveyor's fees, solicitor's costs and travelling expenses reasonably incurred in finding and purchasing another house for occupation was compensatable. In *J Bibby & Sons Ltd* v *Merseyside County Council* [1979] Megaw LJ said that what is a reasonable and direct result of a compulsory purchase is largely a question of fact, although it may to some extent be a question of law. In *Tull's Personal Representatives* v *Secretary of State for Air* [1957] the Court of Appeal held that the loss of an on-licence, which could have been, but was not transferred, was not too remote an item of claim for disturbance.

Unforeseeable losses

In *Hoddom & Kinmount Estates* v *Secretary of State for Scotland* [1992] it was held that where a claimant gave up farming because of impending compulsory purchase, the loss attributable to the later introduction of milk quota was an unforeseeable loss and uncompensatable. The costs of obtaining a certificate of appropriate alternative development (see p206) may be said to be the reasonable consequence of the dispossession, yet in *Hull and Humber Investment Co Ltd* v *Hull Corpn* [1965] the Court of Appeal disallowed such costs on the basis that they were not reasonably incurred in ascertaining the value of the land but incurred so as to increase the value of the land. It is submitted that this case might be decided differently today, and the dissenting judgment of Russell LJ adopted, as the purpose of a certificate of appropriate alternative development in its present form, following the amendments made by the Community Land Act 1975, must be to ascertain the planning basis upon which the value of the land can be determined. However, such costs are now recoverable in so far as they relate to the costs of applying for a certificate and the costs of an appellant whose appeal succeeds: see section 17(9A) of the Land Compensation Act 1961.

2. *Causal connection between loss and dispossession*

Dispossession

The cost of acquiring the expropriated land is not recoverable as disturbance compensation because such expenditure is not caused by the acquisition: see *Windward Properties Ltd* v *Government of Saint Vincent and the Grenadines* [1996]. It has been seen that disturbance to occupation is necessary before a claim can be made. For that reason the landlord, whose interest is acquired, and who is not in occupation, cannot, subject to section 10A of the 1961 Act, recover his costs of reinvestment; unlike the position of the claimant in the *Harvey* case, who, being an occupier, was able to recover her legal and other costs in purchasing a new house. But see p269 for the changes made by section 10A of the 1961 Act.

Where a person dispossessed from land did not have a formal interest by way of a freehold or tenancy, the decision in *Wrexham Maelor Borough Council* v *MacDougall* [1993] may make it easier for that person to recover a disturbance payment equivalent to disturbance compensation under section 37 of the Land Compensation Act 1973: see next chapter.

Losses incurred before notice to treat

For many years the Lands Tribunal applied a rule that only losses and expenses incurred subsequent to the date of a notice to treat were allowable: *Bostock, Chater & Sons Ltd* v *Chelmsford Corpn* [1973]. That rule has been doubted because it places a claimant in a dilemma: does he await the notice to treat, or should he incur expenses before the notice to treat if he sees an opportunity of minimising his losses? In *Smith* v *Strathclyde Regional Council* [1981], the Scottish Lands Tribunal allowed pre-notice to treat (deemed notice to treat) expenses following the principles established in the *Harvey* case, as well as those in *Venables* v *Department of Agriculture for Scotland* [1932] ('person dispossessed should get compensation for all loss occasioned to him by reason of his dispossession' – Lord Justice Clerk Alness); and in *Birmingham City Corpn* v *West Midlands Baptist (Trust) Association Inc* [1969] (notice to treat no longer determines date of valuation). The Court of Session in Scotland later upheld a Lands Tribunal decision that a claimant who had incurred expenses in buying a replacement house, nearly five years before the notice to treat, and even before the resolution to make the compulsory purchase order, was entitled to disturbance compensation for those expenses: *Aberdeen City District Council* v *Sim* [1982].

The English law appears to have been brought into line by the Court of Appeal in *Prasad* v *Wolverhampton Borough Council* [1983] in a case concerned with the entitlement to a statutory disturbance payment under section 37 of the Land Compensation Act 1973: see next chapter. The *Prasad* case was approved by the Privy Council in *Director of Buildings and Lands* v *Shun Fung Ironworks Ltd* [1995]: profits lost during the shadow period before possession may be compensatable. In *Prasad* the court saw no reason to doubt the correctness of the Scottish cases on the entitlement to disturbance compensation under rule (6). In interpreting section 37, it was said that 'displaced from ... and in consequence of the acquisition of the land' indicated a causative connection between the displacement and the acquisition: 'in consequence of' did not mean after acquisition, it meant 'because of'. A claim can only be made if a notice to treat is ultimately served, and the claimant will have to establish that the loss is not too remote, and is the natural and reasonable consequence of the dispossession: *Harvey* v *Crawley Development Corpn* [1957].

However, in *Emslie & Simpson Ltd* v *Aberdeen City District Council* [1994] the Court of Session (First Division) in Scotland rejected a claim for trading losses incurred in the year prior to acquisition on the ground that a causative loss had not been established; accordingly the lost profits were attributable to the indiscriminate effects of blight and were irrecoverable.

3. Duty to mitigate

A claimant must take all reasonable steps to mitigate his losses. This duty is an objective one. In *Bailey* v *Derby Corpn* [1965] a claimant was too ill to re-establish his business. It was held by the Court of Appeal that he must, for compensation purposes, be regarded as under a duty to re-establish in order to mitigate his losses. In *Bede Distributors Ltd* v *Newcastle upon Tyne Corpn* [1973] LT, the dispossessed business occupier did not move into some suitable alternative premises at a time that would have reduced to a minimum his expenses and other losses; his claim was reduced to a sum that would have adequately compensated him had he so moved. This duty to mitigate usually arises in relation to relocating businesses at the earliest opportunity to reduce possible loss of profits. However, if relocation takes place before a notice to treat is served, the claimant will have to await such notice before claiming disturbance compensation under *Prasad* v *Wolverhampton Borough Council* [1983]: there is always the danger that no acquisition takes place.

The question of the duty to mitigate arose in *Lindon Print Ltd* v *West Midlands County Council* [1987] LT. The claimants were obliged to give up possession within eight weeks of the confirmation of the compulsory purchase order. The Tribunal decided that, in all the circumstances, it was not reasonable to expect the claimants to find accommodation to relocate in such a short period of time. No obligation to mitigate arose before the order was confirmed, and the claimants were entitled to be compensated for the total extinguishment of their business. It did not matter that they had had several years notice of the impending compulsory purchase, nor that they had no resources to buy alternative premises.

In the *Lindon Print* case implied approval was given to the principles for the recovery of damages at common law in relation to the duty to mitigate (Chapter 7, *McGregor on Damages*):

(a) a claimant must take all reasonable steps to mitigate the loss to him consequent upon the eviction and cannot recover compensation for avoidable loss;

(b) the onus is on the acquiring authority to prove that the claimant has failed reasonably to mitigate his loss;

(c) a claimant is only required to act reasonably and the standard of reasonableness is not high; and

(d) a claimant will not be prejudiced by his financial inability to take steps in mitigation.

That part of the decision in *Lindon Print*, which suggests that there is no duty to mitigate prior to the confirmation of a compulsory purchase order, must now be reconsidered in the light of *Director of Buildings and Lands* v *Shung Fung Ironworks Ltd* [1995]. Under that case a loss suffered after the commencement of a scheme (which could well be prior to the confirmation of a compulsory purchase order) is compensatable if casually connected, not too remote and could not have been avoided by mitigation. It may follow from these principles that there is duty to mitigate anticipated losses.

4. Value for money

There are circumstances where a claimant incurs expenditure that is due to the compulsory purchase, but in respect of which he receives value for money. If this is the case, he cannot claim compensation for such expenditure. That was the case in *Lindon Print Ltd* v *West Midlands County Council* [1987], when the Tribunal disallowed the cost of this book on the ground that the claimant had obtained value for his expenditure. This will also occur when a claimant carries out structural alterations to new premises, and this constitutes improvements: see *Smith* v *Birmingham Corpn* [1974]; or pays a higher rent for alternative premises, but enjoys better advantages: see *Bibby & Sons Ltd* v *Mersey County Council* [1977].

In *Service Welding Ltd* v *Tyne & Wear County Council* [1979] CA Bridge LJ said:

> when an occupier, whether residential or business, does, in consequence of disturbance, rehouse himself in alternative accommodation, *prima facie* he is not entitled to recover, by way of compensation for disturbance or otherwise, any part of the purchase price which he pays for the alternative accommodation to which he removes, whether that accommodation is better or worse than, or equivalent to, the property from which he is being evicted. The reason for that is that there is a presumption in law, albeit a rebuttable presumption, that the purchase price paid for the new premises is something for which the claimant has received value for money. If he has made a good bargain and acquired premises which have a value in excess of what he has paid for them, that is not something for which

the acquiring authority is entitled to any credit. If the claimant has made a bad bargain and has paid a great deal more for the new premises to which he is moving than they are really worth, that is not something for which the acquiring authority can properly be charged.

5. *Extinguishment or removal of a business*

In *Wright* v *Municipal Council of Sidney* [1916] it was said that in estimating the compensation payable to claimants 'they were not entitled in any event to more than the total value to them of the business carried on on the land in addition to the ordinary market value of the land'. This proposition is sometimes relied on in support of an argument that the compensation payable to a claimant in respect of the removal of business premises cannot exceed such sum as would have been payable if the business had been totally extinguished. In the *Wright* case Gordon J said that the proposition was indisputable in that it could not be prudent or reasonable to pay more than the whole of the business was worth in order to move a business to new premises, or to put the same matter in other words, to avoid losing the old site which was compulsory acquired. However, he accepted that it depended upon the circumstances of the particular case. The real issue is whether it is prudent and reasonable for the particular claimant in his particular situation to decide to remove to alternative premises rather than extinguish his business. Thus, where there is a business where the profits have been low, or even where there have been losses, it may still be prudent and reasonable for the owner of the business to remove to new premises where there are prospects of improving profitability even where the value of the goodwill of the business based on historic profits is less than the cost of removal: see further *Festiniog Rly Society* v *CEGB* [1962] and *A&B Taxis Ltd* v *Secretary for Air* [1922].

The position advanced in the preceding paragraph above (which appeared in the 4th edition of this book) has now been fully confirmed by the Privy Council in *Director of Buildings and Lands* v *Shun Fung Ironworks Ltd* [1995]. There is no rule that a claimant can never be entitled to compensation on a relocation basis if this would exceed the amount of compensation payable on an extinguishment basis. As Lord Nicholls said:

> In the ordinary way, the expenses and losses incurred when a business is moved to a new site will be less than the value of the entire business as a going concern. Compensation payable on a relocation basis will

normally be less than compensation payable on an extinguishment basis. But this will not always be so and a rigid limitation as contended by the Crown could lead to injustice.

Lord Nicholls gave the example of a businessman spending large sums setting up a new business. If the business premises are then compulsorily acquired before the business has proved itself and established a profit record, the business might be worth little and compensation on extinguishment basis paltry. But a reasonable businessman spending his own money might consider it worthwhile relocating the business. Fairness required that he should be entitled to his reasonable costs incurred in the removal of his business. It would be different if no reasonable businessman would incur the cost of moving the business and setting up in a new property. Lord Nicholls said that it depends on how a reasonable businessman, using his own money, would behave in the circumstances: 'However when considering these matters the tribunal or court might allow a moderate degree of latitude in approving as reasonable the relocation of a family business for the reasons set out by Wells J in *Commissioner of Highways* v *Shipp Bros Pty Ltd* (1978) 19 SASR 215 and 222'.

In any event whether the relocation is of the same business is a question of fact and degree: see the *Director of Buildings and Lands* case and *Lamba Trading Co* v *Salford City Council* [1999]. For a case where the Lands Tribunal accepted the claimant's evidence that it was entitled to refuse to relocate to a property suggested by the acquiring authority, because it was too expensive, see *John Line & Sons* v *Newcastle upon Tyne Corporation* [1956].

The cases show that where it is not practicable to relocate the business, compensation is payable for the total extinguishment of the business in a number of situations: where the alternative premises were too expensive to be profitable: *Knott Mill Carpets* v *Stretford Borough Council* [1973]; where the claimants had made genuine efforts to find alternative premises but had found nothing they could afford: *Lindon Print Ltd* v *West Midlands County Council* [1986]; where no alternative premises were available: *Barlow* v *Hackney Corporation* [1954].

6. Tax

The question of whether the compensation should be increased or decreased to take into account tax that may be payable on the lump sum received, or would otherwise have been payable on the 'lost' profits, is dealt with in Chapter 22. However a claim for compensation for a capital gains tax liability was dismissed in *Harris* v *Welsh Development Agency* [1999] on the grounds that such a liability was a contingent liability not caused by the acquisition and was too remote.

The reader is referred to Chapter 22 for the treatment of VAT.

7. Benefits

Although a claimant is obliged, as a matter of general principle, to set off benefits against expenses, this will not apply where the benefits are of a totally different nature. Thus, in *Palatine Graphic Arts Co* v *Liverpool City Council* [1986] CA, a regional grant paid to the claimant for moving to a development area was not to be deducted from the disturbance compensation.

8. Effect of the scheme

In *Ullah* v *Leicester City Council* [1996], where the claimant's property had been used for light industry purposes, it was held that the cessation of that use two years prior to the valuation date was due to the making of the compulsory purchase order. In the no-scheme world the claimant would not have abandoned his business, and he was entitled to be compensated on the basis that his property had continued to be used for that purpose.

9. Burden of proof

The burden first lies on a claimant to prove loss; it then shifts to the acquiring authority to show, for example, that the item claimed is too remote: see *Bede Distributors Ltd* v *Newcastle-upon-Tyne Corpn* [1973].

17.5 Disturbance: particular compensatable losses

While the categories of losses that can be compensated must not be regarded as closed, the following items are well established.

1. Goodwill

Goodwill can be defined as 'the price which a purchaser of a business is prepared to pay, above the value of the premises and stock, for the probability that customers or clients will continue to resort to the old place of business, or continue to deal with the firm of the same name: it is the benefit or advantage which a business has in its connection with its customers' (see *A Concise Law Dictionary* PG Osbon). Goodwill may be attributable to the personal qualities of the entrepreneur; the reputation attached to a particular firm; or the position or location of the enterprise. Goodwill can therefore be a saleable asset addition to the value of any land.

Goodwill may diminish if a firm changes its address and loses established customers; on the other hand, the relocation of a business close to its previous address may have an insignificant effect on goodwill. With a business that primarily deals with its custom through the post, a change of address may have no effect on goodwill at all.

Depending, therefore, on the facts in each case, a diminution or complete loss of goodwill which is the consequence of the compulsory purchase is compensatable. However, a claimant is required to mitigate his losses and if alternative premises are available to which he could reasonably remove to minimise the diminution of goodwill, he will be unable to recover as compensation further loss of goodwill that could have been so avoided. Compensation therefore only becomes payable where the business cannot be relocated and is forced to close down, or the business is removed, but the value of the goodwill is depreciated. In *Bailey* v *Derby Corpn* [1965] the Court of Appeal disallowed a claim for loss of goodwill; the inability to relocate the business was due to the claimant's ill health and was not due to acquisition.

Goodwill is assessed on a value to owner basis, and therefore a business running at a loss may still have a value to the owner: *Koch* v *Greater London Council* [1969].

Total loss of goodwill: person over 60

If the following conditions are satisfied, a person may be compensated for the total loss of goodwill. The claimant is over 60 on the date he gives up possession, his premises have a rateable value not exceeding a 'prescribed amount' (currently £18,000), he has not disposed of the goodwill of the whole of the trade or business, and undertakes not to dispose of the goodwill nor directly or indirectly engage in, or have any interest in, any other trade or business of the same or substantially the same kind as that carried on by him on the land. The claimant may then be compensated for the total extinguishment of his business if, as a consequence of compulsory acquisition he gives up possession of the whole of the premises or land on which he carries on his trade or business: section 46 of the Land Compensation Act 1973.

Business includes a company where the majority shareholder is over 60 years, and any minority shareholder is either over 60 or is a spouse of a majority shareholder. The requirement that before a person can claim section 46 compensation the claimant must be required to give up possession is satisfied by the service of a blight notice and the 'process of acquisition'; it is not necessary that there must be a notice of entry: see *Glossop Sectional Buildings Ltd* v *Sheffield Development Corporation* [1994].

Calculating value of goodwill

Because the claim for disturbance compensation was specifically excluded by rule (6) from the application of rule (2) – the market value rule – goodwill is valued on a 'value to owner' basis, not in terms of the market value: see *Afzal* v *Rochdale Metropolitan Borough Council* [1980]. The Tribunal may, where appropriate, take a robust approach to the assessment of compensation: see *Lindon Print Ltd* v *West Midlands County Council* [1987]. There is a well-established practice that is approved by the Tribunal in valuing goodwill in the case of a one-man business. It is well illustrated in *Reynolds* v *Manchester City Council* [1981]:

> Stage 1: The ascertainment of a figure of historic profit, which is customarily (but not necessarily) taken as the average of the three previous years' trading.
> Stage 2: Adjustment of this historic profit by deducting:
>
> (a) an allowance for rental value if not charged to accounts in computing annual profit;
> (b) an allowance for interest on capital (in a one-man business it is not customary to deduct the owner's notional wages).
>
> Stage 3: The capitalisation of the adjusted annual profit by applying an appropriate multiplier in terms of a year's purchase – usually between two and five.

Example (the *Reynold*'s case):

Annual profit (average of last three years)		£8,500
Less rental value	£950	
Interest on capital, 10% of £5,150	515	
Adjusted annual profit		£7,035
× 3.5 YP		
Value of goodwill		£24,650

In *Sceneout Ltd* v *Central Manchester Development Corporation* [1995] the acquiring authority's answer to a claim for total extinguishment was that there was no principle that required the value of goodwill to be based on the value to the owner. That was not accepted by the Lands Tribunal which decided that the proper measure of compensation was the value of what was lost to the owner. The value of the business to the owner was payable, even if it is greater than the market value. In that case a robust approach was adopted to assessing the value of the goodwill; the Tribunal went straight to a figure without employing the classic method explained above.

In the case of businesses that are larger in scale than a one-man business, the classic method set out above is not really appropriate. An accountant will normally value the business on accountancy principles. This may involve finding an appropriate multiplier to apply to net earnings derived from tables of comparable share prices or from valuations of comparable businesses made for the purposes of acquisitions and mergers. Where appropriate the value of any property or other assets is then deducted. There is an example of this approach in *Lion Nathan Ltd* v *CC Bottlers* [1996] where a price/earnings method was used to value the goodwill of a business, although the method is not necessarily the only method: see *Senate Electrical Wholesalers Ltd* v *Acatel Submarine Networks Ltd* [1998] where a price/earnings ratio method was appropriate to assess damages where the valuation experts agreed the method or it was the method used to value or calculate the original price or value prior to the dispute.

Partial loss of goodwill

Where a business is relocated to new premises, there may be a partial loss of goodwill, and therefore a permanent loss of profits. Such a loss is recoverable: see *London County Council* v *Tobin* [1959].

Summary of Lands Tribunal decisions on valuing loss of goodwill 1955–2002

	Multiplier	Business type	Adjustments to net profit
Perezic v Bristol Corpn [1955]	2	Grocery	No deduction for personal remuneration of one-man business
Zarraga v Newcastle-upon-Tyne Corpn [1968]	2	Fish and chip shop	Wife's wages not deducted
Afsal v Rochdale MBC [1980]	4		
Lindon Print Ltd v West Midlands CC [1987]	robust award of £125,000	Printing	Accounts for preceding years did not reflect potential
Sceneout Ltd v Central Manchester Development Corporation [1995]	robust award of £50,000 on annual adjusted profits of £28,324 equates to multiplier of 1.77	Laundry business	Various including bad debts
Klein v London Underground Ltd [1996]	3.25	Hairdressing	Declining profits in last year not due to scheme

	Multiplier	Business type	Adjustments to net profit
Shevlin v Trafford Park Development Corporation [1998]	2.5	Steel treatment	Director's remuneration added back Depreciation not added back
Aslam v South Bedfordshire DC [1998]	20% discount rate on DCF method 3.81 on traditional method	Slaughterhouse	Adjustments to reflect income stream risks
Crista v Highways Agency [2000]	3.25	Light engineering	Director's remuneration added back
Halil v Lambeth LBC [2001]	3	Hairdressing and sauna	Wife's earnings not deducted from profits

If a company or business has a number of branches, and one is compulsorily acquired, and head office charges cannot be proportionally reduced, compensation is payable in respect of the head office charges: see *Reed Employment* v *London Transport Executive* [1978].

2. Profits

There is frequent confusion of terminology in this area of disturbance compensation. The author has used 'goodwill' to cover the value of a business to its owner over and above the value of the land. Sometimes the Tribunal will speak of 'loss of profits' (as in the *Reynold's* case) or 'loss of goodwill' (as in the *Nuttal* case): the Tribunal is usually referring to the same thing. Where a claimant has a business that has a value to him over and above the value of the land, he may be entitled to loss of total or partial goodwill, as described above.

A purchaser of business premises or land (including agricultural land), when paying a price for the value of the premises or land, will be purchasing the right to use the property for making profits. The purchase price of land, therefore, includes an element for the profits that can be made from that land: land values reflect the profitability of land.

Obviously the expropriated owner of land, used for business purposes, will be denied the profits that he might have continued to earn from that use but the compensation for the market value of the land should reflect those profits:

> *Wimpey & Co Ltd* v *Middlesex County Council* [1938] DC
> Land being developed by the claimant company was compulsorily acquired. It was held that the company could not recover as compensation the profits they would have made by completing their development scheme; market value of the land was the proper compensation as it would reflect the profitability of the land.

See also *McEwing* v *Renfrew County Council* [1959] where a builder's loss of profits was not recoverable as disturbance compensation. Thus, when a farmer buys agricultural land, he does not pay extra above the price for the right to make the profit that he will be able to earn from the land: the market price is the price for the right to make those profits. When he loses the land to compulsory acquisition, he is entitled to the market value of the land and is not entitled to any additional sum for the profits he would have earned.

As Lord Moulton said in *Pastoral Finance Association Ltd* v *The Minister* [1914]: 'no man would pay for land in addition to its market value the capitalised value of the savings and additional profits which he would hope to make by the use of it.'

However, the next case shows that although future loss of profit must be reflected in the market value of land, profits lost as a direct consequence of the expropriation, which would not be reflected in market value, can be recovered as compensation:

> *Watson* v *Secretary of State for Air* [1954] CA
> Part of the claimant's farm was acquired. He claimed, as compensation for disturbance, the loss of profits of a cereal crop he was unable to harvest in the year of compulsory acquisition and, additionally, the loss of profit he would have made from that land in the following year (for the purposes of his case the last year of his tenancy). But the claimant was entitled to the market value of his interest in the land, and although he could be compensated for the loss of his cereal crop and profit thereon in the first year, the market value of his interest would reflect the profits that could be earned in a subsequent year. 'If the figure is properly arrived at under Rule (2)', said Lord Evershed MR, 'it seems to me that any further sum (for loss of profits) is necessarily excluded, for otherwise he would be having the same thing twice over.'

Thus, although the permanent loss of profits will be reflected in the market value of the land, loss of profits of a temporary nature and as a direct and natural consequence of the compulsory acquisition can be recovered as compensation. Examples would include the loss of profit on a particular farm crop (as above), loss of profit from cancelled or varied contracts and temporary diminution of profits as a consequence of the relocation of a business to new premises. See *Bede Distributors Ltd* v *Newcastle Corpn* [1973] – drop in profits during and after removal of business for a temporary period multiplied by 1.5 YP.

3. Other business or trade loss

The relocation of a business will involve other expenses that can be recovered as compensation. Examples include: depreciation in the value of stock, losses on forced sale of stock, notification of new address to customers, new stocks of stationary and cost of new telephone. Compensation is also payable for a temporary loss of profits during the relocation period provided those losses are due to the disturbance from possession. This is not an exhaustive list; every loss must be considered on its merits and should be recoverable if a natural and direct consequence of being disturbed. In *Chiltmead Ltd* v *Reading Borough Council* [1981] the Lands Tribunal approved a basis for calculating the loss on the forced sale of stock by first assessing the aggregate retail value of the stock, then deducting a substantial discount to reflect the time it would have taken to sell the stock, before deducting the sale proceeds. Whatever basis is used for calculating these additional losses, there should not be double-counting. A claimant cannot claim for loss of profits *and* for loss of *retail* prices on a forced sale.

4. Relocation or extinguishment

See p278 above for a discussion of the decision of the Privy Council in *Director of Buildings and Lands* v *Shun Fung Ironworks Ltd* [1995]. Relocation costs are recoverable where a reasonable business would relocate the business. However, such costs are only recoverable if it is the same business which is relocated (*Director of Buildings*); relocating in a distant locality will not necessarily be a continuation of the same business: see *Blake* v *Newcastle-upon-Tyne Corpn* [1966].

5. New premises and their adaptation

Where new premises are acquired to relocate a business, the cost of adapting those premises for the particular requirements of the claimant's business may be claimed, provided the adaptations represent the facilities originally in the premises expropriated. However, if the adaptations carried out represent an improvement on the old facilities a deduction may be made:

> *Tamplin's Brewery Ltd* v *County Borough of Brighton* [1971] LT
> A bottling plant, originally on the land compulsorily acquired, was relocated on land made available by the acquiring authority. The claimant company took the opportunity of the relocation to install a more modern bottling plant but as this was considered more profitable than the old, the compensation recovered was the cost of replacement less the annual savings in running costs multiplied by 10-years' purchase.

However, there will be many circumstances where expenditure on alternative premises should not be allowed. In *Service Welding Ltd* v *Tyne & Wear County Council* [1979] Bridge LJ said:

> ... there is a presumption of law, albeit a rebuttable presumption that the purchase price paid for new premises is something for which the claimant has received value for money.

Bridge LJ accepted that where part of the purchase price is spent on adapting new premises, the presumption will apply; but it will be rebutted where such expenditure does not enhance the value of the property. See also *Smith* v *Birmingham Corp* [1974] and the decision in *Harris* v *Welsh Development Agency* [1999] where the costs of adapting new premises were disallowed, as the claimant had received compensation for the value of the accommodation acquired, and to demand additional compensation for providing the equivalent accommodation elsewhere was double-counting.

If the new premises cost more to purchase or to rent than the premises compulsorily acquired, the claimant is taken to have obtained value for that extra expenditure, and he will not be entitled to compensation for it:

> *J Bibby & Sons Ltd* v *Merseyside County Council* [1979] CA
> The head office of Bibby was compulsorily purchased and the firm acquired a leasehold interest in a new building; this involved the claimants in increased operating costs by reason of a higher rent and rates, and capital expenditure on making the building suitable for occupation. In the course of his judgment, Brandon LJ said that: (1) extra operating costs could be awarded as compensation in certain circumstances; (2) the circumstances would be where the claimant, as a result of compulsory purchase, had no alternative but to incur the increased operating costs and he had no benefit as a result of the extra operating costs which would make the incurring of them worthwhile; and, (3) in order to succeed in a claim for extra operating costs, the claimants must first show they have suffered a loss, and if so, that the loss was consequential upon the compulsory purchase. Bibby failed in respect of the higher rent and rates, and the capital expenditure; they paid extra for these items; 'they got value for them; they have therefore, suffered no loss'.

The point was clearly made by the member of the Lands Tribunal when he said, 'having received their compensation for the value of the land [taken] ... the claimants were at liberty to do what they wished and they chose to put their money into a new building'; to the extent that the alternative premises are more costly, there is no compensation if the extra costs produce extra benefits; compensation is payable for losses, and there are no losses if extra costs produce benefits or value for money: see also *Powner & Powner v Leeds Corporation* [1953] where it was suggested that a claim for the cost of a new factory might be accepted if alternative premises were not available in the market. It may always be possible to reach an agreement with an acquiring authority over the need to relocate. In *Wilson v Minister of Transport* [1980], the acquiring authority agreed to purchase an area of land to site some sheep pens following the acquisition of part of a farm. Compensation may now be paid in money or money's worth: see section 3 of the Compulsory Purchase Act 1965.

6. Removal expenses, legal costs and other fees

These can be recovered as compensation by business and other claimants and, following the *Harvey* case, the costs of finding a new house and abortive expenses spent on an intended purchase of a comparable house that fell through, can also be recovered. Legal costs will include the costs of the conveyance of a comparable substitute property and stamp duty; other fees will include those payable to surveyors or architects in connection with the survey or adaptation of substitute premises.

An investment owner, whose reversionary or other interest is expropriated, can now be compensated for those expenses: see p269 above.

In *Sadik & Sadik v Haringay London Borough Council* [1978] the claimants were entitled to claim £254 towards the cost of the services of an interpreter and translator used during negotiations for compulsory purchase.

7. Personal time

A claimant may spend a great deal of personal time in dealing with a claim, finding alternative accommodation etc. Compensation is payable for the personal time of the claimant: see *Ministry of Transport v Pettit* [1969]. In the case of businesses, the wage costs of directors or employees attributable to the acquisition are not usually compensated directly; these costs should be reflected in the claim for temporary loss of profits: see *M&B Precision Engineers* v *Ealing London Borough Council* [1972]. A claim may be rejected unless fully supported: see *Harris* v *Welsh Development Agency* [1999].

8. *Interest paid and charges*

A claimant, in acquiring alternative property to replace that compulsorily purchased, may incur bank interest or other charges if he needs to borrow money. This may arise if the claimant seeks alternative premises before he is required to leave those to be acquired, and compensation will not, of course, have been paid; or, the claimant is dispossessed by a notice of entry and compensation cannot be agreed.

Interest and bank charges incurred are not compensated if the claimant receives value for money:

> *Service Welding Ltd* v *Tyne and Wear County Council* [1979] CA
> The claimants acquired a site and had constructed a new factory to replace that being compulsorily purchased. As compensation for the land taken was not paid until the replacement factory was built and the old premises vacated, money was borrowed, and interest charges incurred to finance the acquisition and building costs. The Court of Appeal accepted the Tribunal's finding of fact that one of the necessary elements in the cost of erecting a new building is the interest charges incurred; in other words, the purchase price paid for new premises includes an element for interest. That being so, the court reversed the decision of the Tribunal, and decided 'that the purchase price paid for new premises is something for which the claimant has received value for money'. This was a rebuttable presumption in law; the claimant had not shown that he had not received value for money.

Quite clearly, if the claimants in this case had purchased a new factory from a developer the purchase price would have reflected the developer's costs, including any interest, and a claimant could not claim, as compensation, any element of that purchase price to the extent that he received value for money.

In *Simpson* v *Stoke-on-Trent City Council* [1982] the claimant bought a house before compensation was agreed on the house being compulsorily purchased; he incurred interest on a bridging loan and claimed this as part of his claim. The interest was disallowed because the Tribunal said that a claimant could avoid delays by making an early reference to the Tribunal; if possession was taken by the authority, the claimant is also entitled to the advance payment of 90% of acquiring authority's estimate (see Chapter 11), and there was no need to borrow the money, and in *Harris* v *Welsh Development Agency* [1999] a claim for a bridging loan was dismissed as the claimant had failed to apply for an advance payment.

Interest charges may be an appropriate item of a claim if reasonably incurred (see *Cole* v *Southwark London Borough Council* [1979]), but in making arrangements for the relocation of a business, the claimant should not speculate at the acquiring authority's expense: in *Thomas & Son Ltd* v *Greater London Council* [1982] abortive development charges and interest was disallowed.

9. General interference

In *Budgen* v *Secretary of State for Wales* [1985] the Lands Tribunal allowed a claim for compensation for noise, dust and general interference suffered by the claimant in respect of his retained land during the construction of the scheme. The legal basis of this claim seems doubtful; it was not damage to the value of land, nor was it a consequence of being disturbed from occupation of the land taken. Possibly it compensated a loss of a cause action in nuisance. Whatever doubts one may have of its legal pedigree, it was probably justified on the merits.

10. Loss of rents

Where a claimant is an investment owner, or has a business, letting out accommodation, he will be entitled to compensation for the value of the property under rule (2) (see Chapter 12). The rule (2) compensation will usually represent the value of the loss of the right to rents, as was explained in *Mallick* v *Liverpool City Council* [1999], so that there can be no further claim for compensation for future loss of profits derived from rents. The rule (2) basis recognises the total extinguishment of the renting business.

11. Summary

The tests, for determining the eligibility of items of claim for disturbance compensation, were summarised by the member of the Lands Tribunal (RC Walmsley) in *Cole* v *Southwark London Borough* [1979] LT:

(a) the loss must be shown to have been sustained;
(b) the loss must be the natural and reasonable consequence of the dispossession; and
(c) the loss must not be too remote.

He added that the claimant must take all reasonable steps to mitigate the loss, and cannot recover for loss he could have avoided. The *Cole* case involved an extensive list of 87 items of claim in respect of disturbance following the compulsory purchase of the claimant's two houses; the case is worth reading for the reasons for allowing or disallowing those items.

17.6 Other matters under rule (6)

The second limb of rule (6), 'or any other matter not directly based on the value of land', appears to allow the payment of compensation for all other matters that are not related to being disturbed from possession and are not related to the value of land. Some of the heads of loss or expenditure that are compensatable under this limb of rule (6) are considered in other Chapters. There is authority in *London County Council* v *Tobin* [1959] that professional fees are compensatable under rule (6): see Chapter 18. There are circumstances where a claimant, who is not disturbed from possession, but suffers losses, may recover the same under this rule. This was the position in *Wrexham Maelor Borough Council* v *MacDougall* [1993] where the loss of a service contract with a company was compensated: see Chapter 18.

The compulsory acquisition of land may have the effect of increasing the tax liability of a claimant. This is explained in Chapter 22, where the question whether any increased liability is compensatable under rule (6) has been considered in at least three Lands Tribunal cases.

There is one type of loss that seems, potentially, compensatable under rule (6), but in respect of which there is, as yet, no decided and published authority. It is best explained by the following illustration. Assume that an investment landlord holds a number of shops in a shopping area that has been identified by the local planning authority for a redevelopment scheme. Such schemes often progress rather slowly and various areas of such a scheme may be acquired over a period of time so as to cause a general blight over the area. Retail tenants may choose not to renew leases or may be successful in having their leases acquired following the service of blight notices. This merely adds to the blighting affect. The investment landlord will, increasingly, suffer rent voids and an inability either, to trigger rent reviews, or to secure rent increases that might otherwise have been the case in the absence of any blighting. Although such a landowner will be entitled to the open market value of his property interest disregarding the scheme, he will incur real losses prior to the valuation date. The landowner is not in possession and not entitled to disturbance compensation under the first limb of rule (6): see **17.3 Persons entitled to disturbance compensation** above. Can these losses be compensatable under the second limb of rule (6)? One argument, that is advanced against any such claim, is that such losses are related to the value of land because they are, in effect, losses of rent, and rent is related to the value of land.

The words 'the value of land' were clearly used in rule (6), when the six principal rules were adopted by the Acquisition of Land (Assessment of Compensation) Act 1919, to differentiate the rule (6) claim from that under rule (2). The rule (2) claim is the claim for the open market value of the land taken – in other words the capital value. The words 'the value of land' in rule (6) must be a reference to the same words in rule (2). It follows that a claim that was in some way value-related, such as rents, would not be outside rule (6).

Chapter 18

Additional Payments

Introduction
Legal costs and other fees and losses
Home-loss payments
Statutory disturbance payments
Statutory discretionary payments, re-housing duty and loans
Interest
Loss payments

18.1 Introduction

An expropriated owner is entitled to compensation for the land acquired from him and, if he was in occupation, he is also entitled to compensation for being 'disturbed'. Together, these two claims represent the price or compensation for the land compulsorily acquired. The owner will, additionally, be paid his legal costs and other professional fees incurred in preparing a claim for compensation. This chapter also deals with certain other payments, provided for under the Land Compensation Act 1973: these were enacted to make good some deficiencies in the pre-existing compensation provisions, and are payable to certain categories of persons displaced from land.

18.2 Legal costs and other fees and losses

1. Conveyancing costs

Under the Compulsory Purchase Act 1965, section 23, the costs of all conveyances of the land subject to compulsory purchase shall be borne by the acquiring authority. The costs, which are confined to the conveyancing costs, include all charges and expenses incurred on the part of the expropriated owner of deducing, evidencing and verifying title, making out and furnishing such abstracts and attested copies as the acquiring authority may require; and, of preparing all conveyances of any of the land. Disputed claims must be referred for assessment to a master of the High Court.

2. *Other professional fees*

A claimant, however, may well seek legal advice following the receipt of a notice to treat, and he may need the advice of a valuation surveyor or accountant in preparing and sustaining his claim for compensation. Although there is no express provision in the 1965 Act for the payment of these fees, there is clear judicial authority, such as in *London County Council* v *Tobin* [1959] CA, that where legal and accountancy fees are incurred as a result of the service of a notice to treat, in advising the claimant and preparing his claim, they are recoverable as compensation. In the *Tobin* case, the fees were necessarily and reasonably incurred in preparing a disturbance claim. In *Lee* v *Minister of Transport* [1965] CA, Lord Denning MR said that fees payable to a surveyor, valuer or agent in preparing a claim have always been allowed on a compulsory acquisition; they are not part of the disturbance claim. He considered that section 5, rule (6), of the 1961 Act safeguards the payment of fees following the change to market value in 1919:

> Rule (6): The provisions of rule (2) shall not affect the assessment of compensation for disturbance or any other matter not directly based on the value of land.

Section 17(9A) of the Land Compensation Act 1961 provides that the fees and expenses incurred by a claimant in connection with the issue of a certificate of alternative development, and of any successful appeal, shall be taken into account in assessing compensation.

Where a claim is made under Part I of the Land Compensation Act 1973, reasonable valuation and legal fees are payable: see section 3(5).

Fees for preparing and negotiating a claim are normally allowed on what is called Ryde's Scale. A surveyor is entitled to charge his client such fees as are agreed, and in default of agreement, reasonable fees: see *Grafton* v *Secretary of State for Air* [1956]. The Lands Tribunal is increasingly prepared to allow reasonable fees actually charged, rather than Ryde's Scale fees: see *DB Thomas and Sons Ltd* v *Greater London Council* [1982] and *Matthews* v *Environment Agency* [2002]. Sometimes claims may be aggregated for the purposes of calculating fees: see *Johns* v *Edmonton Corpn* [1958]. If Ryde's Scale fees are less than the reasonable fees, the surveyor may recover the excess from the client: *Francis* v *Harris* [1989]. Fees will be disallowed or reduced if the surveyor is not involved in negotiating the claim, or some part of it: see *Mahood* v *Department of the Environment for Northern Ireland* [1986].

In *Phipps* v *Wiltshire County Council* [1983] LT, in connection with the acquisition of land suitable for tipping, the claimant incurred over £22,000 in pollution consultants' fees in the preparation of his claim. Although it was held that the services of the consultants were properly and reasonably incurred, the fees were reduced after disregarding certain inadmissible items.

The costs of a reference were held to be recoverable under the equivalent of rule (6) in *Lesquende Ltd* v *Planning and Environment Committee of Jersey* [1998].

3. Other losses

Where a claimant is not disturbed from occupation, and therefore cannot make a claim for disturbance compensation, he may be able to rely on section 5, rule (6), of the 1961 Act to claim compensation for losses consequential to an acquisition. The Court of Appeal in *Wrexham Maelor Borough Council* v *MacDougall* [1993] decided that the owner of a lease which was acquired could claim compensation for the loss of a service contract with a company which had occupied the property, even though the claimant had not been in occupation and was not entitled to disturbance compensation.

18.3 Home-loss payments

The Land Compensation Act 1973, sections 29–32, provides for a payment to be made to a person who is displaced from a dwelling. The sum payable is in addition to any other compensation, and is a small recognition that a person is being compelled to leave his home. A number of changes were made by the Planning and Compensation Act 1991 in respect of displacements on or after November 16 1990. There are several requirements to be satisfied if a person is to be entitled to such a payment:

1. Cause of the loss of the home

The person must be displaced from a dwelling in consequence of (section 29(1)):

(a) the compulsory acquisition of an interest in the dwelling; the interest acquired need not necessarily be that of the home-loss claimant; a tenant, whose landlord's interest is acquired, and who is displaced, will be entitled, if he, the tenant, satisfies the other requirements;

or
(b) the making or acceptance of a demolition, closing or obstructive building order under the Housing Acts;
    or
(c) the carrying out of redevelopment on land that has been previously acquired by an authority possessing compulsory powers or appropriated by a local authority and for the time being held by the authority for the purposes for which it was acquired or appropriated;
    or
(d) the carrying out of improvements to the land by a housing association which has previously acquired the land;
    or
(e) the making of a possession order on grounds 10 or 10A of Part II of Schedule 2 to the Housing Act 1985.

In (c) above, if land was being held for housing purposes, and the local housing authority resolved to demolish the existing houses, this would be regarded as redevelopment and any local authority tenant displaced from a dwelling as a consequence is eligible for a home-loss payment: see *R* v *Corby District Council, ex parte McLean* [1975]. 'Redevelopment' includes site clearance preparatory to a sale, and the compensation claim is not lost if the purpose for which the land was acquired or appropriated has been abandoned: *Greater London Council* v *Holmes* [1986]. Compensation may therefore be payable to tenants of a local housing authority required to move to enable works to be carried out: see the cases on the meaning of 'displacement' below.

The claimant will be eligible if he is displaced as a consequence of the compulsory acquisition of an interest and that acquisition follows a service by him of a blight notice: see the repeal of section 29(5) of the 1973 Act. A claimant will not be eligible if, in the case of a compulsory acquisition, he vacates his dwelling before the date of the confirmation of the compulsory purchase order. But after that date there is no obligation that he must be required to give up possession: see section 29(3).

2. *The occupation of the dwelling*

A claimant must also satisfy the following requirements as to his occupation of the dwelling, section 29(2):

(a) he has been in occupation of the dwelling, or a substantial part of it, as his only or main residence, throughout a period of not less than one year ending with the date of displacement; and

(b) his interest or right to so occupy the dwelling was freehold, leasehold, statutory tenancy or restricted contract under the Rent Act 1977, or a right to occupy under the terms of his employment: see section 29(4).

A claimant, who has had different rooms at some time during the one-year period, but in the same building, will still be eligible. The Act also provides that if a person has been in residence throughout the one-year period, but does not satisfy all the conditions, or only for some shorter period, he, or she (a widow is a good example), may add any immediately preceding period, when those conditions were satisfied by a person in occupation, to their own qualifying period: see section 32(3) and (5). A person who has not been in occupation for the full one-year period may in appropriate circumstances, be able to add his predecessor's period of occupation: see section 32(3A).

A spouse who has acquired rights of occupation under the Matrimonial Homes Act 1983 may claim the home-loss payment where the spouse who would otherwise be the proper claimant is no longer in residence: see section 29A.

3. Displaced from occupation

A person is displaced if he has no real choice and leaves the premises, a formal notice to leave may not be required; whether a person is displaced in a question of fact: see *Caplan* v *Secretary of State for the Environment* [1980] and *Follows* v *Peabody Trust* [1983]. A person who willingly leaves, but not because a move is inevitable, may not be 'displaced': see *Ingle* v *Scarborough Council* [2002].

4. The amount of home-loss payment

Where the date of displacement is on or after January 1 1989 and before November 16 1990, the amount is equal to the rateable value of the dwelling multiplied by 10, subject to a maximum of £1,500 and a minimum of £1,200.

Where the displacement is after November 16 1990, there are two levels of home-loss payment. A claimant who is the owner of a freehold or a lease exceeding three years, is entitled to 10% of the market value of his interest, subject to a maximum of £15,000 and a minimum of £1,500: see section 30(1). Any other claimant is entitled to £1,500: see section 30(2). Market value means the amount which is assessed for the purpose of the acquisition of the claimant's interest, or would be so assessed.

The Secretary of State has power to vary the multiplier and to prescribe a different maximum or minimum. The indication is that a flat rate will be introduced following the abolition of domestic rating. If the dwelling forms part of a hereditament, the valuation officer certifies an appropriate apportionment of the rateable value.

Where there are two or more persons entitled to make a claim to a home-loss payment in respect of the same dwelling (joint occupation or interests), the full payment is divided equally between each claimant.

5. The claim

The person displaced from a dwelling, and who satisfies the requirements so far considered, must make his claim within six years of the date of displacement: see section 32(7A). The claim must be in writing and shall be supplemented by any further particulars the authority concerned reasonably requires to enable them to determine entitlement.

The home-loss payment must then be made by the authority on or before the latest of the following dates: the date of displacement; the last day of the three-month period from the date of the claim; and, where the amount is by reference to the market value, the day on which the market value is agreed or determined: see section 32(2). Where, upon the date when payment should be made, the market value of the interest has not been determined, an advance payment shall be made in the lesser amount of the maximum payment or 10% of the acquiring authority's estimate of market value: see section 32(2B). It is clear from the Act that a person may vacate his dwelling, in the case of a compulsory acquisition, at any time after the confirmation of the compulsory purchase order; he need not wait for the authority to require him to give up occupation, he will still be eligible to make a claim.

6. Acquisition by agreement

There is no right to a home-loss payment if the dwelling is acquired from the claimant by agreement. But provided the authority possesses compulsory purchase powers, it has a discretion, and may make a payment corresponding to any home-loss payment which they would be required to make to him if the acquisition were compulsory: see section 32(7).

18.4 Statutory disturbance payments

A person who has an interest in land, which is compulsorily acquired, is entitled to claim compensation for losses or expenditure, which are a natural and reasonable consequence of being 'disturbed', in accordance with the criteria of the preceding Chapter 17.

The Land Compensation Act 1973, sections 37–38, makes provision for the payment of compensation to persons who are displaced from land and have no interest in the land entitling them to compensation in the ordinary way. Examples would include tenants holding over after the expiring of their leases (although a business tenant holding over under a continuation tenancy under the Landlord and Tenant Act 1954 does have a compensatable interest: *Selborne (Gowns) Ltd* v *Ilford Corpn* [1962]) and residential statutory tenants under the Rent Act 1977 whose contractual tenancies have terminated. Persons displaced from agricultural land are excluded: see Chapter 20.

1. *Persons entitled to a disturbance payment: section 37*

A person is entitled if a number of conditions are satisfied:

(a) He is displaced from land in consequence of the circumstances that give rise to a home-loss payment at p297 above, (a) to (d): a compulsory acquisition of the land, the making, passing or acceptance of a housing order or resolution, and the redevelopment of land previously acquired or appropriated by an authority with compulsory purchase powers. But the surrender of a tenancy is not an acquisition of land: *R* v *Islington London Borough Council* [1984]. For the meaning of displacement see p299 above.

(b) The claimant must have lawful possession of the land from which he is displaced: see section 37(2). 'Possession' means physical occupation with the intention of excluding unauthorised intruders: *Wrexham Maelor Borough Council* v *MacDougall* [1993]. The date for determining whether a person has lawful possession is, in the case of a compulsory purchase order, the date when notice of the order was first published; in the case of land acquired by agreement, the date of that agreement; and in the case of a housing order or resolution, the date the order or resolution was made.

(c) The person displaced in consequence of the acquisition of land must have no interest in the land for the acquisition of which he is otherwise entitled to compensation: see section 37(2)(b).

Any person with such a compensatable interest would be entitled to compensation for disturbance in the ordinary way: see Chapter 17. The combined effect of this and the preceding requirement of lawful possession is apparently to restrict entitlement to a disturbance payment to the following categories – tenancies at will (including a tenant holding over after termination of his lease, but not a continuation tenancy under section 24 of the Landlord and Tenant Act 1954 (*Selborne (Gowns) Ltd* v *Ilford Corpn* [1962]); tenancy at sufferance (tenant holding over after termination of his lease, without consent of his landlord); and a residential statutory tenancy after the contractual tenancy has expired (Rent Act 1977, section 3): in appropriate circumstances, a licensee can have lawful possession and would be entitled: see *Smith & Waverley Tailoring* v *Edinburgh District Council* [1976] and *Wrexham Maelor Borough Council* v *MacDougall* [1993]. But a squatter who has not acquired a possessory title is not: see *Rivers* v *Dorset County Council* [1995]. Thus in *Mills & Allen Ltd* v *Commission for New Towns* [2001] a claimant with an interest in an advertisement site would be entitled to a disturbance payment.

In *McTaggart* v *Bristol and West Building Society* [1985] a claimant, who had served a blight notice, was displaced, not by the acquiring authority, but by a bailiff appointed by his building society.

Finally, in respect of business tenants, if a person is displaced from land in circumstances that would entitle him to compensation from the authority concerned under section 37 of the Landlord and Tenant Act 1954 (compensation from a landlord where an order for a new tenancy of business premises is precluded on certain grounds), he is entitled, at his option, to the disturbance payment or to the compensation under the Landlord and Tenant Act but not to both: see section 37(4). In *Evis* v *Commission for New Towns* [2002] the Lands Tribunal decided that a disturbance payment under section 37(1)(a) of the 1973 Act (acquisition of the land by an authority with compulsory powers) was not precluded by the claimant's entitlement to compensation under section 37 of the Landlord and Tenant Act 1954; but it was precluded under section 37(1)(c) of the 1973 Act (land previously required or appropriated by an authority with compulsory powers and improvements or redevelopment will take place) where the development was not carried out by the acquiring authority.

Section 37 does not apply where land is used for agriculture: see section 37(7).

2. *Amount of disturbance payment: section 38*

The amount of a disturbance payment shall be equal to:

(a) the reasonable expenses of the person entitled to the payment in removing from the land from which he is displaced; and
(b) if he was carrying on a trade or business on that land, the loss he will sustain by reason of the disturbance of that trade or business consequent upon his having to quit the land.

In estimating the loss of any person for the purposes of (b) above, regard shall be had to the period for which the land occupied by him may reasonably have been expected to be available for the purpose of his trade or business and to the availability of other land suitable for that purpose.

In connection with (a) above, the Court of Session in Scotland decided in *Anderson* v *Glasgow Corpn* [1976] that the reasonable expenses of the claimant in removing from the land are not confined only to the expenses of actual removal but include all reasonable expenses reasonably incurred as a direct and natural consequence of being displaced: the costs incurred by a protected tenant in redecorating the house vacated were therefore recoverable as part of the disturbance payment. The limits to be put on a claim were considered by the Lands Tribunal in:

Nolan v *Sheffield Metropolitan District Council* [1979] LT
Because his dwelling had been included in a housing action area, the claimant, a tenant, was required to remove from 167 to 181 Rock Street, Sheffield. He received a home-loss payment and he then claimed a disturbance payment to cover removal expenses, telephone reconnection, connection of gas cooker, purchase of 13-amp plugs, refixing automatic washing machine, refitting burglar alarm, adapting curtains,

redirection of mail, hire of electric kettle and calor gas, notional loss on forced sale of water heater and extractor fan, purchase of paint and filler for repairs, a certain amount of time off work, loss of rose bushes and folding table, and the cost of redecorating where there was evidence of damp; all these items were allowed by the Tribunal. But the Tribunal refused to allow new carpets and kitchen-wall cupboards, replacing fire-place surrounds, loss of fish pond and payment of rent during carrying out of work. The reasons given by the Tribunal for its decision were that the disturbance payment cannot cover expenses which are not incurred as a natural and direct consequence of the necessity to remove from the old dwelling to the new one.

The Lands Tribunal in this case considered that the claim for a statutory disturbance payment was analogous to the ordinary claim for disturbance compensation. Where the person displaced, and this includes a company, is carrying on a trade or business so that (b) above applies, it is likely that a similarly wide view would be taken of what is allowable: see *Wrexham Maelor Borough Council v MacDougall* [1993]. In *Evans* v *City of Glasgow District Council* [1977], the Lands Tribunal for Scotland considered that the principles enunciated in *Harvey* v *Crawley Development Corporation* [1957] in respect of ordinary disturbance compensation were applicable, though subject to the actual statutory wording of the Act. The decision of the Court of Appeal in *Prasad* v *Wolverhampton Borough Council* [1983] has been explained in relation to disturbance expenses incurred before the notice to treat: see p275. In *Goss* v *Paddington Churches Housing Association* [1982] a claim for a new carpet twice the size of the old carpet was rejected. A new carpet was not a natural and direct consequence of disturbance – the correct claim was the cost of lifting and relaying the old carpet or the loss on the forced sale.

Where the displacement is from a dwelling in respect of which structural modifications have been made for meeting the special needs of a disabled person, then the reasonable expenses in making comparable modifications to another dwelling to meet the disabled person's special needs can be claimed.

18.5 Statutory discretionary payments, re-housing duty and loans

1. *Discretionary disturbance payments*

There will still be circumstances where a person is displaced from land and will not be entitled to any disturbance payment or to compensation for disturbance under the normal rules. Examples include lodgers and licensees, who have no lawful possession of land, and tenants found alternative accommodation and displaced too early to be eligible for a disturbance payment.

The Land Compensation Act 1973, section 37(5), provides that the appropriate authority has a discretion to make a disturbance payment to such persons. The matters considered in section **18.4** *supra* otherwise apply. The Lands Tribunal has jurisdiction to determine the amount payable: see *Gozra* v *Hackney London Borough Council* [1988] CA. Although apparently not in Scotland, see *City of Glasgow District Council* v *Mackie* [1992].

2. *Re-housing duty*

Under section 39 of the Land Compensation Act 1973, the local housing authority has a duty to re-house a person displaced from residential accommodation in consequence of the acquisition of the land by an authority possessing compulsory purchase powers, and suitable alternative residential accommodation on reasonable terms is not otherwise available to that person. The duty of the housing authority is to secure that person will be provided with such accommodation. However in *R* v *Bristol Corporation, ex parte Hendy* [1973], it was held that the duty to re-house was discharged by providing such a person with temporary accommodation, and otherwise placing the person's name on the housing waiting list. In other words the duty does not require the housing authority to give any priority over others on the housing waiting list.

3. *Loans to displaced residential owner-occupiers*

The Land Compensation Act 1973, section 41, provides that where a person is displaced from a dwelling in consequence of the circumstances that make him eligible for a home-loss payment, namely acquisition of the land, making, passing or acceptance of a housing order or undertaking, or redevelopment of land that has been previously acquired, the authority may make that person a loan for the purpose of acquiring or constructing another dwelling in substitution for that from which he is displaced.

To be eligible, the person displaced must either have been the freeholder of the dwelling he was displaced from, or have held a lease with not less than three years remaining unexpired at date of displacement. The loan will be secured by a mortgage on the substitute dwelling. The acquisition of a building and its conversion to a dwelling can also be considered.

4. Power to defray expenses

Where a person is displaced from a dwelling in consequence of the acquisition of the land by an authority possessing compulsory purchase powers, the Land Compensation Act 1973, section 43, empowers the acquiring authority to pay any reasonable expenses incurred by the person displaced in connection with the acquisition, by him, of another dwelling in substitution for that from which he is displaced. To be eligible, the claimant must have had no interest in the dwelling he was displaced from, or no greater interest therein than as a tenant for a year or from year to year.

18.6 Interest

1. Acquisition of land

Where an acquiring authority enter and take possession before agreeing compensation, interest, at a prescribed rate, is payable until compensation is paid: Compulsory Purchase Act 1965, section 11. Interest is payable from the date possession is taken of any land the subject of a notice of entry: see *Chilton* v *Telford Development Corporation* [1987]. The handing over of keys is not necessarily entry: see *Simmonds* v *Kent County Council* [1990]. Where a general vesting declaration has been used, and a title has vested with the acquiring authority, it may be some months before the authority takes physical possession. It was held in the Scottish case of *Birrell Ltd* v *City of Edinburgh District Council* [1982], where the analogous expedited completion of title had been used, that interest on the unpaid compensation ran from the date legal title passed, and not a later date when physical possession was given up. The position in England is governed by section 10 of the Compulsory Purchase (Vesting Declarations) Act 1981: interest is payable from date of vesting: see *Singh* v *Rochdale Metropolitan Borough Council* [1992].

The prescribed rate is changed from time to time according to prevailing market rates. Any award of the Land Tribunal carries interest from the date of that award: Lands Tribunal Rules 1996, rule 38.

Where an advance payment is made under section 52 of the Land Compensation Act 1973, interest is payable on the estimated compensation due in respect of the acquisition of any interest in the subject land from the date of entry until payment of the 90% advance: see section 52A(1). If the initial estimate of compensation was too low and an additional sum is payable as a further advance under section 52(4A), interest on the difference between the original and revised values becomes payable. Interest must also be paid on an annual basis on the difference between the estimated (or revised) compensation and the amount of the advances provided the accrued interest payable exceeds £1,000.

2. Claim for injurious affection where no land acquired from claimant

If a claim is made for compensation under section 10 of the Compulsory Purchase Act 1965 for injurious affection where no land is acquired from the claimant, interest is payable on any sum due from date of claim: Land Compensation Act 1973, section 63: see Chapter 23 for this claim. Interest is payable on statutory disturbance claims: see section 37(6) of the Land Compensation Act 1973.

3. Claim or equivalent reinstatement and disturbance

Where compensation is payable for equivalent reinstatement under rule (5), interest is payable on the costs of reinstatement from the date of entry until the date when the compensation is paid. This is so even if resinstatement does not take place until some years later: see *Halstead* v *Manchester City Council* [1998]. There seems no reason why the same principle should not apply to compensation for disturbance under rule (6).

4. Claims within Schedule 18 to the Planning and Compensation Act 1991

Interest is now payable on the compensation claims listed in this Schedule. The claims include those under the Ancient Monuments and Archaeological Areas Act 1979, Land Drainage Act 1991,

Highways Act 1980, Building Act 1984, Water Industry Act 1991 (probably it applies), Town and Country Planning Act 1990 and the Planning (Listed Buildings and Conservation Areas) Act 1990. The relevant decision giving rise to the claim must have been made after a specified date. Interest is payable from the date of a formal claim: see *Bestley* v *North West Water Ltd* [1998].

5. *Limitation period*

The limitation period for the recovery of interest commences on the date when the compensation upon which it is due is agreed or awarded: see *Halstead* v *Manchester City Council* [1998].

6. *Lands Tribunal's general jurisdiction to award interest*

In *British Coal Corpn* v *Gwent County Council* [1995] the Court of Appeal held that the tribunal did not have a general jurisdiction to award interest on claims (as distinct from on awards). However interest can now be ordered on claims and awards under the Lands Tribunal Rules 1996, rule 32.

18.7 Loss payments

The Planning and Compulsory Purchase Bill 2002 is currently before Parliament. Part 7 contains additional sections that will be inserted into the Land Compensation Act 1973 to make provisions for loss payments. A basic loss payment will be payable to a person with a qualifying interest. The payment will be the lower of 7.5% of the value of his interest or £75,000. A qualifying interest is a freehold or a lease that subsists for 12 months before various relevant dates.

The bill provides for two types of occupier's loss payments. An occupier's loss payment for agricultural land based on percentage of land values and a rate per hectare, and an occupier's loss payment for other land also based on land values, but with some rates on areas. Both payments are subject to a maximum amount of £25,000.

Chapter 19

Compensation for Leasehold Interests and Tenancies

Introduction
Compensation for leasehold interests
Compensation for short tenancies: section 20 basis
Compensation for reversionary interests
Business tenancies
Additional payments

19.1 Introduction

The two appropriate methods of acquiring a leasehold interest and obtaining possession were mentioned in Chapter 8; the acquiring authority may either acquire the reversionary interest and serve notice to quit in accordance with the terms of the lease on the lessee, or serve a notice to treat on the lessee and expropriate his interest as an ordinary compulsory acquisition. In the case of what are called short tenancies, where the person in possession has no greater interest in the land than as tenant for a year or from year to year (including a term of years certain which at the relevant time has less than a year unexpired), a notice to treat need not be served; if possession is required by the authority, it can either serve a notice to quit in accordance with the terms of the tenancy, or a notice of entry, of not less than 14 days under the Compulsory Purchase Act 1965, section 11. In the latter case, compensation is assessed by virtue of section 20 of the same Act if the tenant is required to give up possession before the expiration of his term.

Where a lease is acquired by notice to treat, and the tenant is compelled to assign the lease to the acquiring authority, the landlord's consent to assignment (if otherwise required by the lease) need not be obtained: see *Slipper* v *Tottenham & Hampstead Rly Co* [1867].

Although the rules for the assessment of compensation dealt with in the preceding chapters are generally applicable to the acquisition of a leasehold interest, certain matters of relevance to leases and tenancies are considered here. The assessment of compensation for agricultural tenants presents special problems and is dealt with in the next chapter.

19.2 Compensation for leasehold interests

The owner of a leasehold interest, served with a notice to treat, is entitled to compensation for the value of his interest (essentially the value of any profit rent); compensation for severance and injurious affection; and compensation for disturbance. All the rules considered in the chapters on these three heads of claim are applicable to the assessment of compensation for the acquisition of a leasehold interest. Certain additional points can be made. The position of tenancies under the Landlord and Tenant Act 1954 is considered in section **19.5** below.

In the case of a lease where the passing rent is above the current rental value, the lease may have a negative value. That gives rise to the interesting question as to whether the negative value must be set against any disturbance compensation claim on the argument of one claim under which the claimant is entitled to no more or less than his loss: see p168 above. A strict application of the one claim fairness principle would suggest that a negative value should be set off.

However, a negative value is like negative equity in a house; it may be transient, and will disappear with time. The claimant is not choosing to get rid of the lease; he is compelled under compulsory purchase. To set off the negative value against other compensation does not recognise the compulsion and will leave the claimant with uncompensated losses caused by the acquisition. Although the claimant would appear to be fortuitous in having a burdensome lease acquired, he might well have preferred to pay a higher rent in the meantime. It should be remembered that the higher rent will be reflected in lower profits, and therefore a lower claim for loss of profits or extinguishment of goodwill.

If, at the date of the notice to treat, the lease had more than a year to run, then compensation will be assessed on the usual basis, and section 20 (see below) will have no application: see *Runcorn Association Football Club Ltd* v *Warrington & Runcorn Development Corpn* [1982] where notice to treat was served two and a half years before the end of a 14-year lease, but entry was taken when seven months of the lease remained. Because section 20 was said to have no application in the *Runcorn* case, the claimants were entitled to request that the compensation be assessed on the costs of equivalent reinstatement under rule (5), section 5 of the 1961 Act.

1. Date of valuation

The normal rules apply: see section **11.5** in Chapter 11. But the difficulty is that a lease is a wasting asset and if possession is not required, and no agreement as to compensation made, a delay following the service of the notice to treat may have the consequence that the lease loses value. In fact, if the lease expires before possession is taken, the acquiring authority will pay no compensation for the interest as there will be nothing to acquire: *Holloway* v *Dover Corpn* [1960] CA. However, in *Soper & Soper* v *Doncaster Corpn* [1964], where the lease had only some six months to run, the lessee agreed with the lessor prior to the notice to treat, to take a grant of a new five-year lease from the expiry of the current term; the acquiring authority served notice of entry about four months before the expiry of the current term but was required to compensate the lessee on the ground that the agreement for a new lease gave him a compensatable interest which he possessed at the date of the notice to treat.

2. Early determination clauses and options for renewal

Sometimes a lease will contain clauses enabling either the landlord or the tenant to determine the lease before the full expiry of its term. Such a right to determine may have to be exercised by a certain date. The likelihood of early determination is a matter that should be considered in valuing the interest. Similar considerations apply to an option to renew a tenancy. In *Trocette Property Co Ltd* v *Greater London Council* [1974] CA (see Chapter 12) it was assumed a new lease would have been granted but for a proposed road scheme. However, the value of the tenant's right to serve a notice under section 5 of the Leasehold Reform Act 1967 and acquire the freehold or the grant of an extension to the lease cannot be considered if in fact no notice has been served: *Johnson* v *Sheffield City Council* [1981].

3. Severance and injurious affection

Where some land is acquired from a tenant, a claim for compensation can be made for the depreciation in value of any other land held by the lessee due to severance or injurious affection. It is not necessary for the retained and acquired lands to be held under the same lease: see section 7 of the Compulsory Purchase Act 1965. However, the lessee is entitled under section 19 of the Compulsory Purchase Act 1965 to have the rent apportioned between the land taken and the residue of the land: see *Dixon* v *Allgood* [1981].

19.3 Compensation for short tenancies: section 20 basis

It is not necessary to serve a notice to treat on a tenant having an interest no greater than as a tenant for a year, or from year to year; provided a notice to treat is served in respect of some interest in the land (i.e. the reversionary interest) entry can be effected against a tenant holding a short tenancy following a 14-day minimum notice of entry under section 11 of the Compulsory Purchase Act 1965.

The Lands Clauses Act 1845, section 121, provides a basis for the assessment of compensation for short tenancies; this section has been re-enacted in the Compulsory Purchase Act 1965, section 20, and applies to the majority of acquisitions: see Chapter 6 in Part II.

It was held in *Newham London Borough Council* v *Benjamin* [1968] CA that, although a person having no greater interest in land than as a tenant for a year or from year to year (including a term with less than a year unexpired) may be served with a notice to treat, he will only be compensated on the basis set down in the Compulsory Purchase Act 1965, section 20:

(1) ... if that person is required to give up possession of any land so occupied by him before the expiration of his term or interest in the land, he shall be entitled to compensation for the value of his unexpired term or interest in the land, and for any just allowance which ought to be made to him by an incoming tenant, and for any loss or injury he may sustain.

(2) If a part only of such land is required, he shall also be entitled to compensation for the damage done to him by severing land held by him or otherwise injuriously affecting it.

...

(4) On payment or tender of the amount of such compensation all such persons shall respectively deliver up to the acquiring authority, or to the person appointed by them to take possession, any such land in their possession required by the acquiring authority.

'Required to give up possession' means required by a notice. Accordingly, if a claimant leaves after a notice to treat but before a notice of entry, it will not be entitled to compensation: see *R* v *Stone* [1866], *R* v *Great North Rly* [1876], *Frisby* v *Chingford Corpn* [1957] and *Roberts* v *Bristol Corpn* [1960]

1. Date of valuation

The date for assessment of compensation is the date the authority takes possession: see the *Benjamin* case above and *Greenwoods Tyre Services Ltd* v *Manchester Corpn* [1972]. Although section 20(4) contemplates that if the proper amount of compensation is tendered, the tenant shall then give up possession, and therefore suggests the possibility of some agreement prior to entry, it is doubtful whether the date of that agreement should be the date of valuation: as *per* the *West Midlands Baptist* case: see section **11.7.2** in Chapter 11. This doubt arises because section 20 refers to the entitlement to the value of the unexpired term of the tenancy when the person is required to give up possession, i.e. the date of entry. But with a periodic tenancy, the unexpired term is regarded as running to the date the tenancy could have been determined had a notice to quit been served on the date of entry: see *Greenwoods Tyre* case. So, depending on the date of entry in relation to the next latest date for giving notice to quit, a difference of opinion as to the proper date for valuation becomes important. The point, therefore, is not free of doubt.

2. 'Value of unexpired term or interest'

Until 1919 the value of the unexpired term would have been the value to the tenant; the value to owner basis: see Chapter 11. However, it is by no means clear that the statutory rules for the assessment of compensation, now in the Land Compensation Act 1961, apply to the valuation of a short tenancy. The tenancy is not acquired but would appear to merge with the reversion or to be destroyed by the taking of possession by the acquiring authority: the statutory rules apply to a compulsory acquisition of an interest: see section 5.

The length of the unexpired term of a term certain runs from the date of entry; with a periodic tenancy, to the earliest date the tenancy could be determined by a notice to quit served on the date of entry.

However, it is generally assumed that the 1961 Act does apply and the market value of the unexpired term is to be assessed.

Regard should be had to any right of renewal in the tenancy; a right of renewal under statutes is considered below at section **19.4** in relation to business tenancies, and in the next chapter in relation to agricultural tenancies. Regard should also be had to any bar on assignment; this would make the tenancy less valuable.

Normally a leasehold interest is valued by valuing the profit-rent, if any; in *Watson v Secretary of State for Air* [1954] (see next chapter) the Court of Appeal accepted that a short tenancy, if put on the open market, might fetch a price which reflected the profit that could be made from the land. That case involved a claim to compensation under section 20 of the Compulsory Purchase Act 1965. The value of a short tenancy, therefore, may be the value of the right to make prospective profits. This point is important as the 'fag-end' of a lease or a periodic tenancy will not necessarily be marketable as such to enable a market value to be determined in the ordinary way.

Alternatively a lease could have a surrender value to the landlord. The marriage value might be shared and motives and intention of the actual landlord are relevant: see *Walton's Executors v Commissioners of Inland Revenue* [1996].

A statutory tenant under the Rent Act 1977 does not have a term and in any event it has no value on the open market. A business tenant whose tenancy continues under the Landlord and Tenant Act 1954, section 24, is within section 20: *Selborne (Gowns) Ltd v Ilford Corpn* [1962].

3. *'Any just allowance by an incoming tenant and any loss or injury sustained'*

What is usually referred to as disturbance may be claimed under this head. The principles discussed in Chapter 17 are applicable and need not be repeated. In *Minister of Transport v Pettit* [1969] it was said that 'loss or injury' was not confined to financial loss, but was wide enough to cover the inconvenience and upset suffered by a claimant. However, only loss or injury sustained between date of entry and expiry of the term are recoverable; in the case of business and agricultural tenancies, regard is to be taken of security of tenure: see next section **19.5** and Chapter 20.

4. *Severance and injurious affection*

See Chapter 15. In *Worlock v Sodbury Rural District Council* [1961]

LT, it was held that compensation could only be claimed if there was damage to the rest of the land in the same tenancy: if a tenant is required to give up possession of land held by him under tenancy A, he cannot be compensated for any damage by severance or injurious affection to land in tenancy B, even if both tenancies are held from the same landlord. By an amendment by the Planning and Compensation Act 1991, compensation for injurious affection and severance is no longer restricted to damage to the retained tenancy, but also to other interests held by the claimant: see section 20(2) of the 1965 Act.

19.4 Compensation for reversionary interests

The compulsory acquisition of the reversionary interest to a lease may cause special problems. The fact that the property is tenanted, and the tenant may enjoy security of tenure, may have the effect of depreciating the value of the reversionary interest in comparison with an interest in possession. There are also problems concerning repairs, and the proper valuation date.

1. *Effect of security of tenure*

This matter is illustrated in *Pyrah (Doddington) Ltd* v *Northamptonshire County Council* [1982] where the freehold interest belonging to the claimant was valued at £68,500 on the assumption that the claimant could not obtain vacant possession from the tenant under the Agricultural Holdings Acts, but where the value of the freehold interest on the assumption that vacant possession could be obtained was £90,000. It was decided by the Lands Tribunal that as the freehold interest was the subject of an agricultural tenancy on the date of the notice to treat, then the proper compensation for the freehold was the lower sum as it was not possible to obtain vacant possession: see also *Paul* v *Newham London Borough Council* [1991].

Where, by reasons of the scheme, the reversionary interest ceases to be an interest subject to a protected tenancy, and becomes an interest subject to an unprotected tenancy, that is not a matter to be disregarded under the *Pointe Gourde* principle: see *Rugby Joint Water Board* v *Foottit* [1973].

Marriage value of the freehold to the lessee may be taken into account: see *Hearts of Oak Benefit Society* v *Lewisham Borough Council* [1979].

Although where a valuation assumes vacant possession, one should assume the maximum difficulty to obtaining possession from a tenant: see *Harris* v *Commissioners for Inland Revenue* [1961].

2. *Repairs*

If an acquiring authority compulsorily acquires property which is the subject of a lease, the landlord will be prevented from enforcing his repairing covenants. This could be serious if the property is out of repair and this devalues the reversionary interest. The landlord will have been prevented from making the tenant put the property in repair, or of obtaining compensation for the breach of the repairing covenants. It was held in *Hibernian Property Ltd* v *Liverpool Corpn* [1973], in a case where the acquiring authority had itself been the tenant of the subject properties, and through its own lack of repair caused those properties to be declared unfit, that the landlord had a claim for damages for the difference in value between the compensation he was entitled to and the value the property would have had had it been kept in proper repair.

In the Lands Tribunal case of *Leek* v *Birmingham City Council* [1982] the standing property value of premises last used as a shop with offices above was agreed at £3,145 and their value in good repair at £15,000. The freehold claimant submitted that the compulsory acquisition prevented the enforcement of the repairing covenants. The Tribunal was not prepared to allow for the full difference in value to be awarded as part of the compensation, but did, on the evidence presented, allow a speculative 'overbid'. This 'overbid' reflected the value of the tenant's covenants having regard to the fact that the tenant in that case was a subsidiary of an international company of repute. The allowance was 80% of the difference between the two values.

In *Range* v *Buckinghamshire County Council* [1985] the Lands Tribunal applied a discount of £3,000 to reflect disrepairs, producing an investment value of £8,000.

In the case of 'old tenancies', that is those granted before the Landlord and Tenant (Covenants) Act 1995, there is a potential trap for landlords. Once an acquiring authority has acquired the reversion to leasehold property the landlord loses the right to sue on the tenant's covenants and recover damages: see *Re King* [1963]. It follows that if the compensation is less than it might have been if premises had been in a state of good repair the landlord will not be able to sue the tenant for damages for the difference between the compensation he obtains and the compensation he might have obtained. Accordingly a landlord should commence proceedings claiming damages before he parts with his title. However in those cases where the landlord retains the right to sue the tenant for damages for disrepair (either because a claim was issued before the compulsory acquisition in the case of 'old tenancies', or because the lease is a 'new tenancy') the landlord may be able to recover damages from the tenant if the compensation he receives reflects the state of dilapidations, and these dilapidations are due to the failure of the tenant to comply with the repairing covenants. The measure of those damages is limited by section 18(1) of the Landlord and Tenant Act 1927; namely the difference between the value of the reversionary interest, subject to the lease and the existence of the compulsory purchase scheme, but on the assumption that the repairing covenants have been complied with and the value of the reversionary interest, subject to the lease, the actual state of disrepair and the compulsory purchase scheme, but on the assumption that the potential purchaser would pay a price reflecting the right to enforce the repairing covenants. The second valuation will probably be greater than the compensation assessed in accordance with compulsory purchase principles because it will reflect the scheme whereas the value of the reversionary interest for compulsory purchase purposes disregards the scheme. This problem was considered by Buckley J in *Re King*, at first instance [1962].

3. Rent reviews

The scheme underlying an acquisition may have a number of consequences to a reversioner. Tenants may have served blight notices and their leases acquired leaving empty premises; rental values may have fallen so that passing rents are in fact below the rents likely to have been achieved in the absence of the scheme; and rent reviews may not have been triggered for these reasons. In relation to the last matter, the Lands Tribunal decided in *Preseli Pembrokeshire District Council* v *Greens Motors* [1991] that the open market value of a reversionary interest could include an element to reflect the right to trigger rent reviews and collect the reviewed rents in the no-scheme world. As to whether the other losses are recoverable, see paragraph 4 below on reinvestment and other losses.

4. Reinvestment expenses and other losses

The expenses of an investment owner in acquiring another property within one year of date of entry are allowed as disturbance compensation: see section 10A of the Land Compensation Act 1961.

A reversioner may suffer other losses, such as a lower rental income for a period of time prior to the acquisition attributable to the blighting effect of the scheme as tenants move out or rents are reviewed to levels less than they would otherwise be. The principle of fairness restated in *Director of Buildings and Lands* v *Shun Fung Ironworks Ltd* [1995] strongly suggest that a reversioner claimant should be able to recover such losses. The decision of the Court of Appeal in *Wrexham Maelor Borough Council* v *MacDougall* [1993], that section 5, rule (6), of the 1961 Act permitted a non-occupying owner of a lease to recover losses consequential to a compulsory acquisition, could well be applied to enable a reversioner to recover loss of rental income. The only difficulty will be to establish the necessary causal connection between loss and the acquisition; an acquiring authority might well argue that the general blighting effects of a scheme are not compensatable: see *Emslie & Simpson Ltd* v *Aberdeen City District Council* [1994].

5. Date of valuation

The date of interest may be critical if a tenant with security of tenure gives up possession at some point. This question is fully considered in Chapter 11.

6. Notices of entry

If the acquiring authority has served notice to treat in respect of any of the land, the authority may enter and take possession of that land before compensation is agreed. However, before doing so, they must also serve a notice of entry of not less than 14 days on the owner, lessee and occupier of the land. It appears that some acquiring authorities give notice of entry to the reversioner, but fail to give notice to an occupying lessee. The Lands Tribunal has criticised the practice for it means that an owner can lose rental income and will only receive interest on unpaid compensation. If no notice of entry has been served on the reversioner, then he would be entitled to the rent until such notice was properly given: see *Drake* v *Manchester City Council* [1980].

19.5 Business tenancies

1. Security of tenure

The Land Compensation Act 1973, section 47, provides that the security of tenure applicable to tenants within Part II of the Landlord and Tenant Act 1954 is to be taken into account in assessing either the landlord's or the tenant's interest. This section will apply to the acquisition of leasehold interests and the dispossession of short tenancies already considered in this chapter.

It provides that where an acquiring authority acquires the interest of the tenant (or the landlord) in, or takes possession of, any land subject to a business tenancy, the right of the tenant to apply for the grant of a new tenancy shall be taken into account in assessing the compensation payable by the acquiring authority either to the tenant or to the landlord. In assessing the compensation it shall be assumed that the acquiring authority has not acquired or proposed to acquire the land (otherwise it may be considered to have grounds of opposition to a new tenancy).

It is difficult to see how this provision can increase the value of the tenant's interest as, upon the grant of a new tenancy under the 1954 Act, the rent will normally be such that the tenant will be left with no profit rent. However, it may be significant where the tenant has carried out improvements, and the value of these is to be disregarded in determining a new rent under the 1954 Act: the tenant will then enjoy a profit rent. The provision may also be important in assessing the disturbance compensation and in particular loss of profits. The analogous position of agricultural tenants and the *Wakerley* case in Chapter 20 should be considered.

2. Compensation for short tenancies

There is a further point applicable to short tenancies when assessing compensation under section 20: the Landlord and Tenant Act 1954, section 39(2), provides that the tenant, dispossessed under section 20, is entitled to the amount assessed under section 20 of the 1965 Act or under the 1954 Act, whichever is the greater. In other words, a tenant dispossessed and compensated under section 20 should not receive less compensation than he would have received had he been given notice to quit and paid the compensation provided in the 1954 Act.

Under the 1954 Act, if a grant of a new tenancy is opposed on the ground that the landlord intends to demolish and/or reconstruct, or that he requires the premises for his own occupation (and has not acquired his interest within the five years preceding the termination of the tenancy), the court cannot award a new tenancy and the tenant is entitled to be paid compensation amounting to a multiplier of the rateable value; or, if he has occupied the premises for business purposes for at least 14 years, a higher multiplier of the rateable value. These multipliers are varied from time to time by statutory instrument.

3. Compensation following a notice to quit or expiry of term

If the acquiring authority purchases the landlord's reversionary interest and, instead of serving a notice to treat on the tenant (or a notice of entry if a short tenancy), it serves a notice to quit under the terms of the tenancy or allow the tenancy to expire, there will be no compulsory acquisition of the tenant's interest. If there is no compulsory acquisition, the tenant cannot claim any compensation under the Compulsory Purchase Act 1965: *Syers* v *Metropolitan Board of Works* [1877]. If a business tenancy terminates in this manner, section 24 of the Landlord and Tenant Act 1954 may apply and the tenant can remain in possession by virtue of a continuation tenancy under that section. In *Selborne (Gowns) Ltd* v *Ilford Corpn* [1962] LT it was decided that a continuation tenancy under the 1954 Act was an interest within section 20 of the 1965 Act and compensation could be claimed on the basis provided in that section. (A continuation tenancy under the 1954 Act will cease if, for instance, the landlord can show a ground for opposing a new tenancy and the court is thereby precluded from ordering that a new tenancy be granted.)

If there is a provision in a lease for resuming early possession by the landlord, the acquiring authority cannot take advantage of this for the purpose of reducing the tenant's compensation: see *Fleming* v *Newport Rly Co* [1883] HL. However, if a lease contains a provision that upon the compulsory acquisition of the landlord's reversionary interest, the lease will automatically terminate, such a provision will be valid and the landlord will be entitled to claim compensation on a vacant possession basis: *Re Morgan and London and North Western Rly Co* [1896]. A tenant dispossessed in this manner will not have a compensatable interest; he will have no unexpired term and no right to claim disturbance compensation: *Murray Bookmakers Ltd* v *Glasgow District Council* [1979] SLT. He may be entitled to the statutory disturbance payment under section 37 of the Land Compensation Act 1973.

A tenant dispossessed by notice to quit or the expiry of his term will only be entitled to the compensation provided by the 1954 Act (see 2 above) and compensation for any improvements under the Landlord and Tenant Act 1927. But the 1927 Act compensation may be reduced if the landlord intends to demolish, alter or change the use of the premises: an acquiring authority will usually have such an intention. A business tenant who is not eligible to make a claim for compensation under the Compulsory Purchase Act 1965 may be entitled to a disturbance payment: see below.

19.6 Additional payments

Subject to the requirements of eligibility, the additional payments dealt with in Chapter 18 are applicable to the assessment of compensation for leasehold interests and tenancies. The home-loss payment and disturbance payment will be of particular help to the dispossessed residential tenant who has a statutory tenancy under the Rent Act 1977, and therefore no compensatable interest. The disturbance payment will be of benefit to the business tenant whose tenancy has been terminated by notice to quit or effluxion of time and is not eligible for the grant of a new tenancy under the 1954 Act. But a business tenant who has a continuation tenancy by virtue of section 24 of the 1954 Act is regarded as having a compensatable interest, *Selborne (Gowns) Ltd* v *Ilford Corpn* [1962] LT, and would therefore seem ineligible for the disturbance payment.

Chapter 20

Compensation for the Acquisition of Agricultural Land

Introduction
Land acquired from an owner-occupier
Land acquired from a landlord
Land acquired from a tenant
Farm loss payment
Severance of an agricultural unit

20.1 Introduction

Although the rules for determining compensation upon the compulsory acquisition of land, considered in the preceding chapters, are applicable to the taking of agricultural land, it is the author's view (not unconnected with the fact that he once practised as a land agent) that there is some convenience in collecting in one chapter a number of matters concerning agricultural land.

Of course, the basic rules for assessing compensation for the land taken (see Chapter 12) and for injurious affection and severance (Chapter 15) apply, but agricultural land is more susceptible to the consequences of severance; and, where a yearly tenant is involved, the peculiarities of the landlord and tenant relationship merit separate consideration.

20.2 Land acquired from an owner-occupier

1. Land taken

The value of land taken is assessed by applying rule (2) (see Chapter 12); comparable property sales will be important in determining the market value. Two matters deserve special consideration in relation to agricultural land. First, the possibility of lotting a holding; a farm put on the market in two or more lots may fetch more than if sold as one lot.

Second, the question of development value; the statutory planning permission assumptions and any existing planning permissions must be carefully considered, and whichever gives the highest value can be selected; though if the scheme of the acquiring authority enhances the value of the land for development, this may have to be disregarded by the *Pointe Gourde* principle or its statutory equivalent: see *Myers v Milton Keynes Development Corpn* [1974].

Where there exists development value, then following *Horn v Sunderland Corpn* [1941], a disturbance claim is regarded as inconsistent with a valuation on the basis of land sold for development purposes. A claimant is entitled to agricultural value plus disturbance, or development value; as he may take the higher total sum, the former may be to his advantage: for full treatment of this see Chapter 17.

The effect of a milk quota must also be considered: whether it should, or can be, retained or apportioned. But it will be a question of fact whether the loss of a milk quota was caused by the compulsory purchase: see *Hoddom & Kinmount Estates v Secretary of State for Scotland* [1992].

2. *Severance and injurious affection*

The effect of the severance of a farm by a road or other similar public works can be to substantially increase the costs of working the retained land. With arable land, the increased costs of working may not be very significant, with a dairy farm they can be very high. Unfortunately, it is not the increase in the cost of working the land retained that can be claimed, following severance, but the depreciation in the value of the retained land: see *Cooke v Secretary of State for the Environment* considered in Chapter 15.

In some circumstances the market value of a severed farm, considered as two or more separate lots, is not depreciated by the severance: the sum of the separate lots may even be more valuable than the market value of the farm as one lot. Clearly this works as an injustice in respect of a dairy farmer whose land is severed and who faces real and substantial increased working costs; it is no consolation to him that the market value of his severed farm is not depreciated if he has no wish to realise that market value. Whether increased working costs can be recovered as disturbance is considered below.

A final problem can arise in connection with the acquisition of part of a farm. If the land taken is for a road or motorway it will have the shape of a strip through the farm with connections to similar strips through adjoining land. The application of rule (2) requires that the market value of this strip be determined. Quite clearly a strip of this shape, and possibly without access, will not have, necessarily, the same market value as comparable land of better shape and access. In *Fitzwilliam's (Earl) Wentworth Estates* v *British Railways Board* [1967] LT, the claimant owned land with development potential and suitable access; the land without that access could not have been developed by the claimant and would therefore have been less valuable. The acquiring authority compulsorily acquired all the land, other than the access, as it already had a suitable access of its own; it then argued that as that land it was acquiring had no access, on the open market it would be considerably less valuable than the same land with a right of access. The Lands Tribunal decided that an acquiring authority could not reduce the value of the land it was acquiring by deciding not to acquire a small area in the claimant's ownership, which, because it provided access, was the 'key' to the development value of the whole. It is submitted, on the basis of this case, that an acquiring authority cannot, therefore, lower the compensation it must pay because of the shape or lack of access that characterises the land it was acquiring; the market value should, in most cases, be at the same rate per acre as comparable land not disadvantaged by shape or access.

The problems of a highway constructed through a farm were considered by the Lands Tribunal in *Wilson* v *Minister of Transport* [1980]. The owner claimed sums for the onerous obligations of having to maintain more walls and fences and for the land sterilised near a lay-by and underpass. The Tribunal said that a purchaser would make an overall assessment in deciding by how much he would reduce his bid for the land not taken to reflect these factors; he would be unlikely to make detailed calculations under these various heads. A sum of £2,000 was awarded for the depreciation in value of the retained area of 80 acres which had been severed into two parts.

The proper sum of compensation for the injurious affection to an agricultural and shooting estate was in issue in *Cuthbert* v *Secretary of State for the Environment* [1979]. The sum awarded for the effect on the value of land not taken was arranged under the following heads: severance of enclosures; fixed equipment; additional fencing responsibility (capitalised); general injury to farm land; and, general injury to amenity value of land in hand.

In *McLaren's Discretionary Trustee* v *Secretary of State for Scotland* [1987] the Tribunal disallowed a claim for a sinking fund to provide for the maintenance of accommodation works, and awarded a lower sum for the depreciation in market value of the retained land.

3. Disturbance

An owner-occupier, who is required to give up possession of his farm, is entitled to disturbance compensation. The general points discussed in Chapter 17 must be borne in mind. The particular compensatable items will include temporary loss of profits; removal expenses; loss on forced sale of livestock, equipment, produce and feeding stuff; and, any other loss or expense which is not too remote and is a natural and reasonable consequence of the dispossession. In the *Wilson* case, the costs of acquiring a small area of land on which to replace sheep pens was agreed between the parties and allowed as compensation. Compensation was also awarded for the general disturbance to farming operations during the construction period of the road. Noise and other nuisance may be the subject of a claim: see *Budgen* v *Secretary of State for Wales* [1985].

The costs already incurred on the growing crops on the land taken, and any unexhausted manurial value, in that land, may be reflected in the application of rule (2) when the market value of the land is assessed. If that is the case, and market value of agricultural land, with vacant possession, usually does reflect unexhausted manurial values and, depending on the crop, sometimes the growing crops as well, the claimant cannot also receive as disturbance compensation the costs of seeds and labour and the unexhausted manurial value, for otherwise he will be paid twice for the same thing. Much the same point can be made about the loss of profits that would have been made had the claimant not been dispossessed. A prospective purchaser of agricultural land will, when determining the price he is prepared to pay, take into account the prospective profits that he could make from the land. Market value will therefore usually reflect profitability; a claimant is not entitled to receive compensation for loss of profits and the market value of the land: see the case of *Watson* v *Secretary of State for Air* in Chapter 17. The Lands Tribunal will only allow, as disturbance compensation, loss of profits if it considers the market value put forward does not reflect prospective profitability on the basis of vacant possession:

Valentine v *Skelmersdale Development Corpn* [1965] LT
The expropriated owner claimed £250 per acre for the farm land taken. In addition he claimed loss of profits at £25 per acre capitalised at three years. The district valuer put forward two settlements of comparable land supporting a value of £220 per acre and based on the assumption that vacant possession would be given; these values also reflect loss of profits. The Tribunal was not convinced that the market value determined in these two settlements did include the loss of profit element, and allowed, in addition to the £220 per acre, an item for loss of profits based on £20 per acre at three year's purchase.

This case may seem in conflict with the earlier case of *Watson* v *Secretary of State for Air* in which the Court of Appeal said that a claimant cannot have compensation for loss of profits and the market value of the land. Clearly the *Watson* case must prevail as, on points of law, the Lands Tribunal is bound by decisions of the Court of Appeal. However, it can be argued that in the *Valentine* case the Tribunal was not convinced that the loss of profits element was present in the sum put forward for the value of the land and therefore it was entitled to add, as a further item, compensation for the loss of profits. The difficulty with this is that a market value of land with vacant possession must represent and include the profitability of that land: it is the price that purchasers on the open market are prepared to pay to use that land and earn those profits. There must remain doubt about the correctness, in law, of the *Valentine* case.

These points about loss of profits do not apply to temporary loss of profits. A claimant, as discussed in Chapter 17, is always entitled to recover as a compensation, loss of profits on a particular crop, if it is not reflected in the market value of the land, and any temporary diminution of profits that may occur as a result of being 'disturbed' and having to recommence farming elsewhere. If the new farm is less profitable on a permanent basis there is no compensation for this as the market value of his expropriated farm should enable the claimant to acquire a farm of equal profitability. Unfortunately, this is not always the case in practice, as the price of a farm may reflect such things as location, development potential or other matters unrelated to the profitability of the land solely for farming purposes.

4. *Home-loss payment*

If the occupier of an agricultural unit is displaced from his home, then, provided he can satisfy all the requirements, he will be entitled to a home-loss payment: see Chapter 18.

20.3 Land acquired from a landlord

If agricultural land is let and the landlord's interest is compulsorily acquired, the freehold must be valued as if 'on the open-market', and subject to the tenancy; if there is a possibility of vacant possession because of the age or circumstances of the tenant, this may be taken into account. In *Pyrah (Doddington) Ltd* v *Northampton County Council* [1982], the controlling shares in two companies were held by the same shareholder; one company owned the freehold to a farm, the other held an agricultural tenancy. The Tribunal held that as the freehold was subject to an agricultural tenancy at the date of the notice to treat, it must be valued on that basis, and it could not be assumed that vacant possession would be obtained.

1. *Agricultural Holdings Act tenancies*

If the tenancy is one within the meaning of the Agricultural Holdings Act 1986, then, under the Land Compensation Act 1973, section 48, the right of the landlord to serve an effective notice to quit is to be disregarded if the reason the notice to quit is effective is that the land is required for a non-agricultural purpose by the acquiring authority. This new rule reverses the case of *Rugby Joint Water Board* v *Foottit* [1972] where the House of Lords had decided that as the land was required for a reservoir, the landlord could serve an effective notice to quit because the land was required for a non-agricultural use for which planning permission had been granted; the tenant could be considered as having no security of tenure and the landlord's interest would therefore have a higher value. Any notice to quit already served is also disregarded under this section if the only reason it is effective is, again, because the land is required for a non-agricultural use by the acquiring authority.

Apart from the rule just considered, if there is any other ground for serving an effective notice to quit under the Agricultural Holdings Act 1986 which, by increasing the possibility of vacant possession enhances the value of the landlord's interest, this may be taken into account. In the Scottish case of *Anderson* v *Moray District Council* [1980], the tenanted land had development value, and it was held that a notice to quit would have been effective: the tenant was entitled to the capitalised value of his profit rent for a period of two years. Presumably the landlord could have relied on the possibility of an effective notice to quit to enhance the value of his interest. The provisions for succession on the death of a tenant contained in the Agricultural Holdings Act 1986 can restrict the effectiveness of a notice to quit served following the death of a tenant if there are eligible persons who wish to succeed to the tenancy.

2. Farm business tenancy

The landlord's reversion should be valued in the normal way having regard to the terms of the tenancy and any entitlement to a deferred vacant possession value. A term and reversion valuation will usually be appropriate.

3. Severance and injurious affection

A landlord may claim compensation if any retained land is depreciated in value following an acquisition. He may also be able to serve a notice requiring the purchase of any retained land: see section **20.5** below.

4. Other payments

A landlord is not displaced from occupation: he is therefore not entitled to disturbance compensation, a farm-loss payment or a home-loss payment. But he may claim re-investment costs.

20.4 Land acquired from a tenant

Where the tenant of an agricultural holding has only a yearly tenancy, he is not entitled to a notice to treat: see Chapter 19. An acquiring authority will therefore take possession in one of the following ways:

(a) acquire the landlord's interest, then, as landlord, serve the tenant an effective notice to quit under the Agricultural Holdings Act 1986 – the usual ground will be that the land is required for a non-agricultural use for which there is planning permission (no longer possible for open-cast coal-mining: see Case B, as amended by Part II of Schedule 3 to the 1986 Act); or

(b) serve a notice to enter on the tenant under the Compulsory Purchase Act 1965 – the tenant can be required to give up possession before the expiration of his unexpired term.

In the case of farm business tenancies under the Agricultural Tenancies Act 1995, there will either be fixed term tenancies or yearly tenancies. These tenancies are considered separately below.

1. Dispossession by notice to quit – Agricultural Holdings Act basis of compensation

If the acquiring authority has acquired the interest of the landlord, it can serve a notice to quit; the tenant is entitled to the usual period of notice which cannot terminate his interest before the expiration of 12 months from the end of the current year of the tenancy. The Agricultural Holdings Act 1986, section 25, provides for this period of notice to quit. It also permits a shorter notice if possession is required for a non-agricultural use and the tenancy agreement contains an appropriate provision. Such a provision is known as an early resumption clause.

Compensation following notice to quit

A tenant dispossessed following the service of an effective notice to quit is entitled to the following items of compensation:

(a) 'Basic' compensation for disturbance

Under the Agricultural Holdings Act 1986, section 60, a tenant is entitled to 'basic' compensation amounting to one year's rent of the holding; if he can prove that his loss or expenses due to quitting and incurred upon or in connection with the sale or removal of his household goods, implements of husbandry, fixtures, farm produce or farm stock, and other expenses incurred in preparing his claim exceeded one year's rent, the tenant may claim an amount of up to two years' rent by first serving a notice on his landlord one month before the termination of the tenancy.

(b) *'Additional' compensation for reorganisation*

The Agricultural Holdings Act 1986, section 60(4) provides that a landlord must make an additional payment of four times the annual rent of the holding to assist the tenant in the reorganisation of his affairs. The sum is apportioned if part only of the holding is given up.

(c) *Compensation for improvements*

The Agricultural Holdings Act 1986 specifies the circumstances and the measure of compensation that is to be paid to a tenant by his landlord, on the termination of the tenancy, for certain improvements carried out by the tenant. This embraces what is usually called tenant right.

Tenant's option for notice of entry compensation

A tenant dispossessed by notice to quit and compensated under the foregoing heads of claim, though having the advantage of at least 12 months' notice before having to give up possession (unless his contract of tenancy specifies a shorter period for resumption for a non-agricultural use), is likely to receive a lesser sum by way of compensation than he could recover if his interest was determined by a notice to enter served under the Compulsory Purchase Act 1965. The Land Compensation Act 1973, section 59, gives the tenant the right to opt for notice of entry compensation in the following circumstances:

(a) the tenant, served with a notice to quit, is in occupation of an agricultural holding and has no greater interest therein than as a tenant for a year or from year to year; and,

(b) the notice to quit is served after an acquiring authority has served notice to treat on the landlord, or, being an authority possessing compulsory purchase powers, has agreed to purchase the landlord's interest in the holding; and,

(c) either the tenant cannot serve a counternotice to the notice to quit because the land is required for a non-agricultural use, for which there is a planning permission, or the Agricultural Lands Tribunal has consented to the notice to quit on the ground that the land is required for a non-agricultural use.

If the tenant gives up possession of the holding to the acquiring authority on or before the date on which his tenancy terminates in accordance with his notice to quit, he may elect in writing at any time before giving up possession to have his compensation assessed as if his interest was terminated by a notice to enter under the Compulsory Purchase Act 1965. Section 20 of this Act provides for the compensation; this is considered below. A tenant who opts for this basis cannot get notice to quit compensation and should therefore make some careful calculations before exercising his right to opt.

2. Dispossession by notice of entry – Compulsory Purchase Act 1965, section 20 basis of compensation

When a tenant is required to give up possession by a notice to enter, his interest terminates on the date the acquiring authority takes possession and compensation is assessed in accordance with the Compulsory Purchase Act 1965, section 20. The same basis is used if a tenant, served with a notice to quit, makes the election considered in the previous subsection above. Although the section 20 basis of compensation was fully examined in Chapter 19, the following are the heads of claim which are relevant for a tenant of an agricultural holding:

(a) *Value of tenant's unexpired term or interest in the land*
Although the tenant, in law, generally has a yearly tenancy, the Land Compensation Act 1973, section 48, acknowledges that in practice a tenant of an agricultural holding has security of tenure for life. The section provides, that in valuing the tenant's interest, there must be disregarded the possibility that an effective notice to quit can be served, because the land is required for a non-agricultural use for which planning permission exists; and any notice to quit already served is also to be disregarded if the only reason it is effective is, again, because the land is required for a non-agricultural use for which planning permission exists. In both these cases the notice to quit is only disregarded if the land is required by the acquiring authority for a non-agricultural use. In *Anderson* v *Moray District Council* [1980], the land in question had development potential and it was decided that an effective notice to quit could be served on the tenant, thus reducing his security of tenure.

This rule has already been considered in relation to the valuation of the landlord's interest: section **20.3** *supra*. It means that, despite the possibility of an incontestable notice to quit being served on the tenant under the Agricultural Holdings Act 1986 because the land is required for a non-agricultural use by the acquiring authority, the tenant is still to be regarded as having security of tenure for the purposes of valuing his interest. Two points need to be considered. First, an incontestable notice to quit may be served for one of the other reasons specified in the Agricultural Holdings Act 1986, for example where planning permission exists to develop the land for some purpose other than the acquiring authority's (Case B); where this arises, the tenant will not have security of tenure. Second, even if the tenant is to be regarded as having security of tenure, does that fact make his interest any more valuable? Clearly the landlord's interest is less valuable if the tenant is regarded as having security of tenure; the landlord has a marketable interest. But, although a yearly agricultural tenant may be regarded as having security of tenure for life, his lease is not really marketable; even if it can be considered to be marketable, any profit rent may be eliminated at the three-yearly rent reviews. It becomes extremely difficult to give effect to section 48 when valuing the tenant's unexpired lease, though the section may be more significant in assessing the disturbance compensation: see (c) below.

If the tenant's compensation, as determined in accordance with section 48, is less than it would have been had section 48 not been enacted, it shall be increased by the amount of the deficiency. Where this applies, the Agriculture (Miscellaneous Provisions) Act 1968, section 15, directs that in assessing the tenant's compensation any early resumption clause (see subsection 1 above) shall be disregarded.

However, in *Baird's Exors* v *Commissioners of Inland Revenue* [1991] the Scottish Lands Tribunal in considering the open market value of a non-assignable agricultural tenancy under section 38 of the Finance Act 1975, decided that 25% of the vacant possession value of the land represented the value of the tenancy in the hypothetical open market. In *Layzell* v *Smith Morton & Long* [1992], a case concerned with the assessment of damages arising out of the loss of a tenancy through negligence, the High Court applied a sale-and-leaseback approach to valuing a tenancy: it was assumed that the plaintiff would purchase a farm for £440,000 and sell the reversion for £96,000 after reserving a tenancy, thus putting a value of £344,000 on the tenancy. This decision is flawed as it wrongly assumed that the whole of the marriage value went to the tenant.

In another case under section 38 of the Finance Act 1975, the Lands Tribunal decided, and the Court of Appeal agreed, that in valuing a tenancy, the possibility of the tenancy having a surrender value to the landlord could be considered. Although the open market value hypothesis required the hypothetical vendor and purchaser of the tenancy to be regarded as abstract characters, that did not apply to the landlord. The motives and intentions of the actual landlord were relevant. If he did not wish to acquire the surrender of the tenancy, that was a relevant factor: see *Walton's Executors* v *Commissioners of Inland Revenue* [1996], which was followed in *Greenbank* v *Pickles* [2001].

Although not concerned with the valuation of an agricultural tenancy there are cases on the assessment of compensation under the Wildlife and Countryside Act 1981 which can be of assistance: see *Nature Conservancy Council* v *Deller* [1992] and *Cameron* v *Nature Conservancy Council* [1992].

The usual practice of valuers is to determine the vacant possession value of the holding, deduct the value of the reversionary interest subject to the agricultural tenancy and the difference is split, usually on a 50% basis, between the tenant and the landlord: see *Willett* v *Inland Revenue Commissioners* [1982]. The difficulty with this approach is that it assumes the surrender of the tenancy to the landlord and therefore the giving up of possession by the tenant. This raises the question as to whether a claimant/tenant, receiving compensation on the assumption that he would be giving up possession of the holding, can also in addition obtain compensation for disturbance. In the ordinary way the *Horn* principle would apply: see p267.

If the agricultural tenancy is not valued on the basis of a share of the vacant possession value arising on the surrender of the tenancy to the landlord, then the other valuation approach is on the basis of the *Wakerley* case (see p339) where the loss of profits are identified and multiplied by an appropriate YP for the likely life of the tenant.

(b) Any just allowance by an incoming tenant
Although tenant-right is now largely paid by the landlord, and such a claim would be considered under (c) below, an

incoming agricultural tenant may pay an outgoing tenant for certain matters and these can be claimed for. Live and dead stock is an example, but any loss on a forced sale is also recoverable under (c) below.

In the *Anderson* case, an allowance of £1,000 was awarded for a piggery erected by the tenant; and further sums for fences, gates, grass seed sown and unexhausted fertility.

(c) *Any loss or injury sustained by the tenant*

This item, specified in section 20, will include the claim for tenant right and for disturbance, but the payment of one year's rent is not allowed: see the *Wakerley* case. The tenant is entitled to recover as compensation all the losses he incurs provided, first, they are not too remote and, second, they are a natural and reasonable consequence of the dispossession. For tenant right, see the subsection above on dispossession following a notice to quit; for the general law on disturbance see Chapter 17; and, for the particular position of a person 'disturbed' from agricultural land, see section **20.2.3** of this chapter.

In *Minister of Transport* v *Pettit* [1969] it was said that the words 'loss or injury' were not confined to financial loss, but were wide enough to cover the inconvenience and upset suffered by a claimant. Section 48 of the 1973 Act, considered at (a) above, is also applicable to the assessment of compensation for disturbance: the tenant is regarded as having security of tenure for life, unless, apart from the requirements of the acquiring authority, there is the possibility of an effective notice to quit being served on the tenant. This is significant in assessing a sum for loss of profits as the tenant can be regarded as having a life expectancy of those profits.

(d) *Severance and injurious affection*

Where a tenant is required to give up part of his holding, he is entitled to claim compensation for the depreciation in the value of the retained part caused by the severance or due to injurious affection. In *Worlock* v *Sudbury Rural District Council* [1961], it was held that a claim for severance cannot be made if the retained land is held under a different tenancy from that under which the land acquired is held. However, section 20(2) of the 1965 Act was amended by the Planning and Compensation Act 1991 to remove this restriction: accordingly, any severing of a claimant's interest will found a claim.

If a tenant's retained land under his tenancy is less valuable because of the acquisition of some of the holding, the tenant can, at the next three-yearly rent review, obtain a reduction of the rent to reflect this. This possibility has two consequences: first, the tenant will receive less severance and injurious affection compensation because the anticipated rent reduction will reflect the less valuable retained land, and second, the landlord's interest is the interest most affected in the long term by the severance because of the possibility of the rent reduction, and his compensation should reflect this. In *Minister of Transport* v *Pettit* [1968], the Tribunal acknowledged that the tenant could seek a rent reduction if his retained land was less valuable, but accepted the uncertainty of achieving this at the next rent review; five years was taken as an appropriate period to value the depreciation in the tenant's interest.

In *Gooderam* v *Department of Transport* [1994] it was held that the loss of value of a tenancy on severance of part was best compensated on a 'before' and 'after' valuation rather than by capitalising additional costs. It was also decided that a tenancy containing a non-assignment clause should still be valued in the open market, but subject to a similar clause.

In determining the amount of compensation for severance and injurious affection, it can be assumed that the tenant has security of tenure, unless there is evidence that an effective notice to quit could be served on the tenant in respect of the retained land. This was the situation in the *Worlock* case where the Tribunal found that the landlord could have obtained planning permission for a non-agricultural use and therefore could obtain possession by serving an effective notice to quit.

(e) Reorganisation payment

The claimant is also entitled to the 'additional' compensation of four times the annual rent, under section 60(4) of the Agricultural Holdings Act 1986, to assist in the reorganisation of his affairs; this is applied by section 12 of the Agriculture (Miscellaneous Provisions) Act 1968 as amended. However, the Land Compensation Act 1973, section 48(5), provides that the tenant's compensation, as assessed under paras (a)–(c) above, shall be reduced by an amount equal to the reorganisation payment. This is to prevent the payment of compensation for his interest on the basis that he has compensation for security of tenure and the reorganisation payment. But, if the tenant's compensation, assessed on the basis that he has security of tenure and after incurring the deduction just mentioned, is less than it would have been had it been assumed he had no such security and no deduction was made, then the total compensation shall be increased by the amount of the deficiency: section 48(6). This is to ensure that a tenant is not worse off under section 48 than he would have been before the section was enacted. If compensation cannot, therefore, be assessed on the basis that the tenant has security of tenure, because the landlord could serve an effective notice to quit, a careful calculation must be made to ensure he is not worse off after the deduction of the reorganisation payment.

(f) Other items of claim

A yearly tenant is permitted to make a claim for a farm-loss payment, but he is entitled, if otherwise eligible, to a home-loss payment. Finally, the Agriculture (Miscellaneous Provisions) Act 1963, section 22, contains a power to enable an acquiring authority to make a discretionary payment to a person carrying on a trade or business on agricultural land in respect of his removal expenses and the loss which, in their opinion, he will sustain by reason of the resulting disturbance of his trade or business. This is a useful provision for any person not fully compensated under any of the matters so far considered, as a person displaced from agricultural land is not entitled to the disturbance payment under the Land Compensation Act 1973, section 37: see Chapter 18.

3. The application of the rules

The heads of claim available to the tenant of an agricultural holding have been considered in the following cases; the first two cases are on the pre-1973 Act law, but are still applicable if the tenant cannot be regarded as having security of tenure under section 48.

The market value of an interest will usually reflect the value of the right to earn profits, the claimant cannot then have a separate disturbance claim for loss of profits:

Watson v *Secretary of State for Air* [1954] CA: see section **17.5.1** in Chapter 17

The claimant was a yearly tenant; the year ran from May 12.

Notice to treat had been served on May 18, 1951 (presumably on the landlord) and possession was taken in August and September 1951 before it was reasonably possible to harvest cereal crops. At the date of entry, his interest was one which could not be determined, according to his tenancy agreement, at a date earlier than May 12 1953. It was considered by the court that, so far as the first season was concerned, the claimant was entitled to recover, in effect, the profits which he would have made; the crop had been sown and was waiting to be gathered. As for the further year's interest, rule (2) applied and it must be ascertained what some purchaser in the market would have given for that further year's interest. The profit which could have been made from the land was considered a highly material consideration, because a purchaser minding to buy the interest would have fixed a price he was prepared to pay on the basis of the profits he could have made. It was held that if the claimant was paid, as compensation for the second year of the tenancy, the market value of that year, he could not have, in addition, disturbance compensation for loss of profits in respect of that year, for otherwise he could be having the same thing twice over.

The case went back to the Tribunal; it held that the market value of the whole two years had to be assessed, but the sum for the second year would have regard to the potential profits less a substantial margin for seasonal risk and profit which a possible purchaser would retain for himself. Accordingly, the tenant was entitled to loss of profits on first year (£850); value of the right to farm and earn profits in second year (£450); unexhausted manurial value, and removal expenses.

In computing the annual profits for a disturbance claim, the notional wage of the claimant is not necessarily deducted:

Pearce v Bristol Corpn [1949] LT
The claimant was dispossessed, by notices of entry, of a yearly tenancy of a 123-acre farm. The acquiring authority argued that compensation should be assessed on the basis that the claimant's notional wage should be deducted from the annual profit; he had not lost that part of the profit attributable to his own labour as he could find employment and earn that wage. It was held that it was not reasonable to suppose that a farmer who had been his own 'master' could be expected to find

employment as a farm-hand; no deduction from the annual profits in respect of the tenant's notional wage was made, although a deduction was made for interest on capital; the resulting net profit was multiplied by three-years' purchase (reflecting an agricultural tenant's security of tenure) to produce a figure for loss of profit and employment.

The following case is the first on section 48 and is relevant where the tenant is to be regarded as having security of tenure:

Wakerley v St Edmundsbury Borough Council [1977] LT
The claimant had a yearly tenancy of about 155 acres of farmland; he surrendered his tenancy of this land to the acquiring authority on July 15 1973 and received two licences to continue farming the land pending their requirement of possession. In consideration of the surrender, the acquiring authority agreed to pay the tenant the compensation to which he would be entitled under the provisions of section 48 of the Land Compensation Act 1973. The Tribunal put a token value of £100 as a value of the interest in the land (in the absence of any evidence). The whole of the claim as presented, however, was considered under the heading of disturbance, and in particular, as a claim for loss of profits to which, by virtue of section 48, the tenant was now to be regarded as having a life-expectancy. The Tribunal accepted a figure of £38 per acre as representing net profit after deducting variable costs, acts of husbandry, fluctuation risk, interest on capital and a notional rent. This net profit was capitalised having regard to the tenant's life expectancy of 33.5 years and at a rate of 20% at a YP 4.88 to produce a figure of £24,000 for loss of profits. A claim for one year's rent for disturbance was rejected as having no place in a claim by a tenant dispossessed under the general compensation code. (The Tribunal then deducted the value of the licences granted to the tenant from the compensation so far assessed; on this point the claimant's appeal succeeded and the Court of Appeal has held that on the construction of the deed of surrender no deduction for the benefit of the licences granted should be made.)

The next case concerns an election under section 59 and the applicability of section 48 where an acquiring authority has acquired the interest of the landlord:

Dawson v *Norwich City Council* [1979] LT

The claimant was a tenant from year to year of an agricultural holding. A substantial part of this holding was purchased from the landlord after planning permission had been granted for development following an application by the landlord. Notices to quit were then served by the authority on the tenant in respect of two areas of his holding specifying that the land was required for a non-agricultural use for which planning permission had been granted. In respect of each notice to quit, the tenant served a counternotice electing that section 59 of the 1973 Act should apply and his compensation assessed as if a notice of entry had been served. The Tribunal decided that the election was valid as section 59 applies to notices to quit served by a local authority as well as a private landlord.

A further question involved section 48 and its requirement to regard the tenant as having security of tenure, for compensation purposes, notwithstanding that a valid notice to quit can be served under the Agricultural Holdings Acts where land is required by an acquiring authority for a non-agricultural use. The Tribunal held that section 48 only directs that the acquiring authority's requirement for the land should be disregarded. If, had there been no acquisition, the landlord might have served a valid notice to quit, so that the tenant did not have indefinite security of tenure, that was a matter the valuer could take into account; it was irrelevant that because there was a scheme of acquisition the landlord could not have served such a notice to quit.

4. Farm business tenancies

Farm business tenancies within the scope of the Agricultural Tenancies Act 1995 may initially be granted as either fixed-term tenancies or yearly tenancies. A fixed-term tenancy of two years or under expires automatically on the term date, whereas a fixed-term tenancy for more than two years continues thereafter as a yearly tenancy unless terminated by notice. A notice to quit of not less than 12 months is required to determine a fixed-term tenancy of over two years. The same minimum notice to quit is required in relation to a yearly tenancy, whether granted initially or arising on the expiration of a fixed-term: see generally sections 5–7 of the 1995 Act.

Where a farm business tenant holds a fixed-term with not less than one year to run, the acquiring authority will have to serve a notice to treat for the acquisition of that interest. The tenant will be entitled to the value of the unexpired term plus compensation for disturbance. The value of the unexpired term may depend upon whether the tenant has the benefit of a 'profit rent', because the rent is less than the open market rent, and also upon the other terms of the tenancy, as explained in Chapter 19 above.

Where a farm business tenant has a tenancy that is either a fixed term with less than one year to run, or is a yearly tenancy, whether as originally granted or as a continuing tenancy, the acquiring authority has a choice of procedures for obtaining possession. It can either serve a notice of entry under section 20 of the Compulsory Purchase Act 1965, or it can first acquire the reversionary interest, and then serve a notice to quit or, in the case of a fixed term that was originally granted for no more than two years, wait until that term expires. Where the acquiring authority serves a notice under section 20 of the 1965 Act, the tenant will be entitled to compensation under that section on a basis similar to the tenant of an agricultural holding protected by the Agricultural Holdings Act 1986, and as explained at p332 above. However a farm business tenant does not have security of tenure and therefore section 48 of the Land Compensation Act 1973 is not relevant. Further, the value of a tenant's unexpired term or interest where the tenancy is a farm business tenancy will not proceed on the assumptions made in relation to a tenancy protected by the 1986 Act where the tenant is protected, in effect, for life and there is a substantial marriage value that can be released if the landlord obtains vacant possession. Accordingly it is unlikely that a farm business tenancy will have much value.

However the farm business tenant is not entitled to the 'additional' compensation under section 60(4) of the 1986 Act as section 12 of the Agriculture (Miscellaneous Provisions) Act 1968 does not apply to the Agricultural Tenancies Act 1995.

A farm business tenant is entitled to a farm loss payment.

Where an acquiring authority first acquires the reversionary interest of the landlord, and then proceeds to recover possession *as landlord*, by serving a notice to quit or allowing a fixed term to expire, the tenant is left with a claim for compensation only under the Agricultural Tenancies Act 1995 for such things as compensation for improvements.

20.5 Farm loss payment

The Land Compensation Act 1973, sections 34–36, makes provision for a farm loss payment; this is intended to compensate a displaced farmer for temporary yield losses, change in husbandry practices or other difficulties he may experience in moving to a new farm.

1. *Persons entitled: section 34*

First, the claimant must be in occupation of an agricultural unit, either as owner of the freehold, or as a tenant for a year or from year to year or a greater interest. Second, he must be displaced from the whole or a sufficient part of that unit in consequence of the compulsory acquisition of his interest in the whole of the land; a sufficient part means not less than 0.5 ha or such other area as may be specified by regulations. Third, not more than three years after the date of displacement he must begin to farm another agricultural unit elsewhere in Great Britain.

A claimant will lose his farm loss payment if he leaves his farm before being required to do so. He must be displaced and displacement means: being required to leave by the acquiring authority (notice to enter) or leaving on any date after the making or confirmation of the compulsory purchase order but before being required to do so; leaving on completion of the compulsory acquisition; or, where the acquiring authority permits him to remain in possession of the land under a tenancy or licence of a kind not making him a tenant under the Agricultural Holdings Act 1986, leaving on the expiration of that tenancy or licence: see section 34(3) of the 1973 Act.

The claimant may purchase the freehold or take a tenancy of the new farm, but he will not be entitled to a farm-loss payment if he acquires any such interest or tenancy before the date on which the acquiring authority was authorised to acquire his old farm (date of confirmation of a compulsory purchase order).

If the old farm was compulsorily purchased following the service of a blight notice, a farm loss payment may be payable.

Finally, a person is not entitled to a farm-loss payment if he is entitled to a payment under section 12 of the Agriculture (Miscellaneous Provisions) Act 1968 (additional compensation payable to a tenant – see below).

Two points are worth noting: a claimant is only entitled if displaced from the whole of his old farm, losing part of a farm will not qualify a person for a farm-loss payment; and, the new farm need not be comparable in size or quality nor need the claimant acquire the same type of interest in the new farm as he had in the old one.

2. *Amount of farm loss payment: section 35*

The amount of the payment shall be equal to the average annual profit derived from the use for agricultural purposes of the agricultural land comprised in the land acquired by the authority. The profit shall be computed by reference to the profits for the three years ending with the date of displacement, or if the person concerned has then been in occupation for a shorter period, that period.

If accounts have been made up in respect of the profits of the claimant on a yearly basis, and the last accounting year ends not more than 12 months before the date of displacement, then the payment will be based on the three accounting periods ending with that last accounting year.

Where the claimant has been permitted to remain in possession of the land under a tenancy or licence not making him a tenant under the Agricultural Holdings Act 1986, he may, if on the date of displacement he has been in occupation for more than three years, elect that his average annual profit be computed by reference to the profits for any three consecutive yearly accounting periods ending before the completion of the acquisition of his original interest and the grant to him of the tenancy or licence.

In calculating the profits there shall be deducted a notional rent for the agricultural land based on the land being let for agricultural purposes to a tenant responsible for rates, repairs and other outgoings. This deduction is made whether or not the land is in fact let, and if it is let, the deduction is made to the exclusion of any deduction for the rent actually paid. If the claimant obtains, as compensation for disturbance, a sum representing temporary or permanent loss of profits from any activity, then the profits of that activity shall be deducted in computing the average annual profits for the purpose of calculating the payment. An example would be where a claimant has produced crops of such high quality that they are usually sold as 'seed'; he may claim, as disturbance compensation, for the temporary or permanent loss of profits on this activity if it appears that he cannot recommence this activity on his new farm to produce the same profits in the short or long term. The deduction is made to prevent the same loss being compensated twice-over.

Where the value of the farm compulsorily acquired exceeds the value of the new farm, the amount of the farm-loss payment is proportionately reduced. For the purposes of assessing the value of the agricultural land in each case, it is assumed the land will be used solely for agriculture and as a freehold interest with vacant possession; the value of the principal dwellinghouse, if any, is to be disregarded; and, the valuation is otherwise in accordance with rules (2) to (4). The date of displacement determines the date for valuing the old farm and the date the claimant begins farming as the date for valuing the new farm. If the agricultural land being acquired has development value, the farm-loss payment is limited to an amount, if any, by which the farm-loss payment, as calculated above, plus the existing use value of the agricultural land exceeds the compensation actually paid for the claimant's interest. In this connection, existing use value assumes that planning permission will not be granted for any purposes other than the minor forms of development in Third Schedule to the Town and Country Planning Act 1990.

3. The claim: section 36

This must be made within 12 months of the claimant beginning to farm a new agricultural unit. Any reasonable valuation or legal expenses incurred in the preparation and prosecution of a claim may be paid by the acquiring authority. The farm loss payment carries interest from date of the claimant beginning to farm.

4. Discretionary farm loss payments: section 36(4)

A farm loss payment may be made where an interest in agricultural land is acquired by agreement by an authority possessing compulsory purchase powers, if the circumstances are such that had the acquisition been compulsory, the acquiring authority would have been required to make such a payment.

20.6 Severance of an agricultural unit

1. Counternotice requiring purchase of whole

If an acquiring authority serves a notice to treat in respect of part of the land belonging to an owner, the owner may serve a counternotice, under section 8 of the 1965 Act, requiring the authority to purchase any severed areas of less than half an acre. Of more interest to owners and tenants of agricultural land are the provisions in sections 53–57 of the Land Compensation Act 1973 which enable the service of a counternotice requiring the purchase of the rest of the land in an agricultural unit if that retained land is not reasonably capable of being farmed by itself.

The circumstances that enable a counternotice to be served under either of these two Acts are fully considered in Chapter 8.

2. Accommodation works

There is no statutory basis for a claim to have accommodation work carried out (see Chapter 21), but in practice a certain amount of such work is carried out by the acquiring authority to reduce the claim for severance and injurious affection. The following are examples of such work: new fences and gates, new access routes, underpass or bridge, new water supply and drainage work. The list is not exhaustive and will depend on the particular circumstances. A bridge or underpass to a severed portion of a farm may reduce, partially or completely, any depreciation in the value of the severed land that would otherwise have been recoverable as compensation. In *Wilson v Minister of Transport* [1980], the cost of purchasing land to resite a sheep pen was agreed as part of the accommodation works.

3. Contractor's damage

This can be significant in relation to agricultural land. The principle here is that if the acquiring authority carries out work by using a contractor, it will not be liable for any damage caused by the contractor which is not authorised by the contract. Thus, if the contractor is careless and causes damage to land alongside the works, the claimant must look to the contractor for any recompense under the ordinary law of nuisance or trespass to land. But if the contract authorises work which causes damage to neighbouring land, the acquiring authority will be liable to the extent that such damage is a necessary consequence of the contract.

The acquiring authority is liable for any damage caused by its own workforce, if that liability lies in nuisance, trespass or negligence, and is damage which is not authorised, expressly or impliedly, by the enabling Act of Parliament.

Chapter 21

Special Compensation Procedures

Introduction
Minerals
Common land
Land of statutory undertakers
Land subject to mortgage
Interests omitted from purchase
Accommodation works

21.1 Introduction

Certain interests in land present particular problems for which there are special compensation procedures. The rules of compensation dealt with so far in this part of the book must therefore be considered subject to these procedures, where applicable.

21.2 Minerals

When land is compulsorily acquired, any minerals it contains will pass to the authority. Compensation for the land should reflect the value of those minerals, although their full value will depend upon the availability of planning permission to extract. In *Eden v NE Railway Co* [1907] it was held that the value of the minerals was the full value less the cost of working them. Planning permission is required as mining operations are development for the purposes of the Town and County Planning Act 1990.

If the authority can acquire the land for its purposes without the minerals under it, this may save it compensation and permit the owner to continue his mineral extraction operations (where he has planning permission).

It is possible to achieve this with a compulsory purchase order by incorporating the provisions of either Part II or Parts II and III of Schedule 2 to the Acquisition of Land Act 1981. Part II re-enacts section 77 and Part III re-enacts sections 78–85 of the Railway

Clauses (Consolidation) Act 1845. Part II of the Schedule provides that:

> (1) The acquiring authority shall not be entitled to any mines under the land comprised in the compulsory purchase order unless they have been expressly purchased, and all mines under the land shall be deemed to be excepted out of the conveyance of that land unless expressly named and conveyed.
>
> (2) Sub-paragraph (1) above shall not apply to minerals necessarily extracted or used in the construction of the undertaking.

Mines means mines of coal, ironstone, slate and other minerals, whether deep mining or open cast. The meaning to be given to minerals depends upon the vernacular of the mining world, the commercial world and landowners at the time. For a full review of the cases on minerals see *Earl of Lonsdale* v *Attorney-General* [1983]. Whether a substance is a mineral is a question of fact: see also *Waring* v *Foden* [1932], where gravel was held not to be a mineral for certain purposes.

Part III of the Schedule may be additionally incorporated if it is desired to permit the owner to work the mines under, or within 40 yds, or other prescribed distance of, the land acquired:

(b) the owner or lessee desiring to work the mines must give 30 days' notice to the authority;

(c) the authority owning the surface of the land must then decide if the workings will damage their interest and, if so, whether they are prepared to treat and pay compensation for such minerals that they consider should not be worked;

(d) if the authority is unwilling to purchase the minerals, the owner or lessee may work them subject to certain safeguards.

All these sections can be incorporated in compulsory purchase orders made under the Acquisition of Land Act 1981 and the Housing Act 1985.

21.3 Common land

The procedure for acquiring common land was considered in Chapter 4. When considering the assessment of compensation, the interests of the freeholder and the commoners must be distinguished. The Commons Registration Act 1965 provided for the registration of the ownership of commons and of rights of common.

1. Compensation for the freehold

The freehold of the common is valued by assessing the market value in the usual way. However, the following factors should be considered:

(a) the value of the residue of rights left to the owner of the soil: this could be significant if he is entitled to timber, minerals or has rights in common himself;

(b) whether the registered rights of the commoners have been challenged under the Commons Registration Act 1965, and remain to be decided by the Commons Commissioner – the owner may be denying that any common rights exist;

(c) all commons within the Metropolitan Police District, or within the areas once boroughs or urban districts (as they existed before local government reorganisation in 1974), are subject to a public right of access for air and exercise; and a similar right applies to commons outside those areas if the owner of the soil has made a declaration allowing for this (Law of Property Act 1925, section 193); and

(d) the soil of a common may be owned by the lord of the manor – this is a species of property right in land that can have considerable value.

2. Compensation for the commoners

Schedule 4 to the Compulsory Purchase Act 1965 provides that the acquiring authority shall convene a meeting of the commoners for the purpose of appointing a committee to treat with the authority for the compensation. The committee may negotiate and agree compensation which will be binding on all the other commoners. This avoids having to serve a notice to treat on each commoner. The authority may pay such agreed compensation to the committee, or to any three of them, who shall apportion the sum among the commoners.

Where the acquiring authority has provided exchange land to replace the common land being acquired, the granting of an exchange land certificate does not by itself preclude the payment of compensation: see *McKay* v *City of London Corp* [1966] and *Lay* v *Norfolk County Council* [1997]. In *Lay* v *Norfolk County Council* the Lands Tribunal considered that the value of commoners' rights transferred to the exchange land represented in whole, or in part, the compensation which was payable for the acquisition of the rights in common which subsisted in the land acquired: see *Freeman v Middlesex County Council* [1965].

Most common rights, for example grazing, are appurtenant to land. This means the rights attached to some land. In certain areas the existence of such rights is a significant factor in the value of farm land.

If the land to which common rights are appurtenant is valued, first with those rights and, second, after those rights have been acquired as a result of the taking of the common, the difference can be said to be attributable to the value of the common rights. As the value of common rights over the same common may differ from holding to holding, the procedure of treating for compensation through a committee rather than directly is not always satisfactory.

If there is disagreement among the commoners as to how the compensation sum should be apportioned, the committee may make application in writing to the Minister of Agriculture, Fisheries and Food, who has powers to make an award binding on the parties: Inclosure Act 1852–54 and Commonable Rights Compensation Act 1882.

The payment of compensation does not alter the status of the land as common land. Therefore unless enclosure is authorised, the land remains common land and cannot be enclosed; further the Schedule 4 procedure does not extinguish any public rights of access, only the commoners' rights: see *Lewis* v *Mid-Glamorgan County Council* [1995].

21.4 Land of statutory undertakers

1. *The minister's certificate*

Statutory undertakers include the bodies running railways, road transport and water transport; or responsible for canals, docks, harbours, piers or lighthouses; or supplying electricity, gas or water. Their operational land may be the subject of a draft compulsory purchase order; but the statutory undertaker can make representations to the minister responsible for its affairs and the order can then only be confirmed if the minister certifies that the land can be taken without serious detriment to the carrying on of the undertaking, or if purchased, it can be replaced by other land without serious detriment to the undertaking: Acquisition of Land Act 1981, section 16. If the purchase is under the Town and Country Planning Acts, the certificate may be dispensed with if the statutory undertaker's appropriate minister and the Secretary of State jointly confirm the compulsory purchase order.

2. *Appropriate minister issues certificate: amount of compensation*

The normal rules of compensation apply: if necessary, the statutory undertaker can claim compensation (under rule (5)) for the cost of reinstatement, at the Lands Tribunal's discretion.

3. *Purchase under the Town and Country Planning Acts – no certificate issued: amount of compensation*

A certificate may be dispensed with if land is acquired under the Town and Country Planning Act 1990. Section 280 of that Act provides that the amount of compensation shall be:

(a) the cost of acquiring land, providing apparatus, erecting buildings or doing work for the purpose of any adjustment of the carrying on of the undertaking necessitated by the taking of the operational land; and either

(b) the estimated amount of any decrease in net receipts from the undertaking, either short term or long term, attributable to the acquisition; or

(c) if no adjustment, as is mentioned in (a) above, is carried out, such amount as appears reasonable compensation for any estimated decrease in net receipts from the undertaking attributable to the acquisition.

These provisions do not apply if the reason no certificate was issued was because the land was acquired by agreement and the statutory undertaker made no representation to its appropriate minister: *National Carriers Ltd* v *Secretary of State for Transport* [1978] LT (acquisition of vehicle repair premises for M4 motorway).

The statutory undertaker may, at its option, claim compensation under the ordinary rules in the Land Compensation Act 1961 (except rule (4)): Town and Country Planning Act 1990, section 281.

21.5 Land subject to mortgage

A mortgagee has an interest in land and is entitled to a notice to treat. The acquiring authority may treat with both mortgagor and mortgagee and, when compensation is agreed, the amount of the loan outstanding is paid off, the mortgage is redeemed and the land can be conveyed as an unencumbered interest.

The Compulsory Purchase Act 1965, section 14, contains two alternative procedures for compensating a mortgagee:

either

(a) the acquiring authority may pay or offer to pay to the mortgagee the principal (outstanding loan) and interest due on the mortgage, together with his costs and charges, if any, and also six months' additional interest;

or

(b) the acquiring authority may give notice in writing to the mortgagee that they will pay all the principal and interest due on the mortgage at the end of six months, computed from the day of giving notice, and his costs and expenses, if any.

As was explained in *Shewu* v *Hackney London Borough Council* [1998], the Lands Tribunal has no jurisdiction under the 1965 Act to determine the date when an acquiring authority should have exercised their powers under section 14 to purchase or redeem the interest of the mortgagee in the land.

Section 15 of the 1965 Act makes provision for the situation where the mortgage debt exceeds the value of the land. It provides that the value of the land, or the compensation to be paid by the acquiring authority in respect of the land, shall be settled by agreement between the mortgagee and mortgagor on the one part, and the acquiring authority on the other part. Section 16 makes a similar provision if part of the mortgaged land is being acquired and that part is of less value than the mortgage debt, and the remaining part of the land not being acquired, is not, in the view of the mortgagee, sufficient security for the loan under the mortgage.

If in any of the situations mentioned, the mortgagee is required to accept payment of the principal at an earlier date than that stipulated in the mortgage deed, section 17 provides that the mortgagee is entitled to be paid his costs of reinvestment and to be compensated for his loss if the rate of interest secured by the mortgage is higher than can reasonably be expected to be obtained on reinvestment at the time when the mortgage is paid off.

For a case involving a mortgagee claimant: see *Provincial Building Society* v *Hammersmith and Fulham London Borough Council* [1982].

21.6 Interests omitted from purchase

Section 22 of the Compulsory Purchase Act 1965 provides that if the acquiring authority has entered land subject to compulsory purchase and 'it appears [it] have through mistake or inadvertence failed or omitted duly to purchase or to pay compensation for any estate, right or interest in or charge affecting that land', it may remain in possession of the land. However, it must pay compensation for that omitted interest and compensation for *mesne* profits, to the person entitled, within six months of the acquiring authority having notice of the interest: see *Advance Ground Rents Ltd* v *Middlesbrough Borough Council* [1986] where no steps were taken within six months. The valuation date is the date of entry, and the *mesne* profits (the profits that would have accrued to the owner of the interest) are calculated also from this date. The section does not apply where land outside a compulsory purchase order has been entered.

An acquiring authority can only rely on this section if it failed to purchase the omitted interest through 'mistake or inadvertence'. If it knew of the interest, but omitted to purchase, it can be required to leave the land by injunction unless it entered under the authority of section 11 of the 1965 Act.

21.7 Accommodation works

An acquiring authority may agree to carry out accommodation works. This can reduce the claim for severance and injurious affection, or for disturbance, or make less likely the need for the authority to acquire, following a counternotice, small severed portions of land: see Chapters 8 and 15. Any agreement entered into will be binding if the authority has the necessary powers and the agreement is supported by some consideration or is by deed. But an authority cannot, by agreement, normally restrict its statutory powers and duties; nor can it be compelled to provide accommodation works in the absence of an agreement. The following are some of the more common examples of accommodation works: bridge, tunnel or underpass to connect severed parcels of land; access, fencing, gates or new walls where part of land taken for a new or improved highway; relocation of water supply or other service pipes, drains, sewers or soakaways. In *Wilson* v *Minister of Transport* [1980], the acquiring authority agreed to acquire some land for the construction of sheep pens lost by the construction of a new road.

See Chapter 24 for mitigation works.

It is important to distinguish accommodation works from works which are part of the scheme of an authority. The former are offered by an authority to assist a claimant and to mitigate the effects of severance or injurious affection. The latter are necessary and carried out on land acquired and may or may not have any benefit to a particular claimant. In all cases, in assessing the 'after value', it is the value of accommodation or works which may be taken into account, not the costs.

Chapter 22

Compensation and Tax

Introduction
Compensation sums subject to tax
Allowance for tax in assessing compensation
Value added tax

22.1 Introduction

There are, essentially, two issues concerning tax and the assessment of compensation. First, what items of compensation that have been agreed with the acquiring authority, or assessed by the Lands Tribunal, are then subjected to either income or capital gains tax when paid to the claimant. Second, to the extent that items of compensation are taxed in the hands of the claimant, should the compensation sum be increased to allow for the tax and leave a net sum which represents not less than the claimant's loss to ensure that he is no worse off because of the acquisition; or, should the compensation be decreased, if it relates to items such as loss of profits, or payment of removal expenses, because tax would have been paid on the profits had they been earned or the expenses are tax deductible.

22.2 Compensation sums subject to tax

1. Compensation for land acquired and for injurious affection and severance

This is a capital sum received upon the disposal of an asset, as such, it is subject to Capital Gains Tax. Whether any tax is payable will depend upon the amount of gain: this is computed in accordance with the Taxation of Chargeable Gains Tax Act 1992: for relief, see below. Payment for severance is treated as a part disposal and therefore a proportion of allowable costs can be offset against the disposal proceeds: section 42 of the 1992 Act.

If, in the unlikely event of the sale of part of a taxpayer's land is to a body with powers of compulsory purchase at an undervalue, the small part disposal rule may apply. The tax payer can elect to deduct the proceeds from the base costs of the holding if the proceeds are less than 5% of the value of the holding: see section 243 of the 1992 Act.

Where compulsory acquisition takes place without a contract, the date of the disposal for capital gains tax purposes is the date compensation is agreed or determined: see section 246 of the 1992 Act.

2. *Compensation for disturbance*

Again this is received as a capital sum, but it may contain the following disparate elements:

(a) compensation for expenses, e.g. removal costs;
(b) compensation for temporary loss of profits and goodwill; and
(c) compensation for permanent loss of profits and goodwill.

Section 245 of the Taxation of Chargeable Gains Tax Act 1992 permits the total compensation sum received to be apportioned as to that amount which is of a capital nature, and subject to capital gains tax, and as to that amount which is compensation for temporary loss of profits. The latter is regarded as income and treated as a trading receipt: *Stoke-on-Trent City Council* v *Wood Mitchell* [1978] CA.

Thus, item (b) above represents income that would have been received and upon which income tax (or corporation tax) would have been paid. Accordingly, it falls to be included as a receipt taxable under Case I or II of Schedule D as income (Inland Revenue Statement of Practice SP8/79). Compensation for losses on trading stock and to reimburse revenue expenditure, such as item (a) above are treated in the same way. This may sound strange, but remember that the amount received for an expense is balanced by the amount actually spent: the net effect is that no tax should be payable as such.

Item (c) represents the value of the goodwill of a business; it is therefore a capital sum and subject to capital gains tax.

For disposals after April 1982, there is a special compulsory purchase rollover relief if the compensation is reinvested in land in connection with the replacement of business assets: section 247 of the 1992 Act. The reinvestment must take place between 12 months before and three years after the compulsory acquisition: the proceeds from the disposal will be regarded for capital gains tax purposes as giving rise to neither gain nor loss. This rollover relief also applies to a landlord compelled to sell or to grant extended leases under the Leasehold Reform, Housing and Urban Development Act 1993: see SP 13/93 (Revenue statement).

For a case on the taxation of farm-loss payments, see *Davies* v *Powell* [1977].

22.3 Allowance for tax in assessing compensation

1. *Compensation for land*

Although the compensation received by a claimant for the interest in land acquired from him is, *prima facie*, subject to capital gains tax, it cannot be increased so as to leave, in his hands, a net sum after allowing for the tax payable, to represent the value of the land. This is because rule (2) of the rules for assessment of compensation clearly provides that the compensation for the land shall be the market value.

In practice there is relief from capital gains tax where a trader uses the compensation on acquiring new assets such as land, buildings, fixed plant and machinery and goodwill (see above): he may claim to defer payment of the tax. Gains accruing on the disposal of a person's principal private dwellinghouse, which has been the owner's only or main residence, together with garden and grounds up to one acre in extent, are exempt from capital gains tax.

2. *Compensation for disturbance*

The assessment of compensation for disturbance items is on a different basis: there is no statutory definition. A claimant 'has the right to be put, so far as money can do it, in the same position as if his land had not been taken from him': *per* Scott LJ, in *Horn* v *Sunderland Corpn* [1941] CA.

The decision of the House of Lords in *British Transport Commission* v *Gourley* [1956], where a claim for damages as compensation for injuries suffered in an accident included an item for loss of earnings, this item being reduced by the amount of tax the plaintiff would have paid had he received those earnings, was followed in the compulsory purchase case of *West Suffolk County Council* v *Rought Ltd* [1957] HL: compensation for temporary loss of profits was reduced by the amount of tax that would have been paid had those profits been earned, so as to leave in the hands of the claimant, compensation for his true loss.

The rule established in the *Gourley* and *Rought* cases assumed that the sum awarded or assessed was not itself taxable in the hands of the claimant. These cases were distinguished in *Stoke-on-Trent City Council* v *Wood Mitchell* (see above) on the basis that as compensation sums received by a claimant are now taxable, either as to income tax or as to capital gains tax, there is no longer any need to reduce the compensation to be paid. The taxation of compensation in the hands of the claimant is therefore a matter for the Inland Revenue: an acquiring authority cannot seek to reduce the amount of compensation.

The *Stoke-on-Trent* case was applied in *Pennine Raceway Ltd* v *Kirklees Metropolitan Borough Council (No. 2)* [1989] where the Court of Appeal decided that the Lands Tribunal had wrongly deducted sums for the corporation income tax that would have been payable on a loss of profits.

3. The Golightly case

However, where a claimant receives compensation for the loss of profits that would have been earned over a period of years, he may find that the sum may be the subject of a higher tax rate than would have been the case had the sum been spread over several years. This problem was recognised in *Alfred Golightly & Sons Ltd* v *Durham County Council* [1981] in connection with an excess liability to development land tax because the land taken contained minerals that would otherwise have been extracted. The Tribunal followed *Taylor* v *O'Connor* [1971] and allowed a sum to reflect the increased liability to development land tax as part of the rule (6) disturbance claim. It did, however, deduct capital gains and corporation tax savings which left only a small additional sum to reflect the net excess tax liability. The *Golightly* case established an important principle whenever an acquisition causes an increased tax liability.

However, in *Harris* v *Welsh Development Agency* [1999] the Lands Tribunal refused to follow *Golightly* and dismissed a claim for compensation for a capital gains tax liability as the tax liability was a matter directly based on the value of the land and outside rule (6). That interpretation must be questionable as the reference in rule (6) to value of land was to deal with non-rule (2) market value losses.

4. Tax and licences

In *Pennine Raceway Ltd* v *Kirklees Metropolitan Borough Council (No. 2)*

[1989] a claim was made for loss of profits the claimant would have made in the exercise of a licence to use property as a racetrack. It was held that the claimant had an asset that depreciated in value due to the revocation of a planning permission; the receipt of compensation for the loss of profits was derived from an asset; it was a capital sum subject to a capital gains tax.

22.4 Value Added Tax

1. General principles

VAT is payable under the Value Added Tax Act 1994 on any taxable supply of goods or services that are made by a taxable person in the course or furtherance of a business. The payment of compensation for the acquisition of an interest in land represents a 'supply' from the claimant to the acquiring authority for VAT purposes. It is always important to ascertain both the VAT status of the claimant and of the property. The attitude of HM Customs & Excise is that where a transaction is one that would attract VAT, unless the parties have specifically stated that the consideration payable is exclusive of VAT, the consideration will be deemed to include it. Thus, if the parties agree a transaction at a consideration of £100,000 without mentioning that the transaction is exclusive of VAT, the person receiving the consideration will have to bear VAT out of that sum.

2. Compensation for land and buildings

The transfer of an interest in land is usually an exempt supply, and therefore VAT will not be payable on compensation received for the value of land and buildings. However under Schedule 10 to the Value Added Tax Act 1994, the owner of an interest in land or buildings can elect to waive their right to exemption to VAT; it then becomes a standard rated supply (sometimes zero-rated). The purpose of making such an election is normally to enable recovery of input tax on expenditure on repairs or improvements. The 1994 Act makes provision for exemptions from such an election, the parties who are not bound by an election, and the limited circumstances of its recoverability. It follows that if land and buildings in respect of which an election to waive the exemption has been made are compulsorily acquired from the person who has made that election, VAT will be payable upon the compensation received for their acquisition.

3. *Severance and injurious affection*

Compensation paid in respect of severance and injurious affection does not attract VAT because the compensation is in respect of retained land, and there is therefore no supply of land. The position is the same in respect of compensation paid under Part I of the Land Compensation Act 1973 and section 10 of the Compulsory Purchase Act 1965 (the *McCarthy* rules).

4. *Disturbance items*

The compensation paid for disturbance items raises the following issues. If the claimant is not registered for VAT, but incurs VAT on certain items that are claimable as disturbance, such as removal expenses, he will require compensation in respect of that VAT. As a person unregistered for VAT purposes he will not have been able to reclaim such VAT as an input tax against any supplies that he may have made that attracted an output tax. If, on the contrary, the claimant is registered for VAT purposes, and incurs expenditure on disturbance items that attracted VAT input tax, he would, in most cases, have been able to claim that input tax against any output tax he recovered in making any of his supplies for VAT purposes. In other words if the claimant was recovering VAT output tax on goods and services he was supplying during the relevant VAT periods, then he would be entitled to set against that output tax any input tax that he incurs during the same relevant VAT periods that he paid on expenditure items that will form part of his claim for disturbance. There are two difficulties with that position. First, where a claimant's business is the subject of total extinguishment due to a compulsory acquisition, the claimant may have been unable to make any supplies of goods and services upon which he was able to charge VAT output tax, and against which he could claim any VAT input tax on disturbance items. Second, it is possible that the effect of the acquisition of a claimant's land and business is that his trading income drops away, while his costs remain the same, or rise disproportionately due to the acquisition. Either way the claimant may be left with an insufficient recovery of VAT output tax against which he can claim his VAT input tax. In both these cases the claimant ought to be compensated for what is a genuine loss directly caused by the acquisition of his interest. The additional tax burden should form a disturbance item for compensation purposes under the *Golightly* principle, discussed above in relation to capital and income taxes.

It must be remembered that compensation paid for disturbance items is part of the compensation paid for the land and buildings: see *Hughes* v *Doncaster Metropolitan Borough Council* [1991]. Accordingly if the land and buildings are exempt from VAT, no part of the compensation received, whether in respect of the land and buildings or for disturbance items, attracts VAT. But where the claimant is fully registered for VAT and the supply of land and buildings is standard or zero rated, because the claimant has elected to waive the exemption from VAT, VAT at the appropriate zero or standard rate should be added to the total compensation paid. Under section 33 of the Value Added Tax Act 1994, a local authority will be able to obtain a refund of any VAT that it has to pay on the supply of land and buildings upon which VAT has been added to the compensation as an output tax elected by the claimant (and conversely as an input tax paid by the acquiring authority).

A careful distinction must therefore always be made between the payment of compensation to reflect losses suffered by a claimant by reason of having to pay, or being unable to reclaim, a VAT input tax, and VAT output tax that a claimant is obliged to add to the total compensation payable to him for the acquisition of land and buildings because such an acquisition is a supply that is either zero or standard rated.

5. *Surveyors' and other professionals' fees*

Surveyors and other professionals are likely to be required to add VAT to their fee invoices. A claimant will therefore pay these fees, together with the VAT element. Expenditure on these fees is usually compensatable as they are treated as disturbance or other losses within the meaning of rule (6) of section 5 of the Land Compensation Act 1961. Accordingly the guidance set out above in relation to general disturbance items has equal application to surveyors' and other professionals' fees.

6. *Statutory interest on compensation*

The payment of statutory interest on compensation between the date of entry and the date of payment of the compensation does not attract VAT.

7. *Advance payments*

Advance payments can be made under section 52 of the Land Compensation Act 1973. Up to 90% of the acquiring authority's estimate of compensation payable may be advanced. The advanced payment may include compensation for VAT where such compensation would be paid upon the principles set out above. Similarly the advance payment may itself be subject to VAT in those circumstances where the supply of land and buildings is not exempt, but is at a zero or standard rate.

PART IV

WORSENMENT: COMPENSATION AND MITIGATION

The first three chapters in this Part are concerned with worsenment, its compensation and mitigation. Worsenment describes the depreciation in value of interests in land caused by the activities and decisions of public authorities. The first of the three chapters considers the rights to claim compensation for depreciation in value, or injurious affection, caused by activities of authorities. Such activities are not necessarily associated with the use of compulsory purchase powers and, indeed, the rights described are those available to claimants who have no land acquired from them which is held together with any land affected. The next chapter deals with some of the powers and duties of public authorities to mitigate the injurious effect of public works. The third is concerned with compensation for decisions: a wide variety of public authority decisions, principally in the planning field, can have a substantial effect on land values; there are a number of compensation rights. Chapter 26 deals with compensation payable for wayleaves.

Chapter 23

Compensation for Activities

Introduction
Nuisance
Compensation for injurious affection caused by execution of works:
  Compulsory Purchase Act 1965, section 10: the *McCarthy* rules
Compensation for depreciation caused by use of public works:
  Land Compensation Act 1973, Part I
Compensation for street lights

23.1 Introduction

If a person carries out activities on his land whereby a neighbouring landowner 'is unlawfully annoyed, prejudiced or disturbed in the enjoyment of land; whether by physical damage to the land or by other interference with the enjoyment of the land or with his exercise of an easement, profit or other similar right or with his health, comfort or convenience as occupier of such land', the activities will amount to a nuisance (*Salmond On the Law of Torts*). Forms of nuisance may include the escape of deleterious things on to the complainant's land; water, smoke, smell, fumes, noise and vibrations are examples. A nuisance gives rise to tortious liability, the remedy for which is an injunction and/or damages.

The activities of public authorities will frequently amount to a nuisance by causing an unreasonable interference with the enjoyment of neighbouring land. Depreciation to land values may also be caused by activities that do not amount to nuisance. A view may be seriously affected by an electricity grid pylon; the quiet residential character of a particular street may change if that street becomes part of a ring-road (the noise and vibration may also amount to a nuisance); and, the profitability of a shop on a busy road may be affected if that road is by-passed by a new road or motorway. Unfortunately for the persons concerned, the activities of the public authority are usually immune to an action in nuisance, or, if they do not amount to a nuisance, there is no remedy at law in any event. This chapter is concerned, first, with the liability of a public authority for nuisance, and then with the rights, if any, to compensation in lieu of any remedy at law whether in nuisance or otherwise. In *A-G v Horner* [1884] Sir William Brett MR said: 'it is a proper rule of construction not to construe an Act of Parliament as interfering with or injuring persons' rights without compensation, unless one is obliged to so construe it'. Despite that view, if Parliament makes no provision for compensation for some harm, no compensation is recoverable for harm that is the consequence of the use of statutory powers.

The general approach of the statutes providing for compensation is in terms of depreciation to market values. This land-value approach to the provision of remedies is due to the context of compulsory purchase in the 19th century – railway companies acquiring land held for its income from the large landowners. These owners were primarily concerned with harm to land values. However, readers should not consider compensation only in terms of money, or harm to land values; affected parties may be reasonably satisfied in other ways. Prof McAuslan has argued that the right to participate in the decision-making process is a form of compensation. There are other possibilities, such as the provision of mitigation works.

Depreciation in the value of land may be caused by public works, but, as we shall see, compensation is only available if provided by statute. In *Arrondelle v UK Government* [1982] the applicant owned a cottage one mile from the east end of Gatwick Airport. She was not entitled to serve a valid blight notice and petitioned the European Commission of Human Rights. The case was settled upon payment of an *ex gratia* sum of £7,500. It is assumed that she was not entitled to make any claim for compensation as discussed in this chapter and that is why she went to the commission.

Two distinctions must be made at this stage. First, one must distinguish the owner who has some land compulsorily acquired, and retains other land, from the owner who has no land acquired from him. In the former case, if the owner's retained land was held with the land acquired from him and the retained land is affected by the proposed activities of the acquiring authority, the owner may claim compensation for the depreciation in value of that retained land. This is the claim for injurious affection considered in Chapter 15. It matters not whether the proposed activities amount to a nuisance or otherwise; the owner is fully compensated for the injurious affection to his retained land. Where an owner has no land compulsorily acquired, and his land is affected by the activities of the authority, his claims for compensation are more limited. Essentially, the claims for compensation of an owner who loses no land are in lieu of an action for nuisance. Consequently, there is no compensation for such an owner to the extent that he is affected by the activities of a public authority that do not amount to a nuisance. It is these limited claims to compensation, available to an owner who loses no land (or if he does it is not held with the land affected), that are considered in this chapter.

The second distinction is between the harm caused by the construction or execution of public works (for example, building a motorway or an aerodrome) and the harm caused by the use of the works (traffic or aeroplane noise and vibration). Although both types of harm can amount to nuisance, for the purposes of compensation they give rise to separate claims; an owner may be entitled to both claims if he shows he has suffered both types of harm. This distinction is not relevant in connection with the claim for compensation for injurious affection by an owner where part of his land is acquired (considered in Chapter 15) who can bring a nuisance action or a claim for compensation. The reader may like to contemplate whether this situation is necessarily inevitable and whether the many who suffer and cannot claim should be without any redress.

23.2 Nuisance

We have seen that nuisance is a tort, or legal wrong, that causes an unreasonable interference with a person's use or enjoyment of land. In the early case of *St Helen's Smelting Co* v *Tipping* [1865] it was said:

> ... it is very desirable thing to mark the difference between an action brought for a nuisance upon the ground that the alleged nuisance produces material injury to the property, and an action brought for a nuisance on the ground that the thing alleged to be a nuisance is productive of sensible personal discomfort.

For the purposes of this chapter nuisances can therefore be divided into two groups: nuisances that affect the enjoyment of property, such as noise, dust or vibration, and nuisances that cause material injury or physical interference, such as physical damage caused by vibration, subsidence damage, obstructions to and from the public highway, or along the public highway, and obstructions of rights appurtenant to property such as easements (for example rights of way and rights of light).

If an activity, which is unlawful, gives rise to a nuisance, the activity may be stopped by an injunction and damages paid to a plaintiff for any loss or depreciation in the value of his property. The fact that the activity is of general public benefit is no defence to an action in nuisance. However, a particular activity may be authorised by an Act of Parliament; it is then a matter for consideration whether any nuisance the activity may cause is thereby made lawful and immune from an action in law. The Act may contain clear words expressly providing immunity to an action in nuisance: see section 76 of the Civil Aviation Act 1982. If it does not, such immunity may be a necessary implication of the activity and powers authorised by Parliament.

> *Hammersmith & City Rail Co v Brand* [1869] HL
> The railway company constructed a railway through Hammersmith, under the statutory powers granted to them by the Hammersmith and City Railway Act 1861. No part of the plaintiff's house or garden was taken, but she claimed damage for vibration, noise and smoke from passing trains. The House of Lords decided that there could be no action for nuisance as the use of locomotives was expressly authorised by Parliament.

A similar decision was made by the House of Lords in *Allen* v *Gulf Oil Refining Ltd* [1981]. In the case, Gulf Oil were authorised by the Gulf Oil Refining Act 1965 to compulsorily purchase land near Milford Haven for the construction of an oil refinery. The refinery was built and Mrs Allen, who lived nearby, brought an action in nuisance alleging noxious odours, vibration, offensive noise levels, excessive flames from burning waste gases, all of which caused her ill-health and a fear of an explosion. She claimed an injunction to prevent the acts of nuisance and damages. The Court of Appeal decided on a preliminary point of law that the 1965 Act only authorised the compulsory purchase of land for a refinery and it did not authorise the use of the land for a refinery. There was therefore no statutory authority to commit a nuisance and Mrs Allen could maintain her action. However, the House of Lords allowed the oil company's appeal. The 1965 Act clearly intended that a refinery would be constructed on the land acquired, and it followed that Parliament authorised, expressly or impliedly, that the refinery could be operated. This did not mean that the company could operate the refinery in anyway it chose: if causing a nuisance was the inevitable consequence of operating the refinery, the nuisance was immune, but if it was possible to operate the refinery without causing a nuisance, then the company would not enjoy any immunity from proceedings in nuisance.

If immunity to an action in nuisance is expressly or implicitly granted by Parliament in a statute which authorises a particular activity, then compensation is only available if provided by statute. The two principal statutory claims to compensation are described in this chapter.

However there is a limit on the immunity to an action in nuisance in respect of the carrying out of works under statutory powers. In *Allen* v *Gulf Oil Refining Ltd* [1981] it was said that the undertaker of works authorised by statute must 'carry out the work and conduct the operation with all reasonable regard and care for the interests of other persons'. If that direction is exceeded, the carrying out of the works does not have immunity from legal action, and a complainant should bring proceedings for nuisance rather than pursue a claim for statutory compensation under the provisions considered in this Chapter. Provided that the complainant has a sufficient proprietary interest in the affected property, a claim in nuisance and, if necessary, negligence, can be pursued: see *Butcher Robinson & Staples Ltd* v *London Regional Transport* [1999].

If proceedings in nuisance are taken in respect of nuisances that do not cause direct physical interference with property, or a right to property, such as noise, vibration and dust, the decision in *Andreae* v *Selfridge & Co Ltd* [1938] has implications for building operations. It was said in that case that:

> Where one is dealing with temporary operations, such as demolition and re-building, everybody has to put up with a certain amount of discomfort, because operations of that kind cannot be carried on at all without a certain amount of noise and a certain amount of dust. Therefore, the rule with regard to interference must be read subject to this qualification, and there can be no dispute about it, that in respect of operations of this character, such as demolition and building, if they are reasonably carried on and all proper and reasonable steps are taken to ensure that no undue inconvenience is caused to neighbours, whether from noise, dust or other reasons, the neighbours must put up with it.

The implications of this case in pursuing one of the statutory claims to compensation are considered later in this chapter.

If damage is caused to an adjoining property owner through the negligence of a statutory authority, immunity from a negligence action cannot be implied into the statute under which the authority is operating, and is unlikely to be expressly granted by Parliament. See *Department of Transport* v *North West Water Authority* [1983] where the propositions of law are set out: water authority was not liable in nuisance for the escape of water from a burst pipe because the provision of water was in performance of its statutory duty; it would only have been liable for damage had it been negligent.

23.3 Compensation for injurious affection caused by execution of works: Compulsory Purchase Act 1965, section 10: the *McCarthy* rules

1. The basis of the claim

Section 10 provides:

> (1) If any person claims compensation in respect of any land, or any interest in land, which has been taken for or injuriously affected by the execution of the works, and for which the acquiring authority have not made satisfaction under the provisions of this Act, or of the special Act, any dispute arising in relation to the compensation shall be referred to and determined by the Lands Tribunal.
>
> (2) This section shall be construed as affording in all cases a right to compensation for injurious affection to land which is the same as the right which section 68 of the Lands Clauses Consolidation Act 1845 has been construed as affording in cases where the amount claimed exceeds fifty pounds.

Section 10(1) is, in part, a re-enactment of section 68 of the 1845 Act (the 1845 Act, it will be remembered, still applies to a few compulsory acquisitions not within the 1965 Act). On reading section 10 (or section 68 as the case may be) it is not immediately obvious that this permits a claim for compensation in the circumstances to be considered hereafter; but, as section 10(2) indicates (and preserves), the original wording of the 1845 Act has been construed by the courts as affording a right to compensation in respect of injurious affection to land where no land is acquired from a particular landowner. The conditions for bringing a claim were particularised in *Metropolitan Board of Works* v *McCarthy* [1874] HL; they are known as the *McCarthy* rules.

In *Wagstaff* v *Department of the Environment, Transport and the Regions* [1999] the Lands Tribunal decided that 'the works' for the purposes of a claim under section 10, were those authorised under certain slip- and side- roads orders and the Highways Act 1980 on the land acquired under the compulsory purchase order involved. Indeed certain works outside the boundary of the compulsory purchase order were disregarded for compensation purposes.

It is immaterial whether the works causing the injurious affection are on land that has been compulsorily acquired or acquired by agreement under statutory powers: see *Kirby* v *School Board for Harrogate* [1896] and *Re Elm Avenue, New Milton, ex parte New Forest District Council* [1984].

A claimant will be entitled to make a claim if he has a substantial interest in the property: see *Re Masters and Great Western Rly Co* [1901] 2 KB 84.

2. The McCarthy rules

There is a modern restatement of the law by Lord Wilberforce in *Argyle Motors (Birkenhead) Ltd* v *Birkenhead Corpn* [1974]. The law was also reconsidered by Lord Hoffmann in the recent decision of *Wildtree Hotels Ltd* v *Harrow London Borough Council* [2000]. Each of the following four rules must be satisfied before a claim can be made under section 10.

Rule (i)   *The injury done must be by reason of what is authorised by Act of Parliament*

In the *McCarthy* case itself, the Board of Works were authorised by the Thames Embankment Act 1862 to construct the Victoria Embankment; one of the necessary consequences was the destruction of a dock adjoining the claimant's premises.

If injury is caused by unauthorised work or work improperly or negligently performed, it will not be within statutory powers and there is no claim for compensation under the Act: the claimant must seek a remedy at common law. In *Allen* v *Gulf Oil Refining Ltd* [1981] it was said that an undertaker purporting to exercise statutory powers must 'carry out the work and conduct the operation with all reasonable regard and care for the interests of other persons'; if that direction is not followed, and the works are carried out unreasonably, the conduct of the work will not have statutory immunity and the proper redress for a complainant is an action at common law. Compensation is not payable under section 10 if the undertaker is acting outside its powers: see *Imperial Gaslight and Coke Co* v *Broadbent* [1859]. In *Biscoe* v *Great Eastern Ry Co* [1873] the removal of one house structurally connected with adjoining tenements impaired the stability of a neighbouring house; on the evidence, due precautions could have avoided the damage, and an injunction was granted.

However, if an authority defends a claim for compensation on the ground that the cause of damage was not within the statutory power, such as negligence or actionable nuisance, it must frame such defence in precise terms: see *Uttley* v *The Local Board of Health for the District of Todmorden* [1874]. In *Colac* v *Summerfield* [1893] the Privy Council held that so long as an authority is acting within its powers, negligence is, in any question of compensation, immaterial, and cannot affect the extent of its liability, which is for all damage resulting from the construction or maintenance of its works. There is no support in the case law that an authority can plead its own negligence as an answer to a claim for compensation under a statute: see *Welsh Water Development Authority* v *Burgess* [1974].

Rule (ii)   *The injury must arise from that which would, if done without the authority of Act of Parliament, have been actionable at law*
This rule poses the question: if the injury had not been authorised by statute, could the claimant have obtained a remedy in the courts to prevent or compensate such injury? A remedy is available to redress a legal wrong such as a tort or a breach of covenant. Loss of privacy is not actionable so no compensation can be claimed: *Re Penny and South Eastern Ry* [1857]. It is important to appreciate that this claim to compensation is in substitution for an action at law. Many of the circumstances in which these rules have been applied have involved an injury or harm that would have been actionable as a nuisance.

What is and what is not actionable at law was considered in relation to the law of nuisance at the beginning of this Chapter. It must be borne in mind that, in the case of building operations, a nuisance that does not cause physical interference with land or a right to land will not normally be actionable. Thus, a nuisance causing noise, dust or vibration would not be actionable if carried out in the normal and reasonable course of demolition or building operations: see the *Andreae* v *Selfridge & Co Ltd* [1938] case. Thus, in *Wildtree Hotels Ltd* v *Harrow London Borough Council* [2000] compensation was not payable n respect of noise, dust or vibration. The decision in *Clift* v *Welsh Office* [1999] is probably confined to its special facts.

In the *McCarthy* case, the claimant's right to use the adjoining public dock was a public right: an interference with a public right amounts to public nuisance and, if the claimant suffers special damage over and above that suffered by the public at large, he may have an action in nuisance.

To interfere with a landowner's access onto the highway without statutory authority would be a tort. In the Irish case of *Moore* v *Great Southern and Western Ry Co* [1858], the company was authorised to lower a road adjoining the claimant's cottage. This necessitated the use of a ladder to reach the cottage from the road; he had a claim for compensation. However, temporary obstruction of the highway, or access onto it, will only be actionable if unreasonable in duration or extent; for this reason there was no claim for compensation in *Herring* v *Metropolitan Board of Works* [1865] where hoardings put around works on sewers partially obstructed access to the claimant's business premises for six months.

Compensation is payable for temporary interruptions if they would be actionable but for statutory immunity. This proposition has now been confirmed by the House of Lords in *Wildtree Hotels Ltd* v *Harrow London Borough Council* [2000]. The decision of the Lands Tribunal in *Budgen* v *Secretary of State for the Environment* [1985], that compensation was payable during a period of road construction for noise, dust and other nuisance would not appear justified under section 10. Claims for compensation in respect of temporary interferences were also considered in *Ford* v *Metropolitan and Metropolitan District Railway Companies* [1886] and *Lingké* v *Christchurch Corpn* [1912], a case under the public health legislation. Temporary interruption formed one of the claims in the *Argyle* case.

In *Flanagan* v *Stoke-on-Trent City Council* [1982] the Lands Tribunal allowed a claim in respect of shop premises left in a cul-de-sac, following extensive road works. The claimant 'was deprived of the easy access to his house and premises which he before enjoyed', said the member, quoting from the *Moore* case.

Interference with easements such as rights of way, support or of light are, if unauthorised, actionable as nuisances and therefore are clearly within the scope of this right to compensation.

If the construction or execution of works amount to a breach of a restrictive covenant, the covenantee, the person whose land benefits from the covenant, may also claim compensation: see *Long Eaton Recreation Grounds Co* v *Midland Ry* [1902].

Rule (iii) *The damage must arise from a physical interference with some right, public or private, which the claimant as owner of an interest in property is by law entitled to make use of, in connection with such property, and which gives an additional market value to such property.*

This rule has regard to the words of the statute that compensation is to be paid for injurious affection to land or a right to land; the legal right interfered with must contribute to the value of the claimant's land and not be of mere personal advantage or of trade value:

Ricket v *Metropolitan Ry Co* [1867] HL

Ricket was the occupier of a public house, the Pickled Egg. The company obstructed, with hoardings, for a period of 20 months the adjoining streets and Ricket's business suffered loss of profits for the period because of some deprivation of custom. It was held that because there had been no injurious affection to the value of his interest in the land, he had no claim to compensation for loss of profits. (In any event, the temporary obstructions would not have given rise to a cause of action in nuisance had they been erected without statutory authority.)

This case can be contrasted with the *McCarthy* case where the loss of the right to use the adjoining public dock entry affected the value of the claimant's premises. However in *Becket* v *Midland Railway Co* [1867], the narrowing of a street founded a claim by a frontager.

In the *Wildtree* case the House of Lords saw no reason why a claim for compensation should be restricted to a claim for loss of the open market capital value of the affected property. In cases where compensation was payable for temporary interference with the affected land, or a right appurtenant to the land, a reduction in the open market letting value of the land is sufficient to sustain the claim even where the capital value, after the conclusion of the works, is unaffected.

If a claimant proves loss of profits, he has no claim for compensation for the injurious affection to his land. But it may be open to him to establish that a permanent loss of profits does affect the land value:

> *Argyle Motors (Birkenhead) Ltd v Birkenhead Corpn* [1974] HL
> The reconstruction of the road approaches to the Mersey Tunnel caused both a temporary and a permanent loss of direct access to the claimants' motor car showrooms: they claimed loss of business and consequential loss of profits. The House of Lords disallowed the claim for business loss, but Lord Wilberforce said that if the claimants could 'prove that a loss of profitability affects the value of their interest in the land, they could recover compensation for this loss of value'. The claim was later resubmitted as damage to land value and determined by the Lands Tribunal: *Leake v Wirral MB* [1977].
> We have already seen under rule (ii) that interference with easements is within the scope of this provision; normally these are appurtenant to dominant land and will also satisfy rule (iii). If there is no dominant land, this rule can only be complied with if the right or advantage is an interest in land such as a profit in gross. A person who has a licence (not by deed) to shoot over the land acquired (*Bird v Great Eastern Ry* [1865]), or an exclusive right to sell refreshments in a theatre (*Frank Warr & Co v London County Council* [1904]), does not have an interest in land and cannot claim compensation under this provision (but see Chapters 7 and 8 as to licences).

Rule (iv) *The damage must arise from the execution of the works and not by their subsequent use*
> 'Execution of the works' appear in the section itself and, following *Hammersmith Ry Co v Brand* [1869] HL it is settled law that, unlike the provision (now section 7 of the

Compulsory Purchase Act 1965) concerning injurious affection compensation where some land of the claimant is acquired, this provision does not give a right to claim compensation for the depreciation in value of land caused by the use to which the works are put.

It is this point and the fact that the subsequent use of works is usually authorised by statute, and therefore immune to an action in law (as in *Allen* v *Gulf Oil Refining Ltd* [1981], that required some reconsiderations after public concern about the noise and other harms caused by the use of motorways and airports. Substantial depreciation in the value of properties and interference with the use and enjoyment of land can be caused by the use of land taken for public works; under the *McCarthy* rules there is no claim for this aspect of worsement. (But see the new claim for compensation considered at **23.4** below.)

There must be an execution of works to found a claim for compensation. Thus, in *Jolliffe* v *Exeter Corporation* [1967] compensation was not payable for the effect of a stopping up order made under the Highways Acts. However in *Wagstaff* v *The Department of the Environment, Transport and the Regions* [1999], where a highway authority had made a number of stopping-up and side-roads orders, together with the execution of works forming a by-pass, it was held that compensation was payable. The stopping-up and side-roads orders were construed such that they did not take effect until the works of execution of the by-pass commenced. It was further held in the *Wagstaff* case that no claim for compensation could be made in respect of that part of the works that were carried out outside the boundaries of the compulsory purchase order in question.

There is some doubt whether compensation is payable where a covenant restrictive of some use is breached; compensation should only be payable for the damage arising from the execution of the works, not the use, under *Hammersmith Rly Co* v *Brand* [1869], applied in *Re Simeon and the Isle of Wight RDC* [1937]. But in *Long Eaton Recreation Grounds Co* v *Midland Rly* [1902] the judge thought compensation was payable, as did Chadwick J in *Brown* v *Heathlands Mental Health National Service Trust* [1996]. In *Thames Water Utilities* v *Oxford City Council*

[1999] the judge said that Chadwick J was probably wrong on this point.

3. *The measure of compensation*

As this claim is in substitution for an action in law, the rules concerning damages payable in tort are applicable. The damage must be the natural and probable consequence of the execution of the works and must not be too remote. The amount of compensation awarded must, so far as money can, put the claimant in the same position as he would have been in had no tort occurred. The diminution in the value of the claimant's land is the usual measure of compensation.

The measure of compensation is not limited to the diminution in the open market capital value of the affected property. In cases of temporary interference there might be no, or little, permanent diminution in the capital value of the affected property at the conclusion of the works causing the damage. In those cases the House of Lords in *Wildtree Hotels Ltd v Harrow London Borough Council* [2000] saw no reason why a claim could not be advanced based on a reduction in the open market letting value of the affected property for the period of the interference.

The relevant date for the assessment of compensation must be the date of loss. In the *Flanagan* case, following *Dodd Properties (Kent) Ltd v Canterbury City Council* [1980], this was held to be the date when the works were completed. However, it is arguable that depreciation in land value, or other damage, might occur at an earlier date than the completion of works. It is also illogical, as the Tribunal pointed out in *Flanagan*, that section 63 of the Land Compensation Act 1973 directs that interest on the unpaid compensation is payable from the date of claim; a date that could precede the completion of the works.

A claimant is almost certainly entitled to compensation for future damage: see *Colac v Summerfield* [1893] AC 187. He should include in his claim all damages which are reasonably foreseeable: see *Chamberlain v West End of London and Crystal Palace Rly Co* [1863]. There seems no reason why a claimant cannot make a claim after works have been carried out, even if this is a further claim because of a change in the works causing new or additional and unforeseen damage.

If an easement of light has been obstructed so that further development of the affected site is inhibited, the depreciation in value of the land for that potential development purpose is recoverable (*Griffith* v *Clay* [1912]); damage that can be foreseen should be included as no further claim can be made. In *London, Tilbury and Southend Ry and Gower's Walk School* [1889] it was held that the quantum of compensation for interference to a right of light could include damage from interference to windows without such rights; the Court of Appeal had assumed that cases on injurious affection to land held with land acquired from a claimant, and compensated under what is now section 7 of the Compulsory Purchase Act 1965, where all damage is recoverable, also applied to cases under section 10. But in *Horton* v *Colwyn Bay & Colwyn Urban District Council* [1908], the Court of Appeal distinguished cases on what is now section 7 from those on section 10: the *Tilbury* case being concerned with the latter. The case was regarded as correct only because, in the absence of statutory powers, the claimant could have obtained an injunction to prevent the building from being erected and obstructing his right of light and this would also, coincidentally, have prevented obstruction to his windows without such rights. As he could have prevented the whole building, he was justified in being compensated on the basis of interference to all his obstructed windows.

It is sometimes argued that the *Tilbury* case is authority for the view that if a claim for compensation can be made under section 10 of the 1965 Act, the full depreciation in the value of the affected land can be claimed. Following the *Horton* case, it is clear that this is not so, and that the *Tilbury* case must be confined to its special facts. The quantum of compensation is therefore the depreciation in the value of the affected land attributable to the interference or loss of legal right that gave rise to the claim.

This was confirmed in *Wildtree Hotels Ltd* v *Harrow London Borough Council* [2000] where the House of Lords decided that compensation was only payable for that injurious affection or damage attributable to a matter that would have been actionable; there cannot be a parasitic claim under which all injurious affection, whether actionable or not, is compensatable.

In *Wrotham Park Settled Estates* v *Hertsmere Borough Council* [1993] the Court of Appeal dismissed an appeal from the Lands Tribunal which had decided that in respect of a claim relating to breach of a restrictive covenant the proper measure of damages at law would have been the diminution in value of the claimant's land and would not be related to the profits earned by the council by breaching the covenants. The assessment of compensation, being for a claim in lieu of an action, should be on the same basis.

In *Surrey County Council* v *Bredero* [1993], a case involving a breach of a restrictive covenant, the Court of Appeal held that diminution in value of the plaintiff's land was the true measure of damages in an action at law (not in equity), and the damages should not relate to the profits earned by the contract breaker.

Both cases leave in doubt whether higher damages might be recoverable in equity, and therefore whether a compensation claim would be on a basis reflecting profits gained by the breach. For cases on the basis on profits gained see: *Wrotham Park Estate Co* v *Parkside Homes* [1974]; and *SJC Construction Co* v *Sutton London Borough Council* [1975].

The normal rules of compensation for compulsory acquisition do not apply, so any betterment does not have to be set off against the compensation due: *Eagle* v *Charing Cross Rly* [1867]. The claim under section 10 is for depreciation in the value of the subject land and this means that no claim can be made for loss of profits or business good-will: see *Argyle Motors (Birkenhead) Ltd* v *Birkenhead Corpn* [1974] and *Flanagan* v *Stoke-on-Trent City Council* [1982]. But otherwise the usual approach to valuation applies. Thus in *Wadham* v *NE Railway Co* [1884] where a highway had been stopped up, the compensation was for the diminution of the value of an hotel, *as an hotel*.

Examples

Metropolitan Board of Works v Howard [1889] HL

The claimant was the tenant of a public house on a street some 250ft from old Putney Bridge, Middlesex. The Board of Works constructed a new bridge higher up river and demolished the old bridge. It was held that there was an interference amounting to injurious affection which gave a right to compensation.

Beckett v Midland Rly Co [1867]

The claimant owned a house fronting a public highway. The railway company, acting under statutory powers, constructed an embankment that narrowed the highway from 50ft to 33ft. This materially diminished the value of the claimant's house; he was entitled to compensation for this diminution.

Wagstaff v Department of the Environment, Transport and the Regions [1999]

This case, under section 10 of the 1965 Act, involved a petrol filling station that stood at the junction of a trunk road and a side road. Until a road improvement scheme, access was gained from the side road and by both northbound and southbound traffic on the trunk road. As the result of a road improvement scheme, a new section of dual carriageway replaced the section of the trunk road on which stood the filling station. This carriageway was constructed from a point one kilometre to the south to one kilometre to the north of the station. The side road immediately outside the filling station was closed. There was then no direct access from the new section of the trunk road, and the old section became a service road. The Lands Tribunal decided that the obstruction of the side road founded a claim to compensation under section 10. The claimants' land was injuriously affected, if at all, only by the execution of those parts of the works that obstructed lengths of highway providing access to the land. It was said that loss arising from the use of the new road to the system was too remote to found a claim because it was not properly attributable to such an obstruction. There was therefore no claim for compensation founded on the works to the trunk road as the obstructions to access to the trunk road was, in respect of the south obstruction, outside the area of the compulsory purchase order, and to the north, insufficiently direct direct and proximate.

23.4 Compensation for depreciation caused by the use of public works: Land Compensation Act 1973, Part I

1. *Introduction*

This part of the 1973 Act provides a right to certain owners to claim compensation where their properties are depreciated in value by the use of public works. Public works are defined as a new or altered highway, aerodrome or other public works. This new right avoids the limitation of rule (iv) of the *McCarthy* rules (see above) and the immunity to a legal action enjoyed by an authority in the exercise of its powers, as in the *Brand* case considered at **23.2** above.

However, there are severe restrictions on the measure of compensation that can be claimed under Part I of the 1973 Act; claimants will usually be better compensated under section 7 of the Compulsory Purchase Act 1965 through the severance and injurious affection claim if they could prove that some land is taken from them.

Compensation is not payable under Part I if compensation has been paid under for injurious affection in connection with the acquisition of land: see *Bannocks* v *Secretary of State for Transport* [1995].

2. The right to claim compensation: section 1

A person may claim compensation for the depreciation in the value of an interest in land due to 'physical factors' caused by the use of public works. The 'physical factors' are noise, vibration, smell, fumes, smoke and artificial lighting and the discharge onto the land of any solid or liquid substance.

It is clear that this claim is in lieu of an action for nuisance. First because the 'physical factors' would normally, if unreasonable in effect, amount to a private nuisance. Second, because a claim can only be made under the Act if the authority is immune to an action in nuisance in respect of those 'physical factors' which may be caused by the use of their public works: section 1(6). Although, if the public works are a highway, a claim can be made whether or not there is immunity from action for nuisance in respect of the use of the highway. Clearly if there is no statutory immunity, expressed or implied, the claimant's proper remedy is an action for nuisance. In *Marsh* v *Powys County Council* [1997] it was decided that as the Education Act 1944 did not give immunity in relation to a primary school use, a compensation claim was precluded. However, unlike an action for nuisance where it is necessary to show an interference with the enjoyment of property that is unreasonable, it is sufficient under this provision to show depreciation in value due to the 'physical factors' of not less than £50.

The noise and vibration, or other 'physical factors' caused by aircraft arriving at or departing from an aerodrome are to be regarded as caused by the use of the aerodrome whether or not the aircraft is within the boundaries of the aerodrome. But in other cases the source of the 'physical factors' must be situated on or in the public works. This last point is a severe limitation on the right to claim. For example, if a motorway is built in the locality and an existing road becomes much busier and more noisy because it is used as a feeder-road, the source of the increased noise is not from the public works (the motorway) and residents living in the road now used as a feeder-road will have no claim unless they can show that their road was itself subject to improvement.

In *Blower* v *Suffolk County Council* [1994] the Lands Tribunal decided that the glare created by street lights was a physical factor notwithstanding that the glare could only be seen but did not itself illuminate the subject property.

Where a claim is made in respect of noise arising from alterations to a public highway the physical factors must be from the altered stretch of highway. However, where the increased traffic using the altered stretch of highway is due to new works elsewhere (such as a new bridge), depreciation due to that increased traffic causing more noise on the altered stretch of highway is compensatable: see *Williamson* v *Cumbria County Council* [1994].

No compensation is payable in respect of physical factors caused by accidents involving vehicles on a highway or accidents involving aircraft.

3. *Persons qualifying for compensation: section 2*

The claimant must own a qualifying interest in a dwelling or land before the relevant date. This date, in relation to a claim in respect of a highway is the date on which it was first open to public traffic; and, in relation to a claim in respect of other public works, is the date on which they were first used after completion.

(a) *Dwellings*

A qualifying interest in land which is a dwelling is called an 'owner's interest' and an 'owner's interest' means either a legal fee simple or a tenancy for a term of years certain which at the date of the notice of claim has not less than three years unexpired. A tenant holding a monthly tenancy would therefore not qualify. If the 'owner's interest' carries the right to occupy the dwelling, the claimant must do so as his residence at the date of the notice of claim. Thus, both a landlord and a tenant, if otherwise qualified, could claim, but a claimant in occupation must be in residential occupation. For a claim by a landlord, see *Allen* v *Department of Transport* [1994].

(b) *Land other than dwellings*

If the qualifying interest is in land other than a dwelling, then, although the claimant must have an 'owner's interest' as defined above under dwellings, he must be at the same time an 'owner-occupier'. An 'owner-occupier' in relation to land in an agricultural unit is a person who occupies the whole of that unit while having an 'owner's interest' in the whole or any part of that land; while an 'owner-occupier' of land in any other type of hereditament must occupy the whole or a substantial part of the land while having an 'owner's interest'.

If the land is neither a dwelling nor forms part of an agricultural unit, the rateable value, or, if different, the net annual value, must not exceed a 'prescribed amount'. This limitation, which mainly affects business premises, is the same as that placed on persons entitled to serve blight notices: the amount is presently (2003) £24,600.

(c) Special interests

A mortgagee may make claim without prejudicing the mortgagor's right to make a claim, but if he does, no compensation is payable in respect of the depreciation in value of his interest; he can only claim in respect of the mortgagor's interest (who must, therefore, be otherwise eligible). If compensation is payable in respect of an interest in land which is mortgaged, it shall be paid to the mortgagee on the basis that as the value of the land has depreciated, this affects the mortgagee's security. He, then, applies it as if it were the proceeds of a sale: section 10.

If the interest in land is held by trustees and the person beneficially entitled under the trust is entitled to occupy the land, occupation by that person is regarded as occupation by the trustees and so entitling them to claim if all the other requirements are satisfied: section 10.

A person who acquired an interest by inheritance is eligible to claim even though he inherited after the 'relevant date' provided the person he inherited from had a qualifying interest before that date: section 11.

If a tenant has less than three years unexpired, and therefore is ineligible to claim, he may none the less be regarded as having an 'owner's interest' provided, before the relevant date, the tenant has served on his landlord a notice to have the freehold or an extended lease under the provisions of the Leasehold Reform Act 1967, where he is so eligible, and has not acquired either interest by that date. But if he does not claim compensation under the 1973 Act in respect of his original tenancy until after acquiring the freehold or an extended lease under the 1967 Act, he is still entitled to do so: section 12.

4. *Claim procedure: section 3*

A claim is made by serving on the appropriate authority a notice containing the following particulars:

(a) the land in respect of which the claim is made;
(b) the claimant's interest and date of acquisition;
(c) the claimant's occupation of the land (in cases where occupation is a necessary qualification for a claim);
(d) any other interest in the land known to the claimant;
(e) the public works to which the claim relates;
(f) the amount of compensation claimed;
(g) details of other contiguous or adjoining land owned by the claimant.

Where the claim relates to alterations to public works, details of the alterations must be given.

In *Fennessy* v *City Airport Ltd* [1995] LT it was decided that a claim specified as 'an amount in excess of £50 to be agreed' was not valid. A claim must be particularised: see *Methodist Church Purposes Trustees* v *North Tyneside Metropolitan Borough Council* [1979]. The claim must not be made before the expiry of 12 months after the date the public works were first used or a public highway was first opened to public traffic (the relevant date). The first day after the expiration of the 12 months is the first claim day. In *Davies* v *Mid-Glamorgan County Council* [1979], the issue was when the altered Cardiff Airport was first used following the carrying out of works in three phases. The Tribunal decided that a claim could be made when all three phases had been completed, and it was illogical if a claimant had to submit a separate claim after each of the three phases. There was a single scheme for the improvement of the airport.

Part I of the 1973 Act originally provided a claim period of two years from the first claim day. This has caused some injustice where owners have suffered depreciation due to the 'physical factors' and have not been made aware of this right to claim compensation. The Local Government, Planning and Land Act 1980 amended the 1973 Act by removing this claim period. There were also transitional provisions for allowing claims which were out of time when the 1980 Act became law. The time-limit for making a claim, and referring claims to the Lands Tribunal, is six years from the first claim date: see section 19(2A) of the 1973 Act and section 9 of the Limitation Act 1980.

Where the claimant has entered into a contract during the 12 months preceding the first claim day to dispose of his interest, or, if the land is not a dwelling, to grant a tenancy, he may still be eligible to make a claim. However, he must submit his claim during those 12 months and before he disposes of his interest or grants the tenancy. He need not wait for the first claim day: section 3(3). Where a claimant does dispose of his interest in an affected property, he will not be entitled thereafter to make a claim under the Act. This follows from the decision of the Lands Tribunal in *Donaldson* v *Hereford and Worcester County Council* [1997]. This situation can be unjust as the new purchaser will have purchased the property at the depreciated price, and has no incentive to pursue a claim, and the original owner will have sold at the depreciated price, and will not be entitled to pursue the claim.

5. *Assessment of Compensation (General Principles): section 4*

The compensation is assessed and valuation made with reference to prices current on the first claim day (that is 12 months after use of the public works first commenced).

Although, in assessing depreciation due to the 'physical factors', regard shall be had of the use of the public works on the first day of the claim period, account shall be taken of any intensification that may then reasonably be expected of the use of the works in the state in which they are at that date. For example, there may be some justification for assuming increased traffic flows if a further motorway section or link is completed in the future.

The benefit of any sound-proofing work, or payment of a grant for such work, or works to mitigate the effects of a highway, or other public works, which have been carried out, shall be taken into account in assessing the extent of the depreciation. Such benefit is also assumed if the works could have been carried out, or the grant could have been paid, in respect of sound-proofing, but have not been; though no benefit can be assumed if the authority has a discretion and has refused to undertake to do the work or pay the grant: for works of mitigation, see Chapter 24.

The interest in the land that is the subject of a claim is valued at the beginning of the claim period by reference to its nature and the condition of the land at the date of the notice of claim. But no account can be taken of any value attributable to any building work if the resulting building, or an improved or extended building, is first occupied after the 'relevant date'; the same is true of any value attributable to any change of use of the land after that date.

Rules (2) to (4) of the rules set out in section 5 of the Land Compensation Act 1961 apply to the assessment of values: see Chapter 12. But no account is taken of any mortgage or contract of sale to which the interest is subject, or if a contract is made after the 'relevant date', of a contract to grant a tenancy.

It is the depreciation in the value of the interest by the 'physical factors' that must be assessed. The proximity of the public works, their unsightliness or effect on a view may cause further depreciation in value, but this cannot be claimed. The valuation exercise is frequently expressed as an exercise of finding the 'switched-off' value – that is the value of the affected property, with the works in place, but the physical factors 'switched-off'. The second part of the valuation is to find the 'switched-on' value; the difference between these two values represents the diminution in value attributable to the relevant physical factors. In *Barb* v *Secretary of State for Transport* [1978] LT, the problems of determining depreciation by noise were considered, and expert evidence by noise specialists was given to the Tribunal.

The Tribunal accepted the evidence of an acoustic expert in *Marchant* v *Secretary of State for Transport* [1979] LT and awarded £1,000 compensation in respect of a bungalow worth about £18,000 before the M20 motorway was opened and caused noise just over 600 yds away. However, in *King* v *Dorset County Council* [1997] the Lands Tribunal considered that the evidence of the claimants was a more useful guide to whether there was an increase in noise to that of the noise experts.

In *Shepherd* v *Lancashire County Council* [1977] LT the claimants showed that their bungalow had been depreciated by £5,000 due to the opening and use of a controlled refuse tip on 94 acres of land opposite their property, but they had not proved to the Tribunal that there was measurable depreciation due to the 'physical factors'. The proximity of the tip may have caused depreciation; it is the 'physical factors' and their effect on value which is all that must be considered.

The approach taken in most of the decided cases is to establish a 'no-scheme world' value of the affected property, and then make a judgment as to the proper percentage depreciation that can be attributed to the physical factors. The second step must be more a matter of judgment and opinion than the step which can be based on established valuation methods: see *Maile* v *West Sussex County Council* [1985]. It is irrelevant that the claimant may have purchased the property shortly before the first claim day at a depreciated price: see *Fallows* v *Gateshead MBC* [1993].

6. *Assessment of compensation (assumptions as to planning permission): section 5*

Although the market values must be assessed in accordance with the rules of the 1961 Act, only a depreciation in the existing use value of property is to be compensated; the effect on development value is not the subject of compensation.

Summary of cases

Accordingly it can only be assumed that planning permission would be granted for development of any class specified in the Third Schedule to the Town and Country Planning Act 1990: see p202. It cannot be assumed that planning permission would be granted for any other development; and if planning permission has been granted in respect of any other development, it shall be assumed that it has not been granted in so far as it relates to development that has not been carried out.

Any development in the Third Schedule shall be ignored if a discontinuance order has been made in respect of any development in the Third Schedule and compensation has been paid.

If this right to compensation is in lieu of the common law action for nuisance, by restricting compensation to the depreciation in the existing use value of the land, it means, in certain circumstances a more limited amount of compensation than would be the case if such an action for nuisance were permitted.

7. *Set-off: section 6*

In *Eagle* v *Charing Cross Rly Co* [1867], the claimant obtained compensation under the *McCarthy* rules for injurious affection to land, notwithstanding that other land of his increased in value as a result of the works. The 1973 Act clearly provides that any compensation payable shall be reduced by betterment.

The compensation payable under a claim is reduced by the increase in value of the claimant's land in respect of which the claim is made, and the increase in value of other land, if any,

	Distance from Public Works	% of 'before' or 'switched-off' value and sum awarded as competition
Barb v Secretary of State for Transport [1978]	730m (highway)	7.5%
Rigby v Secretary of State for Transport [1979]	620m (highway)	7.5%
Marchant v Secretary of State for Transport [1979]	582m (highway)	5%
Arkell v Department of Transport [1983]	Viaduct 74m Slip road 158m Inter-change 186m (highway)	10.4%
Maile v West Sussex CC [1985]	14m (highway)	5.7%
Blower v Suffolk CC [1994]	600m and 1,100m (artificial lighting)	1.8% £10,000
Durnford v Avon CC [1994]	24.5m to 136m (second carriageway)	£1,575 to £8,800
Wakeley v London Fire and Civil Defence Authority [1996]	From about 26m (fire station)	6.25% £7,500 to £16,500
King v Dorset CC [1997]	12.5m to 17.6m (altered highway)	22% to 23% £44,280 to £46,920
Whitehead v Leeds/Bradford International Airport Ltd [1998]	130m to 880m (airport runway extension)	11% £2,800
Clarke v Highways Agency [2000]	56m to 84m (new bridge)	1% £600
Nesbitt v National Assembly for Wales [2002]	120m (new bridge)	18.38%

contiguous or adjacent to the land subject to the claim and in which the claimant is entitled in the same capacity on the 'relevant date'. In each case, the increase in value is only deducted if attributable to the public works, their use or prospective use.

In order to determine if there is such betterment, the land which is subject to a claim for compensation must first be valued in the normal way and without the limitations and requirements mentioned in sections 4 and 5 of the Act: see 5 and 6 above. Any betterment to possible development value may therefore be identified and taken into account in the set-off (though, as has been described, worsenment to development value is not compensated).

Where an increase in value of other adjoining land has been taken into account and set off against the compensation payable for the land which is subject to a claim under this Act, that increase in value is not to be left out of account by virtue of section 6 or taken into account by virtue of section 7 of the Land Compensation Act 1961. This means that if there is a subsequent acquisition of the other adjoining land of the claimant, the land that increased in value, it will be the increased value that must be paid and no reduction shall be made because the increased value is due to a scheme of development mentioned in the First Schedule to the 1961 Act. This is fair, as that increased value has already been deducted from the initial claim under the 1973 Act and to allow the betterment provision of the 1961 Act without restriction would otherwise permit the betterment to be deducted twice.

8. *Other restrictions on compensation: section 8*

The first of these restrictions is that if compensation has been paid or is payable under this Act, no subsequent claim for compensation can be made in relation to the same works and the same land or any part thereof; though in respect of a dwellinghouse, this does not prevent a claim in respect of the freehold and a claim in respect of a tenancy.

Second, if part of a person's land is acquired for the purposes of any public works and that person is entitled to compensation in respect of any retained land under section 7 of the Compulsory Purchase Act 1965 (or section 63 of the Lands Clauses Act 1845) for injurious affection and severance, then that person shall not be entitled to any compensation under this Act in relation to a claim made after the date of service of the notice to treat. A notice to treat will usually precede any claim under this Act as a claim is not made until the works have been built and in use for 12 months. In any event, the injurious affection compensation under the 1965 Act is more favourable to a person who is eligible: see Chapter 15.

9. Compensation where existing public works are subject to alterations or a change of use: section 9

This section widens the scope of a claim for compensation under Part I of the 1973 Act. Certain alterations or changes of use of existing public works can be taken into account if they cause depreciation of value due to the physical factors and the depreciation would not have been caused but for the alterations or change of use. The circumstances in which a claim can be made are:

(a) *Highways*
   Where the carriageway of a highway has been altered after the highway has been open to public traffic
   In this connection a carriageway is only altered if, and only if, the location, width or level of the carriageway is altered (otherwise than by resurfacing); or an additional carriageway is provided for the highway beside above or below an existing one. The removal and replacement of the road surface is not an alteration: see *King* v *Dorset County Council* [1997]. The increased use of a highway as a result of a new traffic management scheme would clearly not be included unless the alteration work was also carried out.
   For the purposes of determining the extent of the public works and in identifying the source of the 'physical factors', one considers the full length of the carriageway which has been altered; and if an additional carriageway has been provided, one may take into account the use of both the existing and the additional carriageway as there may be an increased traffic flow over the existing carriageway due to the new additional carriageway.

(b) *Other public works*
   Where any public works other than a highway have been reconstructed, extended or otherwise altered after they have been first used
   Where work has been carried out at an aerodrome, a claim can only be made in respect of physical factors caused by

aircraft if the work was runway or apron alterations. Such major work being defined as the construction of a new runway, the major realignment of an existing runway or the extension or strengthening of an existing runway, or a substantial addition to, or alteration of, a taxiway or apron, being an addition or alteration whose purpose or main purpose is the provision of facilities for a greater number of aircraft. It will be a question of fact whether a series of alterations are one scheme for the purpose of a claim: *Davies v Mid-Glamorgan County Council* [1979] LT.

It will be remembered that in connection with aerodromes, the noise and other physical factors caused by the aircraft using that aerodrome, whether that aircraft is inside or outside the aerodrome boundaries, may be taken into account. If relatively minor alterations are carried out to permit a nosier type of aircraft to use an aerodrome, or to allow a greater number of night flights, there would be no claim under this section. However it is for the minister to certify whether works have been carried within the meaning of section 9. In *R v Secretary of State for the Environment, Transport and Regions, ex parte Plymouth City Airport* [2001], the minister was entitled to have certified that substantial apron works had been carried out.

(c) *Change of use*
Where there has been a change of use in respect of any public works other than a highway or aerodrome

The section specifically excludes the intensification of an existing use as constituting change of use. In any event, if a change of use is to take place there will usually also be some new public works.

10. *Valuation and legal expenses: section 3(5)*

If compensation is payable, the responsible authority shall also pay any reasonable valuation or legal expenses incurred by the claimant for the purposes of the preparation and prosecution of the claim. This does not affect the power of the Lands Tribunal to award, as it thinks fit, any costs or expenses of proceedings before the Tribunal. The first few reported cases of disputed claims under this Act suggest that the evidence of acoustic experts may be very significant in substantiating a claim. While the Tribunal may award such an expert's fees as part of the costs against the authority, if the dispute is not referred to the Tribunal, the duty under this section to pay valuation and legal expenses would not seem to include the expenses of experts other than valuers.

11. *Interest on compensation*

Compensation payable under Part I of this Act carries interest at the same rate prescribed from time to time for interest on compensation for land compulsorily acquired. The interest runs from the date of service of the notice of claim; or, in the exceptional case where a notice of claim can be served before the first claim day, from that day.

12. *Unsuccessful claim (action for nuisance): section 17*

If a responsible authority has resisted a claim under this Part of this Act by contending that no statute confers immunity, whether expressly or by implication, from actions for nuisance in respect of the use to which the public works are put, it cannot then, if an action for nuisance is brought, rely on any immunity in a statute as a defence to the claim.

It will be recalled that, with the exception of highways, immunity to a nuisance action must exist before a claim under the Act can be made. This section prevents an authority from first denying there is immunity, and then seeking to rely on immunity if an action is brought.

13. *Limitation period*

Section 19(2A) of the 1973 Act provides that a person's right of action to recover compensation under Part I of the Act is deemed to have accrued on the first claim day. Under section 9 of the Limitation Act 1980, the period of limitation is six years from this date. Unless both a claim and a reference to the Lands Tribunal is made within this six-year period, a claim will be statute-barred: see the decision of the Lands Tribunal in *Bateman* v *Lancashire County Council* [1999].

23.5 Compensation for street lights

Section 97(3) of the Highways Act 1980 provides that where a person has suffered damage by reason of the execution of works consisting of the pet lights, the highway authority shall pay compensation. Damage would include depreciation in value of affected property.

Chapter 24

Mitigation of Injurious Effect of Public Works

Introduction
Sound-proofing of buildings affected by public works
Sound-proofing of buildings affected by the use of aerodromes
Acquisition of land
Execution of works
Expenses of persons moving temporarily during construction
    works

24.1 Introduction

Certain works of a public nature can cause great inconvenience and discomfort to those living nearby: aerodromes and motorways are obvious examples. The deleterious nature of such works may depreciate the value of any affected land and, to the extent that it does, compensation for such injurious affection may be payable. There are serious objections to the principle of compensation, as well as to its adequacy. Paying compensation will mitigate any land value depreciation but it will not remove the source of the inconvenience or discomfort; compensation is only normally available to those with a substantial proprietary interest in the land – tenants or employees who live or work in affected premises do not share in that compensation; and, where the land affected is not held with any land compulsorily acquired from a claimant, the full depreciation in the value of his land is not necessarily payable as compensation: see previous chapter.

This chapter is concerned with certain powers and duties contained in Part II of the Land Compensation Act 1973 and the Highways Act 1980 to mitigate the injurious effect of public works by sound-proofing, acquiring land, executing works and paying the expenses of persons moving temporarily during construction works. In respect of aerodromes, schemes for sound-proofing are made under the Civil Aviation Act 1982.

393

24.2 Sound-proofing of buildings affected by public works: section 20

1. *Duty or power*

The Land Compensation Act 1973 enables the Secretary of State to make regulations imposing a duty or conferring a power on responsible authorities to insulate buildings against noise caused or expected to be caused by the construction or use of public works or to make grants in respect of the cost of such insulation.

The distinction between a duty and a power is important. If an authority is under a duty to carry out noise insulation or to pay a grant, it is obliged to do that work or pay the grant; if it has a power, it has a discretion as to whether it will carry out the work and make grants. Thus a person will be entitled to noise insulation if there exists a duty, but cannot demand, as of right, noise insulation if the authority is only empowered to carry out the work or make grants. The present regulations impose certain duties and confer certain powers.

The responsible authority is, in relation to a highway, the appropriate highway authority and, in relation to other public works, the person managing those works.

The regulations so far made under this Act only provide for noise insulation to buildings affected by noise from highways; they are now described.

2. *The Noise Insulation Regulations 1975 (SI 1975 No 1763)*

Regulation 3 imposes a duty on highway authorities to carry out or make a grant in respect of the cost of carrying out insulation work in or to an eligible building when the use of a highway causes or is expected to cause noise which exceeds a specified level.

This regulation applies to a highway or additional carriageway first open to traffic after October 16 1972. The specified level means a noise level of L 10 (18-hour) of 68dB(A). The duty arises when the relevant noise level exceeds the prevailing noise level by at least 1dB(A) and is not less than the specified level, and noise caused or expected to be caused by traffic using or expected to use the new highway makes an effective contribution to the relevant noise level of at least 1dB(A), i.e. not all the new noise level need be created by the highway. The relevant noise level is expressed as a level of L 10 (18-hour), one metre in front of the most exposed of any windows and doors in a facade of a building to the new traffic levels and flows.

A noise level of 68dB(A) on an L 10 (18-hour) scale means that a sound level of 68 decibels is exceeded for 10% of each hour of the 18 hours between 06.00 to 24.00 hours on a normal week day: this is quite loud!

An eligible building is a dwelling or other building used for residential purposes and not more than 300m from the nearest point on the carriageway of the highway after its construction.

Regulation 4 empowers a highway authority to carry out or make a grant in respect of the cost of carrying out insulation work in or to an eligible building affected, or likely to be affected, by noise levels exceeding the specified level (see under Regulation 3) and caused by the use of an altered highway. An altered highway means a highway of which the location, width or level of the carriageway has been or is to be altered otherwise than by resurfacing.

If there is a duty to carry out insulation work or make a grant, the highway authority must prepare a map, or list, of every eligible building and make such a map or list available for public inspection within six months of the opening to traffic of the highway. They must then make an offer in writing to the occupier (or landlord) of every eligible building to carry out insulation work or make a grant (a grant equals the actual cost incurred in carrying out insulation work to certain specifications). The occupier may accept the offer to carry out insulation work, or to make a grant, within, normally, six months.

In any event, only 'eligible rooms' in a building can be insulated and these are living rooms or bedrooms having doors or windows affected by the noise levels.

If a person believes he should receive an offer of noise insulation and he has not because his building has not been identified on the map or the list, he may request the authority to make him an offer. The authority must then review all its noise and other calculations and reconsider whether it has a duty or not: Regulation 13.

Provision is now made for the making of regulations to permit the payment of compensation in respect of any dwelling which is not a building which is affected or likely to be affected by noise during the construction or use of public works: see section 20A of the 1973 Act.

24.3 Sound-proofing of buildings affected by the use of aerodromes

Section 79 of the Civil Aviation Act 1982 enables the Secretary of

State to make a scheme requiring the relevant manager of a designated aerodrome to make grants towards the cost of insulating dwellings against noise attributable to the use of the aerodrome.

As each scheme is local in effect, it is not intended to consider this power in further detail.

24.4 Acquisition of land

The object of the powers considered here is to enable an authority to mitigate the effects of its works by purchasing affected land and, if necessary, to carry out screening or sound-proofing works on such land. Further, the powers enable the purchase of land that is not directly required for the scheme but is so affected that compensation cannot adequately mitigate the hardship and purchase is the only just solution.

(A) In connection with highways

1. *Powers of acquisition*

Section 246 of the Highways Act 1980, as amended by the Planning and Compensation Act 1991, contains the following powers of acquisition (again, the distinction between power and duty is important as a landowner cannot compel an authority to purchase his land):

- (a) a highway authority may acquire land compulsorily or by agreement for the purpose of mitigating any adverse effect on the surroundings of a highway constructed or improved by them or proposed to be constructed or improved by them;
- (b) a highway authority may acquire by agreement land the enjoyment of which is seriously affected by the carrying out of works by the authority for the construction or improvement of a highway (the diminution in value of the property caused by the proposed highway must be considered by the highway authority: see *R* v *Secretary of State for Transport, ex parte Owen* [1995]);
- (c) a highway authority may acquire by agreement land the enjoyment of which is seriously affected by the use of a highway which the authority have constructed or improved;
- (d) where a highway authority propose to carry out works on blighted land, it may acquire by agreement land the

enjoyment of which will be seriously affected by the carrying out of works or the used the highway; and

(e) a highway authority may acquire by agreement land which will be seriously affected by proposed highway works (see (b) above and see *R* v *Parliamentary Commissioner for Administration, ex parte Balchin* [1996] where a failure of an authority to consider this power in section 246(2A) of the 1980 Act was a possible act of maladministration).

The powers in (b) and (c) may only be exercised to acquire the interest of a person whose interest, by virtue of section 149(2) of the Town and Country Planning Act 1990, is an interest qualifying for protection under the blight provisions, namely a resident owner-occupier, an owner-occupier of any other hereditament the rateable value of which does not exceed a prescribed limit, or the owner-occupier of an agricultural unit: section 246(2):

2. Time-limits: section 246(3)

The compulsory power of acquisition in (a) and the power in (b), above, must be begun before the date on which the highway, or the improved highway, is first open to public traffic.

The power to acquire land by agreement under the power of acquisition in (a) above, and the power in (c) above, must be begun before the expiration of one year after the date the highway, or the improved highway, is first open to public traffic.

The power of acquisition is 'begun', if it is compulsory, by the first publication of the newspaper advertisement of a proposed compulsory purchase order; if it is by agreement, by the date of the agreement: section 246(4).

3. Compensation

If land is acquired compulsorily under the power in 1(a) above, it is to be assumed that the land is being acquired for the construction, or the improvement, as the case may be, of the highway: section 246(6). This enables any depreciation in the value of the land, due to the highway, to be disregarded in assessing the market value. The same effect can be achieved if the purchase is by agreement. Either way, a home-loss payment can be made in appropriate circumstances.

If the land is acquired by agreement under the powers described at 1(b) or (c) above, the Act is silent as to whether such an acquisition is to be treated as if it were for the construction or improvement, as the case may be, of the highway. This would seem to mean that any depreciation in value caused by the highway could not be disregarded under section 6 and Schedule 1 to the Land Compensation Act 1961: see Chapter 14. However, to the extent that these provisions of the 1961 Act do not cover a particular situation, the *Pointe Gourde* principle probably would; the scheme including not only the land acquired for the highway construction or improvement itself, but also that acquired to mitigate injurious effect. A home-loss payment cannot be made for purchases under (b) or (c).

The purpose of section 246 of the 1980 Act is to enable land affected by highway schemes to be acquired by the highway authority rather than to leave an owner with the sole remedy of claiming compensation for land value depreciation under Part I of the Land Compensation Act 1973: see preceding chapter. Whether the authority decides to acquire, or merely to pay compensation, will depend on the circumstances caused by each scheme, such as physical factors and visual intrusion. Clearly an owner will be financially better off to have his land acquired rather than being paid compensation for depreciation due to the effect of physical factors: unfortunately he cannot insist on acquisition.

(B) In connection with public works other than highways

Section 26 of the Land Compensation Act 1973 contains similar powers to acquire land in connection with other public works. The principal difference is that there is power to acquire by agreement, but not compulsorily, land for the purpose of mitigating any adverse effect which the existence or use of any public works has or will have in the surroundings of the works; this is unlike the case in connection with highways.

The Planning and Compensation Act 1991 extended the power to acquire land where works are proposed on blighted land which will seriously affect the enjoyment of the land to be acquired: section 26(2A).

24.5 Execution of works

Section 282 of the Highways Act 1980 (in connection with highways) and section 27 of the Land Compensation Act 1973 (in connection with other public works) empower the highway, or other responsible authority, to carry out on land owned by them works for mitigating the adverse effect which the construction, improvement or alteration, existence or use of a highway or public works has or will have on the surroundings of the highway or public works.

The works of mitigation may include planting of trees, shrubs or plants of any other description, and the laying outgrassland. Authorities are also authorised to develop or redevelop any land they own for the purpose of improving the surroundings of a highway or public works.

If compensation becomes payable to any person who has made a claim under Part I of the Act, the benefit of works of mitigation under these provisions must be taken into account.

24.6 Expenses of persons moving temporarily during construction works

Section 28 of the 1973 Act provides that if the enjoyment of a dwelling adjacent to the site on which works are being carried out is affected to such an extent that continued occupation of the dwelling is not reasonably practicable, the responsible authority may pay any reasonable expenses incurred by the occupier in providing suitable alternative residential accommodation for himself and members of his household.

The works being carried out include works by a highway authority for the construction or improvement of a highway, and works of a responsible authority for the construction or alteration of any public works other than a highway.

A payment cannot be made unless the appropriate authority have first agreed to the need to seek suitable alternative accommodation. Such accommodation may be necessary for the whole or any part of the period during which works are being carried out. In any event payment can only be made in respect of any expenses additional to those the occupier would have incurred in his dwelling.

This provision has three limitations: it only grants a power to the appropriate authorities – there is no duty to pay such expenses; the authority's agreement must first be obtained before expenses are incurred; and, only dwellings adjacent to the works are included.

Chapter 25

Compensation for Decisions

Introduction
Interference to property rights: is there a right to
    compensation?
Compensation for refusal of planning permission
Compensation for revocation, modification and
    discontinuance under the Planning Acts
Compensation in connection with listed buildings
    and ancient monuments
Compensation in respect of tree preservation orders,
    control of advertisements and stop notices
Compensation for highway decisions

25.1 Introduction

Many decisions of public authorities affect the value of land. A decision to formulate plans and policies which increase the possibilities of development or the more profitable use of land may cause land value increase; other decisions, such as to revoke a planning permission or to prescribe a building line in connection with a highway, may cause land value decreases. Such a land value increase is known as betterment, it may be collected if capital gains tax becomes payable or if rateable values are increased. The described land value decrease is one form of worsenment. This chapter is concerned with, first, the legality of interfering with property rights by decisions, and second, with some statutory provisions enabling compensation to be claimed for land value decreases, or other losses, caused by decisions of public authorities.

Section 31 of the Planning and Compensation Act 1991 repealed several planning provisions for the payment of compensation. A brief description of the repealed provisions is included in this chapter for the sake of completeness.

25.2 Interference to property rights: is there a right to compensation?

In England it is acceptable that Parliament, by virtue of its supreme authority, may authorise the Crown, or indeed any corporate or incorporate person, to take land by compulsory acquisition. Alongside this accepted right is a principle restated by Viscount Simonds in *Belfast Corpn v OD Cars Ltd* [1960] HL:

> It is no doubt the law that the intention to take away property without compensation is not to be imputed to the legislature unless it is expressed in unequivocal terms.

Article 17 of the Universal Declaration of Human Rights states that everyone has the right to own property and shall not be arbitrarily deprived of his property; and the European convention on Human Rights, ratified by the United Kingdom, provides that every person is entitled to the peaceful enjoyment of his possessions and shall not be deprived of them except in the public interest and subject to the conditions provided for by law, but that the State may enforce such laws as it deems necessary to control the use of property in accordance with the general interest.

The taking of property by the acquisition of title, or by possession, is clearly within the principles just stated; and compensation is available for all such situations under enactments authorising compulsory acquisition. But is the right to develop land a property right which, if interfered with by decisions of planning or highway authorities, is to be compensated as of right in accordance with those principles? Clearly every restriction imposed by authorities deprives an owner of rights that he previously enjoyed, and if those rights are restricted to prevent some use or development harmful or dangerous to public interest, the non-payment of compensation is probably justified. However, in an American case, *Pennsylvania Coal Co v Mahon* [1922] and cited in the *Belfast* case, Holmes J said:

> The general rule at least is, that while property may be regulated to a certain extent, if regulation goes too far it will be recognised as a taking.

These words were echoed by Viscount Simonds in the *Belfast* case itself when he had to consider whether certain restrictions on rights of development imposed without compensation amounted to a taking of property without compensation and therefore invalid under the constitution of Northern Ireland: he decided it was not a taking of property, and therefore valid.

In England there is no written constitutional limit on Parliament's powers to authorise restrictions on property rights, and so any Act of Parliament imposing restrictions without compensation is perfectly valid in English law: but that is not to say it may not be contrary to the European Convention. See *Arrondelle v UK Government* [1982] for a case brought by a property owner harmed by the noise of aircraft at Gatwick Airport: the case was settled by an ex-gratia payment made by the government before the Commission had to consider whether a breach of the Treaty had occurred.

In another case, *James v UK Government* [1986], the applicants argued that the Leasehold Reform Act 1967 was a breach of the Convention for two reasons: first because the compensation basis was unfair to landlords because landlords may receive less than full market value; and second because the legislation itself is indiscriminate in its application. Both grounds were dismissed: the Court deciding that there was a margin of appreciation for Parliament in balancing the burden imposed on an individual against the wider public interest in achieving the purpose of the legislation.

A person who is affected by a law which imposes such restrictions on his property as to amount to a breach of the articles or protocols of the Convention may lodge a complaint with the European Commission of Human Rights; or raise the matter in any proceedings under the Human Rights Act 1998. This matter is more fully considered in Chapter 27 below, where both Act and the Convention rights are discussed.

One further difficulty in English law is illustrated by *Westminster Bank Ltd v Ministry of Housing and Local Government* [1970]. The bank had been refused planning permission for an extension because of a proposed road widening scheme; the bank argued that it was *ultra vires* to use planning powers because compensation was not payable for a refusal of planning permission. There was power under section 72 of the Highways Act 1959 to prescribe an improvement line to safeguard land for road widening: the frontager is entitled to compensation for injurious affection if he cannot build inside the improvement line. The bank's argument was founded on the principle that property rights should not be taken away without compensation, and that where there was a choice of statutory powers, the power providing for compensation should be used. The House of Lords rejected the bank's argument:

an authority may decide which of two powers it exercises, and choose the one that has no compensation burden to the ratepayers: a similar point arose in *Hoveringham Gravels Ltd* v *Secretary of State for the Environment* [1975].

Summary

The points discussed can now be summarised. Although Parliament may pass any laws so as to restrict property rights, and a restriction if severe enough may amount to a taking away of property rights, the courts assume that property rights are not taken away without compensation unless the legislation so provides in unequivocal terms. As the United Kingdom is a signatory to the European Convention on Human Rights, its legislation must satisfy the requirements of that convention. This matter is more fully discussed in Chapter 27 below.

25.3 Compensation for refusal of planning permission

The provisions described in this section were repealed by the Planning and Compensation Act 1991.

1. Background

If the rights to develop or use land without restriction are considered as part of the rights of a property owner, then these rights were taken away on July 1 1948 by the provisions of the Town and Country Planning Act 1947. The Act provided that planning permission was required for the development of land (this included building, mining and engineering operations, and the making of a material change of use of land or buildings) and that if planning permission was refused for any development, other than some minor classes of development called 'existing use development', no compensation was payable.

The Act also provided that if planning permission was granted for any development, other than existing use development, 100% of the development value was to be paid, as a development charge, to a body called the Central Land Board.

A landowner, in 1948, who considered he had been deprived of development value by the loss of the rights to develop, either because planning permission would be refused or, if granted, he would have had to pay the development charge, was entitled to make a claim, under Part VI of the Act, for compensation from a fund of £300 m set up for the purpose.

2. Compensation for a refusal of planning permission for 'new' development: Part V of the Town and Country Planning Act 1990

'New' development means any development other than classes of existing use development specified in the Third Schedule to the 1990 Act: see p202.

Part V of the 1990 Act provided for the payment of compensation for the refusal of planning permission or a grant subject to conditions, for the new development of land if at the time of the decision the land has an 'unexpended balance of established development value'.

The 'Part VI claims' under the 1947 Act were, in general, never paid; this was due to a change of government in 1951 and the abolition of the development charge (but not the need to obtain planning permission). The established claims are adjusted to take into account any amounts actually paid out; aggregated together if a lessee and the freehold reversioner of the same land had both made claims in 1948; apportioned if claims are made in respect of land in 1948 which is now in divided ownership; and, then increased by one-seventh in lieu of interest lost between 1948 and 1955, the date the changes were made. The resultant sum, which attaches to the land, was called the 'unexpended balance of established development value'.

Part V of the 1990 Act has now been repealed and no claims can be made after September 25 1991.

3. Compensation for a refusal of planning permission for 'existing use development'

It will be recalled that certain classes of development, called 'existing use development', were excepted from some of the provisions of the 1947 Act: the idea was that the right to carry out minor forms of development in respect of existing buildings, or existing uses of buildings and other land should not, in effect, be nationalised. Although planning permission was required for these classes of development, if it was refused in respect of some of them, or an existing planning permission was revoked or modified, compensation for the loss of development value could be obtained as of right. Also, the value of the right to carry out development of any of these classes was taken into account in the assessment of compensation for a compulsory acquisition of land. The development charge was not payable if planning permission was granted.

The compensation for the refusal of planning permission for 'existing use development' was repealed by the 1991 Act in respect of any planning applications made after November 16 1990.

4. Compensation for refusal of planning permission for development specified in a development order

This right to claim compensation for the refusal of planning permission, or its grant subject to conditions, seems at odds with the general philosophy of the 1990 Act that compensation is not payable for a planning refusal. However, section 108 provides that if planning permission has been granted by a development order, and that permission is withdrawn by the issue of a direction (such as an Article 4 direction under the General Permitted Development Order 1995), then, if a person is subsequently refused planning permission for that development or it is granted subject to conditions, he is entitled to compensation. However, the 1991 Act amended section 108 to provide power to make regulations to exclude the right to compensation. For recent claims see _Slot_ v _Guildford Borough Council_ [1993] and _Bolton_ v _North Dorset District Council_ [1997].

25.4 Compensation for revocation, modification and discontinuance under the Planning Acts

Under the Town and Country Planning Act 1990, section 97, a planning permission already granted may be revoked or modified by an order confirmed by the Secretary of State before the building or other operations to which it relates have been completed, or, if it permits a change of use, before that change has taken place.

Section 102 of the same Act enables a local planning authority to serve a discontinuance order, which must be confirmed by the Secretary of State; such an order can require the discontinuance of any use of land, or impose conditions as to its further use, or require the alteration or removal of any buildings or works.

These powers clearly interfere with rights already enjoyed by persons with interests in the land: the 1990 Act provides for compensation.

1. Compensation for the revocation or modification of a planning permission

Section 107 provides that a person who has an interest in land affected by an order for the revocation or modification of a planning permission, may claim from the local planning authority compensation for the following matters: expenditure incurred on work rendered abortive by the order and other loss or damage directly attributable to that order.

The preparation of plans and other similar preparatory matters can be included in the claim, if such work is also abortive; but any other work done before the grant of planning permission is disregarded. The claim must be made within 12 months of the date of the decision, although the time can be extended: see Town and Country Planning General Regulations 1992.

In *Pennine Raceway Ltd* v *Kirklees Metropolitan Council* [1982] the Court of Appeal decided that a person who had a licence to use land for motorcar and motor-cycle racing was 'a person interested in land' and therefore entitled to claim compensation when an Article 4 direction was issued which stopped the use of an old airfield for these purposes.

Apart from compensation for abortive work already carried out, a claimant, with an interest in the land, is entitled to compensation for the depreciation in the value of his interest by reason of the loss of development rights; but in this connection, it is assumed that planning permission would be granted for development of any class specified in the Third Schedule: see section **25.3.3** above and p405. This presents a problem if the revocation order in fact concerns any such development. In *Canterbury City Council* v *Colley* [1993] the House of Lords were concerned with a claim for compensation for the revocation of planning permission to rebuild a house which had been earlier demolished. It was held that in valuing the land what is now section 107(4) of the 1990 Act required the assumption that there was planning permission to rebuild. Accordingly, it could be the case that no compensation is payable if the assumed permission is the same as that revoked.

Compensation is not restricted to a depreciation in land value; it includes any loss or damage:

> *Hobbs (Quarries) Ltd* v *Somerset County Council* [1975] LT
> A planning permission, granted in 1947, to work limestone in a quarry was revoked. At the time, the reserves of limestone

amounted to 2m tons and it was accepted as almost certain that the claimants, but for the revocation, would have obtained a subcontract for the supply of material for the construction of the M5 motorway. Had that contract been obtained, they would have earned nearly £200,000 in profits; but without that contract they would have earned £84,000 supplying the general market.

The depreciation in the market value of the quarry due to the revocation order was agreed to have been £72,000. The Tribunal decided that the loss of the motorway contract was not too remote; that, although £72,000 was the depreciation in the market value of the quarry, the claimant could not have purchased another quarry to earn the same profits; and, as the company did not claim for the depreciation in value of the land, they could have loss of profits instead, suitably deferred.

See below for the present position in relation to minerals and mining operations.

In *Cawoods Aggregates (South Eastern) Ltd* v *Southwark London Borough Council* [1982], the Tribunal concluded that a loss is recoverable if it is not too remote. It is arguable that the costs of obtaining the planning permission may be recoverable.

There is now provision for the payment of interest from the date of the revocation order, although, if a reference is made to the Lands Tribunal, that body has discretion to award interest from the date of its award: see also *Knibb* v *National Coal Board* [1986]. In *Loromah Ltd* v *Haringey London Borough Council* [1978] LT, it was held that the payment of Development Land Tax on the compensation sum was not attributable directly to the revocation; accordingly, any such liability could not be added.

In assessing any part of the compensation for depreciation in land values, the rules in section 5 of the 1961 Act apply: see Chapter 12.

Where compensation in excess of £20 is paid, it is registrable as a local land charge and repayable if development is subsequently allowed.

2. Compensation in respect of a discontinuance order: section 115

A claim for compensation can be made if any person has suffered damage, in consequence of a discontinuance order, by a depreciation of the value of his interest in the land; he is also entitled to be compensated for damage attributable to 'being disturbed in his enjoyment of the land'.

Additionally, the costs of carrying out any work to comply with the order which have been reasonably incurred for that purpose can also be recovered. In *K & B Metals Ltd* v *Birmingham City Council* [1977], it was held that the acquisition of a scrap bailer between the date of the making of an order and its confirmation could be the subject of a claim.

The rules in section 5 of the 1961 Act will apply to the assessment of compensation for a depreciation in the value of the land.

3. Compensation and mining operations

The Town and Country Planning (Minerals) Act 1981 introduced amendments to the control of mining operations. There are now amended provisions dealing with the revocation or modification of a planning permission for mining and in the use of discontinuance orders. There are also prohibition orders to prohibit the resumption of winning and working minerals, and suspension orders for temporary suspension: see now sections 102 and 116 and Schedules 5, 9 and 11 to the Town and Country Planning Act 1990.

In circumstances where the 'minerals compensation modifications' apply, there is a reduced basis of compensation: see Town and Country Planning (Compensation for Restrictions on Mineral Working and Mineral Waste Depositing) Regulations 1997.

4. Measure of compensation

Section 117 of the 1990 Act applies the rules set out in section 5 of the Land Compensation Act 1961 to the assessment of compensation in relation to the depreciation in the value of an interest in land. In *Loromah Estates Ltd* v *Haringey London Borough Council* [1978], the Tribunal decided that a principle analogous to the *Pointe Gourde* principle must be implied so that the market value of land is determined ignoring the effect of the revocation or other order.

25.5 Compensation in connection with listed buildings and ancient monuments

A building of special architectural or historic interest may be listed under section 1 of the Planning (Listed Buildings and Conservation

Areas) Act 1990. It then becomes an offence if any works are carried out for the demolition of a listed building or for its alteration or extension in any manner which would affect its character as such a building, without obtaining a listed building consent. Compensation is not payable upon the listing of a building. In respect of applications made for listed building consent made before November 16 1990, compensation may be payable if listed building consent is refused. There is no compensation for applications made after this date. Compensation is payable for the revocation of listed buildings consent and in connection with building preservation notices. There are similar provisions in the Ancient Monuments and Archaeological Areas Act 1979 in respect of scheduled monuments: these are considered below.

1. *Compensation for the refusal of listed building consent*

In respect of an application made before November 16 1990, compensation was payable if listed building consent is refused by the Secretary of State, or granted subject to conditions, for the alteration or extension of a listed building: see section 27 of the Planning (Listed Buildings and Conservation Areas) Act 1990. The work proposed must not constitute development within the meaning of the 1990 Act, or, if it does, the development is permitted by a development order; see *Burroughs Day* v *Bristol City Council* [1996]. There is no compensation for a refusal of consent to demolish a listed building: see *Shimizu* v *Westminster City Council* [1996].

Compensation shall equal the difference between the value of the claimant's interest had the consent been granted, and its value subject to the decision of the Secretary of State (including any alternative consent he may have granted or undertaken to grant).

Compensation is not payable for a refusal of listed building consent if an application is made after November 16 1990: see section 31 of the Planning and Compensation Act 1991.

2. *Compensation for the revocation or modification of a listed building consent*

Compensation for the revocation or modification of a listed building consent is payable in the same circumstances as the revocation of a planning permission: see section **25.4.1** above and also section 28 of the Planning (Listed Buildings and Conservation Areas) Act 1990.

3. *Compensation in respect of a building preservation notice*

Under section 3 of the Planning (Listed Buildings and Conservation Areas) Act 1990, a local planning authority may serve a 'building preservation notice' on the owner and occupier of a building. It will do so where it is intended to seek the listing of the building and the building requires temporary protection because it is in danger of demolition or alteration.

If the Secretary of State decides not to list the building, the building preservation notice, and the temporary protection it afforded, lapses. Any person with an interest in the building at the time of the notice may then claim compensation in respect of any loss or damage directly attributable to the effect of the notice: see section 29. The section permits the costs involved in terminating a contract to be claimed where the proposed work, say demolition, is prevented by the notice. However, such expenses cannot be claimed if the building is eventually listed. This can produce severe hardship: in *Amalgamated Investment & Property Co Ltd* v *John Walker & Sons Ltd* [1976] CA, a building sold for development was listed one day after the plaintiff signed a contract to purchase for nearly £1.75m. The effect of listing was to reduce the value of the building to £200,000. *Amalgamated* were bound by their contract and could not seek a reduction in price: the planning legislation provided no right to claim, as compensation, their loss of £1.33m.

4. *Compensation in respect of ancient monuments*

Under the Ancient Monuments and Archaeological Areas Act 1979, the Secretary of State may compile a schedule of monuments; it then becomes an offence to carry out certain works to a 'scheduled monument' without consent. A scheduled monument may include a building, structure or work, or a site comprising the remains of such things. The proscribed work includes work of demolition, destruction, removal, repair, alteration or addition, or flooding or tipping operations: section 1.

If scheduled monument consent is refused, or granted subject to conditions, compensation is payable to any person who has an interest in the monument and who 'incurs expenditure or otherwise sustains any loss or damage in consequence': section 2.

Compensation is only payable for a refusal of consent for the following works:

(a) works reasonably necessary for development for which planning permission was granted before the monument was scheduled;

(b) works which do not constitute development (or, for which permission is granted by a development order), other than works for the demolition or destruction of the monument;

(c) works which are reasonably necessary for the continuation of any use of the monument for any purpose for which it was in use immediately before the application for scheduled monument consent: section 7.

However, in relation to (a) above, the compensation is limited to expenditure incurred or other loss or damage sustained which is due to the fact that development for which planning permission has been granted cannot be carried out because of the scheduling of the monument: section 7(3). Compensation is not available where planning permission is granted after a monument has been scheduled and scheduled monument consent is refused.

In relation to (b) above there is a potential problem where agricultural development enjoys permitted development rights, but which are subject to the prior notification procedure in the General Permitted Development Order 1995. It could be argued that the development would never be permitted and therefore no compensation is payable. That seems unjust if the only reason for refusing permission for the development is the ancient monument as it defeats the purpose of the compensation provisions.

The rules in section 5 of the 1961 Act apply for the purpose of assessing compensation in respect of any loss or damage consisting of depreciation of the value of an interest in land: section 27.

Compensation is to be assessed as at the date of refusal: see *Currie's Exors* v *Secretary of State for Scotland* [1993].

25.6 Compensation in respect of tree preservation orders, control of advertisements and stop notices

1. Tree preservation orders: section 203–204 of the 1990 Act

Section 198 of the 1990 Act empowers a local planning authority to make a tree preservation order for the preservation of specified trees, groups of trees or woodlands. The order may prohibit the cutting down, topping, lopping of trees without the authority's consent; it may also provide for replanting when any part of a woodland is felled in the course of permitted forestry operations.

If consent is refused for any matter prohibited by a tree preservation order, then compensation in respect of loss or damage as a result of that refusal is payable if the order itself permits of this: see section 203 of the 1990 Act. The standard form of order in the Town and Country Planning (Trees) Regulations 1999 restricts compensation to claims made within 12 months and which exceed £500. The order contains a number of other restrictions on the right to compensation.

When payable, compensation may equal the depreciation in the value of the trees: *Cardigan Timber Co* v *Cardiganshire County Council* [1957] LT. It would seem that the capital value of the profits that could have been made from the land by growing Christmas trees had felling taken place cannot be recovered: *Bollans* v *Surrey County Council* [1968] LT: see also *Fletcher* v *Chelmsford Borough Council* [1991] (costs of expert awarded). But the Court of Appeal approved a claim based on the difference in the value of land subject to an order, and its value as agricultural land in *Bell* v *Canterbury City Council* [1988]. However, the Town and Country Planning (Tree) Regulations 1999 standard tree preservation order excludes compensation for loss of development value.

Where consent was initially refused, and later granted, to prune a tree, compensation awarded to a developer included increased borrowing costs attributable to the delay: see *Factorset Ltd* v *Selby District Council* [1995]. And where a property was damaged by the tree roots of a tree which could not be felled, the owner was entitled to compensation for remedying that damage: see *Buckle* v *Holderness Borough Council* [1996]. In *Mooney* v *West Lindsey District Council* [2000] compensation of £5,739 was awarded for stress, inconvenience and loss of earnings in seeking consent to fell two trees which was only granted on appeal.

A licence is required for the felling of timber, with some exceptions, under the Forestry Act 1967: there is provision in that Act for compensation if such a licence is refused.

In respect of a direction made under the provisions of a tree preservation order that replanting should take place, compensation for the loss or damage incurred complying with the direction is payable. However, such compensation is only payable where the Forestry Commission consider the replanting would not be in the interests of commercial forestry and the local planning authority require such replanting in the interest of amenity.

2. *Restriction on advertisements*

The Town and Country Planning (Control of Advertisement) Regulations 1992 are made under section 220 of the 1990 Act. These regulations provide for restricting and regulating the display of advertisements in the interests of amenity or public safety.

No compensation is payable for a refusal of consent to display an advertisement: see above at **25.3.2**(c). But section 223 of the 1990 Act does provide for compensation to any person who carries out work to comply with the regulations in the following circumstances: he is entitled to any expenses reasonably incurred in complying with an order for removing an advertisement displayed on August 1 1948; or for discontinuing the use of a site used for advertisement displayed on that date. A claimant must submit his claim to the local planning authority within six months of completing the necessary work.

3. *Stop notices*

Section 184 of the 1990 Act empowers a local planning authority, who have issued an enforcement notice requiring a breach of planning control to be remedied, to serve a further notice called a 'stop notice'. The stop notice may prevent the carrying out of the activity alleged to constitute the planning breach before the expiration of the period of compliance allowed in the enforcement notice.

If the enforcement notice takes effect, there is no compensation for loss or expense incurred in complying with such a notice, or a stop notice that may have been served with it. However, section 186 of the 1990 Act does provide compensation for loss or damage directly attributable to a stop notice in the following cases: the enforcement notice is quashed on appeal; the enforcement notice is varied so that the matter covered by the stop notice is no longer part of the enforcement notice; and, either the enforcement notice or the stop notice is withdrawn. In such cases, any sum payable in respect of a breach of contract made necessary by compliance with a stop notice is considered to be loss or damage attributable to the prohibition in a stop notice.

A claim must be made within 12 months of the decision of the Secretary of State and an informal letter may constitute such a claim: *Texas Home Care Ltd* v *Lewes District Council* [1986]. In *J Sample (Warkworth) Ltd* v *Alnwick District Council* [1984] LT, a stop notice and enforcement notice were served on the same day. The enforcement notice was quashed on appeal 22 months later without any order as to costs. The parties disputed the meaning of *directly attributable* in connection with the compensation claim, but the Tribunal did not accept that the words were qualified by the concept of reasonable foreseeability. Building delays were directly attributable to the stop notice and the Tribunal awarded as compensation, loss of interest on purchase money and extra labour costs. The costs of the enforcement notice appeal were disallowed.

Before serving a stop notice, and therefore incurring the unknown liability for compensation, the local planning authority ought to be reasonably certain a breach of planning control has taken place. It was held by the Court of Appeal in *Malvern Hills District Council* v *Secretary of State* [1982] that the marking out of an estate road with pegs was a 'specified operation' which kept alive a planning permission under what is now section 56 of the 1990 Act. The cost of delay caused by the stop notice was considered by the Lands Tribunal in *Robert Barnes & Co Ltd* v *Malvern Hills District Council* [1985]; interest on unpaid compensation between the date the stop notice ceases to have effect and the date of the tribunal's award could not be awarded but can now.

Where a loss arises substantially due to the impecuniosity of the claimant, it may be rejected under the *Liesbosch* principle as being too remote: see *Graysmark* v *South Hams District Council* [1989].

Compensation is excluded in two circumstances. First, where loss arises due to a stop notice which prohibited anything which was a breach of planning control during the period the notice was in force: see section 186(5)(a) of the 1990 Act. Second, for losses which could have been excluded had the claimant provided information properly requested by the local planning authority: see section 186(5)(b) of the 1990 Act.

25.7 Compensation for highway decisions

Highway authorities and, to a lesser extent, planning authorities, have certain powers in the Highways Act 1980 and the Town and Country Planning Act 1990, respectively, to make decisions as to the improvement of public highways, access on to them, and as to their status and use.

Such decisions can depreciate the value of adjoining land or otherwise cause loss and expense. Some of the principal rights to claim compensation are set out below. Somewhat confusingly, there are also a number of powers under the Road Traffic Acts to make traffic orders or schemes. These schemes can regulate parking, provide for one-way systems, or prohibit traffic or certain classes of traffic from specified streets. The consequence of these schemes can also depreciate the value of adjoining land, not least business premises, but there is usually no direct right to compensation under the Road Traffic Acts. There are two possibilities in these situations. If some improvement work has been done, a claim under Part I of the Land Compensation Act 1973 may be possible (see Chapter 23), and it is also possible to seek a reduction in rateable value.

1. Stopping up private rights of access

Under sections 124–125 of the Highways Act 1980, a highway authority may stop up any private means of access to premises adjoining or adjacent to the route of a special road, such as a motorway, or stop up a private means of access from any highway to any premises if it is likely to cause danger or interference with traffic. Any person who suffers damage by the depreciation of his interest in the land or by being disturbed in his enjoyment of the premises is entitled to claim compensation: section 126. For a case where a private right of way was interfered with and compensation determined, under section 127 of the Town and Country Planning Act 1971, see *Ward v Wychavon District Council* [1986].

2. Making of new footpaths and bridleways

A new public footpath or bridleway may be created by a 'public path creation order' by a highway authority over any land. Such an order is an exercise of compulsory powers and any person whose interest in the land is depreciated in value or who suffers damage by being disturbed may claim compensation under section 28 of the 1980 Act. In this connection, interest in land includes an interest or licence in the land in respect of sporting rights.

3. Stopping up and diversion of highways

There are powers in the 1980 Act to stop up and divert all classes of public highways (sections 116–120); similar powers are found in the Town and Country Planning Act 1990 in relation to the development of land and in sections 294–295 of the Housing Act 1985.

Only if a public footpath or bridleway is stopped up or diverted by a 'public path extinguishment order' or a 'public path diversion order', made under the 1980 Act, is compensation payable. The right to compensation is that set out in section 28: see 2 above. It may be payable in respect of land once served by a footpath or bridleway, as well as land affected by the diversion.

If an access or other rights to use a highway are interfered with as a result of the execution of works, a landowner may be able to claim compensation for injurious affection under the *McCarthy* rules as in *Flanagan* v *Stoke-on-Trent City Council* [1982]: see Chapter 23 above. But there is no claim if injurious affection is caused by a stopping up order:

> *Jolliffe* v *Exeter Corporation* [1967] CA
> The claimant had a garage and filling station on a busy road. The corporation built a ring road and the road in which the claimant's garage stood was stopped up to facilitate this. The effect of the stopping up was to leave the garage in a cul-de-sac and the plaintiff sustained considerable loss of business. It was held that as the cause of the injurious affection suffered by the claimant was the stopping up order (under the Town and Country Planning Act 1947) and not the works executed for the ring road, he had no claim for compensation for injurious affection under, what is now, section 10 of the Compulsory Purchase Act 1965.

This case was distinguished in *Garrett* v *Department of Environment for N Ireland* [1985].

4. *Materials for repair of publicly maintained highways*

Section 45 of the 1980 Act authorises a highway authority to take gravel, sand, stone and other materials from any waste or common land, or to take stones from any other land for the purpose of repairing a public highway. There are considerable limitations on the exercise of this power and a magistrates' court order is required in certain cases. Compensation is payable to owners for any damage done and, where materials are taken under a magistrates' order, for the value of those materials.

5. *Safety provisions*

A highway authority may provide facilities in a highway for the safety of pedestrians, for example raised paving, walls, pillars, rails and even a footbridge over a highway. Compensation is payable under section 66 and 70 of the 1980 Act to any person who sustains damage by reason of such works: see *Ching Garage Ltd* v *Chingford Corporation* [1961] CA: raised paving obstructed means of access to a highway.

6. Improvement lines and building lines

A highway authority has power to prescribe an improvement line under section 73 of the 1980 Act where a street is narrow or inconvenient and needs widening; and has power to prescribe a building line under section 74 of the same Act as a frontage line for building. In each case no new building or excavation may be carried out nearer to the centre of the highway than the improvement line or building line, as the case may be, without the consent of the highway authority.

Any person whose interest in land is injuriously affected by the prescribing of these lines is entitled to compensation. Generally compensation must be claimed within six months of the date the appropriate line was prescribed. If a planning authority refuses planning permission for development because of a proposal to widen a road and chooses not to prevent such development by prescribing an improvement or building line because the latter method involves the payment of compensation, it is perfectly lawful for it to do so: see *Westminster Bank Ltd* v *Minister of Housing and Local Government* [1971] HL where planning permission was refused for extension of bank premises to safeguard proposed improvement of highway, compensation was not payable for the refusal, though it would have been had an improvement line been prescribed.

However plans by a highway authority to improve a junction did not amount to the prescribing of an improvement line in *Citypark Properties Ltd* v *Bolton Metropolitan Borough Council* [2000], and therefore a claim for compensation was not triggered.

7. Improvements to highways

A number of other powers in the 1980 Act enable highway authorities to alter the level of a highway, require the removal of obstructions to corners, or projections from buildings, and the rounding off of angles at corners. Compensation is generally payable to persons who incur expenditure or otherwise suffer damage.

In *Bigg* v *London Corporation* [1873], it was held that if a road level is altered and this directs traffic away, resulting in less business for the claimant, he could not claim compensation for the injury to his trade, but only for direct physical damage to his property. This situation would now be partly covered by a claim under Part I of the Land Compensation Act 1973 for the effect of 'physical factors'. Alternatively, a claim under section 10 of the Compulsory Purchase Act 1965 may be possible: see *Flanagan* v *Stoke-on-Trent City Council* [1982]. Compensation is also payable where lighting is provided for a public highway: see section 97 of the 1980 Act.

8. Pedestrianisation

The local planning authority has power under section 249 of the Town and Country Planning Act 1990 to reduce the status of a public highway from a road or street for vehicles to an area for pedestrians, cyclists or horse riders – the pedestrianisation of central shopping streets being the most usual example. Although vehicular use can thereby be stopped, it is possible to except certain vehicular use, for example deliveries between stated hours.

Any person, having an interest in land with lawful access to the affected street, may claim compensation for any depreciation in the value of his interest and any other loss or damage attributable to the order giving effect to the decision of the authority. The claim must be made within six months of the decision giving rise to the order.

9. Determination of compensation disputes

The assessment of compensation for depreciation in the value of any interest in land is made in accordance with rules (2) to (4) of section 5 of the Land Compensation Act 1961. Disputes, with some exceptions, are referred to the Lands Tribunal: section 307, Highways Act 1980. The Tribunal is entitled to have regard to the value of any new access provided to replace any access stopped up; and, in respect of a claim for injurious affection caused by the prescribing of an improvement line, it shall take into account any benefit accruing to the claimant due to the improvement of the street concerned; similarly, any benefit due to any improvement to a highway in relation to which a building line has been prescribed is to be taken into account.

The following are the principal exceptions to the rule that compensation disputes are referred to the Lands Tribunal: obtaining materials for a highway; safety provisions for pedestrians; alteration of level of highway and removal of obstructions at corners; and, removal of projections from buildings. In these cases any dispute as to compensation may be referred, by agreement, to arbitration, or to the county court: section 308, Highways Act 1980.

Chapter 26

Statutory Utilities: Compensation for Wayleaves and Damages

Introduction
Oil exploration and exploitation
Coal mining subsidence
Land drainage work
Sewers and water pipes
Gas pipelines
Telecommunications
Electricity
Pipe-lines Act 1962

26.1 Introduction

A number of statutes provide for the right of specified authorities or industries to acquire rights over private land. The obvious example is the right of a water industry company to lay a sewer or water pipe. Such rights are normally called wayleaves; they are not usually technically easements because there is no dominant tenement. However, the effect of the enabling statute is that the authorised authority or industry is entitled to carry out works, and leave pipes, lines or cables, as the case may be, in private land. The right to leave these features is therefore a statutory right or wayleave. Many statutes authorise entry onto land for various purposes and require the appropriate authority or industry to compensate for any damage which has been caused. Coal mining subsidence is an example.

This chapter briefly identifies some of these rights to compensation, and outlines the appropriate procedures.

What is the nature of the interest of a statutory utility in private land?

Under earlier legislation sewers laid in private land vested in the statutory utility under the provisions of the appropriate statute. It was held that such vesting did not give to the statutory undertaker ownership in the appropriate pipe, but only such ownership and such rights as were necessary for the purpose of carrying out the duties of the statutory undertaker. In relation to sewers this was explained in *Bradford* v *The Mayor of Eastbourne* [1896] and in relation to gas and water pipes, the matter was explained in *Newcastle under Lyme Corporation* v *Wolstanton Ltd* [1947].

A possibly inconsistent position was taken in two cases, *Taylor* v *Oldham Corporation* [1876] and *Thurrock, Grays & Tilbury Joint Sewerage Board* v *Thames Land Co Ltd* [1925], where it was decided that statutory sewerage undertakers acquired an interest in land where a sewer was laid under statutory powers. In the *Thurrock* case, this was regarded as an acquisition for the purposes of what is now the Land Compensation Act 1961. These apparently inconsistent legal decisions can be reconciled as follows. A statutory undertaker may acquire the equivalent of a freehold; it is not an actual legal or equitable interest in the land (see the *Newcastle under Lyme Corporation* case), but it has otherwise all the characteristics of a freehold interest save that it comes to an end as soon as the statutory undertaker ceases to require the pipe for its statutory purposes. The pipe, being a fixture, reverts to the landowner. The statutory undertaker will thereafter have no legal or statutory rights in the land.

The position is quite different where a statutory undertaker exercises powers of compulsory purchase and acquires under a compulsory purchase order a freehold interest or a perpetual right equivalent to an easement.

26.2 Oil exploration and exploitation

The Petroleum (Production) Act 1934 nationalised petroleum found under land without the payment of compensation. Companies seeking sites for exploration or exploitation do not usually use compulsory powers and prefer to negotiate terms.

However, the Mines (Working Facilities and Support) Act 1966 applies to the grant of rights for the exploitation of oil (and other minerals) and provides for compensation. Compensation is not subject to the rules in the Land Compensation Act 1961. Disputes about compensation are determined by the High Court; the measure of compensation is 'what would be fair and reasonable between a willing grantor and a willing grantee': section 8 of the

1966 Act. There is an additional allowance of not less than 10% on account of the acquisition being compulsory: see section 3(2)(b) of the 1934 Act.

For a case of the grant of rights and the determination of compensation: see *BP Petroleum Developments Ltd* v *Ryder* [1987].

26.3 Coal mining subsidence

The National Coal Board was liable for subsidence compensation under the Coal Mining (Subsidence) Act 1957. Section 13(2) of the 1957 Act provided: 'Where in any proceedings under this Act the question arises whether any damage to property is subsidence damage, and it is shown that the nature of the damage and the circumstances of such are to indicate that the damage may be subsidence damage, the onus shall be on the Board to show that the damage is not subsidence'.

This provision placed the onus of proof on the Board to show that damage is not caused by its activities. The reason for placing the onus of proof on the Board was necessarily because knowledge of the below-ground workings is peculiarly within the knowledge of the Board. In *Burton* v *National Coal Board* [1983], a claim for subsidence damage to a house constructed on a filled-in tip was rejected as the overwhelming probability was that the damage was caused by the settlement of the fill and not by the mining activities of the Board.

The whole question of compensation for subsidence damage was considered in the Waddilove Report: *The Repair and Compensation System for Coal Mining Subsidence Damage* (1984). The Coal Mining Subsidence Act 1991 gives effect to the recommendations in the Waddilove Report.

Part II of the Act makes provision for remedial action to be taken by the British Coal Corporation in respect of subsidence damage to any property. Section 7 provides for the execution of remedial works following a notice of subsidence damage and sections 8–11 provide for discretionary or obligatory payments in lieu of the execution of remedial works. There are further provisions for payments in lieu and depreciation payments.

Part III of the Act provides for additional remedies. Where a dwellinghouse is rendered uninhabitable there is provision in section 22 for home-loss payments. Sections 26 to 28 provide for farm-loss and crop-loss payments and for payments for tenant farmers. There are miscellaneous remedies including purchase of property affected by blight and compensation rights for consequential loss for small firms.

Section 40 provides that, except as otherwise provided for under the Act, any question arising, in default of agreement, be referred and determined by the Lands Tribunal. By section 40(2) if any question arises whether any damage to property is subsidence damage and it is shown that the nature of the damage and the circumstances are such as to indicate that the damage may be subsidence damage, the onus is on the corporation to show that the damage is not subsidence damage: this follows the policy under the 1957 Act. For cases under the 1957 Act, see *Wombwell Foundry and Engineering Co Ltd* v *National Coal Board* [1979] and *Atkinson* v *National Coal Board* [1974].

26.4 Land drainage work

Both water and local authorities may carry out land drainage or flood prevention work under the Land Drainage Act 1991. Section 14(5) of that Act (see also section 64) provides that:

> where injury is sustained by any person by reason of the exercise by a drainage authority of any of their powers under this section, the authority shall be liable to make full compensation to the injured person; and in case of dispute the amount of compensation shall be determined by the Lands Tribunal ...

In *Penty* v *Greater London Council* [1982], a claim for depreciation in the value of a Grade II listed house was made following flood-prevention works to the riverside nearby. The Tribunal accepted a claim based on the depreciation in value of the property, to which was added a sum for the cost of carrying out certain necessary work. The claim under section 14(5) is in respect of an 'injury' and not necessarily for a depreciation in value. In *Day & Sons* v *Thames Water Authority* [1984], the Tribunal decided that the word 'injury' meant a legal injury and that to be entitled to compensation under the Act a claimant had to establish that at common law the claimant would have had a cause of action in the absence of the statute. In the case, flood damage had resulted because of the failure of a flood gate and the partial blocking of another. On the facts, the Tribunal held that the water authority would have been liable in nuisance at common law, in the absence of the statute, for the damage that resulted from a failure to maintain the flood gates, and that, therefore, the claimants were entitled to compensation.

26.5 Sewers and water pipes

Prior to the change in the law as now found in the Water Industry Act 1991, section 278 of the Public Health Act 1936 provided a right to claim 'full compensation to any person who has sustained damage by reason of the exercise by the authority of any powers under this Act'. In *George Whitehouse Ltd v Anglian Water Authority* [1978] it was held that a claim under this provision could include loss of profits attributable to the laying of a sewer in the road outside the claimant's garage and the use of temporary traffic lights that deterred customers. In *Leonidis v Thames Water Authority* [1979] Parker J held that loss of profits caused by the obstruction of the claimant's motor repair garage during the reconstruction of a sewer could be claimed under this provision. What is now of some interest is whether a similar claim is allowable under the new legislation.

By section 159 of the Water Industry Act 1991 an authorised undertaking, such as a water company, has power to lay 'a relevant pipe' in any land upon giving the appropriate notice. A 'relevant pipe' includes 'any sewer or disposal main': see section 158(7). Schedule 12 to the 1991 Act makes provision for compensation in respect of pipe laying works in private land. By para 2(1) of the Schedule:

> if the value of any interest in any relevant land is depreciated by virtue of the exercise, by any relevant undertaker, of any power to carry out pipe-laying works on private land, the person entitled to that interest shall be entitled to compensation from the undertaker of an amount equal to the amount of the depreciation.

Para 2(2) of the Schedule makes provision for what would ordinarily be compensation for disturbance of an occupier by reason of entry on land by a body exercising powers of compulsory acquisition. By para 3(2) of the Schedule:

> For the purpose of assessing any compensation under paragraph 2 above, so far as that compensation is in respect of loss or damage consisting in depreciation of an interest in land, the rules set out in section 5 of the Land Compensation Act 1961 shall, so far as applicable and subject to any necessary modifications, have effect as they have effect for the purpose of assessing compensation of the compulsory acquisition of an interest in land.

Prior to the privatisation of the water industry, section 278 of the Public Health Act 1936 provided compensation in respect of laying of a sewer. An authority was required to make full compensation to any person who had sustained damage by reason of the exercise of any powers under the Act. However, the 1991 Act appears to introduce into the assessment of compensation for the laying of any relevant pipe slightly different rules than those which pertained under the previous legislation. Accordingly, a 'before and after' approach to the valuation of a claimant's land may be appropriate in assessing compensation.

It follows that in assessing compensation where a sewer or water main has been laid through land for the purposes of providing for new development, the opportunity to sell the easement to lay the appropriate pipe will have been denied by the exercise of the statutory powers. Can a ransom value be demanded? This is certainly arguable in that by rule (2) of section 5 of the Land Compensation Act 1961 the 'before value' could include a ransom value determined by the application of the principle in *Stokes* v *Cambridge Corporation* [1961]. It follows that in assessing the 'after value' the ransom value will no longer be present. Therefore the difference between the 'before value' and the 'after value' will include the loss of the ransom value. However, it is important in assessing the 'before value' to have regard to the possibility that the relevant pipe might be laid upon some alternative route: this will affect the appropriate *Stokes* payment. In *Kettering Borough Council* v *Anglian Water Services plc* [2001] such a claim was rejected on the ground that the existence of statutory powers to requisition a sewer, and to lay a sewer, in private land could not be ignored. That ground is inconsistent with the decision in the *Indian Case* where the Privy Council said that the existence of statutory powers of acquisition were to be disregarded in assessing compensation (*Raja Vyrecherla Narayana Gajapatiraju* v *Revenue Divisional Officer, Vizagapatam* [1939]). Accordingly, the ransom value issue is still arguable.

For a Lands Tribunal case on the assessment of compensation for the laying of a water main, see *St John's College, Oxford* v *Thames Water Authority* [1990] for a decision under the earlier legislation. In that case compensation was payable for damage to land and the Tribunal noted that this would not include a recognition payment for the grant of a right. This point seems relevant under the new legislation. Valuers commonly adopt a rate per yard or metre run, as in *Markland* v *Cannock Rural District Council* [1973], or a percentage of the freehold value of the area of the protective 'easement' strip, as in the *St John's* case.

In *Collins* v *Thames Water Utilities Ltd* [1994] the President of the Land Tribunal said that, although not deciding the point, he was inclined to the view that it is legitimate and inherent in the valuation process, to take account of any enhancement in value attributable to the carrying out of the works of laying a sewer.

In *Donovan* v *Welsh Water plc* [1994] a sewer had been laid by the authority's contractor outside the notified route. It was held that the contractor was the authority's agent and that the Lands Tribunal had jurisdiction to determine the claimant's claim.

In *Cook* v *South West Water* [1995] LT it was held that the valuation date was the date of entry and that the claim could include loss of the prospect of development.

In *Bestley* v *North West Water Ltd* [1998] the Tribunal decided that where a pipe was laid through a garden of a private house, the conventional approach of 50% of the value of the easement strip was not appropriate. The proper compensation was for the depreciation in the value of the affected property.

26.6 Gas pipelines

The Gas Act 1986, as amended by the Gas Act 1995, contains powers authorising a public gas transporter to compulsorily acquire land or any right of new right in land: see section 9 of, and Schedule 3, to the 1986 Act. A public gas transporter is the holder of a licence granted by the Director General of Gas Supply. The procedure and provisions regarding the assessment of compensation are found in Schedule 3 to the 1986 Act.

The Secretary of State for Trade and Industry may authorise a public gas transporter to purchase compulsorily any land; land includes any right over land and the acquisition of rights over land by creating new rights: see para 1. Such land may be acquired to enable a public gas transporter to fulfil its duties. These duties are set out in section 9 and include a duty to develop and maintain an efficient, co-ordinated and economical system of gas supply, and to comply, so far as it is economic to do so, with any reasonable request to give a supply of gas to any premises.

Where a public gas transporter is proposing to lay a new gas pipeline, the usual practice is to select a route and then to invite affected landowners to voluntarily enter into a deed of easement. Standard rates per metre run of pipeline are offered based on agreements with the Country Landowners Association and the National Farmers Union.

Where agreement cannot be reached, and compulsory powers become necessary, the Acquisition of Land Act 1981 will apply: see para 4. Where a pipeline easement is sought, and this would involve the creation of a new right, Schedule 3 to the 1981 Act applies. Accordingly, the procedure considered in Chapter 4 above will be broadly followed.

The Compulsory Purchase Act 1965 has effect with modifications necessary to make it apply to a public gas transporter's compulsory acquisition of the creation of a new right in land. It follows that the public gas transporter must, after obtaining a compulsory purchase order, serve a notice to treat and may effect entry before compensation is agreed following the service of a notice of entry: see Chapter 7 above.

The measure of compensation for the acquisition of a new right in land, such as a pipeline easement, is set out in a substituted section 7 of the 1965 Act:

> In assessing the compensation to be paid by the acquiring authority under this Act regard shall be had not only to the extent (if any) to which the value of the land over which the right is to be acquired is depreciated by the acquisition of the right but also to the damage (if any) to be sustained by the owner of the land by reason of its severance from other land of his, or injuriously affecting that other land by the exercise of the powers conferred by this or the special Act.

This substituted section alters the original section 7 in the 1965 Act in one important way: the compensation of the right granted is not its open market value. The compensation is the depreciation in value of the land through which the new right is acquired. However, the substituted section does preserve the right to claim for injurious affection and severance in respect of any retained land.

Accordingly, it may be difficult to advance a claim for compensation based on the argument that there might be rival public gas transporters willing to pay a price above existing use values in order to lay a pipeline through land which has special advantages for that purpose. It may also exclude the right to advance ransom value. It may be possible to argue in appropriate cases that the 'before' value of the affected land itself reflected some special advantage for the laying of a gas pipeline which adds to its market value and which is not dependent upon the scheme underlying the specific acquisition. That might, for example, apply where a particular landowner owns all the land around a gas supply plant, or owns the most satisfactory or economic route between a gas supply plant and the point where the gas is to be used, say a factory.

Para 13 of Schedule 3 provides that the statutes in force with respect to compensation for the compulsory purchase of land shall apply with the necessary modifications in the case of the compulsory acquisition of a new right. In other words, the Land Compensation Act 1961 applies for the purposes of assessing depreciation in the value of land, injurious affection and severance. Presumably, although this is not clear from Schedule 3, compensation for disturbance is payable for the same reason that it is payable in the case of the compulsory acquisition of land where section 7 of the 1965 Act applies in its unamended form.

The remaining provisions of Schedule 3 to the 1986 Act deal with modifications to the Compulsory Purchase Act 1965. Section 8 of the 1965 Act, which provides a right to a landowner to serve a counternotice where a notice to treat is served in respect of part of his property, applies only in a substituted form.

26.7 Telecommunications

Schedule 2 to the Telecommunications Act 1984 sets out the Telecommunications Code. This contains rights for licensed operators to lay cables and apparatus in private land, and provisions for compensation. The rights required by licensed operators are usually called wayleave agreements. By Code para 2(1):

> The agreement in writing of the occupier for the time being of any land shall be required for conferring on the operator a right for the statutory purposes –
>
> (a) to execute any works on that land for or in connection with the installation, maintenance, adjustment, repair or alteration of telecommunication apparatus; or
> (b) to keep telecommunication apparatus installed on, under or over that land; or
> (c) to enter that land to inspect any apparatus kept installed (whether on, under or over that land or elsewhere) for the purposes of the operator's system.

By Code para 2(2) a freeholder or tenant of any land is not bound by a right granted by an occupier of that land unless such a person is himself the occupier or he has agreed in writing to be bound by the right. However a freeholder or tenant, not being an occupier, may be bound by a wayleave agreement made by the occupier where the agreement concerns the provision of service lines that provide telecommunication services to the occupier from time to time: see Code para 2(3). Where a person grants a wayleave agreement, and owns an interest in the land, any right he grants binds successors in title and those who derive interests from such a person: see Code para 2(4). It follows that if an occupier of land enters into a wayleave agreement in writing with a licensed operator in respect of telecommunication apparatus that *does not* provide services to the occupier, the freeholder and any lessee of the land, not being the occupier, will not be bound by such a right.

If a licensed operator is unable to obtain the agreement in writing of the occupier for the time being to a wayleave agreement, the operator can apply to the county court for the compulsory conferment of an agreement under Code para 5. By Code para 7, the terms and conditions of a compulsorily conferred agreement are determined by the county court. This paragraph provides for compensation as follows:

> Such terms with respect to the payment of consideration ... as it appears to the court to be fair and reasonable if the agreement had been given willingly.

In the county court decision in *Mercury Communications Ltd* v *London & India Dock Investments Ltd* [1994] Judge Hague QC decided that 'fair and reasonable' involved an element of subjective judicial opinion; the court's determination is not necessarily the same as the result in the market would have been if the grant had been given willingly. Accordingly, compulsory purchase principles were not applicable. Further, a ransom value approach, having regard to the profit to be made from the use of the cables involved, was inappropriate. Reliance in that case was placed on other similar agreements made by consent: see also *Finsbury Business Centre* v *Mercury Communications* [1994].

When a freeholder or lessee of premises is not bound by a wayleave agreement in writing entered into by the occupier, either because such a person has not agreed to be bound, or the telecommunication apparatus in the land is *not* apparatus providing services to the occupier, such freeholder or lessee may claim compensation for the depreciation in the value of the relevant interest: see Code para 4. In default of agreement, any question as to a person's entitlement to compensation in such circumstances is referred to and determined by the Lands Tribunal.

Telecommunication apparatus may be in land without the benefit of any agreement in writing satisfying the provisions of the Code, or may be in land under agreements that either do not bind a party with an interest in that land, or upon terms giving a right to require the removal of the apparatus on the expiration of some specified period of time, or on the happening of an event. In any of these circumstances, there may be persons entitled to require the removal of the apparatus as a matter of common law, to prevent the continuation of a trespass, or as a matter of contract. Code para 21 contains a restriction on the right to require the removal of tele-communication apparatus. Where a person entitled to require the removal of telecommunication apparatus gives notice to the operator, the apparatus must be removed unless the licensed operator gives a counternotice within 28 days stating that the person is not entitled to require the removal of the apparatus, and/or specifying the steps which the operator proposes to take for the purpose of securing a right to keep the apparatus on the land. The effect of this paragraph of the Code is to confer on a licensed operator a right to keep apparatus on land. If the operator cannot secure the agreement in writing of the occupier of the land, it will have to seek compulsory conferment of an agreement under Code para 5.

26.8 Electricity

Section 10 of the Electricity Act 1989 applies Schedules 3 and 4 of that Act. Schedule 3 provides for the compulsory acquisition of land by the electricity industry and Schedule 4 deals with the acquisition of wayleaves. The arrangements under Schedule 4 will be explained first as they are more usually met.

1. Electricity wayleaves

Most wayleaves are obtained by a 'wayleave agreement'. These are arrangements entered into with the agreement of the affected landowners usually on a form which has been approved by the National Farmers Union and the Country Landowners Association. Under such an agreement, the owner and occupier consent to the appropriate company carrying out specified scheduled works, such as the erection of a transmission line with poles and pylons. In return, the electricity company agrees to pay the owner rent and compensation in accordance with rates which are agreed from time to time with the National Farmers Union and the Country

Landowners Association. In the ordinary case of agricultural land, it is difficult to negotiate terms different from those that are agreed nationally. In the case of other land it may be far easier.

An owner is not obliged to enter into a wayleave agreement, as described above, and even where he has entered into such an agreement, most agreements can be terminated on six months' notice. An owner who wishes to carry out development on his land may want to terminate an agreement. Where an owner has failed to give an agreement, or has terminated an existing one, the electricity industry is entitled to acquire a wayleave compulsorily under the terms of para 6 of Schedule 4. The Secretary of State for Trade and Industry may grant the necessary wayleave subject to such terms and conditions as he thinks fit. Such a wayleave will then continue in force for such period as may be specified in the wayleave. Because of the compensation obligations considered below, the period specified is usually only 15 years. Para 6 does not authorise the granting of a necessary wayleave where an electricity line is to be installed on or over land covered by a dwelling. However, according to *R* v *Secretary of State for Trade and Industry, ex parte Wolf* [1997], that limitation does not apply where a wayleave is being granted in respect of a line that is already installed.

2. Compensation

Where a wayleave is granted under para 6 of the Fourth Schedule to the 1989 Act, the occupier of the land, and where the occupier is not also the owner, the owner of the land may recover from the company compensation in respect of the grant: see para 7 of Schedule 4. Further, where in the exercise of any right conferred by a wayleave any damage is caused to land or to movables, any person interested in the land or movables may recover compensation in respect of that damage. Compensation is also payable where a person is disturbed in his enjoyment of land: see para 7(2). The Lands Tribunal has no jurisdiction to award compensation where land has been entered by an electricity undertaker without a wayleave granted by the Secretary of State: see *Bolton* v *Southern Electric plc* [1999].

The word 'compensation' is not defined, but questions of disputed compensation are determined by the Lands Tribunal. 'Compensation' was said in *Blundell* v *R* [1905] to include the effect of severance and injurious affection. In *Horton* v *Colwyn Bay Urban District Council* [1908], a case involving similarly worded compensation provisions under the Public Health Act 1875, the Court of Appeal held that the claim to injurious affection compensation was limited to the injury caused by the use of the claimant's land, and did not extend to the authority's use of land not owned by the claimant.

In *Macleod* v *National Grid Co plc* [1998] the claimant was said to be entitled to compensation for all the loss (that is not too remote) that followed from the grant of the necessary wayleave. This included direct loss due to the siting of the pylon and line and indirect loss due to the depreciation in value of land not under the pylon and lines. The Tribunal also confirmed that the Land Compensation Act 1961 (apart from sections 2–4) did not apply to the assessment of compensation; the fundamental principle was equivalence within the principle in *Horn* v *Sunderland Corporation* [1941]. See also *West Midlands Joint Electricity Authority* v *Pitt* [1932].

3. Lands Tribunal Decisions

George v *South West Electricity Board* [1982]: the assessment of compensation for the effect of two above-ground electricity transmission lines supported by towers and pylons placed over an outstandingly beautiful and secluded Devonshire Farm.

Clouds Estate Trustees v *Southern Electricity Board* [1983]: Assessment of the annual rental for overhead electric lines, supporting poles and stays and underground cable on a Wiltshire Estate commanding high agricultural rents.

In *R* v *Department of Trade and Industry, ex parte Healauch Farms* [1995] it was held that there was no entitlement to compensation in respect of the costs of a compulsory wayleave public local inquiry.

4. Compulsory purchase

Schedule 3 of the 1989 Act provides for the compulsory acquisition of land or rights by the electricity industry. With some modifications, the Acquisition of Land Act 1981 and the Compulsory Purchase Act 1965 will apply. Accordingly, the earlier parts of this book will be relevant. Where a right is taken, then under the modified section 7 of the 1965 Act, compensation is payable for the damage caused by the grant of a right over land, but is not payable for the value of the right acquired.

26.9 Pipe-lines Act 1962

This Act contains provisions controlling the construction of cross-country and local pipe-lines. A person proposing to execute works in land for the purposes of placing a pipe-line may apply for a compulsory purchase order to be authorised by the appropriate minister. This will either be the Secretary of State for the Environment, Transport and the Regions or the Secretary of State of Trade and Industry. Part I of the Second Schedule to the 1962 Act sets out the procedure for making the application for a compulsory purchase order: see section 11. A compulsory purchase order shall be subject to special parliamentary procedure: see section 11(5).

There is an alternative procedure under section 12. A person proposing to lay a pipe-line may seek a compulsory rights order. The procedure for seeking a compulsory rights order is set out in Part II of Schedule 2 of the Act.

The assessment of compensation for the acquisition of land under a compulsory purchase order is governed by the Land Compensation Act 1961: see section 1 of that Act. The 1961 Act is modified so that no account shall be taken of any interest in land, or any enhancement of the value of any interest in land, by reason of any buildings or works if the Lands Tribunal is satisfied that the creation of the interest or the erection of the building or works was not reasonably necessary and was undertaken with a view to obtaining compensation or increased compensation: see the Third Schedule to the 1962 Act.

Section 14 of the 1962 Act provides for compensation in respect of compulsory rights orders; there are two heads of claim, depreciation in the value of the claimant's interest in his land by reason of the making of the order. The person to whom the order has been granted shall pay the claimant compensation equal to the amount of the depreciation. The Land Compensation Act 1961 will apply if the right to lay a pipe-line under a compulsory rights order amounts to the acquisition of land. 'Land' is given a wide definition by section 39 of the 1961 Act. In *Thurrock, Grays and Tilbury, Joint Sewerage Board* v *Thames Land Co* [1925], it was held that a right to acquire an easement or right over land compulsorily was an acquisition of land to which what is now the Land Compensation Act 1961 will apply. There is also support in the Lands Tribunal decision of *Padfield* v *Eastern Electricity Board* [1972] where the laying of electricity lines amounted to compulsory acquisition of land for the purposes of the Land Compensation Act 1961, although this case was not followed in *Macleod* v *National Grid plc* [1998].

The measure of compensation is therefore the depreciation in value of the claimant's interest. This would seem to preclude payment for the taking of the right itself. Therefore a 'recognition payment' is not payable: see *St John's College, Oxford* v *Thames Water Authority* [1990]. For the same reason a ransom payment under *Stokes* v *Cambridge Corp* [1961] will also not be payable.

Chapter 27

Human Rights

Introduction
Human Rights Act 1998
European Convention on Human Rights
Article 1 of First Protocol: protection of property
Article 6(1) of the Convention: right to a fair trial
Article 8 of the Convention: right of respect to home

27.1 Introduction

Earlier editions of this book made occasional references to the European Convention on Human Rights and the Universal Declaration of Human Rights. The Human Rights Act 1998 is now in force and gives effect to the rights and freedoms under the European Convention on Human Rights. This chapter gives a brief explanation of the effect this Act and of the provisions of the Convention so far as it effects the compulsory taking of property. Many of the rights enshrined in the Convention, such as the protection of property against a taking, have been recognised in the decisions of the common law courts.

27.2 Human Rights Act 1998

The Human Rights Act 1998 gives effect to the rights and freedoms under the European Convention on Human Rights. So far as possible, legislation must be read and given effect in a way that is compatible with the requirements of the Convention: see section 3. Legislation cannot be struck down, but a court can make a declaration of incompatibility, which should promote legislative change: see section 4. Thus, if a court, and this would include the Lands Tribunal, concludes that there is some existing statutory provision that is incompatible with the Convention, it must make an appropriate declaration. Such a declaration will not necessarily help the particular party raising the issue, but the government might be encouraged to address the problem with new or amending legislation. One example of possible incompatibility of legislation is the lack of any effective procedure in the present laws by which a claimant, threatened with a compulsory taking, can compel the taking and the payment of compensation within any sensible, fair and commercially appropriate period of time, a problem recognised by the DETR publication Fundamental review of the laws and procedures relating to compulsory purchase and compensation (July 2000).

One example of existing rules that are possibly incompatible with the Convention are the rules that preclude a claimant who is not disturbed from possession from obtaining compensation under rule (6) of section 5 of the 1961 Act for all his losses, such as lost rents: see p294 above.

Public authorities, including courts and tribunals, must not act in a way incompatible with Convention rights: see section 6. This means that courts must interpret the common law compatibly with the Convention rights. In the compulsory purchase area of law, most of the decisions of the courts and of the Lands Tribunal are decisions on the interpretation of statutory provisions. Such cases include *Stokes* v *Cambridge* [1961] and *Batchelor* v *Kent County Council* [1990] which are about the meaning of 'value of land' in rule (2) of section 5 of the Land Compensation Act 1961 and section 7 of the Compulsory Purchase Act 1965. Certain decisions on the interpretation of statutory provisions may now have to be reconsidered. For example, where a trader suffers loss of profits due to the blighting effects of a scheme, those blighting effects are disregarded in constructing the profitability of the business for the purpose of determining the value of the loss of goodwill. But although the losses are due to the scheme, the actual losses are only compensatable if attributable to, or the threat of, dispossession (*Emslie & Simpson Ltd* v *Aberdeen City District Council* [1994]). Such traders are therefore bearing a loss for which they are not compensated. Of course there may be other traders, also suffering blight losses, who are not compulsorily acquired and have no statutory entitlement to any compensation at all. The courts may have to decide whether one or both groups are being treated incompatibly with Convention rights.

27.3 European Convention on Human Rights

There are two principal provisions that concern private property.

Article 1 of the First Protocol protects private possession and Article 6 of the Convention provides for a fair trial.

Article 1 of the First Protocol of the European Convention on Human Rights provides that:

> Every natural or legal person is entitled to the peaceful enjoyment of his possessions. No one shall be deprived of his possessions except in the public interest and subject to the conditions provided for by law and by the general principles of international law.
>
> The preceding provisions shall not, however, in any way impair the right of a state to enforce such laws as it deems necessary to control the use of property in accordance with the general interest or to secure the payment of taxes or other contributions or penalties.

Article 6 of the Convention is too long to set out in this chapter; much of the Article is concerned with criminal law. However the first part of the Article, Article 6(1), provides that:

> In the determination of his civil rights and obligations . . . everyone is entitled to a fair and public hearing within a reasonable time by an independent and impartial tribunal established by law . . .

Both these Articles are considered below. The leading and relevant case on these Articles is *Sporrong and Lönnroth* v *Sweden* [1982]. The applicant companies each owned properties that were sterilised for development purposes by the threat of expropriation for periods of 23 and eight years and a ban on construction permits that lasted for 25 and 12 years, respectively. There was no provision for compensation for the inability to develop the properties during the period of 'blight'. The European Court of Human Rights held that there had been violations of Article 1 of the First Protocol and of Article 6.

27.4 Article 1 of First Protocol: protection of property

1. Property

Article 1 (see above) uses the word 'possessions' rather than property. Possessions have been widely defined in the decisions of the European Court of the Human Rights. They include land and interests in land, such as the entitlement to rent and the benefit of a restrictive covenant (*S* v *United Kingdom* [1984]). A claimant must show that he has a property right recognised under English law (*Yarrow* v *United Kingdom* [1983]).

The principal decision of the European Court on Article 1 is *Sporrong and Lönnroth* v *Sweden* [1982]. The court said that Article 1 contains three distinct rules. The first rule, which is of general application, states the principle of peaceful enjoyment of property. The second rule, in the second sentence of the first paragraph, concerns deprivation of possessions, but subject to certain conditions. The third rule, in the second paragraph of Article 1, recognises that the state can control the use of property in accordance with the general interest. The second and third rules need to be considered in the light of the general principle contained in rule 1 (*Lithgow* v *United Kingdom* [1986]).

2. The first rule

This rule applies to an interference with property that does not involve a compulsory taking or a control over the use of land. The complaint about the limitations on the use of blight notices and the creation of noise from an airport in *Arondelle* v *United Kingdom* [1982] concerned this rule.

3. The second rule

In *Sporrong and Lönnroth* v *Sweden* [1982] the European Court of Human Rights said that this rule involved not only the formal compulsory taking of property, but also an investigation of the realities of the situation complained of as it has to be established whether the situation amounted to a *de facto* expropriation. This approach arose in a Privy Council case outside the Convention where Lord Hoffmann said that substance rather than form has to be considered in deciding whether the exercise of an administrative power amounts to the deprivation of property (*Grape Bay Ltd* v *Attorney-General of Bermuda* [2000]).

4. The third rule

This rule applies where there is an attempt to control the use of property, for example through planning, environment or public health laws, or through controls over letting and rents, as in *Pine Valley Developments Ltd* v *Ireland* [1991].

5. The requirements for justifiable interferences

(a) Public or general interest

The second rule permits the taking of private property in the public interest. In the *Sporrong* case it was said that interferences with property within the first and third rules could only be justified in the public or general interest. In *James v United Kingdom* [1986] the European court said that states and public authorities have wide margins of appreciation in implementing social and economic policies, such as leasehold enfranchisement under the Leasehold Reform Act 1967, and there will be no breach of Article 1 unless the decision of the national authority has made a judgment without reasonable foundation.

In *Aka v Turkey* [2001] the European Court of Human Rights decided that a failure to pay adequate interest on a delayed additional sum of compensation was a violation of Article 1. The setting of the rate of interest is within the margin of appreciation enjoyed by the state. But where there was considerable inflation during the delay period, this upset the fair balance between the individual and the state.

There must be a reasonable relationship between compensation moneys and the value of the property otherwise deprivation would be unjustified: see *Gaganus v Turkey* [2002].

(b) Proportionality

The requirement of proportionality is concerned with a reasonable relationship of proportionality between the means employed and the aim being pursued. The European court has to balance the rights of the individual against the public or general interest. Compulsory purchase of private property is an undoubted interference with private possessions, but the public or general interest may require public infrastructure, such as roads, railways, sewers, and possibly airports. In such cases one can see that the balancing exercise will favour the use of compulsory purchase powers. Much more difficult are those cases where commercial development is involved, either directly or indirectly. Taking property compulsorily under section 226 of the Town and Country Planning Act 1990 to redevelop land that is suffering from social and physical dereliction will no doubt be justified. But where, as is not uncommon, a developer or supermarket company persuades a local planning authority to use compulsory powers for what is essentially a commercial scheme, it is less easy to see what the public or general interest is, and if it does exist, whether it should prevail over the private interest.

In *James* v *United Kingdom* [1986] the application of the proportionality principle favoured the government and the leasehold enfranchisement legislation over the individual landowner. The application of the proportionality principle involves a consideration of the provisions, if any, for compensation. The existence of a compensation provision is relevant to all three rules of the Article. In *James* the court said that the taking of private property without compensation could only be justified in exceptional circumstances; compensation terms are therefore important in considering whether there is a disproportionate burden on the individual. The court also said that compensation does not necessarily have to satisfy some test of financial equivalence or market value; there will be cases where the social policy being pursued justifies the payment of less than financial equivalence or market value (see also *Lithgow* v *United Kingdom* [1986]).

(c) Legal certainty

In the second rule the expression 'subject to the conditions provided for by law' is found. This requirement of legal certainty applies to all aspects of the Convention, including the rules in Article 1. What is required here is a set of legal rules governing the taking of or interference with property and necessary procedures that must be followed. In the *James* case the applicants' argument that the Leasehold Reform Act 1967 was indiscriminate and did not provide for any machinery whereby a landlord can seek independent consideration for the justification for the enfranchisement or the principles under which compensation is to be calculated, was not accepted. It was for Parliament to consider the advantages and disadvantages of the policy and the system adopted was not irrational or inappropriate.

The English provisions for compulsory purchase orders do provide for that certainty because they include rights for the affected landowners to object or make representations. However, there are some compulsory taking powers that possibly fail the legal certainty requirement. Non-state, and private, utility companies enjoy wide powers to enter private land and 'take' wayleaves on notice only without any procedural safeguards: see section 159 of the Water Industry Act 1991.

(d) International law

The second rule also includes a requirement that a deprivation of property is subject to the general principles of international law. This requirement applies where the private property of alien owners is compulsorily taken.

27.5 Article 6(1) of the Convention: right to a fair trial

In relation to civil rights, this Article (see above) is about procedural fairness. Civil rights are relevant in relation to the compulsory taking of private property and the assessment of compensation. Claims involving compulsory taking are subject to the right to a fair hearing: see *Holy Monasteries* v *Greece* [1994]. Legislation must allow administrative or executive decisions affecting civil rights, such as private property, to be challengeable in a court or be appealable. The right to challenge a planning decision by a judicial review application satisfied Article 6(1) in *Bryan* v *United Kingdom* [1995].

One supposes that the usual case of an authority making a compulsory purchase order, in respect of which affected parties may object and have those heard by an inspector, will satisfy Article 6(1). There is a right to challenge a decision to confirm a compulsory order on judicial review principles under section 23 of the Acquisition of Land Act 1981.

However the most obvious examples of potential breaches of Article 6(1) involve the taking of, or interference with, private property by non-state utility companies. Thus under section 159 of the Water Industry Act 1991 pipes can be laid in private land under notice. There is no right to make any representations or objections and no provision to appeal or challenge the decision.

27.6 Article 8: right of respect to home.

1. Everyone has the right to respect for ... his home ...
2. There shall be no interference by a public authority with the exercise of this right except such as is in accordance with the law and is necessary in a democratic society in the interests of national security, public safety or the economic well-being of the country, for the prevention of disorder or crime, for the protection of health or morals, or for the protection of the rights and freedoms of others.

This Article has particular relevance in relation to the exercise of planning and statutory nuisance controls: see *Arrondelle* v *United*

Kingdom [1982]. It is also important where compulsory acquisition powers are used. However, in most cases where a home is compulsorily acquired, it will be justified on proportionality grounds of weighing the interests of the individual against the wider interests of society. See the article entitled 'Proportionality and Planning' at [2002] JPL 908.

Index

A

Absent owners 128
Accommodation works 345, 353
Acquisition of rights. 108, 246
   compensation 247
Acquisition procedure 24
Advance payment 125
Advertisements. 414
Agreement. . . . . 75 *et seq*
  see purchase by agreement
  disposal by agreement
Agricultural land. . . . . 323 *et seq*
   accommodation works. 345
   farm business tenancy 329, 340
   farm-loss payment 342
   disturbance 326
   home-loss payment. 328
   injurious affection. 324
   landlord's interest. 328
   loss payment 308
   milk quota 324
   notice to quit 330
   owner occupation 323
   profits loss of 326, 335
   purchase notice. 61
   reorganisation payment. 336
   severance 324, 335, 344
   tenancy. 329
Alternative schemes. 44
Ancient monuments. 411

B

Basic loss payment 308
Before and after. 238
Betterment. 163, 167
   non-statutory. 248

Blight notice 62
    agricultural unit 70
    blight categories 62
    counternotice. 67
    disturbance 271
    highways. 64
    lands tribunal 69
    persons entitled. 65
    procedure 65
    time limit. 65
    withdrawal 71
Business tenancies 319
Bwllfa principle 146

C
Certificate of appropriate alternative development 206
    appeal 209
    application for. 207
    procedure. 206
    relevant date 209
    reliance on 208
    retained land 209
    scheme. 210
Certificate of lawful use. 200
Coal mining subsidence. 423
Common land 38, 348
    commoners 349
    owners. 349
Compensation
    accommodation works. 353
    additional development 82, 212
    advertisements 414
    agricultural land. . . . . 323 et seq
    ancient monuments. 411
    assignment of 93
    building preservation notice 410, 411
    coal mining subsidence 423
    common land 348
    discontinuance order 408
    discretionary payment 305
    disturbance 263
    easements and restrictive covenants. 173
    electricity. 431
    entitlement to 168, 170
    gas pipes 427

goodwill. 280
highways 415
injurious affection. 233
land drainage 424
leaseholds 309
legal presumption. 156
licences. 173
listed buildings 409
market value 159, 165, 182
meaning of. 156
minerals. 347
mining operations. 409
mortgagee 173
mortgages 351
oil exploration. 422
omitted interests 353
potential value 160
principle of equivalence. 157
profits loss of. 286
public works 380
purpose 12
purpose of 155
refusal of planning permission 404
reversionary interest. 315
revocation of planning permission 406
right to. 402
sewers 425
statutory disturbance payments 301
statutory undertakers. 350
stop notices 412
tax. 414
telecommunications 429
tenancies. 310, 312, 319, 329
tenant entitled to. 172
tree preservation orders 413
valuation date 174
value to owner 159
water pipes. 425
wayleaves 431
Compensation procedure. 24
Compulsory purchase
indication of 221
Compulsory purchase order 27
challenge 49
confirmation 37

confirmation principles 48
form 30
notification 29
objections. 32
preparation 28
procedural irregularity. 55
public local inquiry. 33
statement of reasons. 31
special parliamentary procedure. 38
Compulsory purchase powers 9
private act 20
public act 21
royal prerogative. 19
use 3
Contractors damage 345
Contrary to law. 187
Conveyance. . . . . 129 *et seq*
owners without power. 129
Conveyancing costs 295
Corporate veil. 270
Costs
lands tribunal 139
Crichel Down rules 80

D

Damages . . . .
breach of good faith 61
Delaforce effect. 143
Depreciation 380
Development value 186
Disabled persons home 250
Discontinuance order. 408
Discretionary disturbance payments 305
Discretionary payments. 305
Disposal of land . . . . 80 *et seq*
Crichel Down rules. 80
sale price 81
Disturbance . . . . 263 *et seq*
adaptation of premises. 288
agricultural land 326
benefits. 280
blight effect 271, 275
blight notice. 271
burden of proof. 280
consistence. 266

corporate veil 270
discretionary payment 305
dispossession and loss 274
entitlement to 268
equivalent principle 263
extinguishment 278
fairness principle. 264
general principles 272
goodwill. 280
Horn principle 267
interest 291
investment owner 269
legal costs 290
licensee. 270
loss before notice to treat 275
mitigation duty 276
occupation 269
part acquisition 272
personal time. 290
profits loss of. 286
purchase notice 271
relocation. 288
remoteness. 273
removal expenses 290
scheme effect. 280
statutory disturbance payments 301
tax. 279, 355
unforeseeable losses 273
value for money 277
Disturbance payments . . . . 301 *et seq*
amount. 303
blight notice. 302
entitlement to 301

E

Easements. 81, 107, 117, 173
Electricity. 431
Enforcement immunity 191
Entry
advance payment 125
consequences of 125
enforcing 128
general vesting declaration 125
housing 124
powers of. 123

unlawful 126
Equivalent reinstatement 255
    bona fide intention 258
    conditions 256
    devoted to a purpose 256
    disabled persons home 260
    measure of costs 259
    no general demand 257
Established use certificate 191, 200
European Convention on Human Rights and Fundamental
    Freedoms 403, 404
Existing use 202

                                        F
Farm-loss payment 342
    amount 343
    claim 344
    discretionary 344
    entitlement 342
Frustration 93

                                        G
Gas pipes 427
General vesting declaration . . . . 98 *et seq*
    compensation 101
    entry 100
    execution 99
    procedure 98
    severance 101
    severed land 109
    tenancies 100
    vesting date 99
Goodwill 280

                                        H
Highways 415
    compensation 415
    stopping up 416
Home-loss payment 297
    acquisition by agreement 300
    agricultural land 328
    amount 299
    claim 300
    conditions 297
Hope value 192

Horn principle 267
Human rights . . . . 6, 437 *et seq*

I

Improvements 89
Improvement lines 418
Injurious affection 233, 237, 370
    accommodation works 246
    acquisition of rights 246
    compensation measure 238, 377
    effect of whole works 246
    no land taken 370
Interest
    advance payment 306
    compensation claims 306
    lands tribunal 142, 308
    no land acquired 307
    possession 306
Intersected land 112
Investment owner . . . .
    reinvestment expenses 318

J

Judicial review 55

L

Land . . . . 104 *et seq*
    definition 104
    freehold 106
    leasehold 106
    mines and minerals 105
    power to acquire 104
    stratum 105
Land drainage 424
Land reform 3
Lands tribunal . . . . 131 *et seq*
    appeal 150
    arbitration Acts 138,142
    costs 139
    experts 144
    interest 142, 308, 392
    jurisdiction 131
    limitation period 133
    preliminary issue 137
    procedure 135

reference 135
sealed offer 140
simplified procedure 137
small claims. 149
valuation methods 142
written representations. 138
Leaseholds
additional payments. 321
compensation 310
entry. 312, 318
option for renewal. 311
rent reviews. 317
repairs 316
security of tenure 315
severance 311
Legal costs. 295
Legal fees. 391
Licences 173
Limitation period 133, 392
Listed buildings minimum compensation 261
Loans 305
Loss payment 308
Lotting 197

M

Market value 159, 165, 182
case against 168
Marriage value 192
Material considerations 46
Material detriment 111
McCarthy rules 370
Minerals. 104
compensation 347
Mines. 105
Mining code 105
Minister
reasons. 43
Wednesbury principles. 46
Mitigation
acquisition 396
duty of 276
expenses. 399
highways 396
works 398
Mortgages 351

N

National trust 38, 129
Natural justice. 53
New premises 288
No-scheme world 217, 218, 223
Noise 394
Noise nuisance 381
Notice of claim 88
Notice of entry. 116, 318
Notice to treat . . . . 86 *et seq*
   consequences. 88
   contents 86
   deemed 97
   frustration 95
   interests fixed 89
   lessee 87
   licences. 87
   notice of claim. 97
   persons entitled to 87
   possession 92
   service 86
   statutory contract 94
   tenancy for life 87
   tenant. 87
   time-limit. 94
   validity. 95
   valuation date 91
   withdrawal 96
Nuisance 367

O

Occupiers loss payment. 308
Oil exploration 422
Omitted interests
   compensation 353
Option for renewal 311
Option to purchase. 105
Overriding rights 117

P

Pedestrianisation 419
Physical factors. 381
Pipe-line. 109, 432
Planning agreement 185
Planning permission. 199, 200

acquisition for highway purposes............................200
assumptions 201
existing...200
post acquisition...212
see statutory planning assumptions
Pointe Gourde principle....................................223
decrease in value..229
disregard value..224
purchase notice..227
scheme...225
vandalism 230
Possession .... 123 *et seq*
absent owners 128
compelling authority 128
entry..123
Post valuation date evidence................................145
Potential value 160
Pre-emption rights 82
Professional fees 293, 391
Profits..286
Provisional order 22
Public benefit 11
Public local inquiry 33
costs... 37
procedure 34
Public sewer 425
Public works
alterations 390
Purchase by agreement 75
compulsory purchase order................................ 77
no compulsory purchase order 75
subject to tenancy.. 80
Purchase notice .... 57 *et seq*
agricultural land... 61
disturbance 271
housing 61
listed building... 60
Pointe Gourde principle..................................223
procedure 59

R

Ransom value 192
cross-claim..196
Stokes principle 196
Residual valuation 142

Restrictive covenants 82, 107, 173
    scheme 223
Revocation order 406, 407
Royal prerogative 19
Ryde's scale 296

S

Scheme . . . . 217 *et seq*
    disregard of 218
    effect of 220
    planning agreement 223
    Pointe Gourde principle 223
    restrictive covenants 223
    statutory rules 218
Sealed offer 140
Set-off 247
    general 249
    highways 250
    subsequent acquisition 252
Severance 233, 236
    acquisition of rights 246
    compensation 236
    compensation measure 238
    general vesting declaration 101
    interest in land 235
    land held with 234
Severed land 109
    agricultural land 114
    general vesting declaration 113
    purchase of 110
Sewers 425
Sound proofing 394, 395
Special parliamentary procedure 22, 38
Special purchaser 187
Special suitability 187
Statutory contract
    notice to treat 78, 94
    statutory disturbance payments *see* disturbance payments
Statutory objectors 32
Statutory planning assumption
    action area 205
    certificate of appropriate alternative development 206
    development plan 204
    no development plan 201
    third schedule development 202

Statutory powers
    and contractual rights 74
    need 15
Statutory undertakers... 350
Stokes principle 196
Stop notices.. 414
Street lighting 392, 419
Subject to contract 78
Survey and preliminary works 121

T

Tax .... 355 *et seq*
Telecommunications... 429
Tenancies
    compensation 312
    severance.. 314
    valuation date 313
Third party rights
    overriding... 117, 118
Tobin fees 296
Transport and works order 38
Tree preservation orders 413

U

Ultra vires.. 51
Unfit house 260
Unlawful use.. 191

V

Valuation
    basic rules 117, 182
    development value... 186
    evidence.. 142
    lotting... 197
    planning agreement 185
    residual 142
    rule (1) 182
    rule (2) 182
    rule (3) 187
    rule (4) 191
    vacant possession 186
Valuation date
    agreement 176
    entry in stages... 177
    general vesting declaration 178

    lands tribunal reference 178
    leasehold 311
    new rule. 175
    old rule 175
    possession 177
    surrounding circumstances 178
Valuation fees 293, 296, 391
Value to owner 159
Vandalism 230

W

Water pipes 425
Wednesbury principles 46
Willing buyer 185
Willing seller 184
Works order 38